Paul Joannides is Emeritus Professor of Art History in the Department of History of Art at the University of Cambridge. He is a specialist in the painting, sculpture, drawing and architecture of the Italian Renaissance. His publications include *The Drawings of Raphael* (1983); *Masaccio and Masolino* (1993), *Titian to 1518* (2001), *Michel-Ange: Élèves et Copistes* (2003) and *The Drawings by Michelangelo and his Followers in the Ashmolean Museum, Oxford* (2007). He curated *The Influence of Michelangelo: Drawings from Windsor Castle*, an exhibition shown at various venues in the UK and the USA from 1996 to 1997, and (with Tom Henry) *Late Raphael*, shown in the Prado and the Louvre in 2012 and 2013.

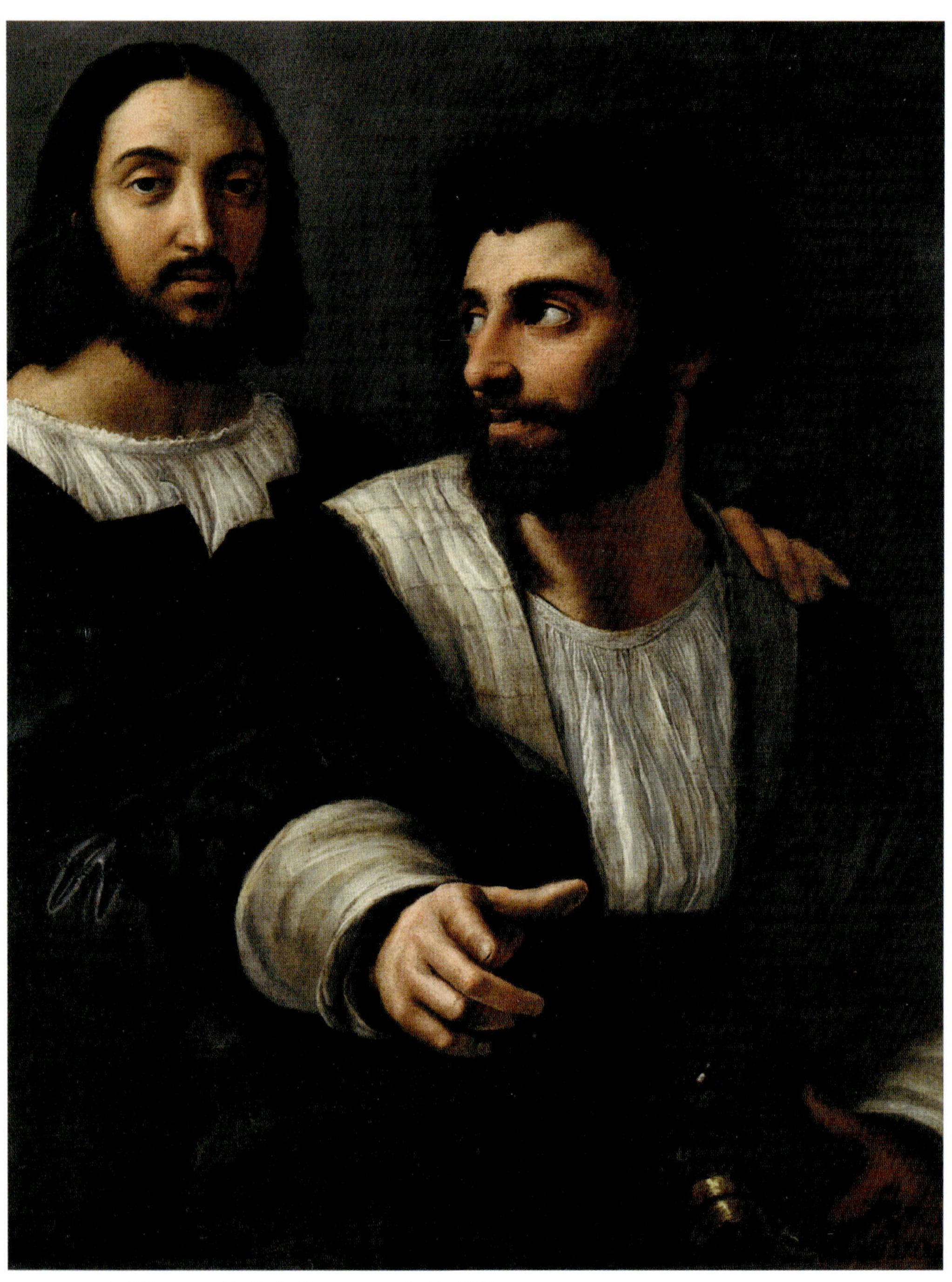

1 *Self-Portrait with Giulio Romano*, probably 1520

World of Art

Raphael

Paul Joannides

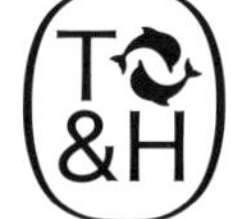

In memory of Sarah Vernon-Hunt

Acknowledgments

I am grateful to all those with whom I have discussed Raphael over the decades, especially Sylvia Ferino-Pagden and Dominique Cordellier, to whose magisterial *Inventaire* (co-written with Bernadette Py) of drawings by and after Raphael in the Louvre I constantly return, and also to Tom Henry, with whom in 2012 I collaborated on an exhibition devoted to Raphael's later work. More immediately, I am profoundly indebted to Sheri Shaneyfelt, David Ekserdjian and James Obelkevich, all of whom, with a commitment over and above the call of friendship, read and commented on earlier versions of this book as a whole or in part. I also wish to thank Dr Guido Cornini who, most generously and in advance of his own publication, supplied me with the previously unavailable dimensions of the four great narrative frescoes in the Sala di Costantino.

First published in 2022 in the United Kingdom
by Thames & Hudson Ltd, 181A High Holborn, London
WC1V 7QX

www.thamesandhudson.com

First published in 2022 in the United States
of America by Thames & Hudson Inc.,
500 Fifth Avenue, New York, New York 10110

www.thamesandhudsonusa.com

British Library Cataloguing-in-Publication Data
A catalogue record for this book is available from
the British Library

Library of Congress Control Number 2021943674

ISBN 978-0-500-20484-9

Printed and bound in China through
Asia Pacific Offset Ltd

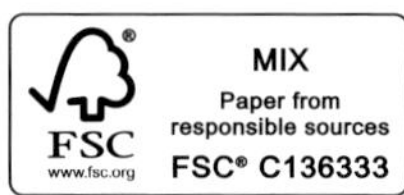

Contents

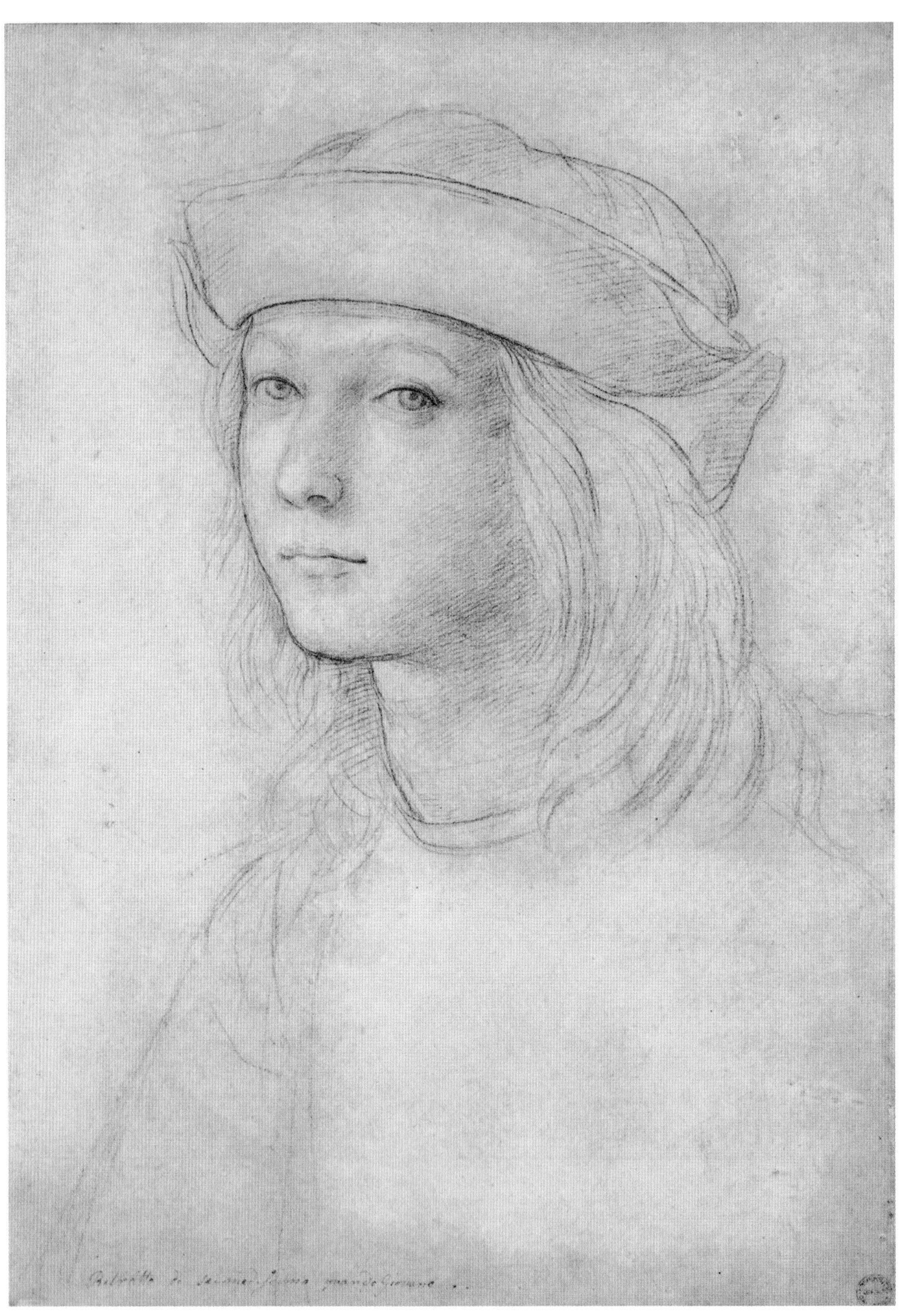

2 *Self-Portrait*, 1499 or earlier

Preface

The aim of this book is to provide an introductory account of Raphael's work and life that students and those interested in Renaissance art might find useful. There exist many general books on Raphael in many languages, including excellent ones in English – among which that by Roger Jones and Nicholas Penny is exemplary – but Raphael was so protean in style, so multifarious in his artistic, architectural, archaeological and theoretical interests, so massively productive and so inventive that no single account can illuminate his work more than partially. Critics and historians respond diversely to his work and to different areas of it, and emphases vary so greatly from one to another that one can read many studies of Raphael consecutively without fatigue and with little sense of repetition.

The starting point of this book is what Raphael drew and painted and designed. The product of many years of studying the work of Raphael and his associates in the original, it concentrates on Raphael's changes of style, his responses to other artists, and the vast expansion of his artistic interests during the twelve years he lived in Rome. It also addresses aspects of his collaboration with others, notably Giulio Romano, whom Raphael, according to Vasari, loved like a son – an artist of a genius and universality that nearly equalled Raphael's own, and whose activity within Raphael's organisation has often been underestimated.

The book is organised chronologically but from the beginning of the Leonine period, as all writers have found, a purely chronological narrative is impractical. Increasingly, Raphael executed and supervised more than one project simultaneously, and to switch from one to another would create confusion and blur appreciation of them. Hence in this book several chapters are devoted to individual – or interrelated – schemes, while others focus on artistic categories, such as Raphael's moveable paintings. There is also a chapter on Raphael's architecture, which has links with some aspects of his painting but whose nature requires separate treatment. Other themes, such as Raphael's projects for Agostino Chigi, run across chapters.

Despite many years of work on Raphael, I was surprised, as I was writing, by how much I did not know. The many lacunae that the reader will find should be taken as incentives to investigate further the literature on Raphael, much of which is deeply rewarding, and, more importantly, to explore those areas of his work that may be less familiar but whose treasures are manifold. Like Rubens, like Bernini, Raphael is a continent still not fully mapped.

Study of Raphael has benefited since the 1960s from the work of many able scholars, but four of them can legitimately be described as great. Philip Pouncey and John Gere, in their 1962 catalogue of drawings by Raphael and his circle in the British Museum, established secure stylistic divisions between the drawings of Raphael and those of his major associates. In a series of articles and books published from 1959 until his death in 2003, John Shearman expanded greatly our knowledge of Raphael's work and his thought processes. A scholar of extraordinary range and erudition, he was particularly successful in establishing the physical, intellectual and theological contexts in which Raphael worked. Shearman's contemporary, Christoph Frommel, whose knowledge of all aspects of Renaissance architecture – and much else – is unequalled, has reconstructed and clarified Raphael's achievement in a field that presents some of the thorniest of all art historical problems. To these four names, many would add that of Konrad Oberhuber, who worked primarily on Raphael's drawings and, less intensely, his paintings. But Oberhuber's achievement is equivocal. In often enlightening writings of the 1960s and 1970s he added the portrait of Julius II and several drawings to Raphael's oeuvre and, in the wake of Pouncey and Gere, shone light on the work of Raphael's assistants, especially Gianfrancesco Penni and Giulio Romano. But from the early 1980s he effectively rejected his earlier conclusions and increasingly gave directly to Raphael almost all the drawings and paintings that he had previously believed to be by assistants. Oberhuber's expansionism was not the result of new discoveries or the coherent rearrangement of existing evidence; it came from a spiritual revelation. Drawings and paintings formerly considered no more than competent suddenly become masterpieces worthy of Raphael. Oberhuber's 'vision', initially greeted with incredulity, has come to exercise considerable influence and has now, in some quarters, become orthodoxy. However, it is the present writer's conviction that the ever inclusive approach of Oberhuber and his followers is misguided and fails to understand the work of both Raphael and his associates. The attributions and stylistic judgments advanced in the present book maintain and, where necessary, develop from a consensus achieved between *c.* 1960 and 1980.

Chapter 1
Urbino

Throughout his life, when Raphael signed his paintings it was generally in the form 'Raphael Urbinas'; and when writing of him, his contemporaries rarely failed to mention his birthplace. Urbino, and particularly its court, was a permanent resource for Raphael. It was there, among the writers, intellectuals, diplomats, aristocrats and members of the power elite who frequented the court, that Raphael made some close and influential friends and established long-lasting contacts.

In legal documents, Raphael is often named as the son of Giovanni Santi, and he seems to have retained a reverence for his father well into his maturity. Although Giovanni was not one of the leading lights of later Quattrocento art, and seems to have left no work in major centres, he was Urbino's most important native-born painter and, in addition, an intellectual of some stature, at least locally. It was Giovanni Santi's example that provided the template for what might be called Raphael's project, and some knowledge of his father's work and career is essential to the understanding of Raphael's mindset.

Giovanni Santi was a man of considerable ambition and wide competence. He was a poet, an historian, a painter and an art theorist; and, although not in the first rank in any of these fields, like his son he constantly tried to improve his capacities and to enlarge his range of knowledge. We do not know how old Giovanni was when Raphael saw the light of day, on Easter Sunday 1483, but he was probably in his mid-40s, perhaps approaching 50. References in his rhyming chronicle to Leonardo da Vinci (1452–1519) and Pietro Perugino (*c.* 1444–1523) as 'giovani' suggests that he was their senior, if not necessarily by many years; he may have been born in the later 1430s.

Little is known of Giovanni's formation. He was probably involved in the festivities mounted to welcome the visit of

Frederick of Aragon to Urbino in 1474, as a designer and perhaps as a librettist, and he was certainly active in the celebrations of the marriage of Guidobaldo to Elisabetta Gonzaga (1471–1526), the sister of Federico II, Duke of Mantua, in 1489. From autobiographical asides in his vast poem, written in *terza rima*, the metre of Dante's *Divine Comedy*, it is likely that Giovanni was a relatively late starter as a painter and that his first calling was literature. His poem, which chronicles the life and achievements of the duke of Urbino, Federico da Montefeltro (1422–82), was probably begun in the 1470s but remained unfinished at his death. It establishes that Giovanni was a serious writer, more committed both to literature and historical writing than any other Renaissance painter.

Famously embedded in the historical narrative and introduced by a brief account of Federico's visit to Mantua, Giovanni includes a short appraisal of the arts of his time that establishes him as a pioneer art historian. He focuses

3 Andrea Mantegna, *The Triumphs of Caesar*, third panel, *The Triumph with Elephants*, 1484–92

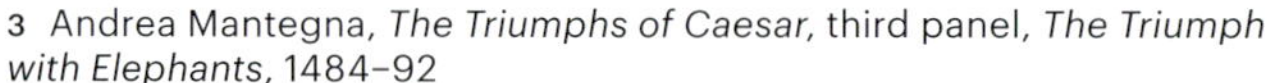

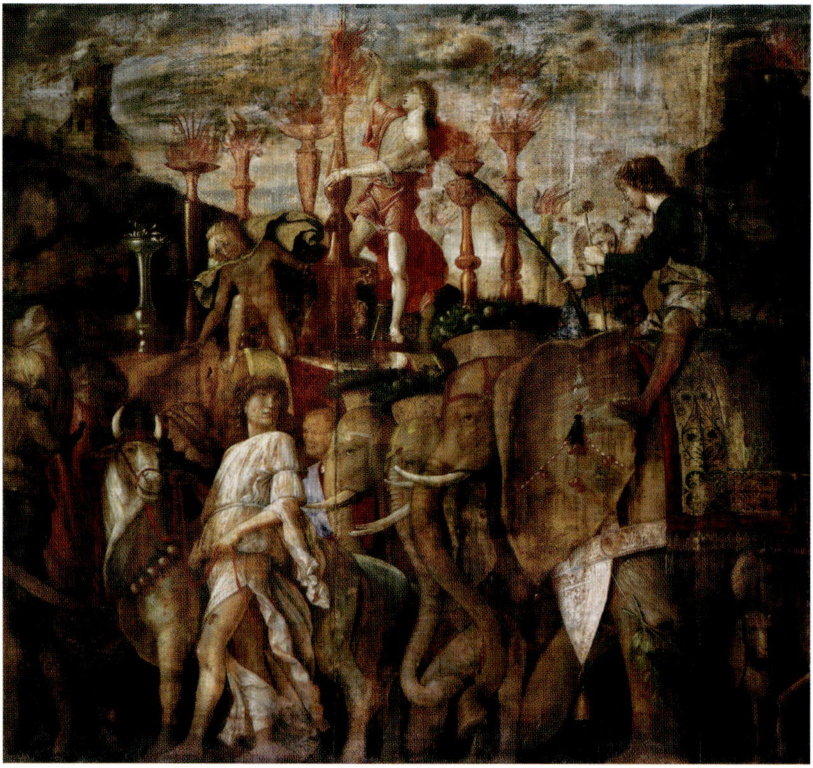

on Andrea Mantegna (*c.* 1431–1506), whom he idolised and considered to be a universal artist and a worthy successor to the ancients, of whose art he has commanding knowledge. Giovanni employs Mantegna as a guide to the central tenets of art. He begins with 'disegno', which he regards as the true foundation of art, and then emphasizes the importance of invention. He praises Mantegna's colour and his command of perspective, both linear and atmospheric, and his ability to foreshorten figures and to show them in movement. He then evokes the importance of graphic art, which he fuses with perspective as a universal and foundational science – and not a mechanical trade – alongside arithmetic and geometry. He speaks of perspective as a scaffolding of vision that allows natural forms to be situated realistically in space, and provides some unexpected examples of forms and substances that might be painted, such as jewels, foliage, water, flowers – in short, the natural world. Such a range of interests coincides with remarks made by Leonardo in his writings on art. It also adumbrates his son's thought process as described by Giorgio Vasari (1511–74) in his *Life* of Raphael, who says that, when Raphael realised he could not compete with Michelangelo in depicting the nude, he reflected that it was vital to know how to portray animals of every type, clothing, hair, trees, fires, clouds, rain, the light of the moon, etc. – in short, to extend art's reach to include the representation of the entire visible world.

Santi proceeds to list, and occasionally to characterise, the leading artists of his time. He begins with Jan van Eyck and Rogier van der Weyden and passes on to reference many of the more important Central Italian and North Italian painters of the period, some of whom – Melozzo da Forlì (*c.* 1438–94), for example – he knew personally. Occasional comments show his preferences: he admired the brothers Pollaiuolo ('gran disegnatori') and makes clear his appreciation of Perugino ('ch'è un divin pictore') and Luca Signorelli (1441–1523; 'de ingegno e spirito pelegrino'). Sculpture also interested him. He cites Donatello (*c.* 1386–1466) first, then Desiderio da Settignano (1428–64), and then moves on to Jacopo della Quercia (1374–1438) and others. He seems particularly to have admired Andrea del Verrocchio (1435–88). Giovanni's knowledge of sculptors is not confined to Central Italy, for he mentions Antonio Rizzo (1430–99) in Venice and, in Milan, Ambrogio Barocci (active *c.* 1470, died after 1516), who had worked in Urbino and whose mastery of low relief he praised. All in all, Giovanni's theory of art and his assessment of artists both living and dead comprise a programme in anticipation of his son, who was to become the supreme aspirant to universality.

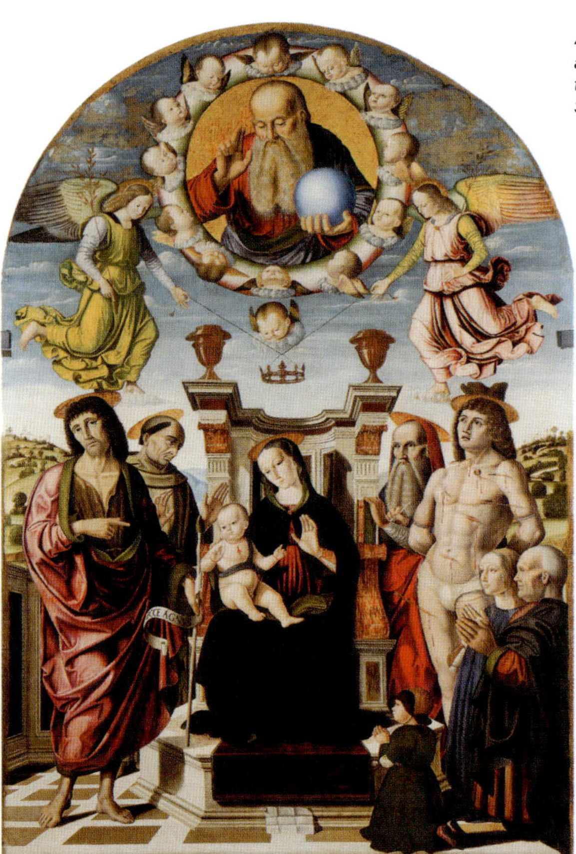

4 Giovanni Santi, *The Virgin and Child Enthroned with Sts John the Baptist, Francis, Jerome and Sebastian (Pala Buffi)*, 1489

If Giovanni took to painting in maturity, as a considered choice rather than a trade, it might explain his theoretical bent and, more significantly, his eclecticism. Not trained from youth by a single master or formed within a specific style, he could approach painting with intellectual independence, ready to make his own judgments, catholic in his interests and liberal in his selection of models. A late entry into the art of painting might also explain a certain lack of fluency in his work, in both design and execution. Painting requires a period of technical preparation, generally from an early age, and its successful practice constant exercise.

It seems that the earliest paintings confidently attributable to Giovanni date to *c.* 1470, meaning that his artistic career stretched over some twenty-five years and was not much longer than that of his son. Vasari considered Giovanni Santi – none of whose work he cites directly – to be a mediocre painter, but

his characterisation of Giovanni as intelligent, thoughtful
and aware of his own limitations offers significant insights
into Raphael's earliest experience. Giovanni was an intellectual
and – given his ambitions as a writer and, inevitably, a thinker,
and the range of influences discernible in his pictorial work,
plus his interest in, and views about, artistic theory – it is likely
that from the beginning he inculcated his son with the value
of literary and historical study and encouraged him to explore
many forms of art.

Giovanni's oeuvre comprises altarpieces – a few of which
are dated or datable – Madonnas and *Pietàs*, as well as single
figures of saints. How much secular painting he executed is
unknown, but he did design and paint several panels in a
series representing the Muses for the ducal palace, probably
in the 1480s (the series is in Florence, Corsini Collection).
His borrowings, for the most part, concern motifs rather than
colours or textures; but Piero della Francesca (*c.* 1415–92), whom
he knew personally and lodged when Piero visited Urbino in
1469, was probably the most important single influence on
his work. Giovanni of course knew the large and innovative
altarpiece painted for Urbino by Justus van Ghent (active
c. 1460–*c.* 1490), who lived and worked in the city in the first
half of the 1470s. He was consequently alert to at least one

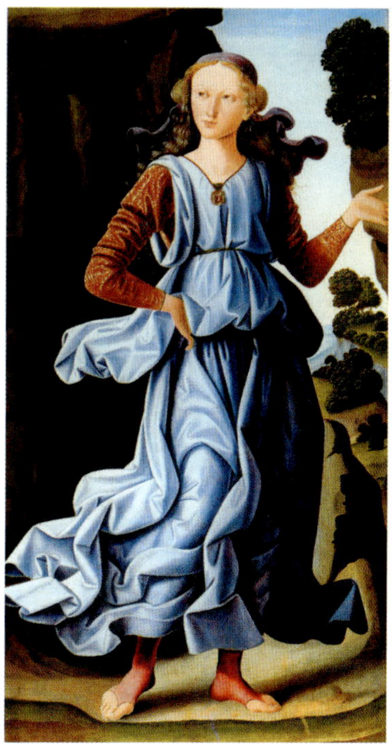

5 Giovanni Santi,
Clio (from the series
The Muses), c. 1480

aspect of the Northern treatment of surfaces and the
representation of materials, and communicated his interest
in Flemish art to his son, some of whose early work shows
an indebtedness to Hans Memling. Justus, together with
the Hispano-Flemish Pedro Berruguete (*c.* 1450–1504), was
responsible for the series of twenty-eight historical portraits
of famous men, shown seated, that decorate Federico da
Montefeltro's *studiolo*. Some of these were innovative in
arrangement and, although Giovanni himself seems to have
remained unaffected, they were to be recalled by Raphael.
By Giovanni we have numerous portraits of donors included
in altarpieces, and a single plausibly attributed individual
panel: the profile of a *Boy* in the Thyssen Collection in Madrid
that follows closely the portrait style of Piero. Once thought to
represent the infant Raphael, it probably depicts Guidobaldo
da Montefeltro (1472–1508) at the age of 5 or 6, underscoring
Giovanni's involvement with the court of Urbino.

Giovanni must have been considered an accomplished
portraitist, and this perception, indirectly, killed him. When
a portrait by his hero Mantegna failed to satisfy the Gonzaga
court, Giovanni was called – or sent by Guidobaldo – to Mantua
in 1494 to take portraits in his stead. The malaria-ridden Po
Valley proved fatal. Returning moribund to Urbino in the
summer of 1494, Giovanni died in August. Perhaps Raphael
had accompanied him on his trip. That Giovanni was favoured
by the court of Urbino is also implied by a commission from
Giovanna Feltria (1463–1513), Guidobaldo's sister, known as
the *prefetessa* from her marriage to Giovanni della Rovere,
prefect of Rome, in 1478. It was to celebrate the birth of
their heir, Francesco Maria della Rovere (1490–1539), that she
commissioned from Santi an altarpiece of *The Annunciation*
for the church of Santa Maria Maddalena in Senigallia,
a della Rovere fief. And she was later to support Raphael.

Giovanni was certainly an effective courtier, an
accomplishment his son inherited in abundance; and
the houses of Montefeltro, della Rovere and Gonzaga
were all to play significant roles in Raphael's career. When,
by 1504, it became evident that Guidobaldo would not sire
heirs, Francesco Maria, whose father had died in 1500, was
named heir apparent to the duchy of Urbino, succeeding at
Guidobaldo's death in April 1508. Thus Giovanni and Raphael
were beneficiaries of a web of contacts that included the
powerful Cardinal Riario (1461–1521) and, of course, Giuliano
della Rovere (1443–1513), the cardinal of San Pietro in Vincoli,
who would later become Pope Julius II and was the brother-
in-law of Giovanna Feltria and uncle to Francesco Maria.

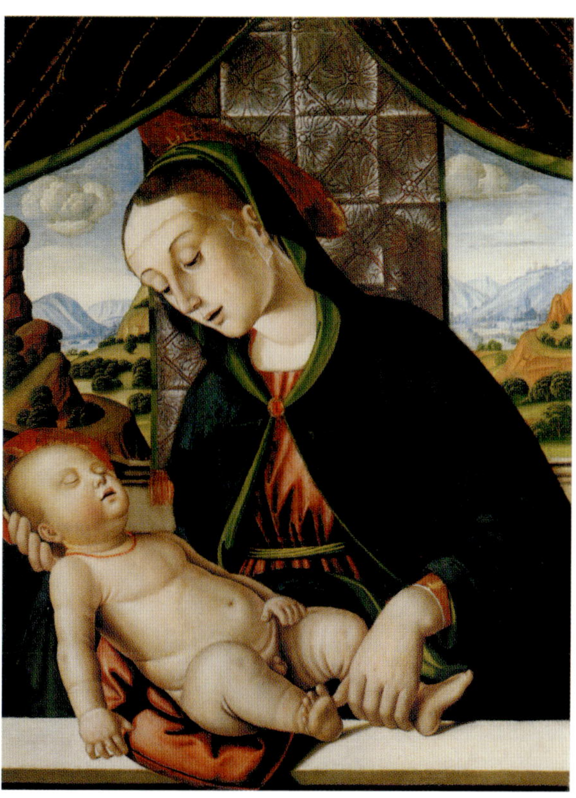

6 Giovanni Santi, *The Virgin and Child*, c. 1488

Any painter favoured by Urbino's ruling dynasty would have access to powerful and cultivated patrons.

Among the artists whose work left traces in Giovanni Santi's oeuvre were Andrea Mantegna himself, as seen in the draperies of some figures, and Giovanni Bellini (*c.* 1438–1516): the Child in Santi's *Madonna* is based on a model by Bellini, and Bellini was the inspiration for several other figures in his work. Neither Bellini nor Mantegna worked in Umbria, but Giovanni, who knew the Adriatic coast, no doubt saw Bellini's great altarpiece at Pesaro; he also knew Alberti's church of San Francesco at Rimini.

Giovanni also had some – perhaps extensive – awareness of Florentine art and may have spent time in Florence during the 1460s, when he seems to have been absent from Urbino. Surprisingly for an Umbrian painter, he was much affected, although he accords them limited mention in his chronicle, by Antonio Pollaiuolo (*c.* 1433–98) and even more so by his brother, Pietro (*c.* 1443–96), notably in colour, poses and female facial

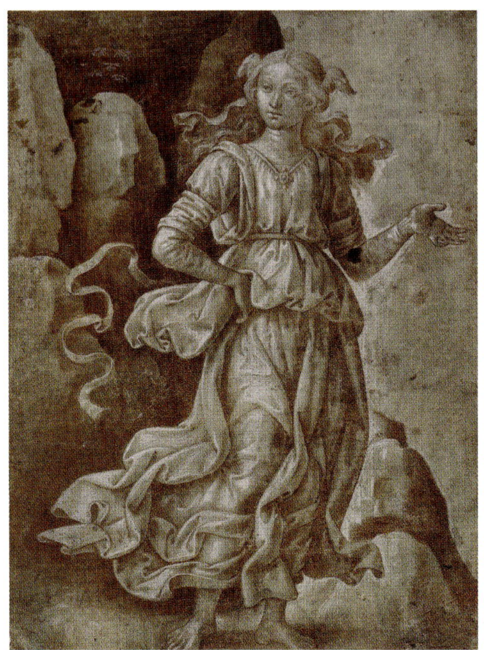
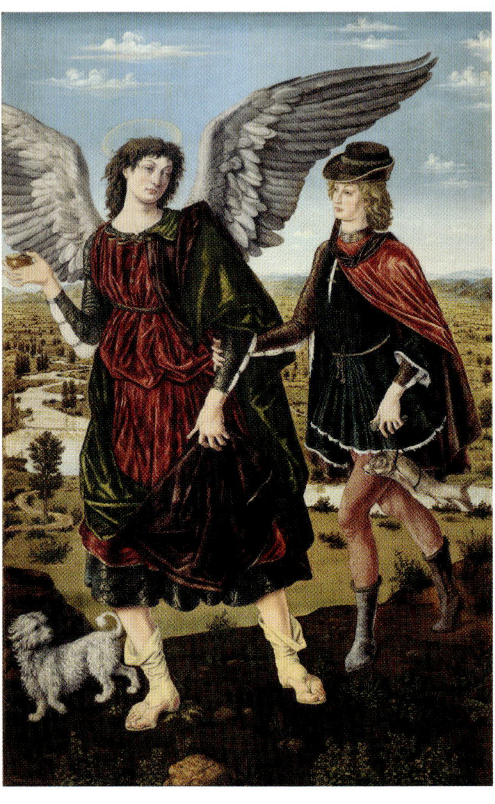

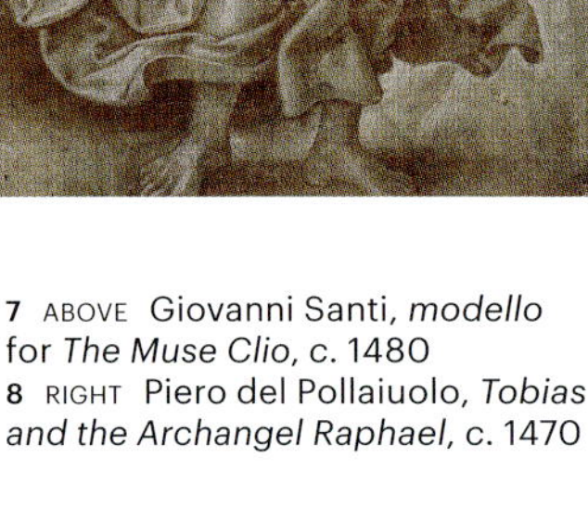
7 ABOVE Giovanni Santi, *modello* for *The Muse Clio*, c. 1480
8 RIGHT Piero del Pollaiuolo, *Tobias and the Archangel Raphael*, c. 1470

7　types. The pose of *Clio* – for which there is a fine drawing, the single example securely attributable to Giovanni – is similar in
8　pose to that of the archangel Raphael in Piero's *Tobias and the Archangel Raphael*.

Probably in the later 1480s Giovanni fell under two strong influences, both of which were to be important for his son. One was Luca Signorelli (1441/45–1523), active widely in Central Italy, who delivered a double-sided banner to Urbino in the year of Giovanni's death. Signorelli's interest in energetic movement is echoed in Santi's Senigallia *Annunciation* and was also to affect Raphael. More important was the work in Umbria and
10　the Marches of Pietro Perugino, whose style came to dominate Central Italian art in the last two decades of the Quattrocento. Fascination with Perugino is demonstrated in Giovanni's *Pietà with Saints* in Breslau, which follows closely Perugino's *Pietà with Sts John the Evangelist, Mary Magdalene, Nicodemus and Joseph of Arimathea* (Florence, Uffizi) of the early 1480s. Perugino's influence is also strongly felt in one of Giovanni's

most accomplished projects, the well-preserved chapel in
San Domenico, Cagli, a few kilometres from Urbino, painted
for the Tiranni family. Undocumented, it is sometimes placed
in the first half of 1480s, shortly after the patron's death. But
the pose of the Virgin and Child in the limpidly spaced *sacra
conversazione* that occupies the lower half of the wall is based
on a famous invention by Perugino, of which the earliest secure
example is the Pala dei Decemviri in Perugia, finished in 1495
but under way for several years. St Peter in Giovanni's fresco
is also based on Perugino.

The chapel contains two notable organisational features.
One is the boldness with which Gabriel and the Virgin in the
tondi in the spandrels break out of their roundels and Christ
looks down from his vault upon the *sacra conversazione* below,
which indicates that Giovanni was thinking in terms of three-
dimensional scenography. The other is the large and dramatic
Resurrection that surmounts the *sacra conversazione* – an
astonishing conception that juxtaposes a dramatic scene
with a static assemblage. Such a conjunction was anticipated
only, perhaps, by Piero della Francesca, who placed a large
Annunciation above a conventional polyptych in his altarpiece
for the church of Sant'Antonio da Padova in Perugia (Perugia,
Galleria Nazionale dell'Umbria). Giovanni's *Resurrection* shows
several guards in complex sprawling poses, and it contains
a direct borrowing from an engraving of a composition of
Hercules and the Giants by Antonio Pollaiuolo. The seeds
of Raphael's consistent interest in cross-spatial linking
and complex and powerful double-level compositions
(as, for example, in his final painting, *The Transfiguration*)
were sown in the Tiranni Chapel and, while it may be no
more than sentimentalism, the suggestion that Giovanni left
a portrait of his son, named after an Archangel, maybe only 9 or
10 years old but already promising brilliance, as a young angel
standing to the left of the Virgin's throne is not to be excluded.

If the Tiranni Chapel illustrates a bold turn in Giovanni's art,
it illustrates too one of his weaknesses: his tendency to repeat
himself. Thus John the Baptist at the lower right, who is a
repetition of a figure Giovanni painted some years earlier, and
Christ in the upper zone are virtually identical in pose. In this
respect Giovanni sometimes descends from artist to artisan,
a lapse of which one could never accuse Raphael.

Giovanni Santi left paintings on canvas and panel and in
fresco, and Raphael would have learnt the technical rudiments
of all three from infancy, and would probably have begun
to draw as soon as he could walk. He was surely precocious:
a small fresco of *The Virgin with the Sleeping Child* in the Casa

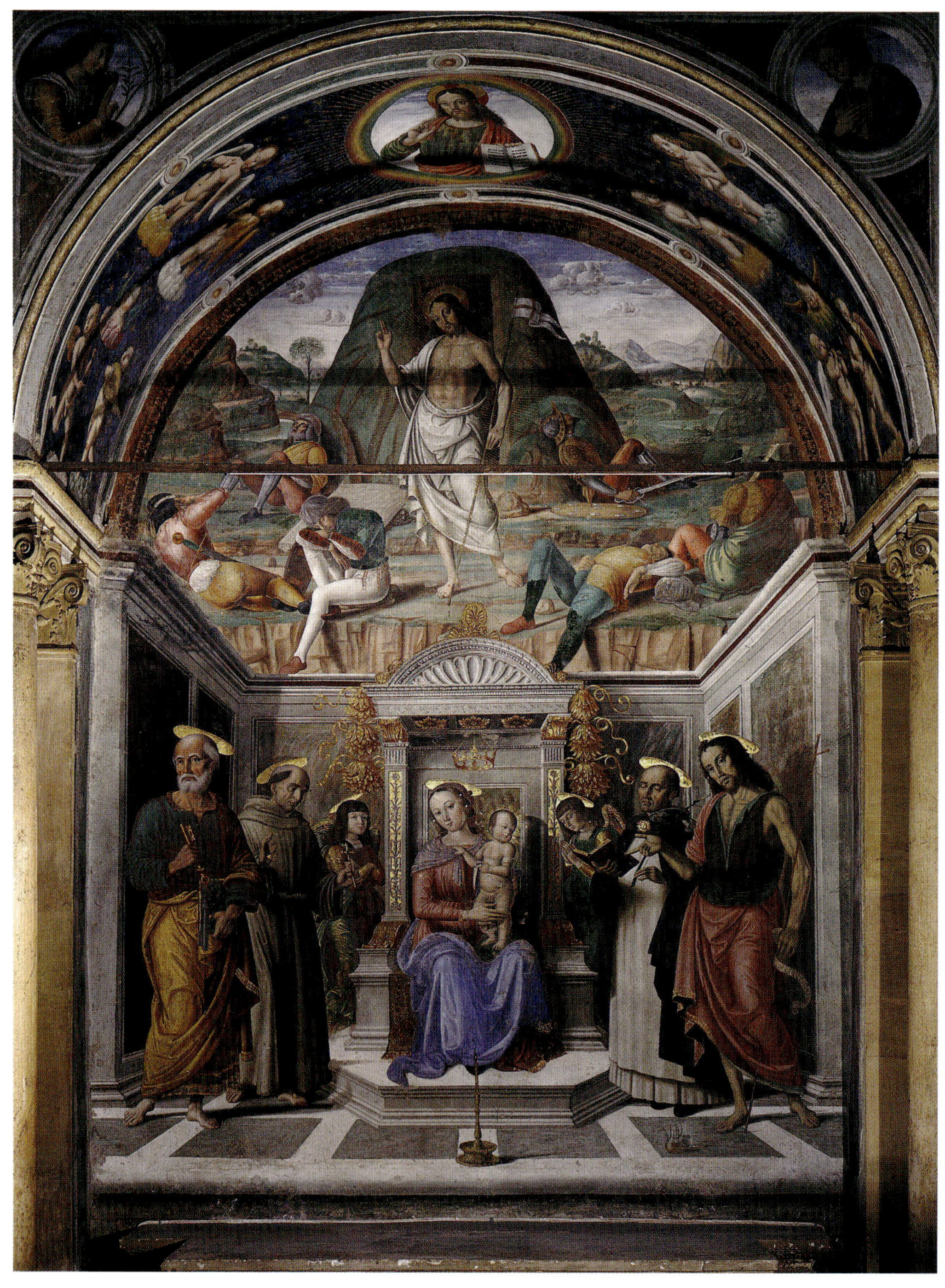

9 ABOVE Giovanni Santi, *The Tiranni Chapel*, probably 1493

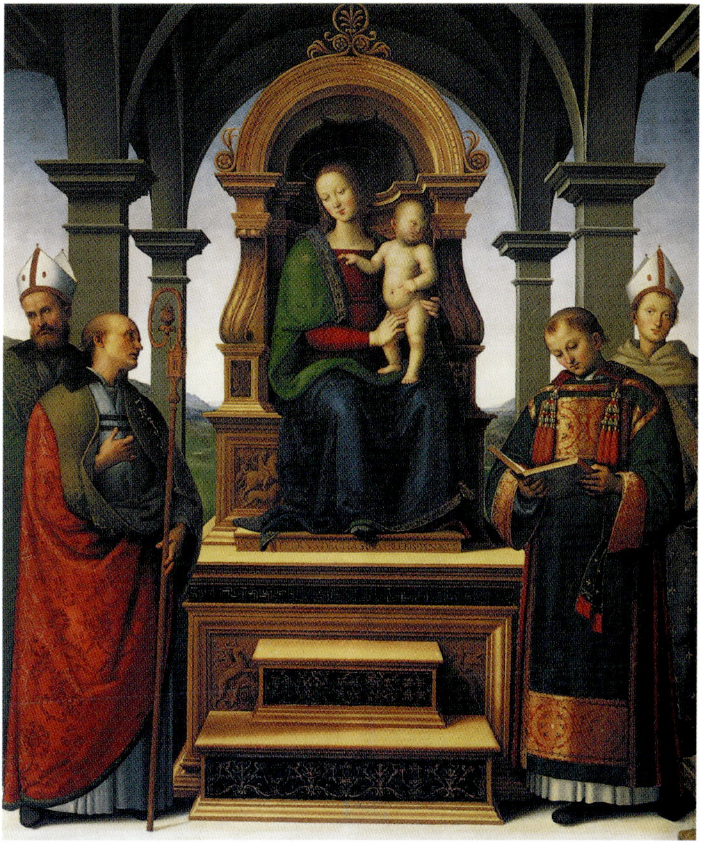

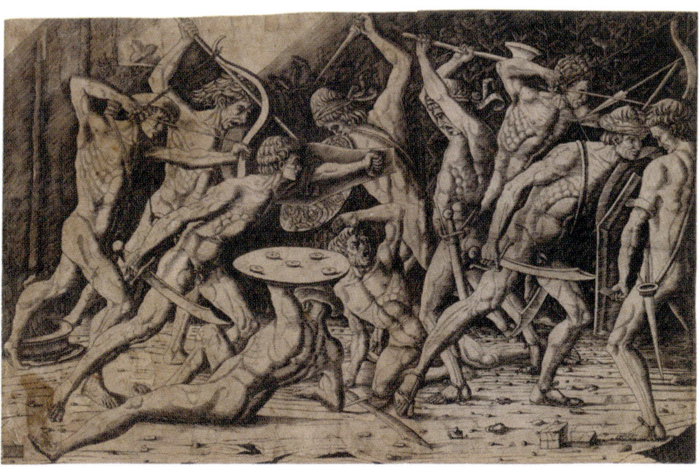

10 ABOVE Pietro Perugino, *The Virgin and Child Enthroned with Sts Ercolano, Costanzo, Lawrence and Louis of Toulouse (Pala dei Decemviri)*, 1495–96
11 BELOW After Antonio Pollaiuolo, *Hercules and the Giants*, c. 1475

di Raffaello in Urbino is traditionally given to the very young Raphael, an attribution that, while unprovable, is not implausible: the soft forms of mother and child and the group's tender emotion are rather different from those of his father, the only other plausible candidate – unless one were to evoke Giovanni's associate, the shadowy Evangelista da Pian di Meleto (*c.* 1460–1549).

His father's death in 1494 occasioned a long-running dispute between Raphael – with his paternal uncle Bernardino acting, maybe over-zealously, on his behalf – and his stepmother, Bernardina, whom Giovanni had married in 1492. We have no precise knowledge of Raphael's financial situation but, notwithstanding this family feud, it seems clear that he was sufficiently well provided for not to be reliant on bread-and-butter commissions. At the time of his father's death, Raphael, although only 11 years old, was exceptionally well informed artistically, experienced beyond his years and gifted by nature with supreme intelligence. He seems to have had considerable freedom of manoeuvre and he had high-level contacts.

Even if *The Virgin with the Sleeping Child* is by Raphael at, say, 10 or 11, it offers few hints of the qualities of design and of the forcefulness of execution he was to display a few years later. So how did Raphael develop between Giovanni Santi's death in August 1494 and December 1500, when he received his first recorded artistic commission: an altarpiece representing *The Coronation of St Nicholas of Tolentino* for the church of Sant'Agostino in Città di Castello?

There are currently two competing reconstructions of Raphael's early career, although they are not wholly mutually exclusive. One follows, in broad terms, the account of Vasari, who states that Giovanni Santi, observing that his son was outstandingly gifted and realising that he could not teach him further, resolved to place him with Perugino. Vasari describes Giovanni as engineering a meeting with Perugino, who was then working in San Francesco in Perugia; his story, often dismissed, may contain a kernel of truth, although it cannot be trusted for dates or details. There is no record of Giovanni Santi having worked in San Francesco (although Raphael did), but Giovanni did paint *The Visitation* for Santa Maria Nuova in Fano, where Perugino also worked, and Vasari may have confused the two churches. Giovanni might well have approached Perugino around 1490, when Raphael was about 7 years old. Vasari says that Magia Ciarla, Raphael's mother, wept when her son left home, and this anecdote is often discounted, especially since Magia died, probably in childbirth, in 1491, when Raphael was 8. But children of 6 or 7 years old

were, and are, frequently sent from home, mothers habitually
weep at partings, and there is nothing inherently improbable
in Raphael's having had a period of training (and further
education) in Perugino's workshop in his childhood. But only
a chance documentary find is likely to bring any clarification.
That Vasari was unaware of the deaths of Raphael's parents
throws doubt on his account, but Raphael might well have been
sent a second time from Urbino following his mother's death
– and more likely still after that of his father. If so, Raphael
would have worked in association with Perugino, and with
Perugino's own associates and colleagues, such as Bernardino
Pinturicchio (*c.* 1452–1513), at one or more stages in the 1490s.
It might be added that Vasari, in his life of Perugino, says that
Giovanni Santi and Raphael collaborated with Perugino.

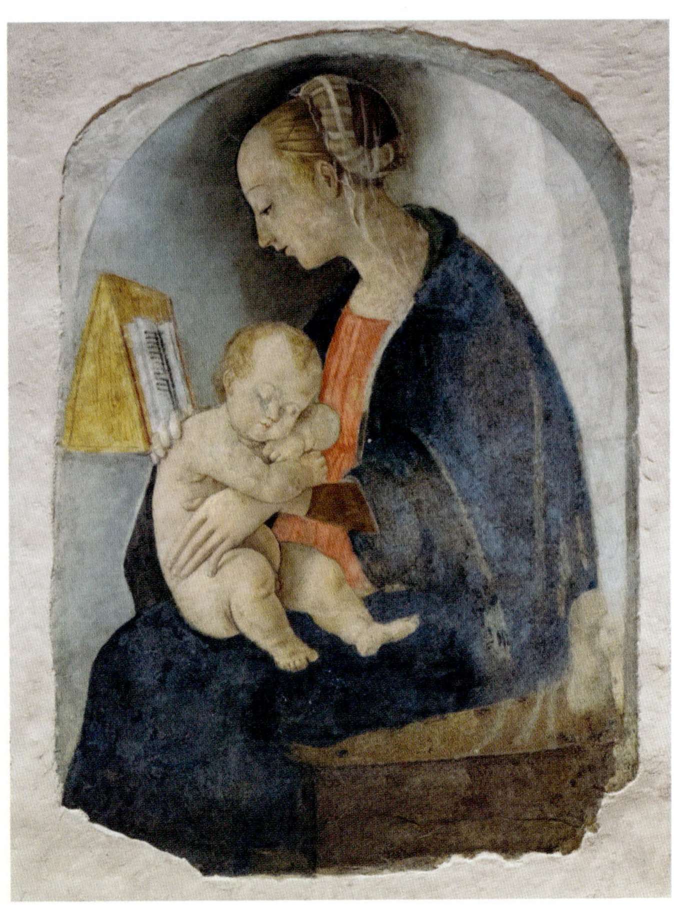

12 *Virgin with
the Sleeping
Child,* 1495?

The other view, based on presupposition rather than evidence, is that following Giovanni's death Raphael continued to work in the family *bottega*, which maintained operations, and only after the turn of the century formed an association with Perugino. This might explain why his earliest documented work contains elements derived from Giovanni Santi. But against such a reconstruction is the fact that it is hard to account for Raphael's extraordinary flowering if he had remained in Urbino, where there was a dearth of court patronage through the middle and later 1490s; Guidobaldo was absent, on military campaigns and, for a period, held a prisoner. And how could Raphael – without external influence – have acquired the astonishing skills as a draughtsman that were evident by 1500 and the command of spatial construction visible in his earliest recorded work? Not from Timoteo Viti (1469–1523) or Girolamo Genga (*c.* 1476–1551), still less Evangelista. It was only in the ambience of Perugino, in Perugia and Città di Castello, that Raphael could have developed as he did and, whatever non-Peruginesque traits may be detected in Raphael's early work, Perugino's presence is by far the strongest.

A further argument against Raphael having lived and worked in Urbino in the later 1490s is the fact that there is no trace in regional literature or tradition that he, the city's most famous artistic son, left any early work there. One would have expected local historians to be alert to youthful efforts by the great man. The fact that in 1500 in Città di Castello Raphael teamed with his father's workshop associate Evangelista da Pian di Meleto is not surprising. He would have known Evangelista from infancy and may have wished to collaborate with someone whom he could trust completely and who, devoid of ambition, would not attempt to dominate him. This was a pattern for later collaborations, notably with Timoteo Viti in Rome. It was at one time thought that, following his father's death, Raphael might have worked with Viti, who returned to Urbino from Bologna – where he had trained with Francesco Francia (*c.* 1450–1517) – around 1495. Timoteo certainly knew some of Raphael's drawings as well as his paintings, but no close connection can be established between them in the years around 1500, and there is no evidence that they collaborated. Girolamo Genga, also based in Urbino, certainly knew Raphael, but where influence can be detected, as with Viti, it flows from, not towards, Raphael.

It seems likely that Vasari, despite his obvious errors, is broadly correct: the young Raphael did spend some time with Perugino before his father's death and during much

of the second half of the 1490s worked alongside him, less
as an assistant than as an associate. During this period he
formed long-lasting friendships with several young Perugian
painters who moved in Perugino's circle: Domenico Alfani
(1479–1553), Eusebio di San Giorgio (*c.* 1470–*c.* 1550) and Berto
di Giovanni (1475–1529) among them. All three were a little
older than Raphael but all were influenced by him, and he
gave them drawings. Vasari says that Raphael travelled with
friends, and he may have left work in Umbrian locations of
which no record survives. He could have moved more widely
in the Marches, perhaps as far as Venice. But unless and until
documentation or visual clues are found, we remain in the
dark. The most important piece of evidence is a documentary
reference discovered only recently. While Raphael is mentioned
with some frequency in court records in Urbino in the 1490s,
none of them unequivocally establishes either his presence or
absence in the town. Only on 4 May 1500 is he specifically noted
as present, and then, in a remarkable adjective, he is referred
to as 'illustris', a surprising accolade for an artist who had just
turned 17 – the age at which the famously precocious Mantegna
had earned his first significant commission. 'Illustris' suggests
an already high reputation – more plausibly one acquired
outside than inside Urbino. On 13 May Raphael was absent
once more.

2

It might be that Raphael's famous *Self-Portrait* drawing,
a formal self-presentation based in its arrangement on
Pinturicchio's fictive panel self-portrait in fresco in the
chapel at Santa Maria Maggiore, Spello, was made about
this time, although it might be earlier: the artist could be
as young as 14 or 15 years old.

Another possibility discounted in recent years is that Raphael
might have contributed to the design and/or execution of some
paintings produced in the Perugino shop. There does seem to be
a resurgence of vitality in Perugino's work around 1500. Paintings
such as *The Resurrection* (Vatican, Pinacoteca) commissioned
in 1499, the panels for the Certosa di Pavia (London, National
Gallery), and some of the figures in the Collegio del Cambio in
Perugia, frescoed by Perugino and his team in the second half
of the 1490s, have an energy and strength of pose that might
suggest the intervention of a new mind and, perhaps, hand. This
is an intuitive appreciation and hardly subject to argument; but
if the young Raphael were becoming known in Perugia, it might
explain why he received his first commission in Città di Castello,
in the Perugian hinterland.

While a direct relation between Raphael and Perugino
in painting cannot be proven, Perugino is the only artist

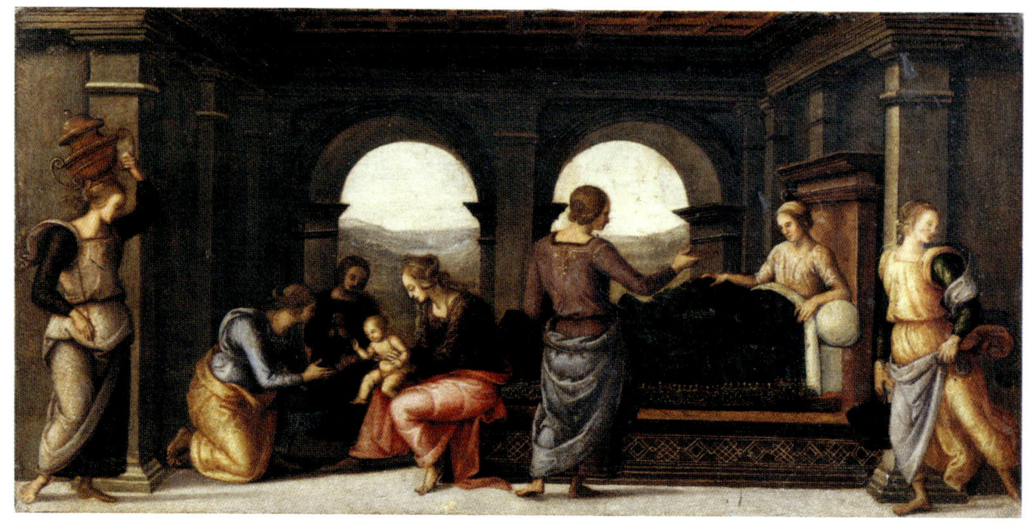

13 Perugino or Raphael, *The Birth of the Virgin*, 1497 or later, predella panel from Pietro Perugino, the Altarpiece

14 BELOW LEFT Study for *The Birth of the Virgin*, 1497 or later
15 BELOW RIGHT Studies for *Holy Family Groups*, 1498–99. The sketch upper right shows St John supporting the Christ Child on a pack saddle

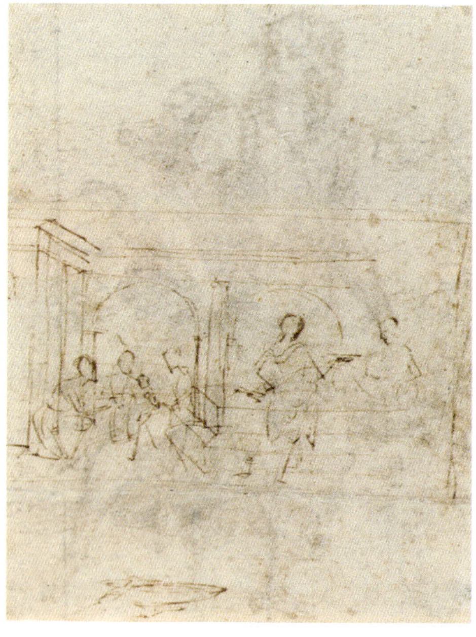

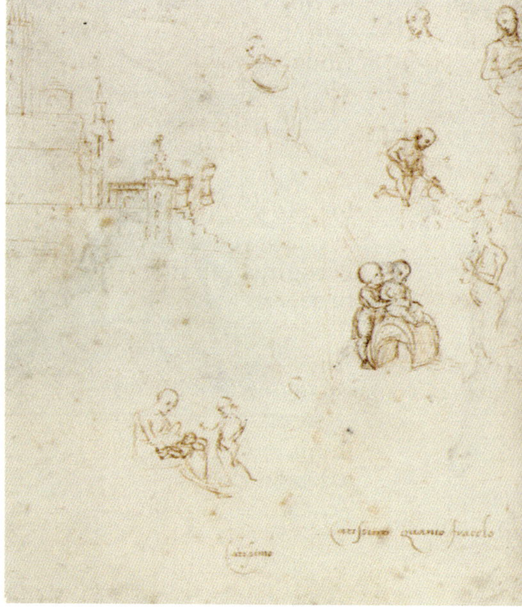

whose drawings might be mistaken for those of Raphael, and vice versa. The relation between their drawings leads us to a controversial subject. In 1497 Perugino delivered an altarpiece of *The Virgin and Child with Saints* to Santa Maria Nuova at Fano, the church for which Giovanni Santi painted his *Visitation*. That year is usually taken to be the date of the predella too, but predellas were often commissioned and delivered separately. It would allow a little more maturity on Raphael's part for his participation in the predella if it were executed closer to 1500. A local tradition of Raphael's involvement was revived in 1955 by the great art historian Roberto Longhi, who proposed that Raphael executed one of its five Marian narratives. He noted that the type of the woman seated at the end of the bed in *The Nativity of the Virgin* was like that of the *Virgin* in the Casa di Raffaello fresco. He might have added that the group of women in this area, and the assured division of the composition by the woman seen from the rear who holds out a plate, is a clever piece of design, simultaneously complex and fluent, which is not paralleled in Perugino's work.

In 1983 four pen drawings related to *The Nativity of the Virgin* and the adjacent panel of her *Marriage* were recognised (Florence, Uffizi). These drawings must be by the artist who designed *The Nativity*, although not necessarily the person who executed it, and they are inseparable from one by Raphael (Oxford, Ashmolean) that shows the same stick-like formation of the figures. This page of sketches – the verso of a study of God the Father for *The Creation of Eve* on the banner made in Città di Castello a year or two later – depicts the infant Baptist supporting the Child on a packsaddle, in which Raphael animated a Perugino prototype; he developed it further in a finished drawing (Oxford, Ashmolean) made in preparation for a now unlocated predella panel by another artist.

Naturally, the Uffizi drawings have been attributed to Perugino, but no drawings resembling them have been related to secure works by the artist. The matter remains open, but if it is accepted that Raphael was involved with the design of this predella, which he certainly knew intimately – and which was copied in 1508 by his friend Berto di Giovanni – then he was collaborating with Perugino before 1500. At this stage in his career, Raphael was probably more accomplished as a designer than as an executant.

Chapter 2
Umbria

Between the end of 1500 and autumn 1504, Raphael
seems to have worked primarily in Città di Castello and
secondarily in Perugia. Probably residing initially in Città,
he is recorded in Perugia in January 1504. He no doubt
returned occasionally to Urbino but not, one imagines,
during the temporary expulsion of Guidobaldo by Cesare
Borgia during the middle months of 1502.

Raphael's Umbrian period is measured in altarpieces.
He completed four, all round-topped, between 1501 and 1504.
Three of them – *The Coronation of St Nicholas of Tolentino*, the
Gavari (or Mond) *Crucifixion* and *The Marriage of the Virgin*
(the *Sposalizio*) – were made for Città di Castello; only *The
Coronation of the Virgin*, the most complex, was for Perugia.
It was probably painted in 1503, when Raphael may have been
attempting to expand his activity in the town. Two further
altarpieces, both *sacre conversazioni*, were commissioned
for Perugian sites: *The Virgin and Child with St John the Baptist
and Nicolas of Bari*, also round-topped, painted for the Ansidei
family chapel in the church of San Fiorenzo; and the so-called
Pala Colonna, rectangular but surmounted by a lunette. Both
were probably laid in before Raphael left for Florence in the
autumn of 1504 but were finished only in 1505 on his return
to Perugia; they reveal a few traces of what he had learnt in
the interim. Raphael then committed himself to further work
for Perugia; on 12 December 1505 he was contracted to paint
a second *Coronation of the Virgin*. This was for the high altar
of the nunnery of Santa Maria de Monteluce. *The Coronation of
the Virgin* of 1486 by Domenico Ghirlandaio (1448–94) at Narni,
which had considerable resonance in Umbria, was cited as a
model. It should not be assumed that Raphael was intended
to follow Ghirlandaio's composition verbatim, but we have

no drawings that can securely be connected with this project. The Monteluce commission became an incubus. It dragged on until 1516, when a new contract was drawn up, but it was finally fulfilled posthumously, in a hybrid form executed by Raphael's heirs, and delivered only in 1525.

231 The Monteluce contract evokes Raphael's reputation and activities at the age of 22. He is described as the best painter in Umbria – a considerable compliment given that Perugino, Pinturicchio and Signorelli were active. It is further specified that Raphael might execute the painting elsewhere than in Perugia: Assisi, Gubbio, Rome, Siena, Florence, Urbino and Venice are listed as possible locations for consultative meetings, which suggests that Raphael was energetically peripatetic. The contract stipulates that the predella was to be executed by Raphael's friend Berto di Giovanni, who made frequent use of his designs. Berto remained in contact with Raphael and was instrumental in negotiating the new contract of 1516. Perhaps as a reward, Raphael gave Berto a drawing for another, different *Coronation*, a rectangular composition intended for the church of Sant'Agnese in Perugia. And Berto did indeed paint the predella of the Monteluce *Coronation* when finally it arrived, making use of Raphael School designs.

At the opposite end of the scale and clearly commissioned by a sophisticated patron are two pairs of portable miniatures
45, 46 on wood: *St George and the Dragon* and *St Michael Vanquishing*
48 *Satan*, and *The Knight's Dream* and *The Three Graces*. It is not clear whether they made up two diptychs or whether they were the fronts and backs of two double-sided panels. They probably date respectively to 1503 and 1504. It is plausible that the first pair was painted for Guidobaldo, in reference to the orders worn by his father, Federico. The second, with its educational theme and its references to Roman texts and antique forms, was probably for Guidobaldo's designated successor, the young Francesco Maria della Rovere, of whom Raphael was to paint a portrait in 1504–05.

In addition to these small, independent panels Raphael executed several predellas. It is not clear whether the *St Nicholas* altarpiece had a predella, nor, if it did, whether it was painted by Raphael; two panels of scenes from St Nicholas's life that are not by Raphael survive in Detroit, but they cannot firmly be attached to Raphael's picture. The Gavari *Crucifixion*, however, did have an autograph predella, two of whose three panels are known; one of them includes a figure in the same pose as *The St Michael Vanquishing Satan*. *The Coronation of the Virgin* likewise had three predella panels, all of which survive.

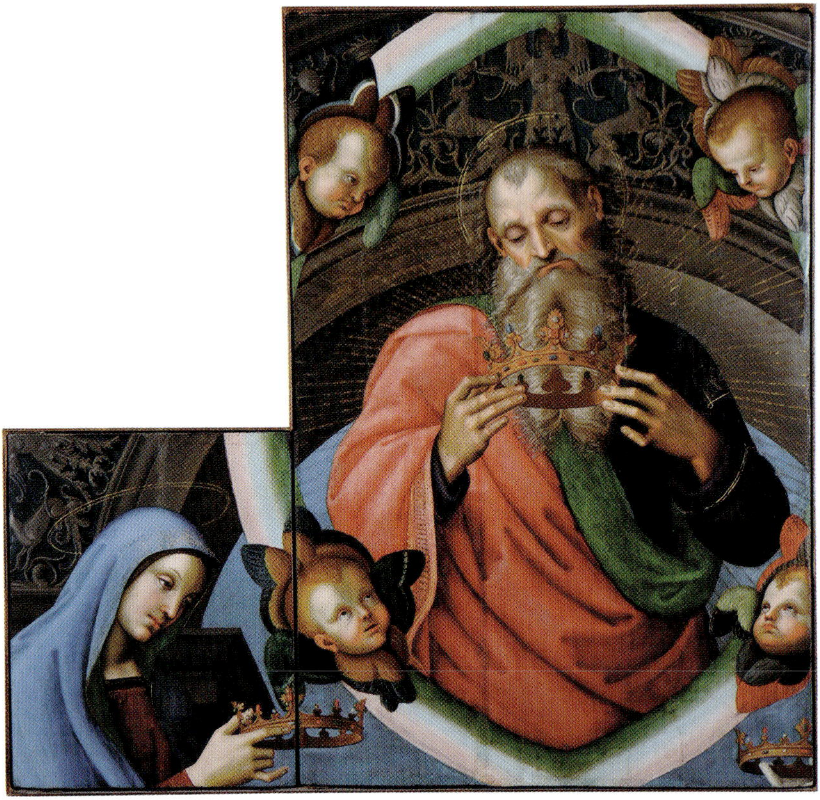

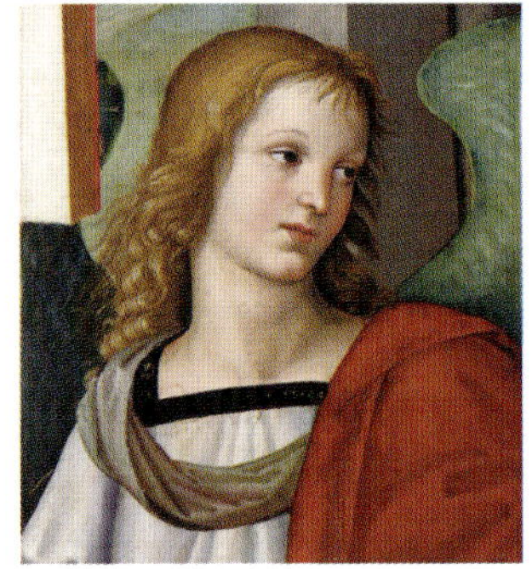

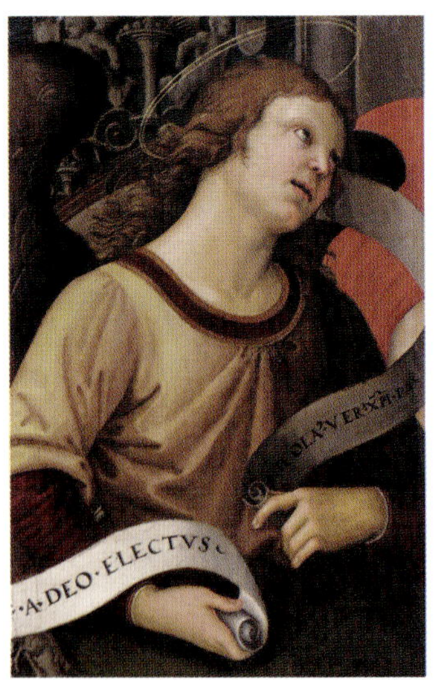

16 TOP *The Coronation of St Nicholas of Tolentino*, 1500–01
17, 18 LEFT AND ABOVE *An Angel* (fragment), 1501

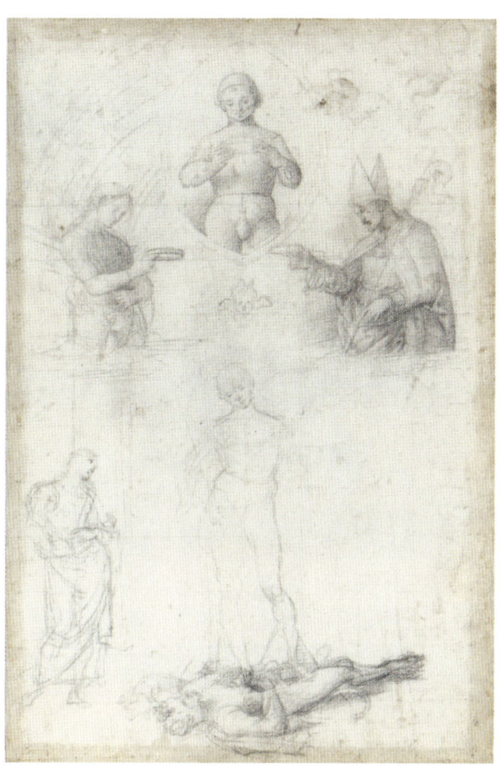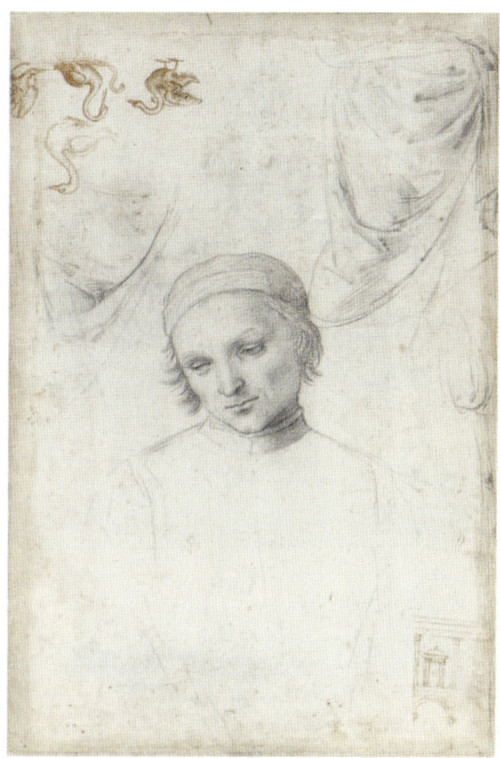

19 ABOVE LEFT Compositional study for *The Coronation of St Nicholas of Tolentino*, 1500
20 ABOVE RIGHT Study for details in *The Coronation of St Nicholas of Tolentino,* 1500

The contract for *The Coronation of St Nicholas of Tolentino*, for the church of Sant'Agostino in Città di Castello, was signed on 10 December 1500. It is the earliest document of Raphael's activity as a painter. He and his collaborator, Evangelista da Pian di Meleto, Giovanni Santi's former assistant, are collectively called 'magistri' or 'magistris' both in the contract and the document of final payment, dated 13 September 1501. Raphael must previously have achieved some recognition, as the word 'illustris' employed in May 1500 implies. He may have chosen Evangelista as a collaborator because he required a mature supporter, but Raphael was the dominant partner, and the design was entirely his. No paintings by Evangelista have been securely identified, but he had a long career and presumably some basic competence. Evangelista's part in what remains of the painting, shattered in an earthquake in 1789 and now in four fragments, is uncertain. The most likely hypothesis is that he executed the cherub heads in the mandorla around

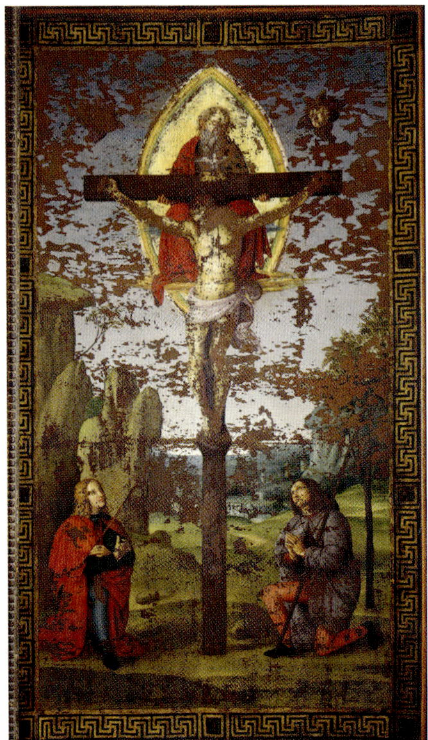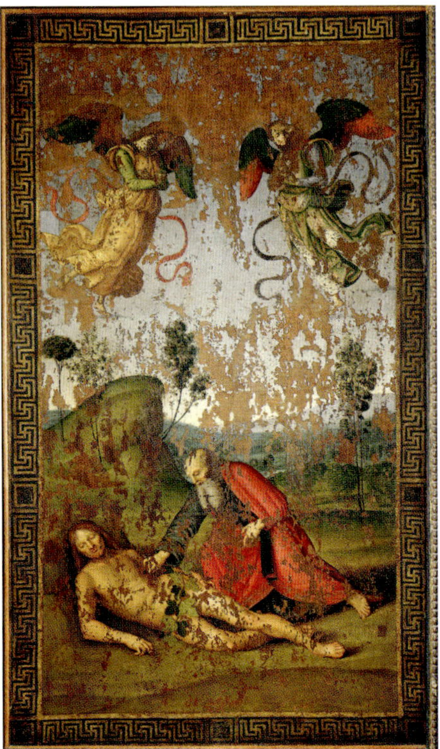

21 ABOVE LEFT *Christ Crucified with God the Father, Sts Sebastian and Roch (Gonfalone della Santissima Trinità)*, 1499–1500
22 ABOVE RIGHT *The Creation of Eve*, 1499–1500

God the Father: they resemble closely those in Giovanni Santi's Buffi altarpiece of 1489, and their surfaces are thinner, their forms less convincing and their characterisations duller than the other surviving parts.

The Coronation of St Nicholas, commissioned by the merchant Andrea Baronci, was one of Raphael's two largest altarpieces. The other was *The Transfiguration*, completed just before his death; the two panels bookend his career, and to compare them makes manifest the distance that he travelled in twenty years. To obtain such a large, although not well-paid, commission, Raphael must already have given proof of his abilities, presumably in Città. This may have been the double-sided banner on canvas – the normal support for *gonfaloni* (paintings to be carried in procession) – still in the town. The front shows *The Crucifixion* (or *Trinity*) with, kneeling to either side, Sebastian and Roch, apotropaic saints associated with the plague. It seems likely that the banner was painted either in a

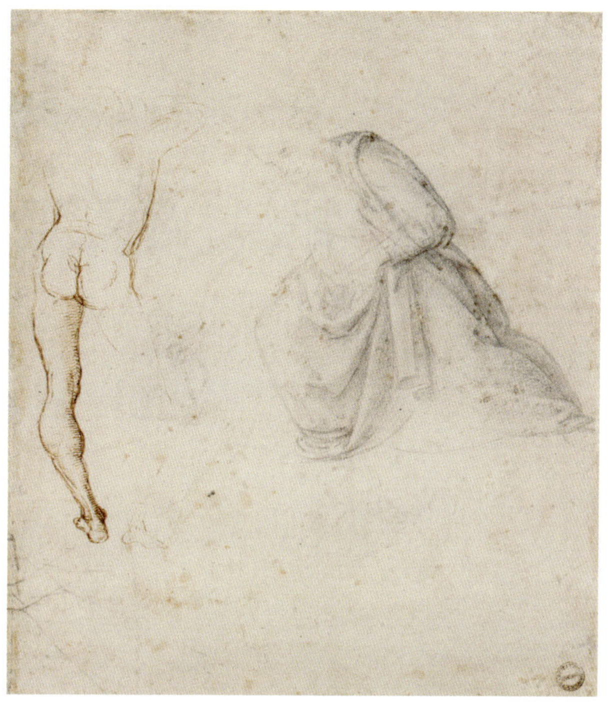

22

time of pestilence or in thanks for its cessation. The back
shows *The Creation of Eve*, presumably evoking the Fall,
the source of human woes. Above hover two slim angels,
Peruginesque in type but subtly differentiated: they were
not painted from reversed cartoons but perhaps follow two
sides of a plastic model.

The banner's dating is contested. Recent scholarship tends
to place it *c.* 1501–02, following *The Coronation of St Nicholas*;
previously it was dated 1499–1500. In favour of the earlier date
is that Roch and Sebastian are more uncertain and stiffer in
arrangement than any other comparable figures by Raphael.
Similarly, the coordination of the landscape with the figures
and with the crucified Christ – who, for the only time in
Raphael's work, is framed by a mandorla – is less precise
than one would expect. On the other hand, the arrangement
of Eve's creation is notably novel: God the Father is customarily
shown standing and was so in a discarded preliminary drawing
(London, British Museum), but here he is half-kneeling,
which implies that Raphael thought through narrative in an
original manner. It seems that Raphael was already making
studies from posed models: the physical type of Adam is

rather Peruginesque, but the flexibility of his body suggests observation of life.

15

The Father's drapery was prepared on the other side of the page of pen sketches of the Holy Family with the packsaddle. Densely and regularly hatched, it is more solid than the chalk drawings of Perugino. It conveys something of the texture of the drapery, which is stretched by the Father's movement. It also shows a control of successive wave-like profiles that animate what could have been a dull contour. Signorelli, whose work Raphael knew in both Urbino and Città, was the Umbrian draughtsman who most favoured black chalk, and it may be that Raphael was taking a lead from one of his denser designs. He was certainly thinking of Signorelli at this moment, for the

23

pen sketch on the same page copies an archer in Signorelli's *Martyrdom of St Sebastian* in San Domenico, Città di Castello, of 1498. Signorelli was one of the few Umbrians to make life studies of both draped and nude figures, and his drawings influenced Timoteo Viti as well as Raphael himself.

The Coronation of St Nicholas was planned with an astonishing and, it appears, unprecedented precision. The

19, 20

upper part of the compositional drawing is handled densely, with extensive stylus indentation, made freehand under the figures, and compass-controlled under the architectural parts. Raphael measured out his surface to gear the inherent geometry of the panel to the organisation of his painting and make it the generator of his composition. By extending the arched top into a circle, he created a dynamic cohesion in the upper half of his painting, often a weak area in Umbrian altarpieces (although not so in his father's work), which penetrates and organises the rectangle formed by the lower section. Raphael continued to use the frame-generated circle as a structural organiser in other Umbrian altarpieces and recalled it in Florence, in *The Belle Jardinière* of 1507, and in his earlier years in Rome in *The Madonna di Foligno* of *c.* 1511, where the Virgin is set against a golden sun, as in Ghirlandaio's Narni *Coronation*. It is a powerful device and gives Raphael's altarpieces a coherence that those by his contemporaries lack.

The circle centres on the navel of God the Father, and the half-length Virgin and St Augustine fit into the circumference. The lower perimeter intersects with the head of St Nicholas and thus focuses attention on it while also establishing the upper horizontal of the lower rectangle. Significantly, the lower section is only loosely sketched; once the upper part had been established, that area could be treated at leisure.

Piero della Francesca had constructed his altarpieces geometrically but not with such energy. Geometry controls the whole surface, but it is dynamic, not static. Perugino, too, spaced his compositions with great clarity, but his geometries did not control full surfaces, and he made no serious use of the power of the circle to condense and expand the viewer's attention. In comparable paintings he tended to line up the figures on the lower level and not show them participating in drama. We have, of course, lost the lower part of Raphael's picture, but the heads of two of the angels accompanying St Nicholas are not symmetrical: they interact both with the saint and with the heavenly manifestation, to which an angel now in the Louvre turns his gaze.

The compositional study is notably uneven in finish: the models who posed for God the Father and the Virgin are studied in modern dress, whereas St Augustine appears in ecclesiastic robes. This drawing must have been preceded and followed by others – perhaps many others – of equal complexity, and it and the other sketches related to the picture demonstrate Raphael's thorough preparation. The verso is a mélange: a light preliminary sketch for a standing angel neighbours a densely drawn portrait head, no doubt intended to serve for St Nicholas, varied in texture with different modes of chalk application for the skin, hair and cap. In addition to its technical accomplishment, it reveals Raphael's gifts as a portraitist, for the head has compelling immediacy. Also on the sheet is a light pen sketch of a colonnade. This resembles the courtyard of Urbino's ducal palace, but not in its finished form: it may follow a project for the palace by the polymathic painter, sculptor, architect and theorist Francesco di Giorgio (1439–1502), who had been known to, and was praised by, Giovanni Santi, and in whose architecture Raphael was to demonstrate a lasting interest. Also depicted is a group of swans, lively but probably not from life (perhaps after an embroidery). Looking at the sheet, one has the sense of a wide-ranging and intellectually curious draughtsman. Some of the drawings are naive and clumsy and might seem the work of a less developed draughtsman. But this results from their functions, not their date, and function is, indeed, the key to understanding Raphael's draughtsmanship.

The half-length figures of the upper section are a legacy of Giovanni Santi, in whose work they can be found quite frequently, while they are rare in Perugino. They have been taken as evidence that Raphael had not previously been in close contact with Perugino. But all the physical types are Peruginesque, especially God the Father and the two angels; indeed, the Louvre fragment was once falsely inscribed with Perugino's name. But if Perugino is the main influence, it is not exhaustive. Thus God the Father is much more three-dimensional than the Peruginesque prototype, with arms stretched out to hold the foreshortened crown symbolically above the saint's head, creating a near-circular form in depth to complement that on the surface. Form-enclosing space was to characterise Raphael's work from beginning to end.

The organisational principle of a rectangle intersecting with and surmounted by a circle served as a template for the other altarpieces of this period, such as *The Crucifixion* commissioned by Domenico Gavari – an associate of Andrea Baronci – for the church of his name saint in Città di Castello. It stood on the last altar at the right of the nave, directly opposite Signorelli's *Martyrdom of St Sebastian*, set in a stone frame inscribed with Gavari's name and the date MDIII, generally – and probably rightly – taken as the year of its completion. Vasari remarked that it would be mistaken for a Perugino were it not signed, and three of the figures in the lower half of the painting are strongly Peruginesque: St Jerome follows the St Jerome in Perugino's Pala Tezi of 1500, and the pose of the Virgin is close to that on the front of the double-sided panel commissioned for San Francesco al Monteripido, near Perugia, in 1502 (both Perugia, Galleria Nazionale dell'Umbria), as is that of the Magdalen. But here priority is uncertain: Perugino's Monteripido altarpiece may not have been started before 1504 and may even have followed Raphael's picture.

The Gavari *Crucifixion* is compositionally cohesive. The circle whose circumference is the panel's top is centred on Christ's navel, and just encloses his feet. Unifying the upper part of the picture, this circle seems to fit into the concavity formed by the heads of the four saints in a cup-and-ball effect. But *The Crucifixion* is a painting in two parts. The figures on the lower level are routine in conception. Each one is isolated in contemplation; they do not convey tragedy, and their poses could serve equally well in other contexts. The contrast in invention with the upper section is striking. The elongated Christ – much larger than the figures below – dominates the painting. His forms are powerfully modelled, and he differs in pose from any prototype by Perugino. The flanking angels, although apparently mirror images, are in fact marvels of three-dimensional drawing and subtle differentiation: they perform an aerial ballet of a complexity and elegance that Perugino never attained. Both collect the blood that drips from Christ's left and right hands, and the angel at left also gathers the blood that spurts from his side. They demonstrate a capacity for representing movement not previously seen in Raphael's work, and this is also a feature of the surviving predella panels,

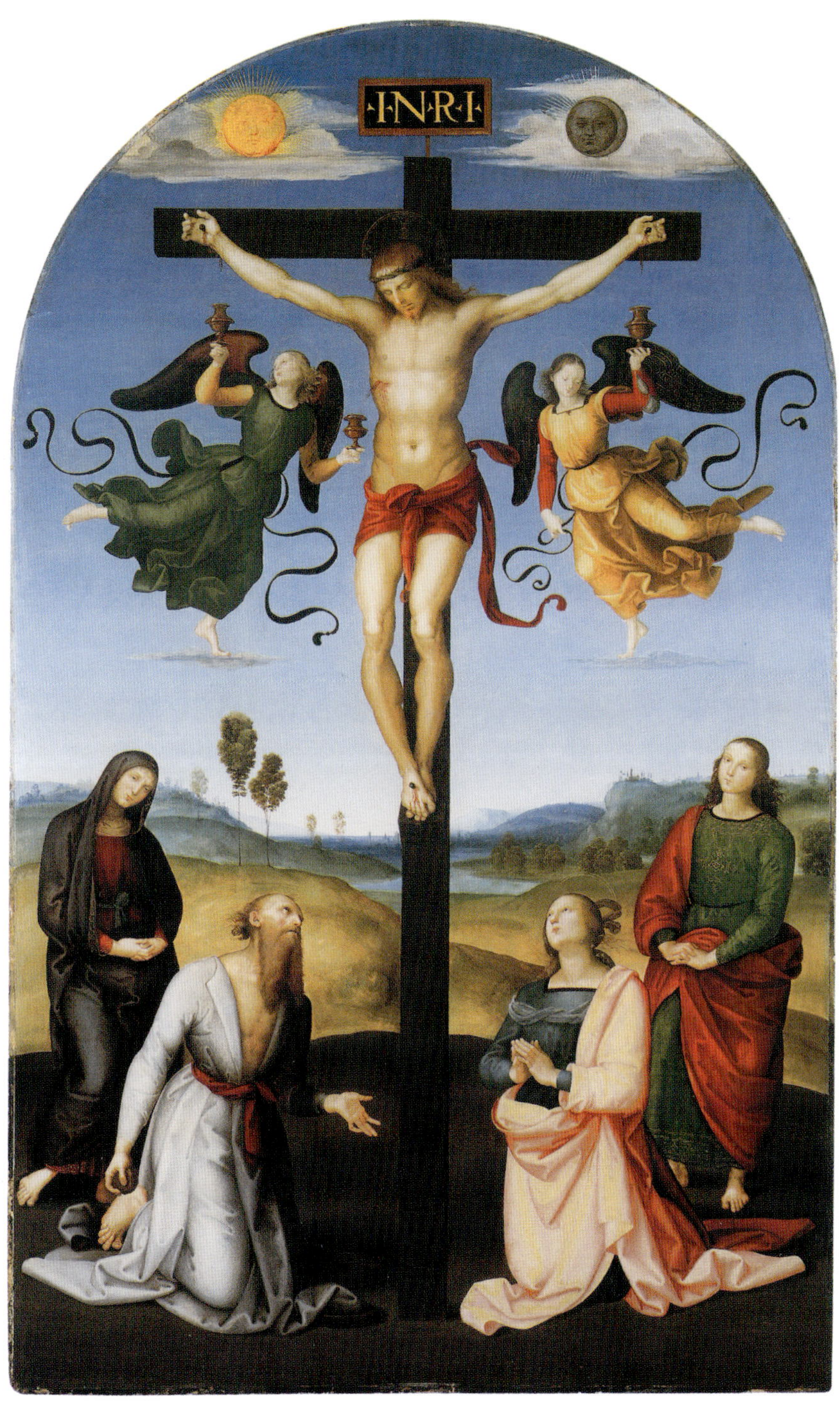

24 *The Mond Crucifixion*, 1502–03. The Crucifixion is Raphael's first suriviving painting to bear a signature (signed RAPHAEL VRBINAS P, but not dated)

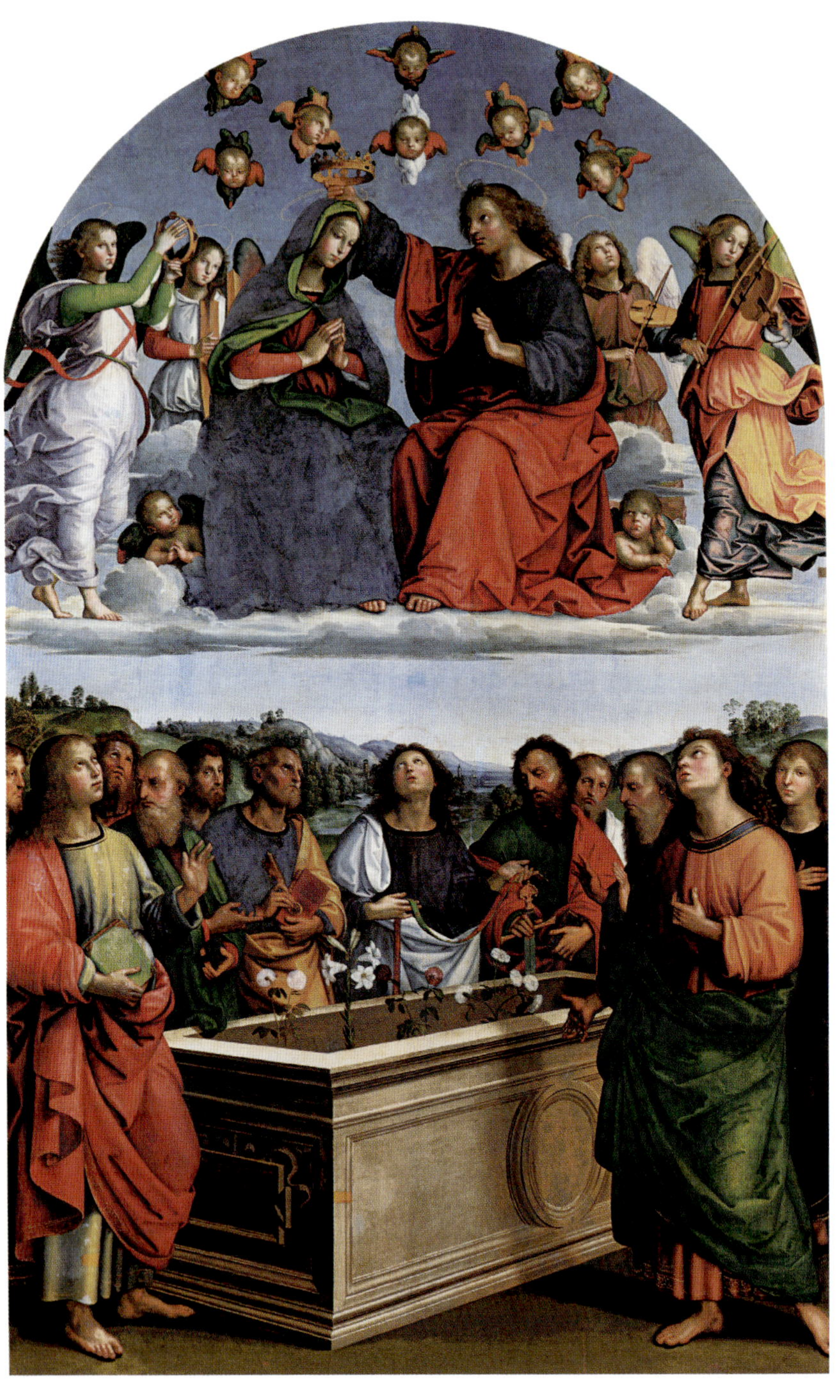

25 *The Coronation of the Virgin with the Apostles* (Pala degli Oddi), 1503–04

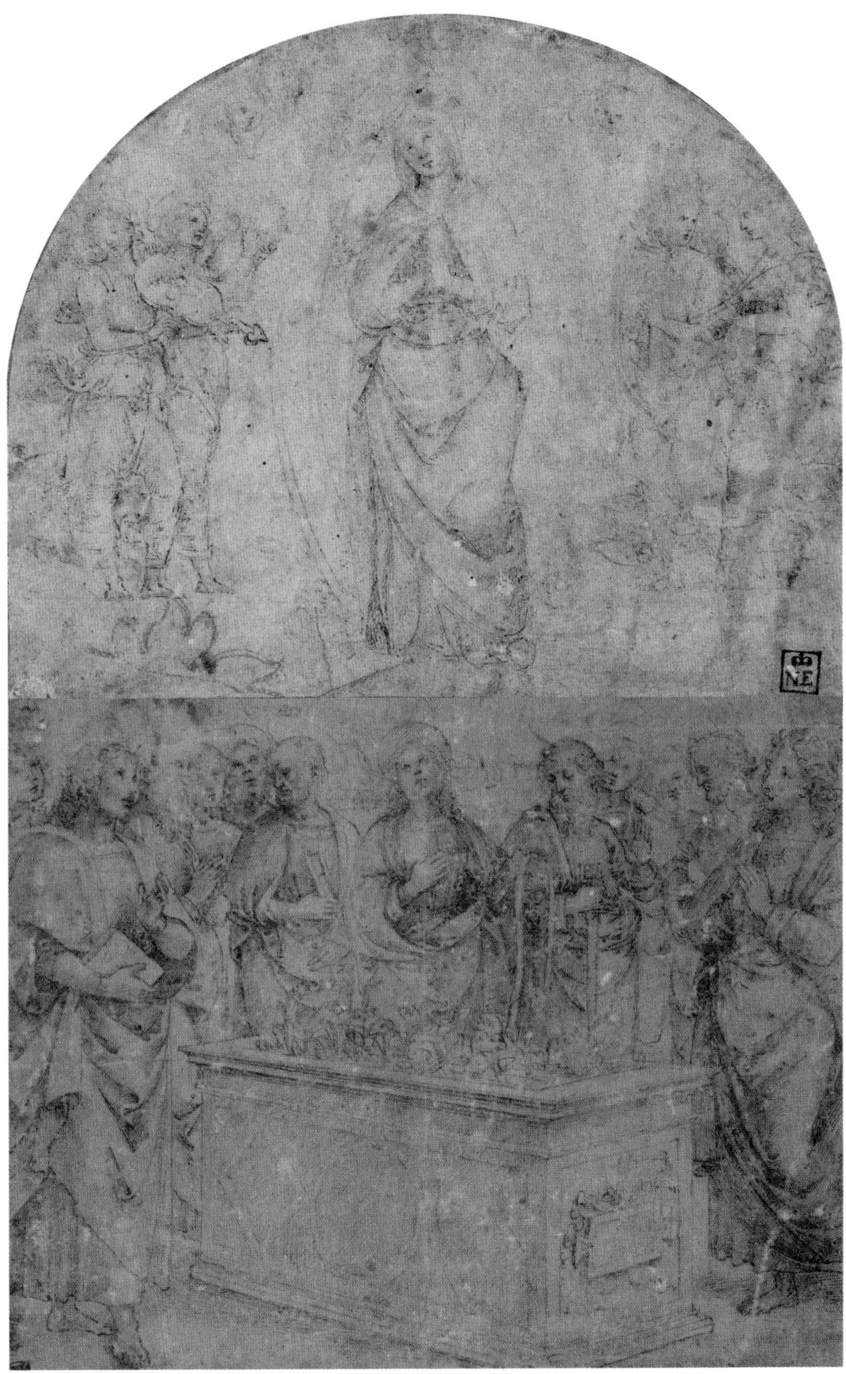

26, 27 *Modello* for *The Coronation of the Virgin*, 1503. Raphael's *modello* was divided at an unknown date

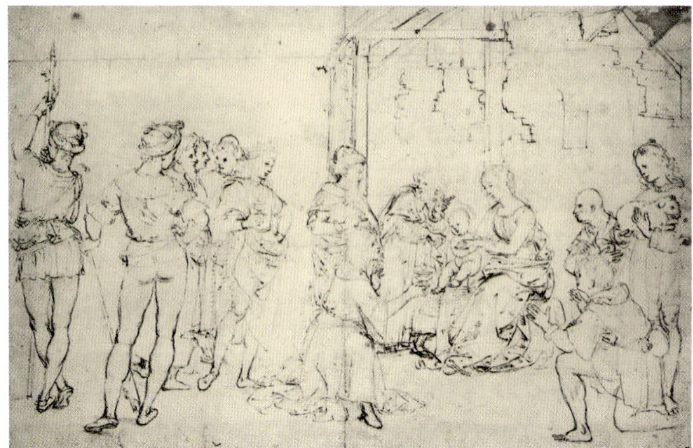

28 ABOVE *The Adoration of the Magi and Shepherds*, 1503
29 OPPOSITE TOP Predella panel, *The Annunciation*, from *The Coronation of the Virgin*, 1503
30 OPPOSITE MIDDLE Predella panel, *The Adoration of the Magi and Shepherds*,
from *The Coronation of the Virgin*, 1503
31 OPPOSITE BELOW Predella panel, *The Presentation of Jesus in the Temple*,
from *The Coronation of the Virgin*, 1503

both quite loosely conceived, which show two rarely depicted
posthumous miracles of St Jerome.

The background is more loosely handled, with long sweeps
of landscape and soft execution: Raphael seems to be using
oils with greater freedom, and *The Crucifixion* illustrates his
ability to paint broadly as well as precisely. These are modes
that he can deploy concurrently, and they may perhaps have
depended on cost and time: it does seem that the commission
was executed rapidly.

Why should a young artist who had already demonstrated
advanced powers of organisation and figural invention have
imitated Perugino's figure types so directly in *The Crucifixion*'s
lower section? Was it a requirement of the patron? Was the
commission initially offered to Perugino and then transferred
to Raphael on the condition that his design be followed –
at least for the lower part? It might be argued that it simply
reveals a moment of creative lassitude, were it not for the
comparative brilliance of the upper section. For whatever
reason, the internal discrepancies in the Gavari *Crucifixion*
remain difficult to elucidate.

25   *The Coronation of the Virgin* was probably executed in 1503.
The main panel has been transferred to canvas, but its three
predella panels remain on wood. Commissioned by the degli
Oddi, one of the leading families in Perugia, for the church of
San Francesco al Prato, it would have outshone contemporary

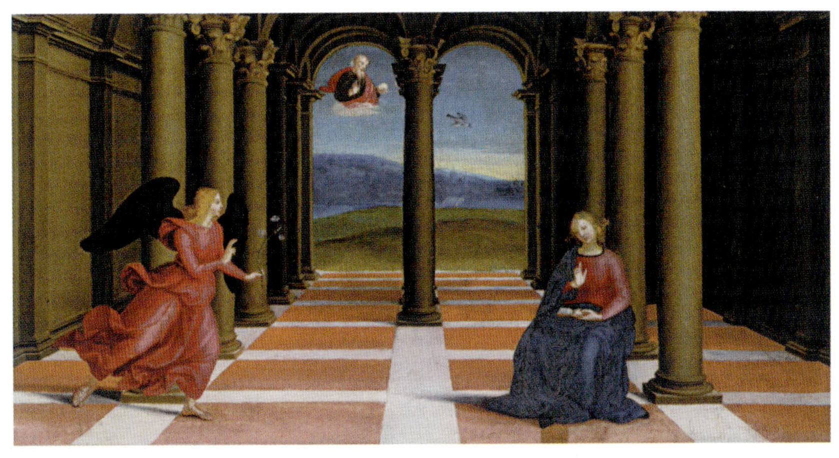

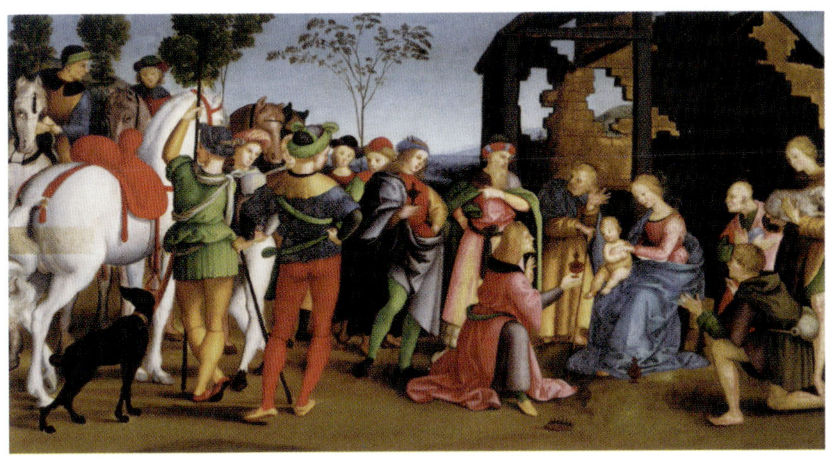

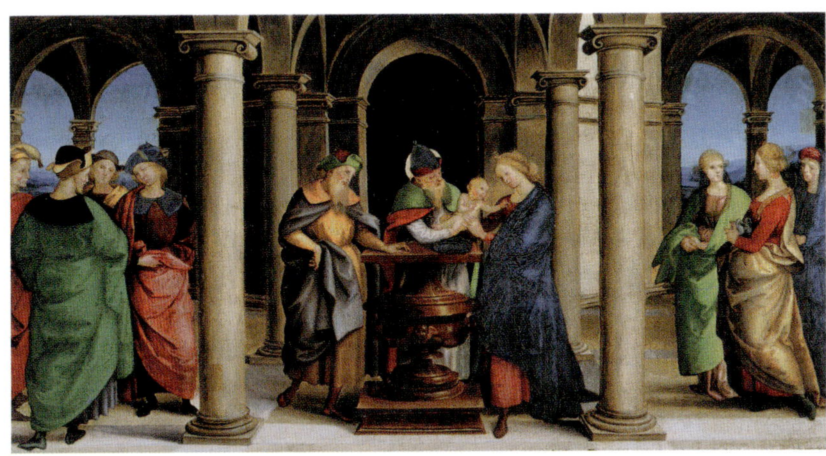

work in the city in its complexity and ambition. Although homogeneous in execution, its final appearance – indeed, its subject – results from a change of plan. The initial project was the Virgin's Assumption, to which the degli Oddi altar is dedicated – not her Coronation. In principle – as seen in treatments of the subject by Ghirlandaio and Perugino – the Coronation takes place in heaven, inaccessible to the eyes of the Apostles, who can contemplate it only mystically. But the Assumption, the Virgin rising from the tomb to rejoin her son in heaven, is an event – most famously seen in Titian's great altarpiece in the Frari, Venice – that the Apostles can witness. In Raphael's *modello*, the Apostles are arranged in their final positions, but they witness the Virgin's Assumption, standing around her sarcophagus, which has no place in a Coronation. Taking a hint from Pinturicchio's *Assumption* in Santa Maria in Aracoeli in Rome – the church for which he would later paint *The Madonna di Foligno* – Raphael angles the sarcophagus obliquely to manage the deployment of the Apostles. Only the two framing apostles are shown full-length, and their draperies are modelled with great density. Raphael focuses the viewer's attention on the three central actors, Peter, Thomas and Paul, seen at bust length, and treats the others as carefully differentiated heads, no doubt studied from life: their acuity implies that Raphael was already making portraits. The individuality of expressions and types far exceeds that in any comparable work by Perugino, and the variation of focus and spacing is an implicit criticism of Perugino's figural parades.

The change from *Assumption* to *Coronation* was made while execution was under way. Raphael did not redesign the upper section but made a series of local adjustments. Thus the studies, drawn from models, for the music-making angels celebrating the Virgin's arrival in heaven follow the Assumption *modello*; but when the new, wider central group was inserted, the lateral angels were squeezed to accommodate it, not reformulated. The heads of Christ and the Virgin are now set at a lower level than the head of the Virgin in *The Assumption* project, so eight cherubs were inserted above them to fill an otherwise empty space. But in compensation for this clumsiness, there were certain benefits: by pushing two of the angels behind Christ and the Virgin, Raphael created for them a notional semi-dome, congruent with the depth created by the angled sarcophagus. The degli Oddi *Coronation* exemplifies improvisation superimposed upon careful planning, a quick-witted flexibility that was to serve Raphael well in his Roman commissions. An iconographical change imposed or requested by the patron, or a new idea by Raphael himself, could lead

to adjustments when the project was too advanced wholly to
be redesigned.

For *The Coronation* Raphael made drawings in pen, black
chalk and metalpoint with and without added bodycolour.
The *modello*, in densely hatched pen, is the prototype of others
made during Raphael's Florentine period and the ancestor of
the first drawings that he was to make for engraving. But it
was an unnecessarily laborious technique, and increasingly
Raphael's *modelli* were in brush and wash. Figure studies for
the angels were executed in metalpoint with white bodycolour,
and a few studies of heads were made in black chalk. One large
head study, for St Thomas holding the Virgin's fallen girdle in
the lower centre, is in metalpoint, presumably because Raphael
sought a crisp three-dimensionality in this saint, pivotal to
the composition and central to its narrative. The preparation
also extends, perhaps for the first time in Raphael's work, to
the creation of auxiliary cartoons: studies made on separate
sheets of paper following the outlines created by powdered
chalk forced though the pricked holes in the cartoon proper.
All were intended to characterise significant facial expressions.
Earlier artists had employed auxiliary cartoons, but not to
the extent that Raphael would do; and while many studies
for *The Coronation* must be lost, the survivors demonstrate
that he employed different media for different stages in the
development of his composition and for different effects
within those stages. They anticipate the graphic elaboration
that was to characterise the Stanza della Segnatura. Aged 20,
Raphael was as thoughtful and meticulous in the preparation
of his painting as a structural engineer.

The Coronation is in sharper focus than the Gavari
Crucifixion: the figures are more powerfully sculptural, and
eye-catching shot colours are abandoned. *The Coronation* is
incomparably more mature. Although the actors are not as
fluently related to one another as they would become, the
complexity of the lower part is far more sophisticated than
anything in either Perugino or Pinturicchio, although some
debt is owed to both.

The fourth in the sequence of altarpieces and Raphael's final
commission in Città di Castello, the *Sposalizio*, is prominently
signed and dated. It was executed for the chapel of St Joseph
in the church of San Francesco. About two-thirds the size of
The Crucifixion, it is an accomplished narrative: note the delicate
inclination of the high priest as he guides the Virgin's finger
into the ring held by Joseph, which shows a human awareness
that Raphael had hitherto little opportunity to express. Raphael
had, of course, treated the Virgin's marriage in the predella of

32

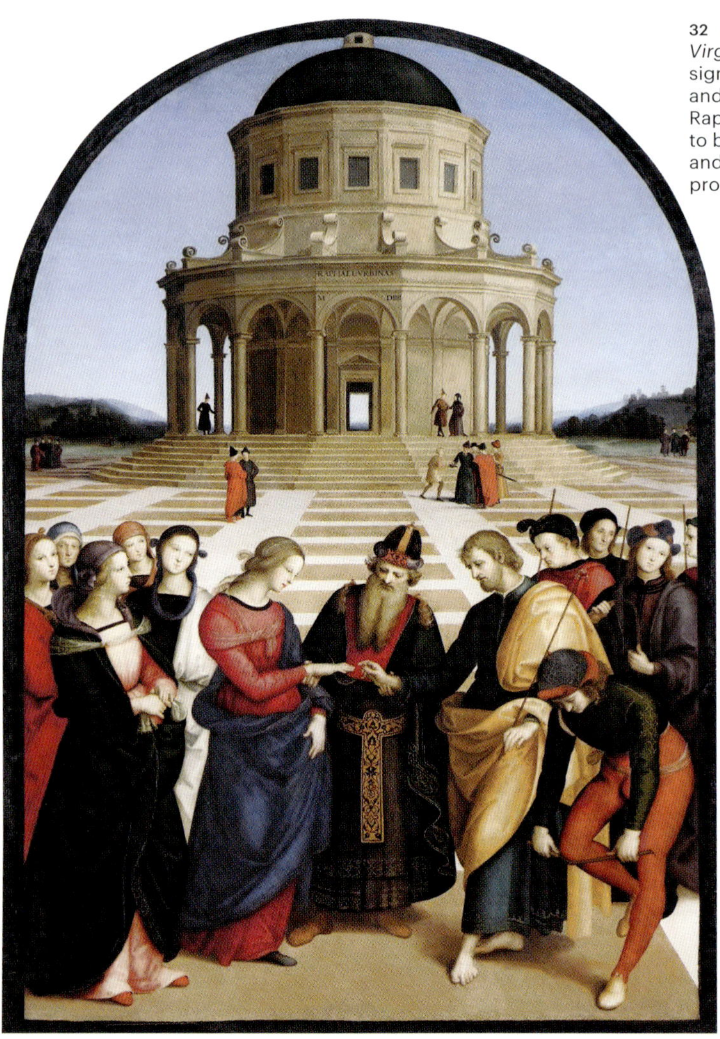

32 *The Marriage of the Virgin (The Spozalizio),* signed RAPHAEL VRBINAS and dated MDIIII (1504). Raphael's first painting to bear both a signature and a date, both displayed prominently

the degli Oddi *Coronation*, but the *Sposalizio* allowed him to test his mettle in an altarpiece treating the same subject as one Perugino currently had under way for the cathedral of Perugia. Now Raphael competes with rather than complies with the older man's ideas, and his figure grouping contrasts favourably with the prosaic line-up and anatomically bizarre high priest in Perugino's painting. The astonishing sixteen-sided temple constructed in the background is an evident and successful effort to surpass in complexity the temples designed by Perugino in his *Sposalizio* and in the Sistine *Delivery of the Keys*.

33

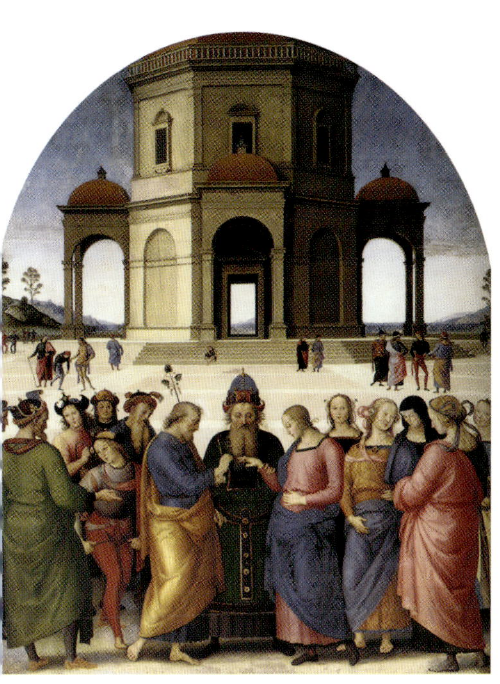 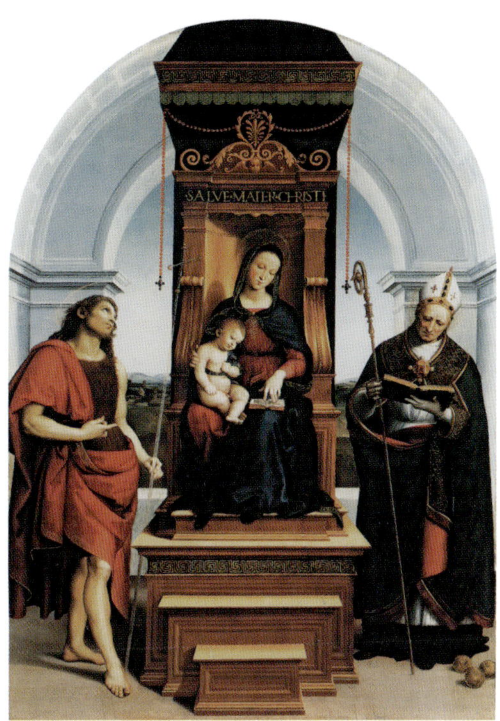

33 ABOVE LEFT Perugino, *The Marriage of the Virgin*, 1499–1504
34 ABOVE RIGHT *The Virgin and Child with Sts John the Baptist and Nicholas of Bari* (*The Pala Ansidei*), not signed, dated MDV (1505)

Nevertheless, Raphael's painting was something of a cul-de-sac. The treatment of the attendant figures is unimaginative, and their responses to the central event lack intensity. The willowy Virgin is strangely elongated, as is the more rigid Joseph, whose feet are set at a balletic right angle. This elongation and the unusual leg position immediately recall those of the Baptist in the Pala Ansidei, whose date of 1505 must be that of its completion, since it was likely designed contemporaneously with the *Sposalizio*. It has never satisfactorily been explained why the saints in the Pala Ansidei are based on those in Verrocchio's rectangular Pistoia altarpiece (completed in 1485), which presumably Raphael knew from a copy – perhaps one by his father or by Perugino, who had been in contact with Verrocchio in the 1470s. There was improvisation in this painting too: the enclosing architecture was a late addition, replacing an open-air setting. But its form, which still reflects the influence of Perugino, suggests that Raphael added it before his first Florentine

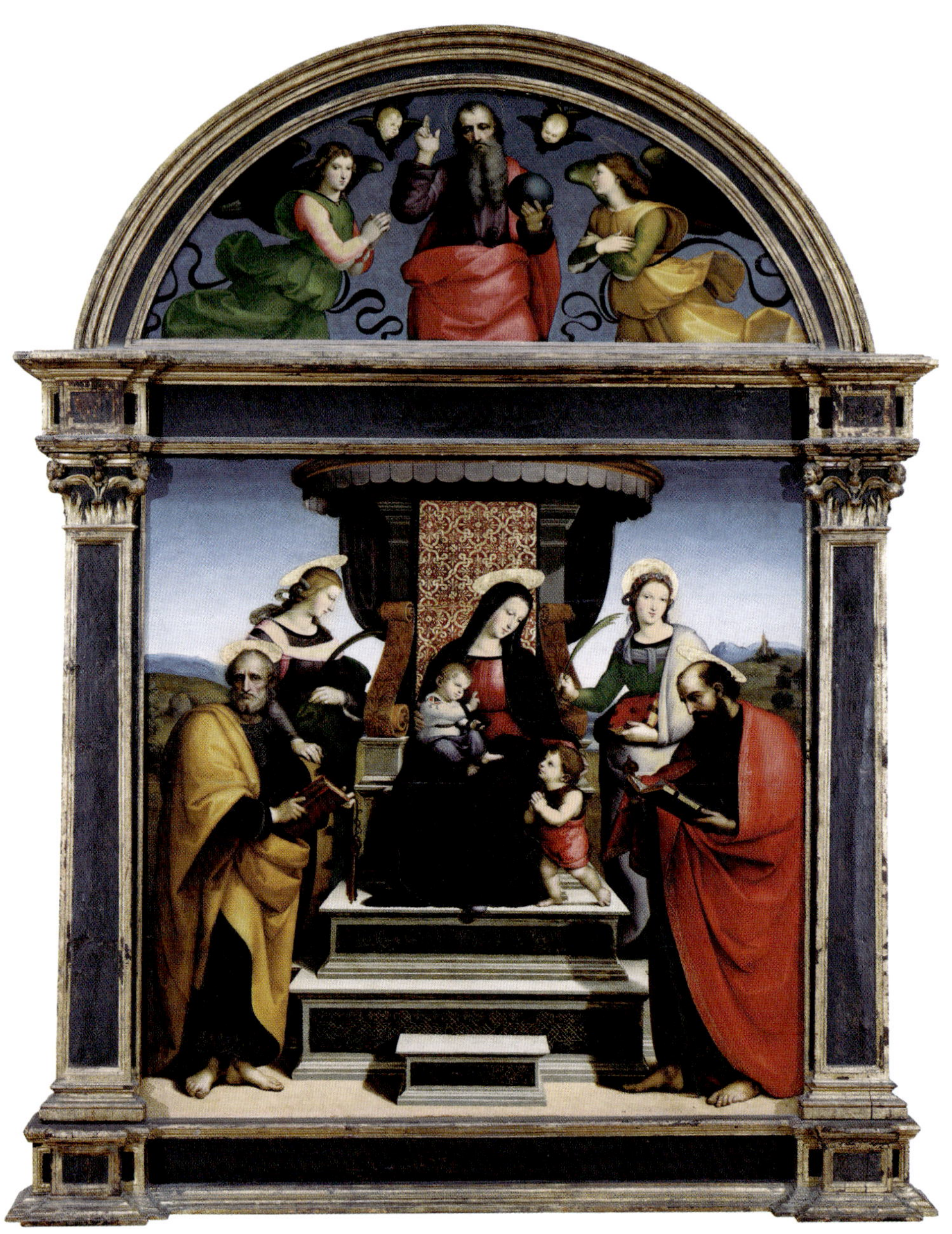

35 ABOVE *The Virgin and Child with Sts John the Baptist and Peter, Paul, Cecilia and Catherine, with God the Father flanked by angels in the Lunette (The Pala Colonna)*, 1504–05

36, 37, 38, 39, 40 OPPOSITE Predella panel to the Pala Colonna, 1504–05: *St Francis of Assisi* (opposite top left); *The Agony in the Garden* (opposite top right); *The Procession to Calvary* (opposite middle); *The Lamentation over the Dead Christ* (opposite below left); *St Anthony of Padua* (opposite below right)

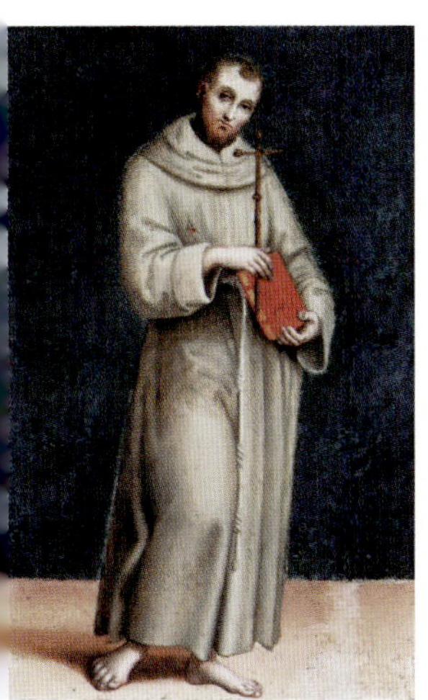

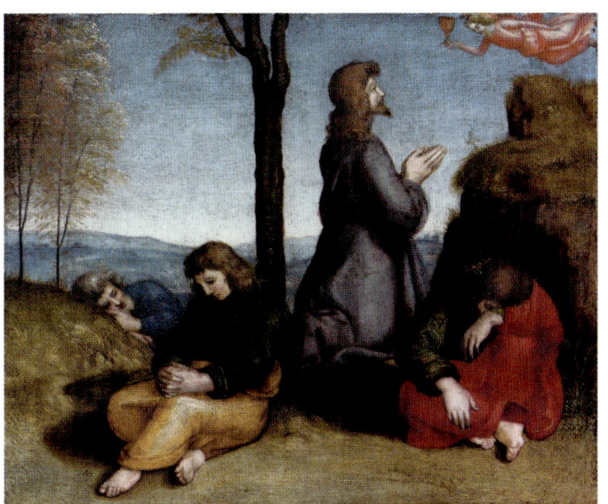

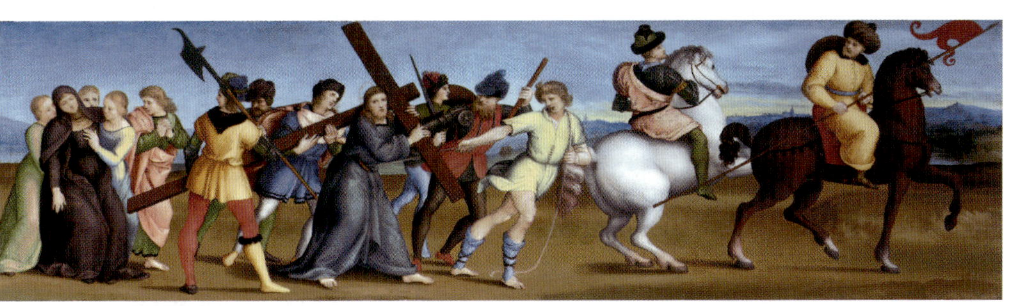

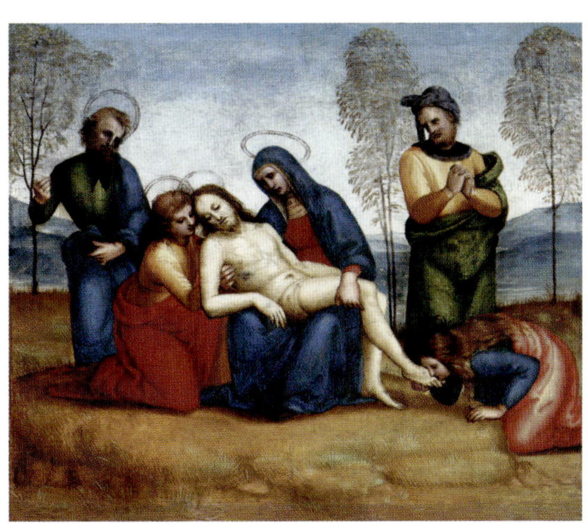

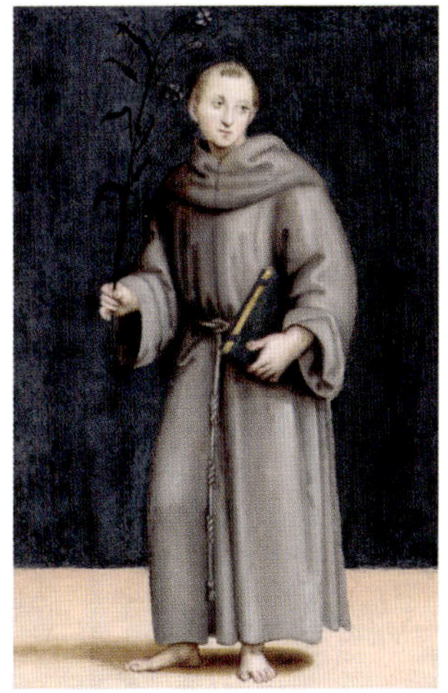

sojourn. The upturned face of John, gazing at his tall cross but simultaneously past the Virgin and Child to the source of illumination, evokes the painting's context and anticipates later responses to out-of-field manifestations by Raphael's actors.

35–40   The Pala Colonna, too, was surely completed in 1505. In fulfilling this commission for the nuns of Sant'Antonio in Perugia, according to Vasari Raphael clothed the Christ Child to spare their modesty. Its design is spatially more adventurous than that of the Pala Ansidei: the circular baldachin creates depth from above rather than below, like a ceilinged set. The female saints are bland and under-characterised, and might be by a collaborator – perhaps Raphael's friend Eusebio di San Giorgio – but the powerful, stocky forms of Peter and Paul contrast greatly with the brittle elongation of the Ansidei saints.

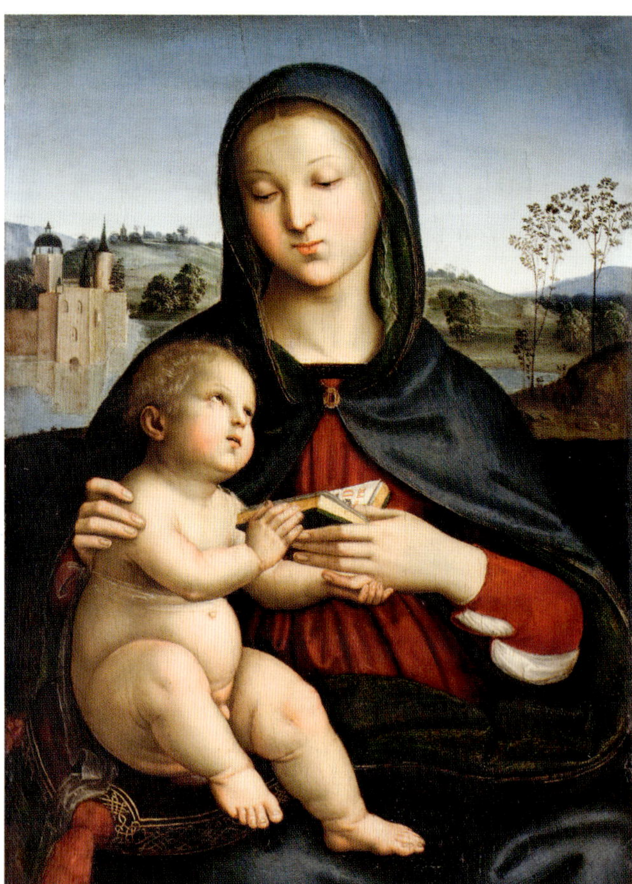

41 *The Virgin and Child at Nones*, probably 1503. Nones, the ninth hour or the mid-afternoon prayer, is indicated in the prayer book that the Virgin shows to the Christ Child

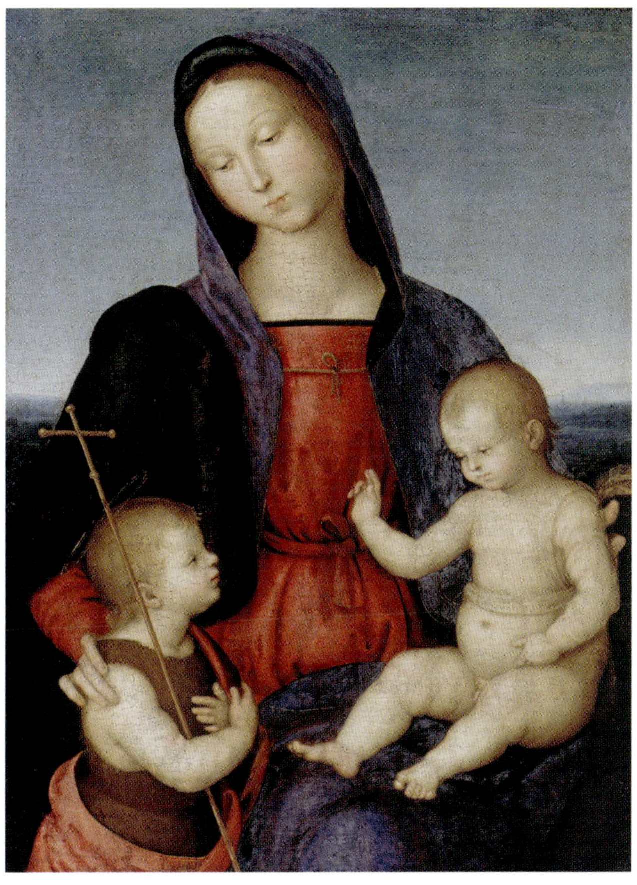

Both paintings probably remained unfinished in Perugia when Raphael went to Florence and were completed on his return in 1505. The Ansidei altarpiece may have lacked only its predella, in which some influence from Florentine models can be detected, but the sinuous movement of the Virgin's left hand might have been revised from a sketch by Leonardo. There was more work to be done on the Pala Colonna; Sts Peter and Paul must have been designed – and not simply painted – on Raphael's return. With a new solidity, they take their place in the Florentine tradition of Masaccio and Ghirlandaio, mediated through a particular friend of Raphael, Fra Bartolommeo. The compact and forceful designs of the predella panels also suggest Florentine influence, and the two standing saints who once separated them, although slight, are related in their types to the figures in Raphael's

fresco of *The Trinity and Saints* of 1505 in the small church
of San Severo, Perugia.

During this span of years Raphael also painted half-
length Madonnas: five of them survive. We know nothing of
the circumstances of these pictures, some of which may have
been painted speculatively rather than on commission. Most
of them came to light in Perugian familial collections and may
have been commissioned or acquired by forebears. While all
are competent and possess a psychological cohesion that is
not found in Perugino, none of them shows awareness of
Florentine forms. Some – like the Solly *Madonna* and the
Diotalevi *Madonna* – are softer in texture, but this may be
due to abrasion: *The Virgin and Child at Nones*, which is
in better condition, appears sharper. But differences in
execution may also correspond to differences in price. In the
Diotalevi *Madonna* the infant St John enters from the left, and
the composition, which is articulated on two levels, comes
close to that of Pinturicchio's *Madonna* in the Fitzwilliam
Museum, Cambridge – but which way the influence runs is
conjectural. Compared with interest shown by his Umbrian
contemporaries in the Madonnas that Raphael painted in
1504–05, at the beginning of his 'Florentine' period, there was
little response to those that he actually produced in Umbria.

Within the relatively closed arena of Umbrian art,
Raphael's artistic output was more varied than that of any of
his contemporaries, and he exercised considerable influence
on them. Had he died in 1505, he would be categorised as
Perugino's most inventive follower and a painter with a
promising future. But no one could have predicted what
he would achieve in Florence, still less in Rome. Compared
with the rapidity of his development in later years, the period
1500–04 is relatively static. Raphael seems to have sought little
inspiration from other centres, and few traces of Florence or
Rome or Venice can be seen in these years, save for the fact that
the horse in his *St George and the Dragon* is derived from one
of those on the Quirinal. Whether this reflected a conservative
pool of patrons or was a matter of choice is debatable. Raphael
was not a perpetual motion machine, and some periods
of his work are slacker than others; but it is hard to believe
that he was lazy, and his comparative lack of adventurousness
between 1500 and 1504 remains unexplained. However, he
was not isolated from knowledge, and some of it may have been
disquieting. Perugino had established a studio in Florence by
the 1490s and worked there extensively, sometimes neglecting
Perugian commissions. But he inadvertently provided a
warning. Perugino made few modifications to his style and

approach in his Florentine works. When he unwisely – and
ineptly – completed Filippino Lippi's *Deposition* after the latter's
death in April 1504, his work was greeted with a contumely
that terminated his Florentine career and virtually drove him
from the city. When he then attempted to update his approach
by seeking designs from other, younger artists, it was too late.
It may be that perception of Perugino's stagnation stimulated
Raphael to take on new challenges while there was still time
to do so.

However, there are exceptions to this picture of relative stasis:
in two schemes, one small, one large, Raphael displayed powers
of design that outstrip anything one might have expected in
Umbria and that equal – indeed surpass – anything being done
at that date in Florence, save by Leonardo. It was in predella
panels, which dealt with narratives and multi-figure subjects,
that Raphael allowed his inventiveness freest reign, and the
most spectacular instance of this is *The Adoration of the Magi
and Shepherds*, the central panel below *The Coronation of the
Virgin*. Raphael composes a rich figure group with the most
subtle differentiation and paragraphing. Within the overall
descent towards the Virgin and the blessing Child, which
lends a cohesion to the figures' attention not seen in any of
the Adorations painted by Perugino, Raphael introduces counter-
movements that interrupt – and thereby increase – the energy of
the flow. Raphael makes the viewer understand the importance
of the event, but simultaneously evokes the casualness of some
of the participants in this wedge-shaped assemblage. Mirrored,
the composition would resemble the lower level of *The Disputa*.
In principle, it would seem an impossible achievement for any
painter who had not seen Leonardo's *Adoration of the Magi*,
but it would be by no means an easy inference, even from that.
How Raphael devised this scheme remains unexplained; he
may already have had some awareness of Donatello's Padua
reliefs, with their dynamic and powerfully organised crowd
scenes, but they could not have provided a precise model.
The Adoration is, by any standards, a major design achievement,
and one without obvious precedent. Neither of *The Coronation*'s
other predella panels, although they are effective, displays this
level of brilliance.

The large scheme is one with which Raphael's involvement,
while undocumented, is attested by Vasari and by surviving
drawings. This was the decoration of the Piccolomini Library,
which opens off the North aisle of Siena Cathedral. In 1502
Bernardino Pinturicchio received a novel and major
commission: to paint a biographical narrative cycle, in ten
episodes, of Aeneas Sylvius Piccolomini, poet, intellectual,

papal diplomat and, finally, pope, as Pius II. It was ordered
by his nephew, Pius III, whose reign lasted less than a month.
The frescoes were large, and there was no obvious precedent
for a biographical cycle of a near-contemporary on such a scale,
although Mantegna had produced a modern scheme in the
Camera degli Sposi in Mantua.

Vasari says that Pinturicchio requested Raphael to assist
him not – as one might have expected – with the cycle's
execution, but with its design. A young man of 19 or 20 was
asked to provide designs for a well-established artist thirty
years his senior. It is hard to think of any art historical parallel
for such a collaboration, and Vasari's account would have been
dismissed as fantasy had not several drawings for the scheme
unmistakably by Raphael survived: *modelli* for, respectively, the
first and fifth episodes in the cycle, *The Journey of Aeneas Silvius
Piccolomini to Basel* and *The Introduction of Eleanor of Portugal
to Emperor Frederick III* (New York, Morgan Library); a copy of
a lost *modello* for the fourth episode (Chatsworth, Devonshire
Collection); figure studies for the third, *The Coronation of
Aeneas Sylvius as a Poet on the Capitol*; and a sketch implying
that Raphael also helped to devise the scheme's layout
(Oxford, Ashmolean). Vasari says in one place that Raphael
made designs for all the episodes and, in another, for only
some of them, which may be more likely, but we cannot be
certain. Nor is it clear when Raphael's participation occurred.
It is usually taken to be at the beginning of the project, in 1502,
but the execution of the library was protracted and the scheme
was not completed until 1508. Raphael may have provided
designs in instalments: the sketches for *The Coronation of
Aeneas Sylvius*, for example, are likely to have been made
in Florence, while the *Introduction* is close enough in design
to the *Sposalizio* to suggest that it is contemporary. The cycle
demonstrates an impressive command of characterisation,
of inventiveness, for none of these events had been depicted
previously (although Perugino had provided a precedent
for 'conference' scenes). Raphael's ability to find ways of
representing new subjects would stand him in good stead
when he met with unrivalled opportunities in Rome.

The most impressive illustration of Raphael's capacity
as a designer is his *modello* for *The Journey to Basel*. Raphael
understood that the introductory episode in the history
needed to be active, to draw the viewer in, so the procession
advances rightwards with nothing to slow the eye. Movements
of horses and men are lively, appropriate to a scene focused
on a young man, and the definition of forms is, throughout,
precise but not pedantic. Raphael includes some seven riders

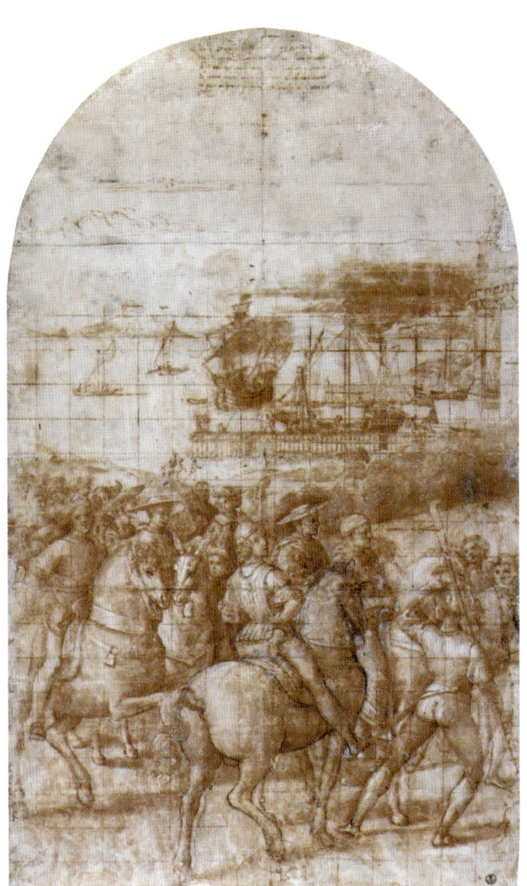
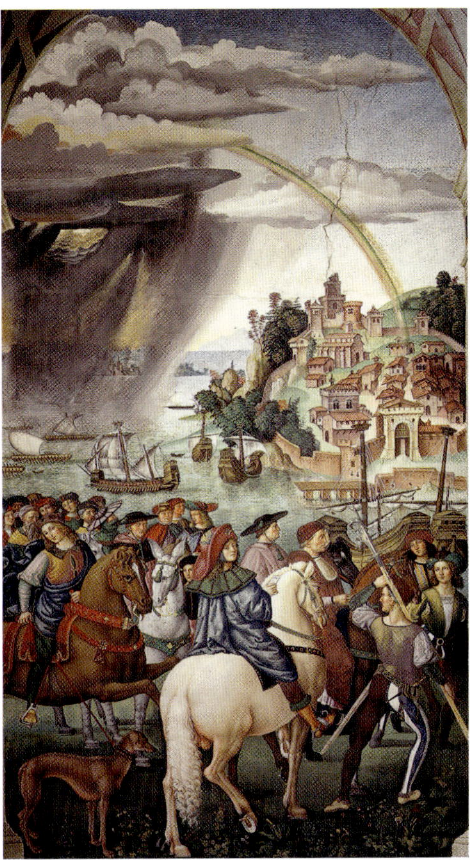

43 ABOVE LEFT *The Journey of Aeneas Silvius Piccolomini to Basel*, probably 1503
44 ABOVE RIGHT Pinturicchio, *The Journey of Aeneas Piccolomini to Basel*, c. 1505

and four horses without congestion, and adds, at the lower
right, a foot soldier in a complex turning movement that
is both natural – he is checking that the procession is in
order – and avoids abruptness. His pose, incidentally, has
some relation to that of the fleeing soldier in the predella
panel (to the Gavari *Crucifixion*) of *St Jerome Rescuing Bishop
Silvanus*. The actors' varied gestures are well integrated into
the landscape setting and the view of the port of Ancona,
which reminds us of an under-appreciated aspect of Raphael's
work: his interest in topography – demonstrated also in the
view of Perugia in the background of a drawing of *The Penitent
St Jerome* of *c.* 1504 (Oxford, Ashmolean).

But while Pinturicchio – aware that his approach required
rejuvenation – was intelligent enough to employ Raphael,

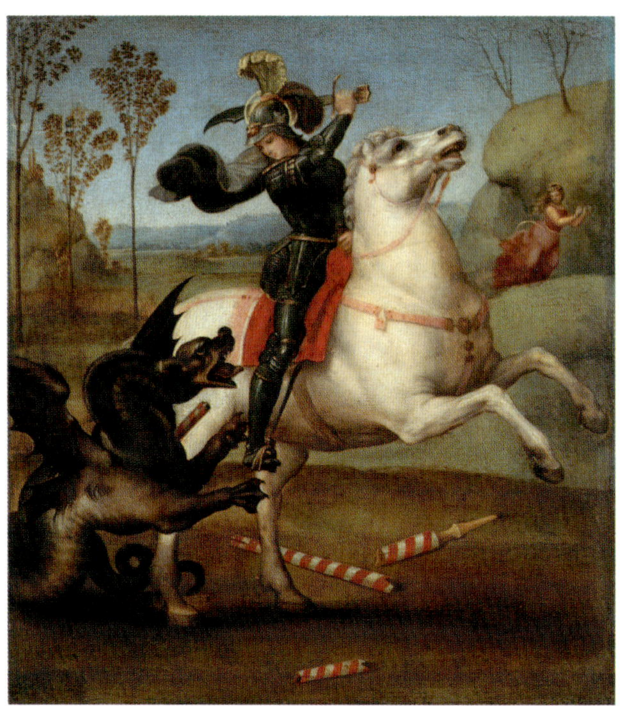

45 LEFT *St George and the Dragon,* probably 1502–03
46 BELOW *St Michael Vanquishing Satan,* probably 1502–03

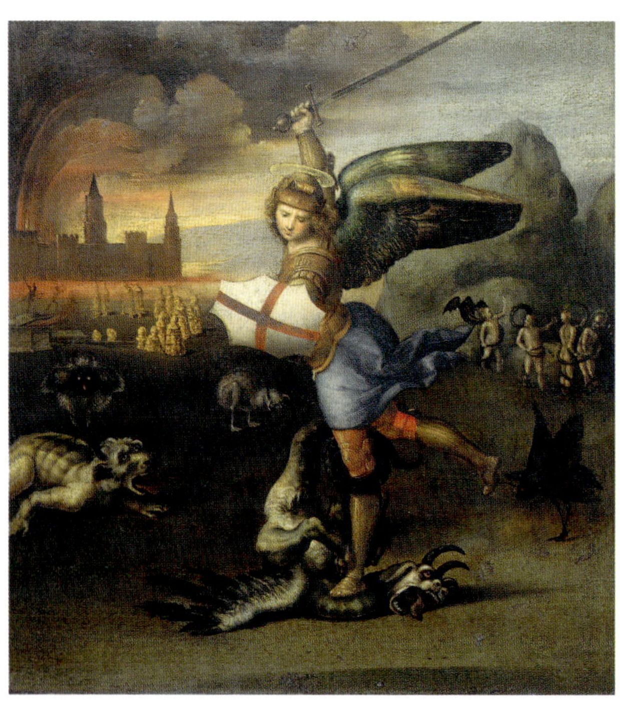

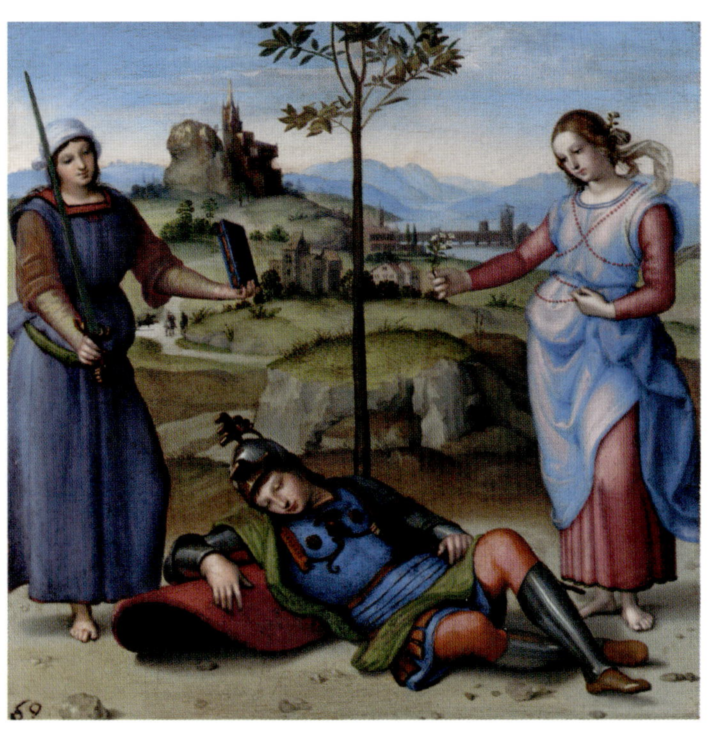

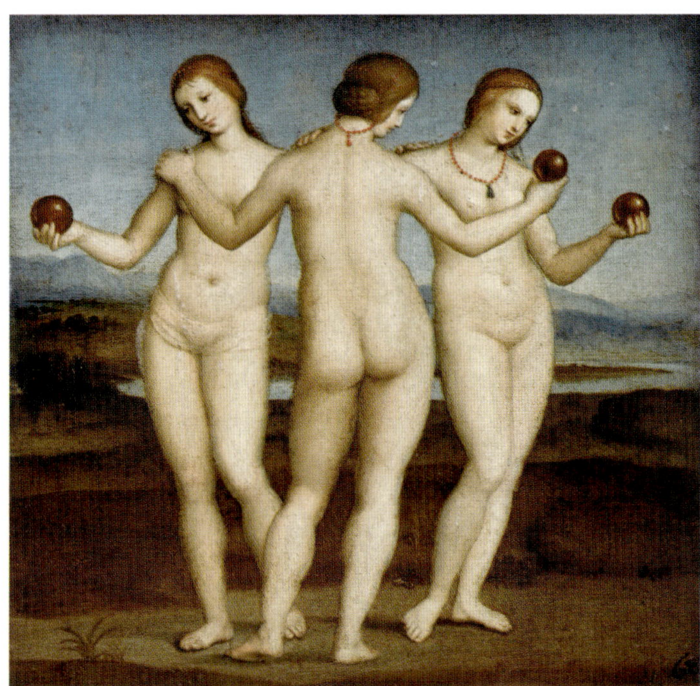

47 ABOVE *An Allegory of the Choice between Virtue and Comfort (The Vision of a Knight)*, probably 1503–04
48 RIGHT *The Three Graces*, probably 1503–04

he was not intelligent enough to make full use of Raphael's mind. The fresco of *The Journey of Aeneas Piccolomini to Basel* compromises Raphael's *modello*. Pinturicchio was evidently concerned about the empty area at the lower left and did not appreciate Raphael's purpose, so to fill it he inserted a hound; had it been shown running, the addition might have been an acceptable accompaniment to the riders, but, entirely static and in profile, it destroys any effect of movement. And instead of the onward procession shown by Raphael, Pinturicchio arrests the young horseman, evidently Aeneas, who looks out at the viewer in a way that is unnatural and quite unlike Raphael's quick glance. In place of the horse's lively flicking tail, he paints a long drooping tail that once more arrests movement. Examples of Pinturicchio's incomprehension of Raphael's ideas could be multiplied. Raphael's Piccolomini designs show a command of form and action, an understanding of relevant composition and a control of facial expression and mobile body language that outstrips any of his contemporaries. But we would be hard pressed to divine it from the surviving paintings of his Umbrian period. This was to change rapidly when he encountered Florence.

An insight into at least some aspects of Raphael's course of study in the period *c.* 1500–05 is offered in a disassembled sketchbook now in Venice. It contains many drawings, mostly after details of compositions and single figures by artists that Raphael knew well – Antonio Pollaiuolo, Mantegna, Signorelli and Perugino, among others – plus a drawing, probably the latest in the book, that records an otherwise unknown variant of Leonardo's *Madonna of the Yarnwinder*. There are also several copies after *The Famous Men* in the *studiolo* of Federico da Montefeltro. Some nineteenth-century scholars believed this sketchbook to be by Raphael and, although this view is now rejected, occasional but unconvincing attempts are made to give one or another drawing to him. But even if nothing in it is by Raphael himself, the book must have been made by a close associate: it features a copy of both the recto and verso of a fragmentary sheet of drawings by Raphael (Oxford, Ashmolean Museum), although not in their original relation. The draughtsman's identity remains elusive, but his sketchbook mirrors Raphael's artistic interests on the eve of his Florentine adventure. It also suggests that, when it was made, Raphael had little foreknowledge of what he would see in the city.

Chapter 3
Raphael's Florentine Period

According to Vasari, Raphael decided to go to Florence – apparently on his own initiative – because he had heard of the battle paintings being prepared by Leonardo and Michelangelo (1475–1564) for the hall of the Great Council of the Palazzo della Signoria. It was probably his first visit: none of the few traces of Florentine art seen in his work before 1505 requires residence in Florence. But he would have learnt of Leonardo from his father and from Perugino, and during his visit to Siena might have heard something of Michelangelo, who in June 1501 had been commissioned to complete the statuary of the Piccolomini altar, adjacent to the library in Siena Cathedral. But no statues were delivered until 1504, and it is improbable that Raphael knew any paintings by Michelangelo.

In principle, Raphael's desire to study innovatory Florentine treatments of military subjects might have been prompted by an impending Perugian commission: an historical cycle for the Palazzo di Priori. However, Raphael's drawing of *The Siege of Perugia*, probably of 1505 (Paris, Louvre), is an exercise in the manner of Antonio Pollaiuolo, without reference to the designs of Leonardo or Michelangelo. Primarily, Raphael must have been eager to see and study the latest achievements in what was, at the turn of the century, the most artistically advanced city in Italy.

Raphael's friend Timoteo Viti may also have spent some time in Florence, perhaps in Raphael's company, but nothing that he learnt affected his art more than superficially. Viti's occasional collaborator Girolamo Genga, a more powerful designer, alsospent time in Florence and produced some compact and complex Holy Family groups, but he was little interested in life

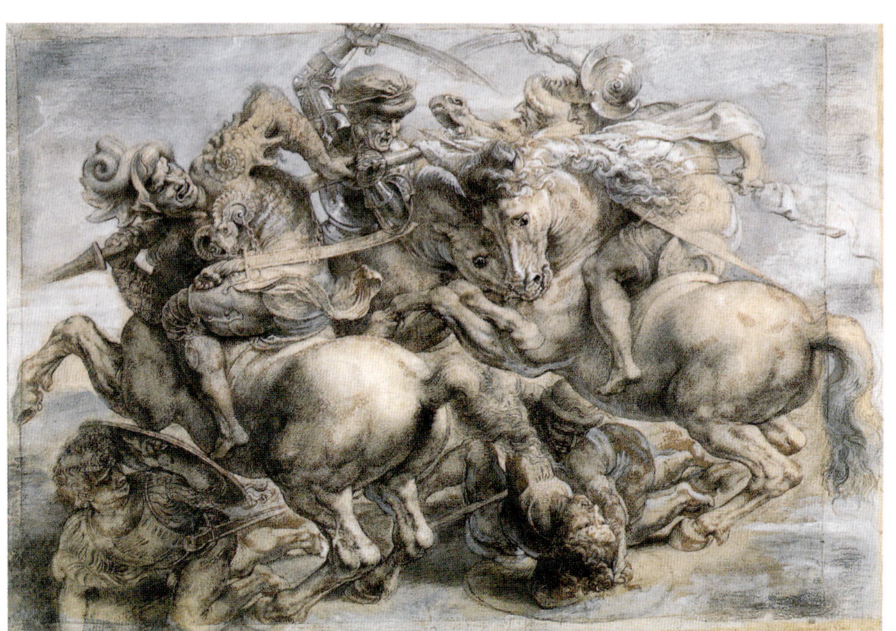

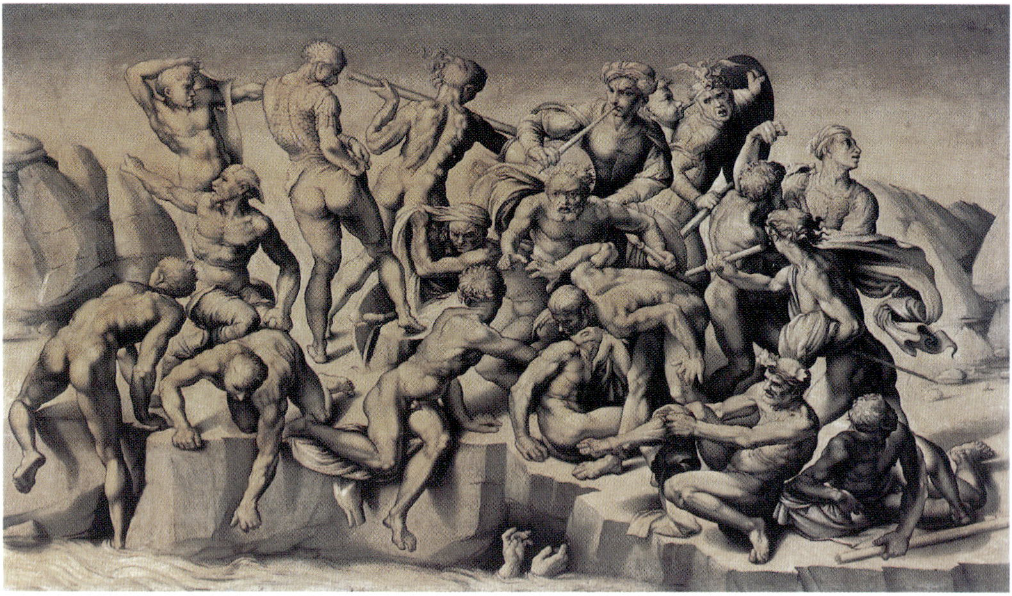

49 TOP Peter Paul Rubens after Leonardo da Vinci's composition
of 1504–05, *The Battle of Anghiari*, c. 1603, reworked later
50 ABOVE Aristotile da Sangallo after Michelangelo's composition
of 1504–05, *The Battle of Cascina*, 1542

study and did not achieve the human directness of Raphael: indeed, his eccentric individualism in some ways anticipates the expressive distortions of Jacopo Pontormo (1494–1556).

Raphael, whose ambitions, talents and, above all, intellect were of a wholly different order from those of his Umbrian and Marchigian contemporaries, probably arrived in Florence in October 1504. The date comes from a letter of recommendation, written on Raphael's behalf, by Giovanna Feltria della Rovere, addressed to Pietro Soderini (1451–1522), the *gonfalonier* of Florence and the driving force of the Palazzo Vecchio commissions. Some critics have dismissed the letter as a confection by Giovanni Bottari, who first published it in 1754, or by one of his contemporaries. But although it contains anomalies (Giovanni Santi is referred to as though he were still alive), they are probably the result of erroneous emendation. The date is appropriate; that the letter was sent to Florence's head of state fits the high-level support that Raphael's career, in Florence as elsewhere, implies; and the language, which has created suspicion – 'a Firenze ad imparara' ('has come to Florence to learn') – is paralleled in a letter of 1508 from Michelangelo to his brother Buonarroto, recommending the young Alonso Berruguete (*c.* 1488–1561) who is coming to Florence 'per imparare'.

During his time in Florence, which was far from continuous, *imparare* was what Raphael emphatically did – and, according both to Vasari and the visual evidence, with unprecedented velocity. Leonardo and Michelangelo, whose reputations drew Raphael to Florence, are, by universal consent, two of the greatest post-medieval Western artists, and their influence was incalculable. Both were great innovators, and both were supreme draughtsmen. That Raphael – from a relative backwater, where he could have had minimal technical or conceptual preparation for their art – was able to address, absorb and combine their vastly different temperaments and ideals is a tribute to both his abilities and his vast self-confidence: any other artist would have returned to Umbria defeated or have ignored what he saw.

Raphael's initial stay in Florence probably lasted no more than five or six months. Vasari says, wonderingly, that Raphael's transformation came about in a matter of months owing to astonishing assiduity in study. A measure of Raphael's progress is *The Holy Trinity with Saints* that he frescoed, probably in spring 1505, in the small Perugian church of San Severo. He completed only the upper section, but it is nevertheless pivotal. It contains nothing of Perugino, which makes it cruelly ironic that it was Perugino who, *c.* 1521, completed the lower section,

51

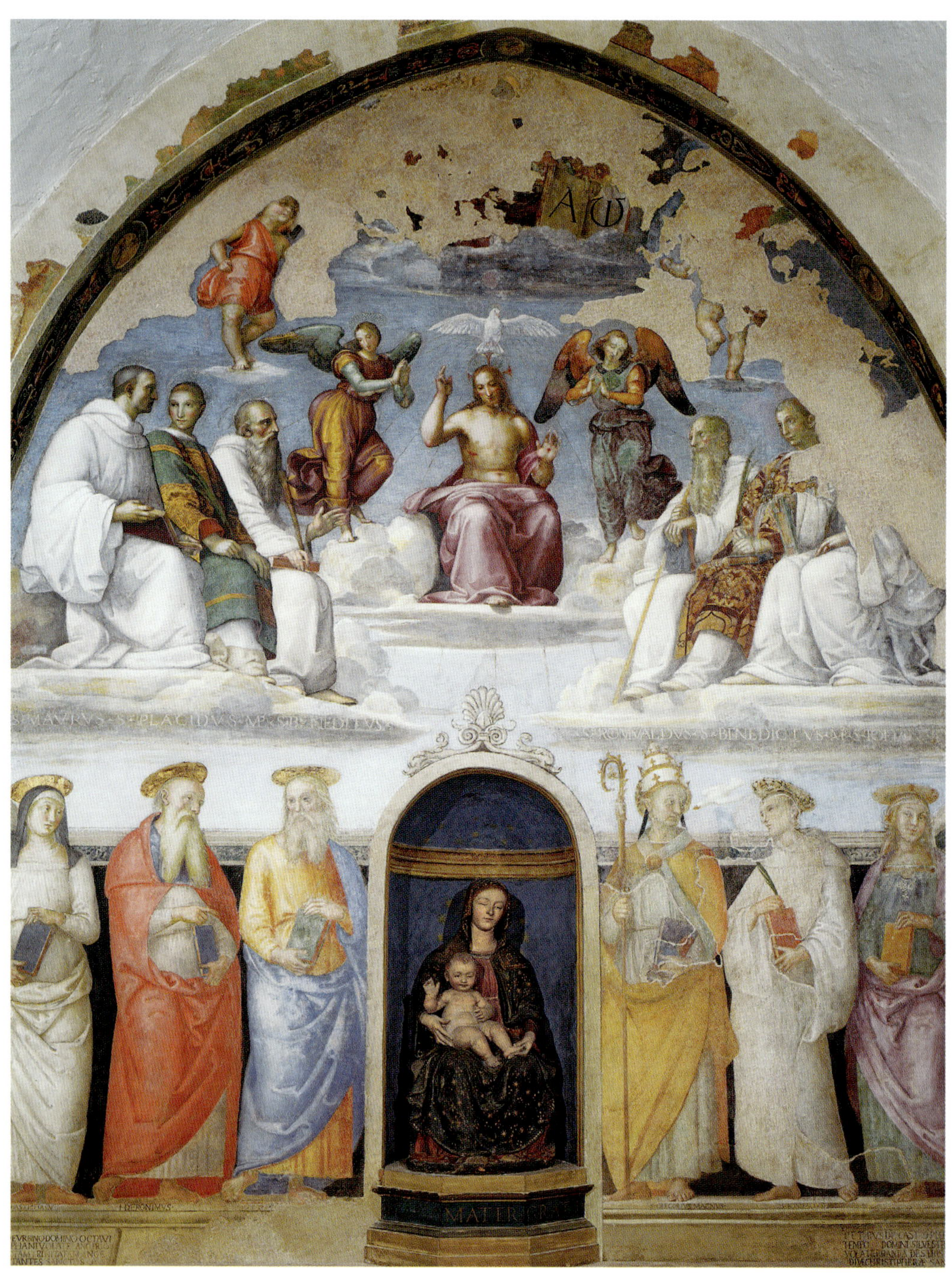

51 *The Trinity with Saints*, 1505. The lower section with six standing saints was executed in 1521 by Perugino, who certainly did not follow, and may not have known, Raphael's plans for this area

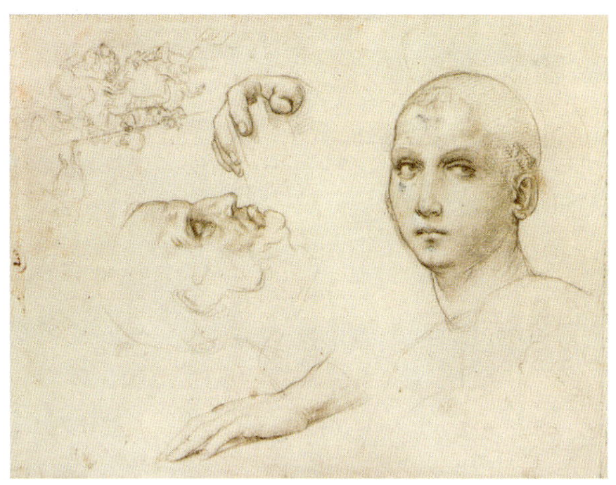

for his simple parade of saints sabotages his former pupil's intentions. On the lower level Raphael would have constructed an apse-like space formed by standing, and perhaps seated, saints – probably the same as those painted by Perugino – arranged in depth that would have supported the notional semi-dome above. Raphael would have projected a tightly geometrical scheme, and the saints would no doubt have contemplated the divine presences above, as in the degli Oddi *Coronation*.

Raphael had certainly studied Fra Bartolommeo's and Albertinelli's *Last Judgment* of 1500 in San Marco, Florence, the upper half of which deployed a semi-dome construction, and it was that fresco which inspired his scheme. A further link with Fra Bartolommeo is the heavy and voluminous forms of the draperies: Peruginesque pot-hook folds, not fully discarded in 1504, are avoided. A different trace of Florence can be seen in two head studies for the fresco. One, a profile, evokes forceful maturity; the other, a young man with an egg-shaped head as pure as a Brancusi, communicates intense idealism. Both are made with the utmost precision in metalpoint, and the contrast between them, and the type of the older man, show Raphael's awareness of the contrasted pairing characteristic of Leonardo. Leonardo is cited directly in the small sketch at the upper left of the same page that records the central group of the 'Fight for the Standard' from *The Battle of Anghiari*, under way in 1504. Raphael no doubt saw some of that ill-fated project on the wall, but his sketch was taken from one of Leonardo's drawings, for it includes a horse seen from the rear that was not carried into

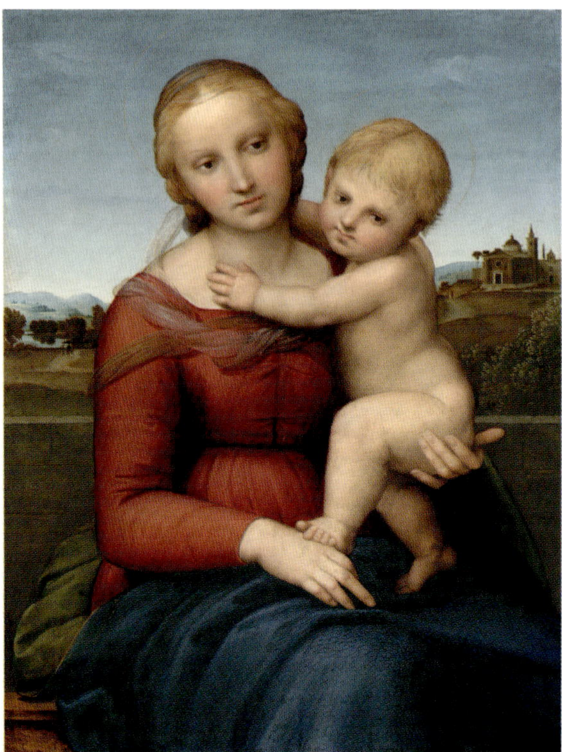

the mural. Raphael must already have had the entrée to Leonardo's studio.

In summer 1505 Raphael may have returned to Urbino. It seems likely that the so-called *Small Cowper Madonna* was then delivered to Guidobaldo, for whom, Vasari says, Raphael painted two Madonnas. Its provenance is unknown, but the inclusion in the background of Francesco di Giorgio's church of San Bernardino, commissioned by Federico da Montefeltro as his mausoleum, suggests Guidobaldo's patronage.

Raphael probably spent the remainder of 1505 and 1506 in Florence. We do not know where he lived and worked, but he may have shared the studio of his exact contemporary Ridolfo Ghirlandaio (1483–1561), the son of Domenico. It was with Ridolfo, when he quit Florence in 1508, that Raphael left the large *sacra conversazione* known as *The Madonna del Baldacchino*; and Vasari adds that Ridolfo completed an unfinished Madonna abandoned by Raphael – probably the Colonna *Madonna* in Berlin.

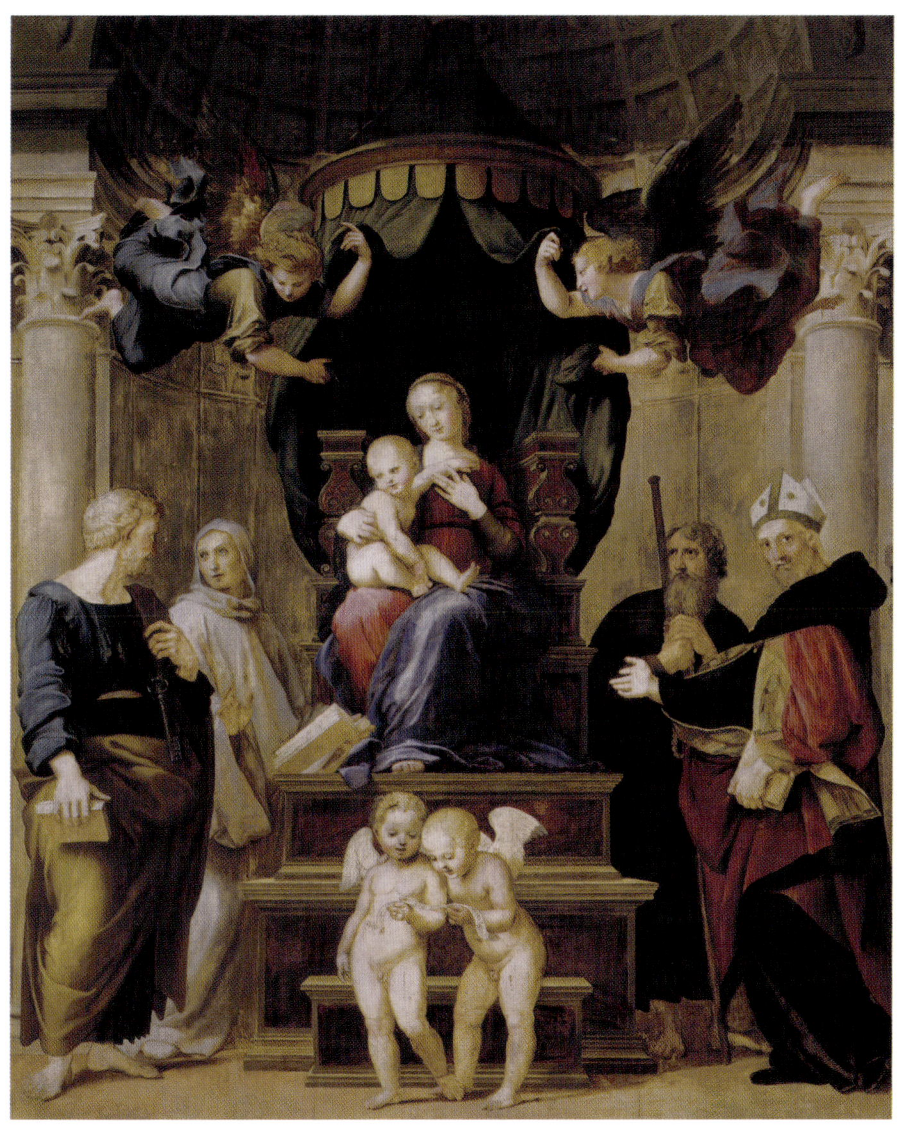

54   *The Madonna del Baldacchino*, commissioned in 1506 for the Dei family's chapel in Santo Spirito, was Raphael's largest Florentine painting and the only one intended for a public site, but he never completed it. The Dei waited until after Raphael's death to replace it but, when they did so, they commissioned an altarpiece from Rosso Fiorentino (1495–1540) in a style that was dramatically new and aggressively un-Raphaelesque, perhaps a

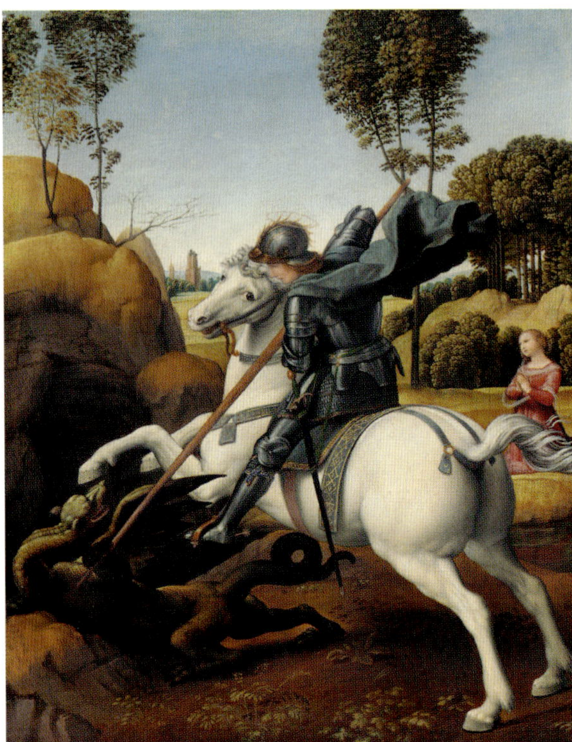

sign of their annoyance. The original panel was acquired
by Baldassare Turini (1486–1543), a Roman friend of Raphael
and one of his executors, who placed it in his family chapel
in Pescia Cathedral (it must have been among the first
obviously unfinished paintings to be placed on public
display), as much a relic of Raphael as a religious image.

Raphael returned to Perugia in 1507 to paint the Borghese
Entombment, which is dated that year. It was destined for the
Baglioni Chapel – dedicated to St Matthew – in the church of
San Francesco al Prato. Raphael probably took the opportunity
to make a return visit to Urbino, where he may have executed
the second *St George and the Dragon* (Washington, National
Gallery of Art), again for Guidobaldo. Perhaps it was at this time
that he made designs for silverware for the court of Urbino:
pieces by Raphael were offered to Isabella d'Este in July 1516,
some of which she purchased. The most probable executant
of Raphael's designs would have been his friend the silversmith
Cesare (or Cesarino) Rossetti (d. 1527), mentioned in a note by
Raphael of, probably, late 1507 on the verso of a drawing that he

sent to Domenico Alfani (Lille, Musée des Beaux-Arts). Raphael was probably back in Florence by the end of 1507 and remained there until he left for Rome in summer 1508.

It has been suggested that Raphael made a brief reconnaissance to Rome in either 1506 or 1507, but the evidence is fragile and the argumentation tortured. The trip, if it occurred, had only slight reverberations in Raphael's art, little more than the Roman views seen in the backgrounds of the *St George and the Dragon* and the unfinished Esterhazy *Madonna*. Two drawings of the Pantheon (Florence, Uffizi) – showing part of the interior and the porch – are generally dated before Raphael moved to Rome and seem to be indirect.

II

Raphael's assimilation of what he saw in Florence was of unequalled rapidity, but it was not instantaneous: some of the paintings and sculptures that he observed and the ideas that they inspired had delayed fruiting. He certainly studied as much as possible of Leonardo and Michelangelo. Raphael's copy of Leonardo's *Leda* (Windsor, Royal Collection), like his sketch of the 'Fight for the Standard', was probably made in Leonardo's workshop from a drawing rather than the painting; in it, following Leonardo in technique as well as form, Raphael uses 'bracelet' hatching: lines that curve round the form and establish its three-dimensionality and volume. A drawn portrait of a young woman (Paris, Louvre) is an adaption of the *Mona Lisa*.

Leonardo was undoubtedly the single most important source for Raphael, and he was probably Raphael's personal mentor. That Leonardo painted so little was not a drawback. In his drawings and in the paintings that his assistants and followers developed from them, Leonardo left a vast reservoir of ideas that Raphael continued to interpret and reinterpret at different moments and in different ways until his death. But we do not know quite how extensive was Raphael's awareness of Leonardo's work, for many of his study drawings are lost. Thus we have no copies by Raphael after any of Leonardo's three versions – or their preliminaries – of *The Virgin and Child with St Anne*, but he must have made them, for motifs from one or other of the compositions recur in his work. He must also have studied Leonardo's San Donato a Scopeto *Adoration of the Magi* assiduously: no copies by him survive, but he cites details from it in many of his paintings, and it fathered compositional devices that he made his own. It underlays the design of *The Disputa*, and Raphael's final painting, *The Transfiguration*, is in part a meditation on Leonardo's unfinished composition.

From Michelangelo's cartoon of *The Battle of Cascina*
Raphael copied two energetic figures (Vatican Library), and no
doubt others. Among Michelangelo's sculptures, he copied the
David, in rear view, and the *St Matthew* (both London, British
Museum), and the unfinished roundels begun for Bartolommeo
Pitti and Raphael's friend Taddeo Taddei, which he no doubt
saw in their owners' houses; he made two drawings of the
latter (Paris, Louvre, and Chatsworth, Devonshire Collection).
Echoes in his work make it clear that Raphael knew the
Bruges *Madonna* – or perhaps a model for it – and the Doni
Tondo of 1506, seen in the house of Angelo Doni and his wife,
Maddalena Strozzi. What Raphael probably valued most about
Michelangelo, in addition to his unrivalled realisation of the
expressive potential of the male nude, was his ability to create
individual figures of unequalled emotional and moral intensity.
Michelangelo's poetry of form alerted Raphael to new strata of
spirituality. But Raphael also responded to Michelangelo's skill
as a composer of compact forms, in which he rivalled Leonardo.

Raphael's attention was not confined to the greatest of his
contemporaries. He looked closely at Quattrocento art. Among
sculptors, he studied Donatello, revered by both Leonardo and

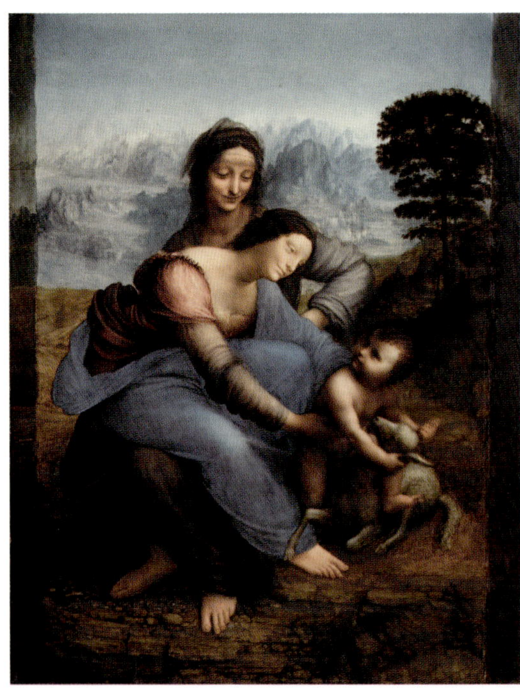

56 LEFT Leonardo, *The Virgin
and Child with St Anne and a
Lamb, c.* 1505–19. Although
Leonardo worked on this painting
until his death and continually
revised it, the composition
was largely finalised by 1505
57 OPPOSITE Leonardo, *The
Adoration of the Magi,* 1480–82
(unfinished)

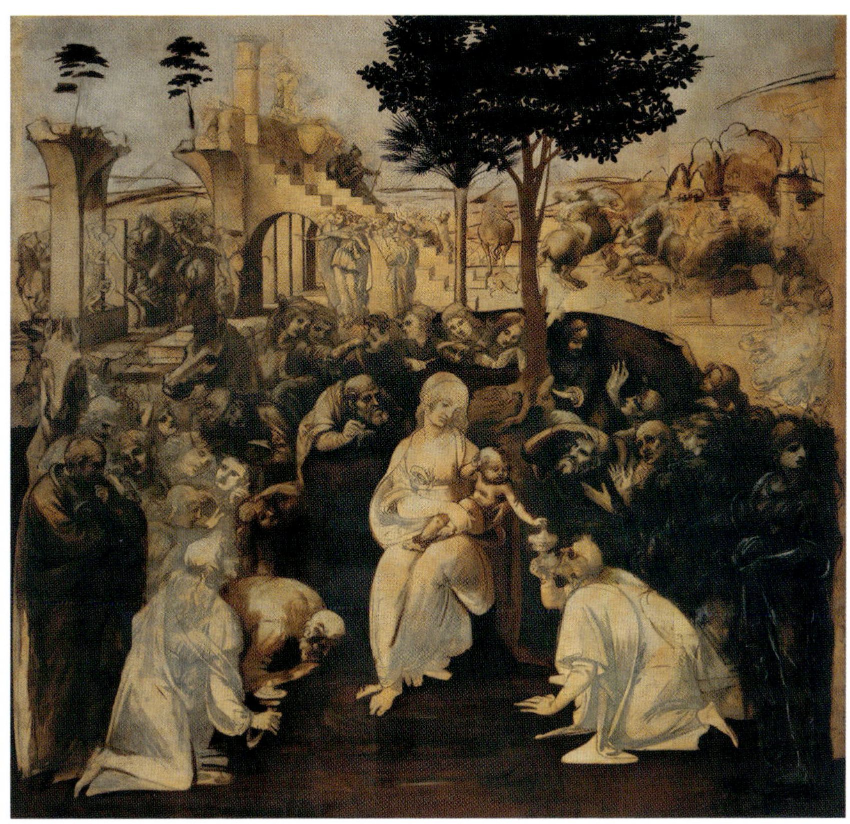

Michelangelo, whose *St John the Evangelist* he already knew,
indirectly, by *c.* 1500: his drawing of it (Paris, Louvre) looks to
have been made after a copy by Perugino. Raphael must have
studied the encyclopaedia of debating gestures in the bronze
doors of the Old Sacristy, of San Lorenzo, and no doubt many of
the other sculptures left by Donatello in Florence, including the
most famous and influential, the *St George* from Orsanmichele,
which is quoted in one of Raphael's drawings (Oxford, Ashmolean).
And Luca della Robbia – whose lunette relief over the main door
of San Domenico in Urbino Raphael would have known from
childhood – stimulated his half-length Madonnas.

Among earlier painters, Raphael studied carefully the frescoes
in the Brancacci Chapel by Masaccio (1401–28), the founder
of the second phase of Renaissance art; his later tapestry
cartoons are keyed to Masaccio's impassive grandeur. And
the work of Domenico Ghirlandaio, whose Narni *Coronation*
he already knew, was of particular interest. The influence of

Ghirlandaio, Florence's leading planner and executant of grand fresco schemes, is apparent in Raphael's Roman work. Raphael also copied the wild vault frescoes by Filippino Lippi (*c.* 1457–1504) in the Strozzi Chapel in Santa Maria Novella (Paris, Louvre), who may have prompted the cloud-borne *Evangelists* that he designed in 1517–18 for an unknown purpose. His father's son, Raphael was not wedded to a particular aesthetic, and little escaped him, even if he did not make immediate use of it.

Raphael's most important initial interlocutor was Fra Bartolommeo (Baccio della Porta; 1472–1517), his senior by just over a decade. Fra Bartolommeo's broad and simplified colour schemes, stately and limpid forms, sense of grand spacing, and easy deployment of Leonardesque *sfumato* would have been immediately accessible to Raphael, for Perugino's work was, to some extent, also the Frate's starting point. Fra Bartolommeo had returned to painting from monastic seclusion only shortly before Raphael arrived in Florence; in the interim his ideas were actualised by his associate Mariotto Albertinelli (1474–1515), with whom Raphael was well enough acquainted to lend the substantial sum of 50 ducats. Vasari records Raphael's friendship with the Frate, to whom, he says, Raphael taught perspective (a questionable claim, because the Frate's perspective constructions were already accomplished), and from whom he learnt richer and broader colouring (which is plausible, particularly for the paintings of 1505). *The Madonna del Baldacchino* is obviously an exercise in and a meditation on Fra Bartolommeo's manner, but Raphael enlivened his picture by vivacious interaction among the standing saints, foreshadowing the conversations in *The Disputa*. He also added a pair of child angels, studying a script before the Virgin's throne, who develop a theme much favoured by Giovanni Bellini and other Venetians: perhaps this insertion was an encouragement to the Frate to visit Venice in 1508. The energetic angels who swoop into the field at top left and right differ in style from the rest and were probably painted during a second campaign of work, shortly before Raphael's departure, in 1508.

Otherwise, Raphael's commissions during these four years, whether in Florence or elsewhere, were for small and medium-size paintings. Raphael painted or began at least twenty-five panels, some now known only from copies. These included three world-famous iterations of the Virgin in a landscape, and three complex Holy Family groups. He also executed half-length Madonnas in different formats – including two roundels – ranging from small and exquisitely finished to life-size and broadly painted; his representations of the Virgin gradually

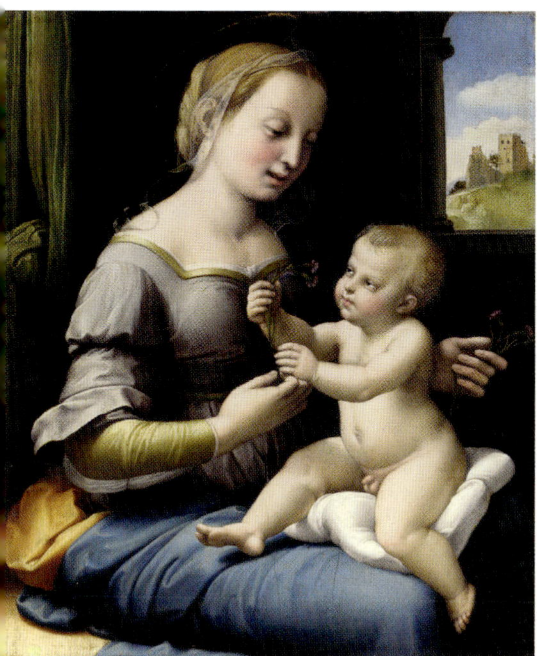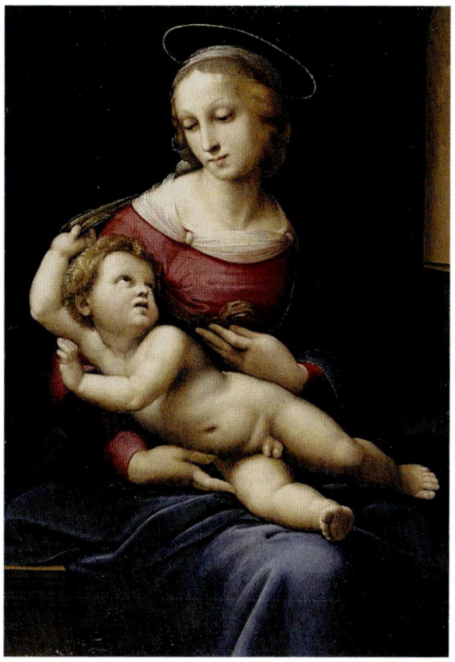

58 ABOVE LEFT   *The Virgin and Child (The Madonna of the Pinks* or *La Madonna dei Garofani)*, probably 1507
59 ABOVE RIGHT   *The Virgin and Child (The Bridgewater Madonna)*, probably 1507

increase in energy – but not on a regular trajectory. He made many drawings of Madonna and Holy Family groups; most are sketchy, but some are carefully finished, and his fertility of invention in treating women and children was inexhaustible. Some of the more elaborate ones may have prepared paintings now lost, or planned but not executed.

For the court of Urbino, probably in 1505, Raphael made portraits of the duchess, Elisabetta Gonzaga, and of the young Francesco Maria della Rovere, while towards the end of his time in Florence he painted the coordinated portraits of Angelo Doni (1474–1539) and his wife, Maddalena Strozzi (*c.* 1490–1546) (Florence, Pitti), as well as portraits of other unidentified women; one, the unfinished *Girl with the Unicorn* (Rome, Galleria Borghese), like the *Maddalena Strozzi*, is based on the *Mona Lisa*, which clearly haunted Raphael. But, rather surprisingly, his production of portraits in Florence does not seem to have been extensive.

Two of Raphael's half-length Madonnas, both painted in 1507, reflect Leonardo's inventions directly. The perfectly preserved *Madonna of the Pinks* is a same-size reworking of

58

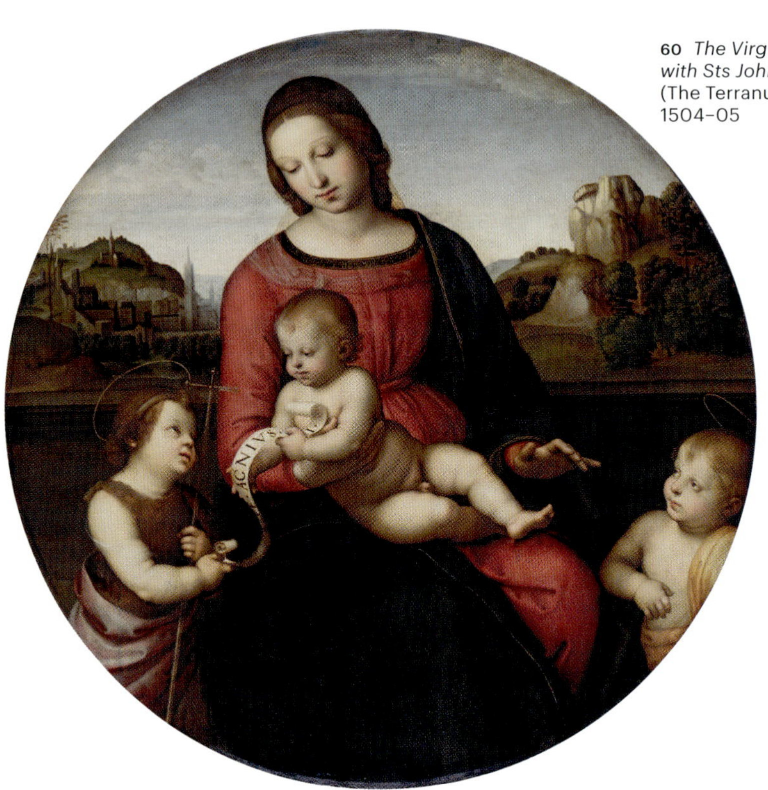

60 *The Virgin and Child with Sts John and Thaddeus?* (The Terranuova *Madonna*), 1504–05

Leonardo's Benois *Madonna* of *c.* 1474 (St Petersburg, Hermitage), which had probably remained in Florence, although Raphael's Child is not the swollen baby created by Leonardo. The Bridgewater *Madonna*, on the other hand, riffs on Leonardo's much more recent *Madonna of the Yarnwinder*: Raphael's interest extended over Leonardo's entire career.

In short, Raphael was highly productive, but in Florence he received only one commission for an (unfinished) altarpiece, and none for murals. Whether Raphael was considered an outsider and overlooked for public and ecclesiastical commissions, or whether, as a peripatetic painter-scholar profiting from his *wanderjahre*, he was reluctant to be tied down to large tasks, especially of relatively conventional type, is an open question. Working for private clients who were as much friends as patrons and frequenting their palaces, Raphael was not constrained by routine commissions or by the conservatism of institutional patronage.

In drawings, however, Raphael did investigate more ambitious projects: thus a drawing for a *Last Supper* (Oxford,

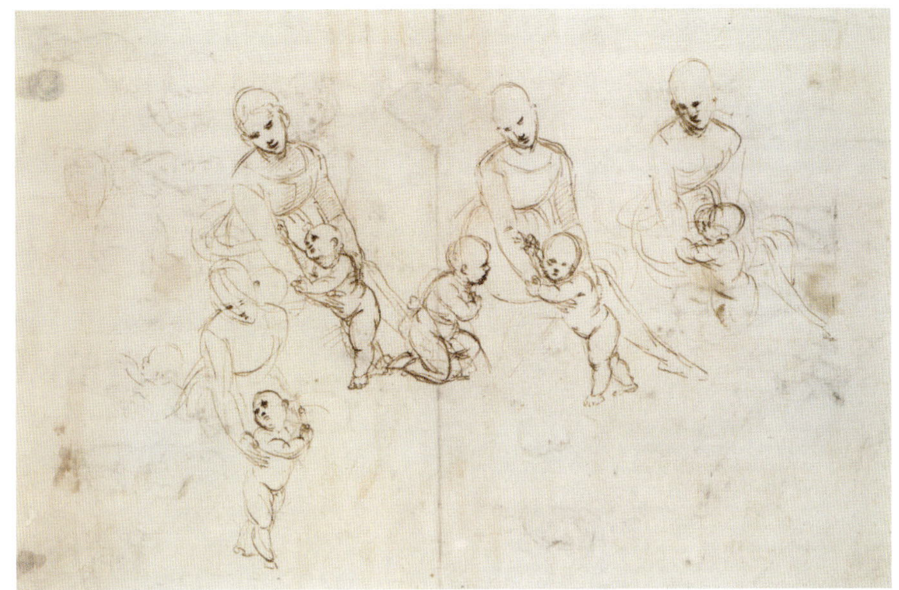

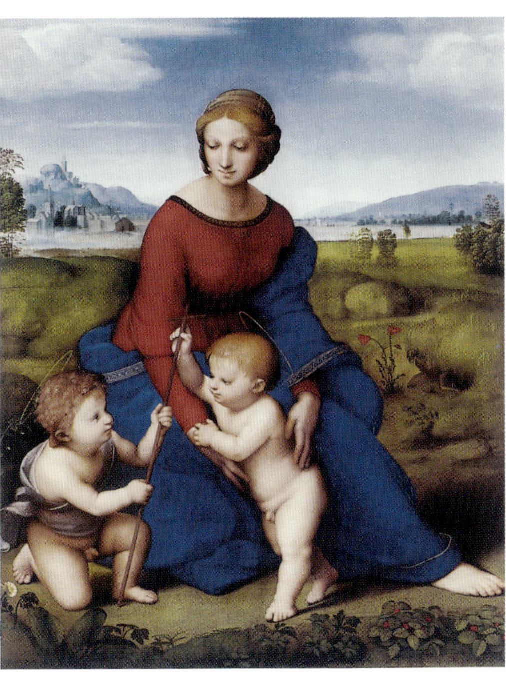

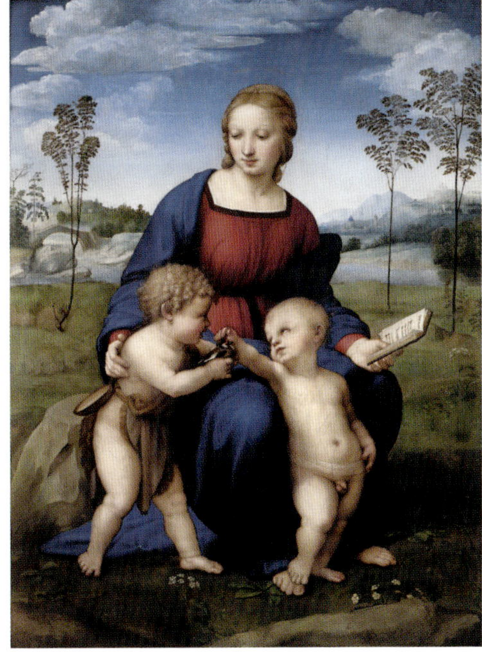

61 TOP Studies for *The Madonna del Prato*, 1505
62 ABOVE LEFT *The Virgin and Child with St John (The Madonna del Prato)*.
Not signed but dated MDV (1505). The date is sometimes read as MDVI (1506)
63 ABOVE RIGHT *The Virgin and Child with St John (The Madonna del Cardellino
[goldinch])*, 1505–06

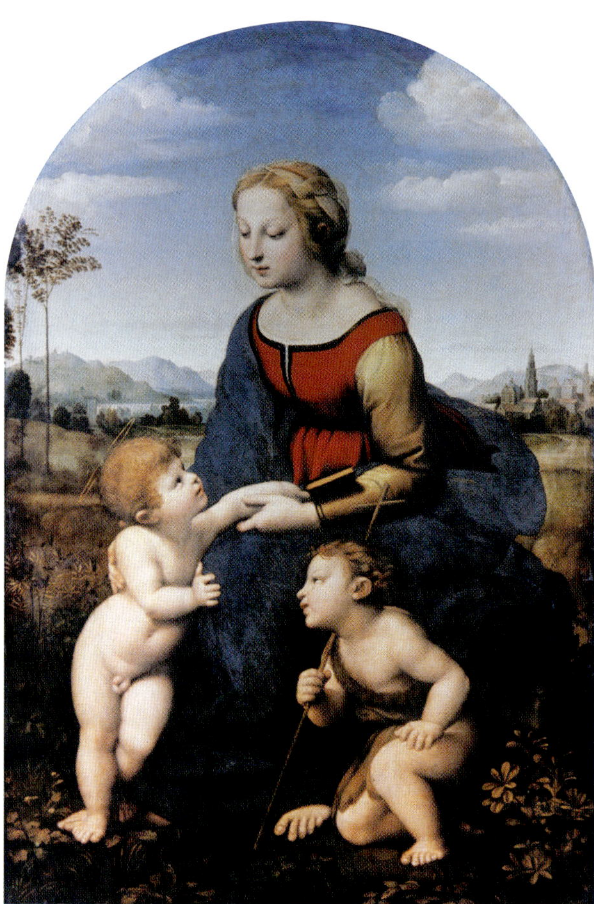

64 *The Virgin and Child with St John (The Belle Jardinière),* signed in the unusual form RAPHAELLO VRB and dated MDVII (1507). The date is sometimes read as MDVIII (1508)

Ashmolean) suggests that he was angling for a monastic commission, but if so nothing came of it. It is also probable that Raphael competed for a grand *Annunciation* for the Company of San Zanobi, for which he made a large and detailed drawing (Stockholm, Nationalmuseum), but the project was allocated to his friend Albertinelli, whose majestic painting was finished in 1510.

In all his treatments of the Virgin and Child, Raphael is alert to both the psychological and the sacramental implications of the relations between mother and child. Like Michelangelo, who also lost his mother in childhood, Raphael was exceptionally sensitive to the poignancy of attachment and inevitable loss, and he made rich use of exchanged glances. But he did not see the relation in the tragic terms of Michelangelo or Donatello. Raphael's Florentine Madonnas have gained so

universal a currency, are such mature versions of the mother
of the Saviour, that it is hard to believe that they were created
by a man in his early twenties.

It is not possible – however desirable it might be, for this
group of panels includes some of the most familiar and beloved
images in Raphael's oeuvre – to discuss them all in detail. But
Raphael's stylistic development and the enlargement of his
ambitions over this period should at least be outlined.

Probably the earliest painting that Raphael executed
in Florence, maybe in winter 1504–05, was the ambitious
roundel known as the Terranuova *Madonna*. The type of the
Virgin retains traces of Perugino, as do the types, poses and
draperies of the infant Baptist at the left and the child saint
at the right. But the Virgin's movement and her outstretched
hand, hovering above the Child, reveal Raphael's awareness
of Leonardo's *Virgin of the Rocks*, of which he would have
seen drawings in Leonardo's studio. The craggy landscape,
lit at the right as though by a rising sun, connects with his
portraits of Francesco Maria and, especially, Elisabetta
Gonzaga (both Florence, Uffizi). If, as has been suggested,
the right-hand infant is St Thaddeus, the Terranuova *Madonna*
may be one of the two pictures Vasari records as painted for
Raphael's patron and friend the cultivated wool merchant Taddeo
Taddei (1470–1529), to whom Raphael refers warmly in a letter of
1508 to his uncle. *The Madonna del Granduca* (Florence, Pitti),
whose patron is unknown, is probably also of 1504–05.

One of most important lessons that Raphael learnt in
Florence was to base his compositions on movement and
counter-movement. His increasing command can be seen in
his three great paintings of the Virgin with the Child and the
infant Baptist: the *Prato*, the *Cardellino* and the *Belle Jardinière*.
In all three the Virgin is seated at full length in open
countryside and observes, and to an extent controls, the
interaction between St John and the Christ Child.

Such arrangements of a seated Virgin and two children
are rare in Umbria. There are a couple of examples by Perugino
and his school in which groups (extracted from altarpieces)
are set in the open, but there is little interchange among their
actors, or of the groups with their surroundings. Leonardo
may have treated the theme – an early drawing seems to
adumbrate the kind of arrangement that Raphael painted
– but did not develop it. However, the theme of the seated
Virgin with two children had been anticipated in a design
made by Michelangelo, probably in the mid-1490s, for his friend
Francesco Granacci (1469–1543) to execute as a painting (Dublin,
National Gallery of Ireland). Raphael would have encountered

Granacci at the gatherings held by the architect and designer
Baccio d'Agnolo (1462–1543), a central figure in the artistic
world of Florence, which both men attended – and there
are several overlaps between the Madonnas of Raphael and
those of Granacci. Michelangelo pursued the theme further
in drawings during the first decade of the Cinquecento,
and in the Bruges *Madonna*, under way before Raphael
arrived in Florence, had represented the Child descending
from the Virgin's lap to take his first steps. But the Frate
was the Florentine who developed groups of the Holy Family
in pastures most extensively, creating grand pyramidal
compositions; and while the dates of his paintings are not
certain, it is likely that he and Raphael worked in tandem.

The Madonna del Prato of 1505 is the earliest and most
limpid of the three. It is as though the Virgin has strolled
out for air and has briefly set the Child down. Holding him
in a loose calliper-like grip, she watches the kneeling St John,
who presents the Child with a cane cross, which he accepts.
The Virgin's emotions, inevitably, are tinged with foreboding
as she appreciates the action's symbolic import.

The Virgin's right leg, extended across the surface, is taken
from Leonardo's Louvre *Virgin and Child with St Anne*, which
must already have been under way and which, a couple of
years later, Raphael would cite more dramatically. But here
the borrowing is not geared to movement, for the Virgin's
figure is static, composed of a series of arcs (note the neckline
of her dress).

The *Prato* (the meadow gives the painting its nickname),
whose arrangement looks effortless, was in fact prepared with
a host of drawings in different media: a suite of pen sketches
on a large sheet was followed up by a carefully worked pen
drawing (Chatsworth, Devonshire Collection), a brush and
wash drawing (Oxford, Ashmolean), and a red chalk study
developed from it (New York, Metropolitan Museum). Whether
such extensive preparation was typical of Raphael's Florentine
Madonnas is conjectural.

In *The Madonna del Cardellino* – painted for another Florentine
merchant, Lorenzo Nasi, probably on the occasion of his marriage
in February 1506 to Sandra Canigiani – the Virgin, who looks up
from her book at St John's arrival, occupies less of the picture
surface. She is compact and sculptural, and evidently based on
the Bruges *Madonna*. The painting follows Michelangelo again
in the assertive movement of St John, taken from his Taddei
Tondo. Finally, in the *Belle Jardinière*, whose patron is unknown,
Raphael set the Virgin in motion: no longer seated, she rises and
bends forward towards her child, whose pose, of course, is again

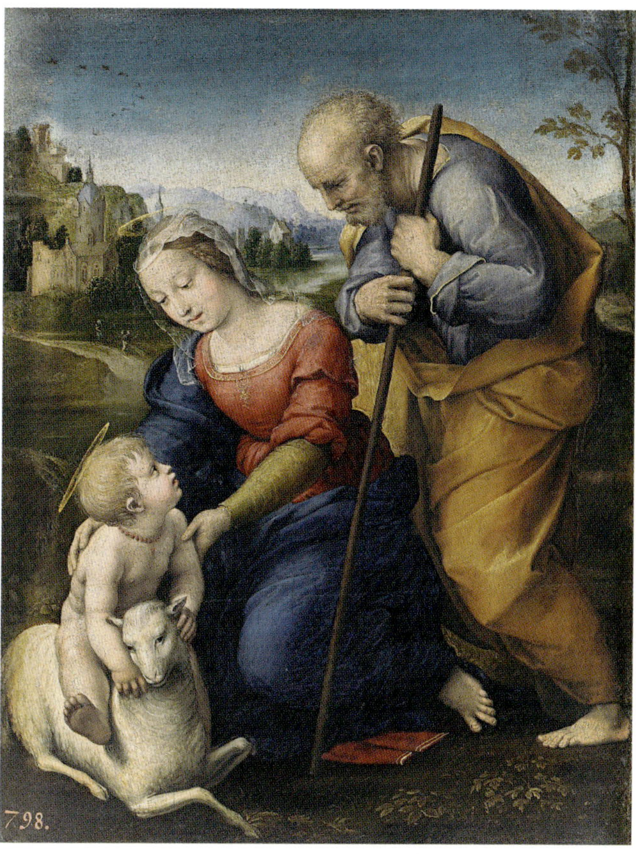

taken from the Bruges *Madonna* and introduces individuality
and complex movement to the Child's action.

The high point of Raphael's interest in mobile compositions
comes in two complex paintings of 1507. In the small *Holy
Family with a Lamb*, Raphael was clearly looking again at
Leonardo's *Virgin and Child with St Anne*, but he substituted
Joseph for the Virgin's mother – a change that allowed him
to tighten the picture's form and emotion. Joseph, elderly but
powerful, leans forward, resting on his staff, and establishes
direct eye contact with the Child who, supported by the
inclining Virgin, is seated on the lamb – 'that sacrificial animal
that signifies the Passion', in Fra Pietro de Novellara's words
about Leonardo's cartoon for the church of SS Annunziata.
Raphael ties the composition together by this exchange of
gazes and creates the cohesion of a family group, unified
rather than disrupted by counterbalancing movement.

The same is true of a large panel painted for the Canigiani, the family of Lorenzo Nasi's bride. (One has the sense of a closely related group of alert merchant collectors patronising the brilliant young artist, keeping him employed within their circle – an aesthetic avant-garde.) In the Canigiani *Holy Family*, Raphael fused three adults and two children (Leonardo had contented himself with four figures in the National Gallery cartoon, and Michelangelo three in the Doni Tondo) into a single pyramid in which four of the actors lean in towards each other, with St Joseph as the keystone stabilising the group and directing attention downwards. The effort of the virtuosic construction perhaps limits the painting's emotional

66 *The Holy Family with Sts John the Baptist and Elizabeth* (The Canigiani *Holy Family*), signed RAPHAEL VRBINAS but not dated, probably 1507

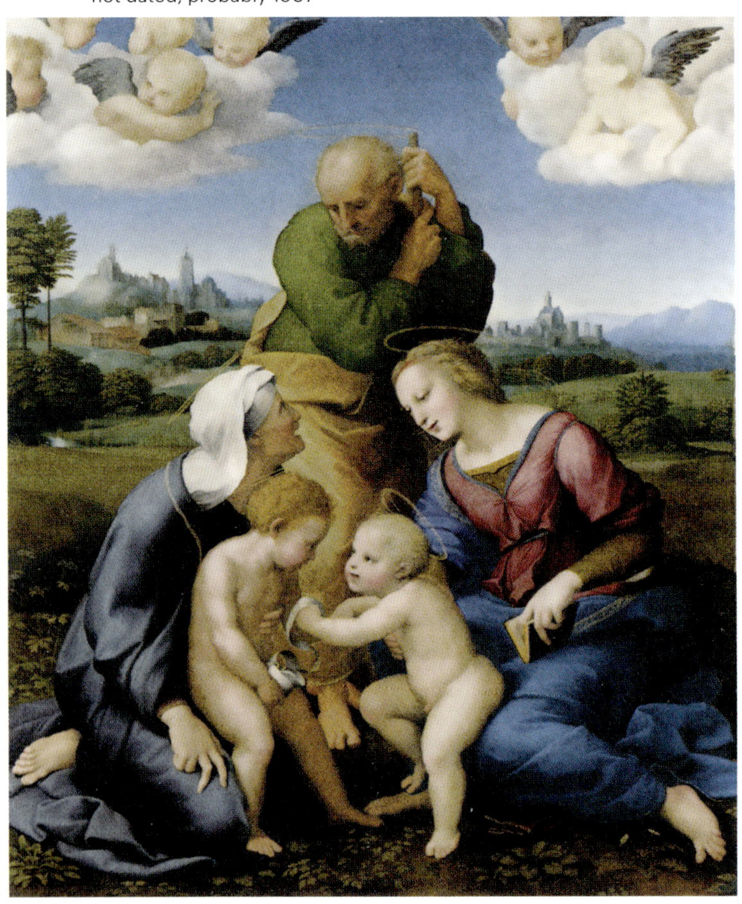

life, but it is an unparalleled triumph of design. Within three years of Raphael's arrival in Florence, he had equalled both Leonardo and Michelangelo in constructive intelligence and far outstripped anything produced by his Florentine contemporaries.

Similar progression can be seen in Raphael's half-length Madonnas. *The Madonna del Granduca*, one of the most reproduced of all Madonnas, retains something of the stained-glass colour areas of Perugino. Interestingly, a preparatory drawing (Florence, Uffizi) shows that Raphael considered painting it in an oval, a format that he seems never elsewhere to have employed and obviously rejected – but the fact that he contemplated it is indicative of his experimentalism. With its three-dimensionality of form, sweetness of emotion and alert Child, prepared from life studies, looking directly at the viewer, the painting surely reveals Raphael's interest in the Madonnas of Luca della Robbia (1400–82), as well as real mothers and real children. The bodies of mother and child are placed side by side: the two are linked physically and psychologically by the latter's movement, and formally by their arms, without diagonals. *The Small Cowper Madonna*, probably painted a few months later, is similar in structure.

But then things change. In the Orléans *Madonna*, probably of 1506 (Chantilly, Musée Condé), the Child leans back against the Virgin's embrace to evoke weight and tension. The unfinished Colonna *Madonna* of 1507–08 (Berlin, Gemäldegalerie) develops the same idea, and in the Bridgewater *Madonna*, probably of 1507, Raphael goes further: the large Child squirms across the Virgin's lap in a complex swimming movement. The composition narrowly skirts disruption and, while the figures cohere psychologically, they do not do so formally. It is as though the Virgin, who now barely supports the Child, is astonished at his force and energy, which may already anticipate his resurrection. The Child's pose stayed with Raphael: he adapted it for the cupid in the foreground of his Roman fresco of *The Triumph of Galatea* in 1512.

The head of Galatea in the same fresco is anticipated in another panel of *c.* 1507: the *St Catherine*, the only single figure of a saint that Raphael painted in Florence. Catherine's voluptuous, near three-quarter-length pose, which owes a debt both to Leonardo's lost *Leda* and to the antique *Venus pudica* type, invites the viewer's gaze to spiral towards the upper left corner, where golden rays confirm her divine mission: the spiral elevates her from physical to spiritual.

The St Catherine and *The Madonna of the Pinks* – fortuitously housed together in the National Gallery, London – show an

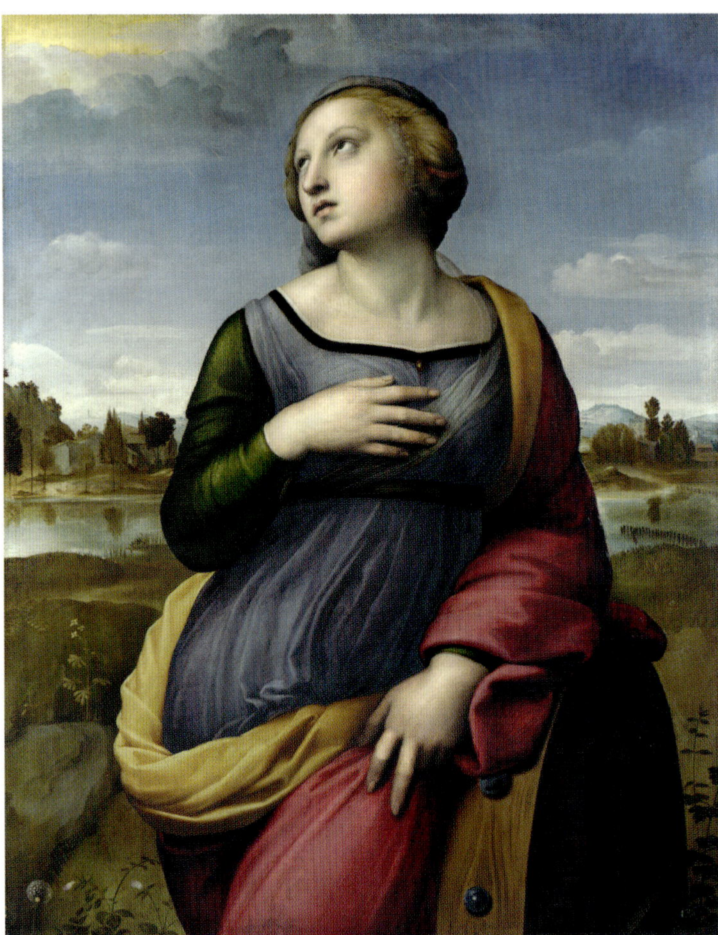

67 *St Catherine of Alexandria*, probably 1507

apparently short-lived colouristic experientialism. Instead of
red and blue, the Virgin's bodice in the *Pinks* is grey with a
yellow lining, and her skirt is blue-grey. Catherine too wears
a blue-grey robe with green sleeves, and her faded rose cloak
also has a yellow lining. These colour combinations have some
correspondences in *The Entombment* but otherwise seem to be
confined to a particular moment.

III

As a draughtsman, Raphael came to Florence technically well
prepared but narrow in his range. He learnt enormously from
both Leonardo and Michelangelo. Raphael's Umbrian drawings,

however refined and accomplished, are limited in energy. And furthermore, few life studies – and fewer nude studies – were made in Umbria, whereas they were fundamental to Florentine draughtsmanship.

Comparatively speaking, few 'artistic' drawings by Leonardo survive: a painting such as *The Last Supper* must have generated dozens, but only a few are known. The supremely complicated compositions of the Virgin, Child and St Anne, of which Leonardo made three distinct versions, must also have generated many lost studies. It is salutary to appreciate that the losses are vast, for it compels us to accept that we can never know the full extent of what Raphael learnt from Leonardo. But what is clear is that one of the most important lessons was the study of movement. When Raphael's earlier drawings are considered, even when figures are studied more than once, they are seen as discrete forms. From Leonardo Raphael learnt the practice of *pentimento* or 'brainstorm' drawing, and the accentuation or diminution of contour. When Leonardo wished to change a figure's pose or the elements of a pose, instead of making a new study he worked over his drawing. This resulted in reduced clarity but increased organic continuity. This method can be seen in several drawings made by Raphael during his Florentine period, notably in treatments of the Virgin and Child, and he continued the practice in Rome. However, such working drawings survive in small numbers compared with the many that must have been made and lost.

Raphael developed from Leonardo a compositional fluency, with forms generating forms in a series of internal rhymes, as in the studies for *The Madonna del Prato*. Combined with the tonal and colouristic unity and the subtle treatment of surfaces that he would have learnt from both Leonardo and Fra Bartolommeo, it gave Raphael's designs a coherence that those of his contemporaries could not match.

From Michelangelo Raphael would have learnt the power of plastic form, which could be created *ex novo* by the most flexible and variegated hatching, simultaneously sensitive and rugged. Raphael did not use cross-hatching as extensively as Michelangelo, but some of his pen drawings are closely meshed. Michelangelo also used pen in many other ways: there are wonderfully economical thumbnail sketches that construct forms only by flexed outline. Once again, Raphael made some use of this technique, but he generally employed pen in rangier ways: fast line work and elastic contours are frequent in his Florentine period. Raphael would have known Leonardo's interest in metalpoint – not used by Michelangelo – as a sketching medium, but his approach seems more vital and more fluid than surviving examples by Leonardo. He came to use it more frequently towards the end of his Florentine period and early in Rome, to create forms that were hard and crisply modelled but frequently warmed by pink grounds.

It is easy to forget that, although Leonardo and Michelangelo were the greater virtuosos, Fra Bartolommeo was also a masterly and prolific, if repetitive, draughtsman. We have more drawings by him, in pen, black and red chalk and charcoal, than by Leonardo and Michelangelo combined. The Frate built up his compositions perhaps more systematically than any earlier artist, making many sketches of figures and heads and then elaborate drapery studies, sometimes of beautiful airiness. He also made – surprisingly – many delicate landscape studies in pen, some of still-identifiable sites; at one time these were attributed to Raphael, by whom very few landscape drawings are known but who must have made them. One of the lessons that we can learn from the Frate is the sheer number of drawings that an artist might make: over a quarter-century of work, his surviving graphic output reaches about 2,000 drawings, even if, for the most part, his compositions are less complex than Raphael's and much less dynamic. One can only wonder, yet again, how many drawings Raphael might have made.

IV

Raphael's most ambitious and innovative project of the Florentine years was not for Tuscany but for otherwise conservative Perugia. It was probably in 1505 that Raphael contracted with Atalanta Baglioni, the matriarch of one of the city's most powerful families, to execute an altarpiece in commemoration of her son Grifone, generally known as 'Grifonetto', killed in 1500 in one of the internecine conflicts that wracked Perugia. Even though Grifone was a murderer who was actually rejected by his mother, she mourned him deeply.

Raphael at first designed a static *Pietà* modelled on Perugino's famous treatment of the same theme of 1494 for the Florentine nunnery of Santa Chiara. He probably did so at Atalanta's request, for it is doubtful whether Raphael in 1505 would have followed on his own initiative a Perugino composition of a decade earlier. Raphael drew two variants: the first is large and elaborate (Paris, Louvre); the second, looser but more compact, was later engraved by Marcantonio Raimondi – a rare printed record of a pre-Roman design by Raphael. Then Raphael reconsidered his project. He certainly knew Mantegna's engraving of *The Transport of Christ's Body to the Tomb* (partly copied in the Venice sketchbook) and may

68

have been reminded of it by news of Mantegna's death in September 1506. He also perceived the relevance of, and copied, an ancient Roman relief in which Atalanta rushes forward to raise the dead Meleager's hand, perhaps prompted by the coincidence with his patroness's name.

Raising the body of Christ from the earth simultaneously raises the dramatic temperature: the composition passes from static and contemplative to active and dramatic, and Raphael made many drawings on the way to finalising his picture. The disciples perform a physical task, in which they express different facets of grief. In its final redaction the Borghese *Entombment* has great intensity, with all the figures in movement. Emotionally, if not formally, it recalls the late styles of both Donatello and Botticelli. Three men struggle to carry Christ's body while St John looks on with clasped hands. The Magdalen, her grief uncontrolled, lunges forward to raise Christ's hand. In the middle ground the Virgin Mary collapses, prevented from falling by her attendants. This group was the result of a late change of design, and its placing and construction are novel. In contrast to the action in the foreground, depicted in relief mode, the Virgin and her supporters resemble a project for a multi-view statuary group. It is the first example of Raphael's exploiting a juxtaposition of foreground and background.

The drama extended further, but its impact was lost with the separation of *The Entombment* from its original context in 1608. It is undeniable that there is a certain awkwardness in the grouping of the bearers' legs, but the often criticised juxtaposition of the heads of Joseph of Arimathea (the most probable identification) and Christ, tilted at the same angle, was deliberate. Above the main panel was a smaller one of *God the Father Blessing his Son*, which remained in Perugia when the rest of the ensemble was removed to Rome. The original arrangement may suggest that Raphael was thinking of Giovanni Bellini's great *Coronation of the Virgin* at Pesaro, in which a rectangular *Pietà* sits above the cornice. But in Raphael's ensemble, unlike Bellini's, the two parts are coordinated.

Christ's head tilts upwards to his Father and the promise of resurrection, and his bearer becomes aware, through his grief, of God's presence. If not unprecedented, such dramatic interlinking across different fields is novel and not seen even in the work of so dramatic a composer as Botticelli. It recalls, distantly, the spatial connections of Giovanni Santi's Tiranni Chapel, and is also a harbinger of the spatial interrelations in Raphael's later decorative schemes and, in general, the practice

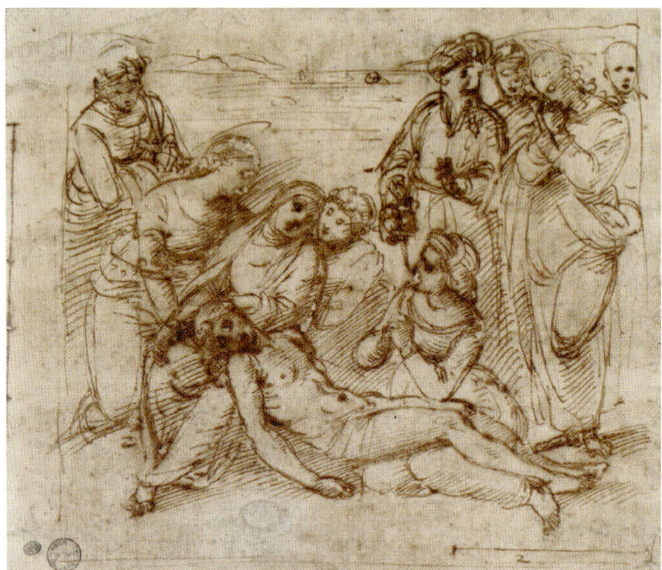

68 LEFT Study for
The Entombment,
c. 1505–06. This drawing
shows one of Raphael's
initial ideas for *The
Entombment*, when it
was still conceived as
a static Lamentation
69 OPPOSITE *The
Entombment*, signed
RAPHAEL VRBINAS
and dated MDVII (1507)

of establishing continuities across boundaries that was to
characterise his architecture. God the Father is powerfully
conceived and, when he devised the blessing *God the Father*
(Paris, Louvre) in the chapel of Leo X's villa, La Magliana
(*c.* 1518), Raphael recalled this figure.

The half-length Father may have been left in Perugia
because it was seen to be by another hand. Perhaps Raphael
ran out of time and, needing to terminate the project, handed
it to his friend and colleague Domenico Alfani. Domenico's
collaboration raises again the issue of the involvement of
associates in subsidiary parts of Raphael's ensembles, but to
what extent remains difficult to elucidate. Domenico, however,
probably did collaborate with Raphael intermittently, and it
seems that they remained in contact, for he certainly knew
some of Raphael's Roman work.

The Entombment's predella, which might seem less important
than the pinnacle, is, by contrast, autograph and something of
a manifesto. It consists of three roundels framed by standing
putti supporting baskets, representing the three Cardinal Virtues
of Faith, Hope and Charity. All are painted to resemble marble,
and *Charity* is based specifically on Michelangelo's Pitti Tondo:
Raphael thus simulated Michelangelo's preferred medium as
well as borrowing one of his compositions.

The main panel too is more overtly Michelangelesque
than anything Raphael had painted hitherto. Christ's body,

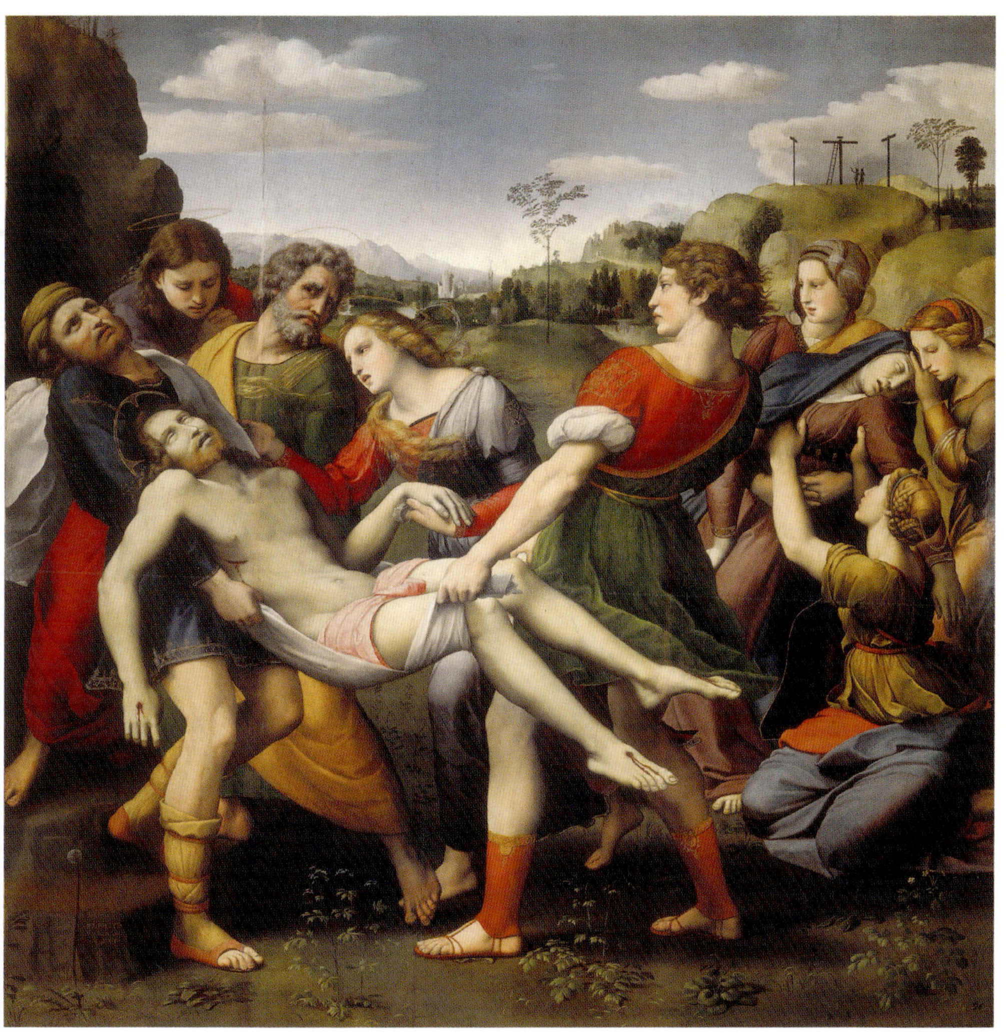

in its forms and idealism, strongly evokes the Christ in
Michelangelo's *Pietà* in St Peter's; and although Raphael
could, in principle, have known the sculpture in copies, the
similarity does furnish an additional argument in support of
a trip to Rome in 1506 or 1507. More significant is the pose of
the kneeling Mary supporting the fainting Virgin, who is taken,
with undisguised insolence, from the Virgin in the Doni Tondo.
No more complicated figure existed, and that Raphael felt able
to adapt it, if not wholly successfully, indicates a confidence
bordering on arrogance: if Michelangelo ever became aware

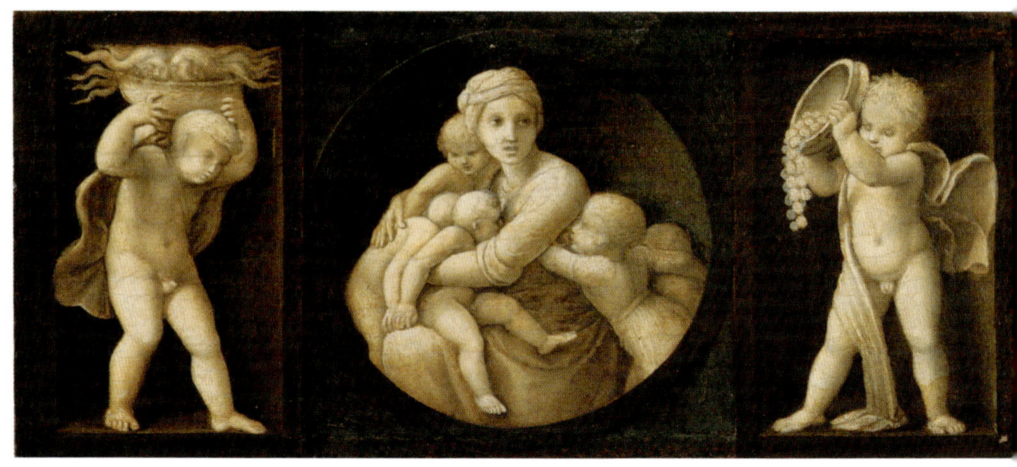

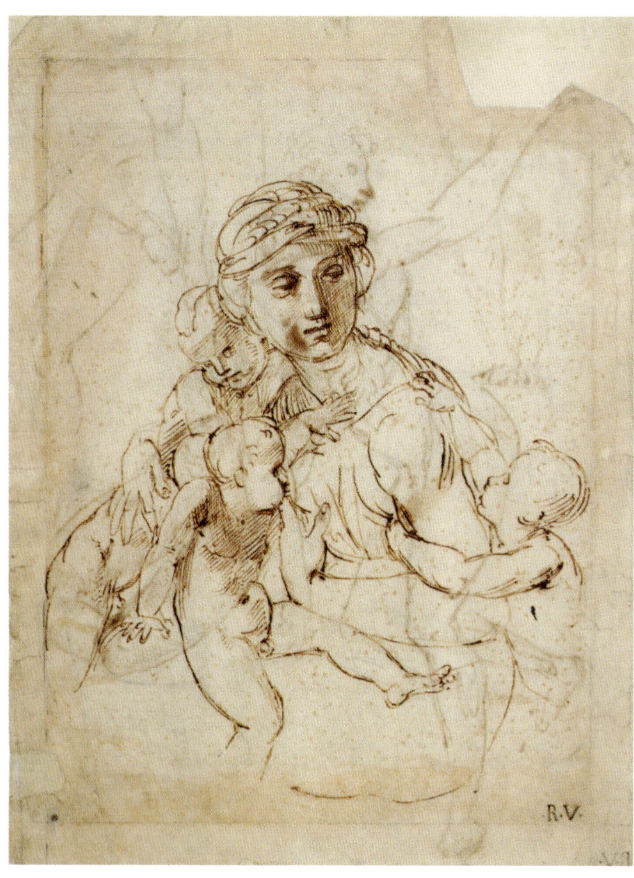

70 ABOVE The predella of the *Entombment* (detail) *Charity (Caritas)*, 1507
71 LEFT Study for *Charity*, 1507

of this borrowing, it is unlikely to have pleased him; indeed, it might have initiated a wariness of Raphael that later became hostility.

Vasari says that Raphael executed the cartoon for *The Entombment* in Florence but the panel itself in Perugia, so he must have been there for several months in 1507. The final picture is bolder and more dramatic than anything currently being painted in Florence, but it seems to have been unknown there. Had it been displayed in a Florentine site, it would surely have changed the tenor and direction of the city's art. In Perugia it seems to have stunned local artists and had no repercussions.

The large (larger than the painted form) and vigorous pen drawing in which Raphael prepared *Charity* evokes Michelangelo's looser and less finished pen drawings. But it could not be mistaken for a drawing by Michelangelo: the line lacks his structural solidity and three-dimensionality. *The Charity*, however, does serve to introduce a suite of pen drawings made by Raphael towards the end of his Florentine period. In these he seems to be developing a style suitable for tackling violent themes, and one that can vie with rugged sculpture, in contrast to his harmonious designs of more ingratiating subjects. Examples of this rough style comprise three of Hercules' Labours (London, British Museum; Windsor, Royal Collection) – there is no evidence that Raphael envisaged more – and three drawings of the taking and maltreatment of prisoners (Oxford, Ashmolean; London, British Museum). The latter may be for the same scheme as his *Siege of Perugia*, but they are much wilder than that drawing, and if related to it they must postdate it: they anticipate some elements in *The Battle of Ostia*, produced seven or eight years later.

In their size (some are unusually large), vigour and relative coarseness – their pen style influenced that of Baccio Bandinelli (1493–1560) – the *Hercules* drawings seem to vie with Michelangelo, but rather naively. Although roughly handled, they are finished designs and were likely intended for marble sculpture, probably a sequence of small reliefs to furnish a study or to decorate the base of a statue. There are, indeed, several reliefs of this kind from about this date in the Bargello, although these have no direct connection with Raphael's drawings. Like the study for *Charity*, they show Raphael's interest in designing both real and simulated sculptures. He would have opportunities to design both in Rome.

Raphael acquired a great deal in Florence and, in his understanding of the artistic possibilities that the city had to offer, he far outdistanced native Florentines. Put simply, his

intelligence, technical ability, capacity for assimilation and
ambition were infinitely greater than theirs. Ridolfo Ghirlandaio
executed a few portraits that loosely resemble Raphael's, but he
derived little else from his friend. But Raphael's Madonnas did
affect the earlier work of the greatest of the younger Florentines,
Andrea del Sarto (1486–1530) and his friend Marcantonio
Franciabigio (1482–1524). Madonnas painted by both artists
up to about 1510 depend heavily on Raphael's ideas. To Giuliano
Bugiardini (1475–1555) Raphael may have been personally closer:
several paintings by Bugiardini adapt Raphael designs, and
at least one of his portraits has been attributed to Raphael.
Nothing is known of their relations, but it is possible that
for a while they too shared a studio.

Chapter 4
The Stanza della Segnatura

I

Raphael is first recorded in Rome on 13 January 1509, when he received the considerable sum of 100 ducats 'ad bonum computam picture' ('for the satisfactory completion of paintings') in the middle of the three 'Stanze' – the chambers that comprised the main suite of the pope's new apartments. This room, originally Julius's private library, later came to be known as the Stanza della Segnatura. The payment, which implies that a good deal of work had been accomplished, was witnessed by Raphael's friend the Perugian goldsmith Cesare Rossetti, whom Raphael had mentioned in his note to Domenico Alfani of 1507; Raphael and Cesare were to collaborate in 1510.

We do not know when Raphael arrived in Rome, but it was probably in summer 1508. In a letter written from Florence to his maternal uncle Simone Ciarla in Urbino, dated 21 April, Raphael refers to a 'stanza' to be decorated and requests the aid of Francesco Maria della Rovere in securing the commission. If this reference is to the Stanza della Segnatura, as seems likely, Raphael probably quit Florence precipitately, maybe in May or June, leaving *The Madonna del Baldacchino* incomplete. Raphael's new patron, Pope Julius II della Rovere, was the nephew of Sixtus IV, whose memory he cherished, and the uncle of Urbino's new duke, so Francesco Maria della Rovere would have been an obvious intermediary. Julius's preferred architect, Donato Bramante (1444–1514), also hailed from Urbino and may have been a distant kinsman of Raphael;

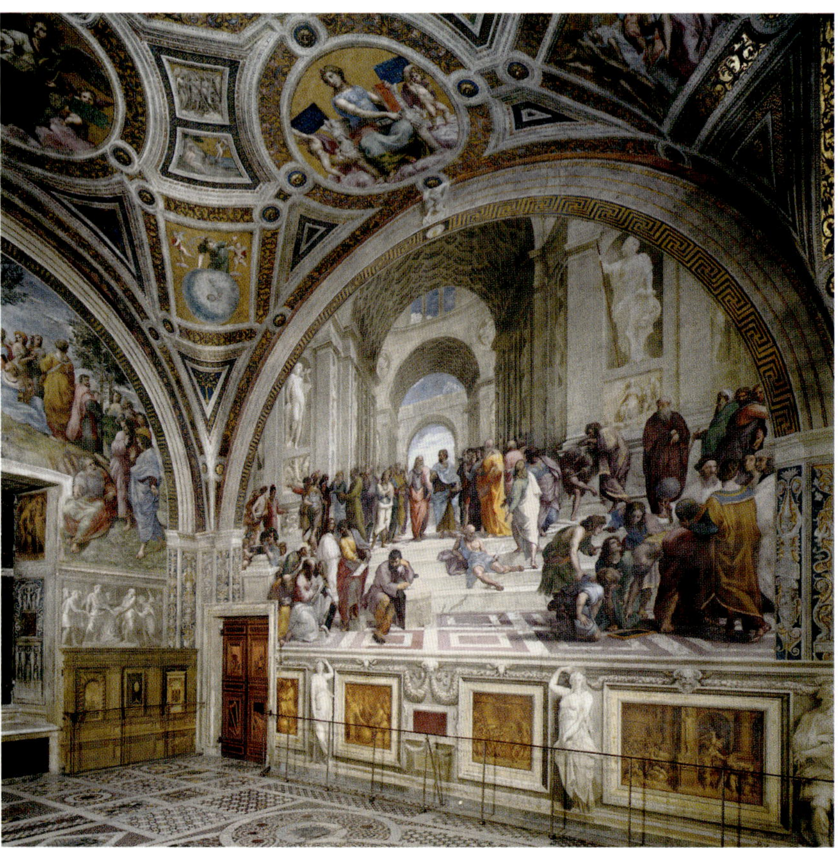

73 The Stanza della Segnatura, 1508–11

he would certainly have known Giovanni Santi. Bramante had worked in Umbria and the Marches and, like Leonardo, had spent many years in Milan – a history that may account for the selection of at least some of the painters employed in the Vatican, whom he probably recommended.

Rome in 1508 was the perfect place for Raphael at the perfect time. The fascination of the city, which still possessed the aura of the *caput mundi*, with its imperial past, its myriad of antiquities of all periods, its gigantic and magnificent ruins, by turns exemplary, melancholy and romantic, and the continual discoveries that emerged from its soil (the most famous of all Hellenistic statuary groups, *The Laocoön*, came to light early in 1506) – would have been a stimulus for any artist or architect. But in the Quattrocento the city's inherent attractions had not produced a great school of either art or architecture. Major artistic schemes had been created, major buildings, sacred and secular, had been erected, but the greatest architects and artists, although they might have visited and worked in Rome, did not reside in the city long-term.

That was to change, animated by the leadership of one of the most determined and energetic of all the occupants of the papal throne. By 1508 Julius II – the Caesarean name is significant – had already stamped his personality on the sleeping giant that was Rome. Autocratic by nature, a warrior by temperament, and a pontiff determined to recover the territories of the papal state and to eject foreign powers from the peninsular, Julius infused a dynamism through all branches of the state and its art. He combined the spiritual authority of the papacy with the energy of a military leader. And, as even his enemies recognised, although self-aggrandising, Julius was also relatively disinterested: he did not exaggeratedly promote the interests of his own family, and his projects were keyed to the grandeur of the church-state. With the church's finances improving, aided by the great banker Agostino Chigi, whose arms Julius allowed to be quartered with his own, he embarked on a transformation of the city, its amenities, its churches and, above all, the Vatican. Julius promoted the reorganisation of the Via Giulia, an early essay in clarifying Rome's streets that bears his name, and commissioned the law courts from Bramante (executed only in part) that were to stand on it. He also encouraged wealthy supporters to undertake architectural works to beautify the city and to compete with one another in doing so. Outside Rome proper, he was concerned with the fortification of the vital port of Ostia and, through his relative Cardinal Raffaelle Riario, its decoration by Cesare da Sesto.

In 1505 Julius commissioned an enormous tomb from Michelangelo, by far the most ambitious sculptural project of its time. It was to prove a tragedy for Michelangelo, and Julius soon became distrustful of it – perhaps coming to feel that it was too egocentric. But the tomb's combination of large neo-Roman reliefs and some thirty over-life-size statues, comprising standing nude prisoners, seated prophets and sybils, and two-figure victory groups, was intended to vie with the monuments of antiquity. Julius also commissioned Bramante to restructure the choir of the della Rovere church of Santa Maria del Popolo to house facing tombs designed and erected by the best Florentine sculptor of the period after Michelangelo, Andrea Sansovino. The vault was painted by Pinturicchio and the glass designed by Guillaume de Marcillat. Another major sculptural project promoted by Julius was the marble casing – designed by

Bramante – of the Holy House in Loreto, which spread a Roman style to North-East Italy.

But Julius's most daring and far-reaching scheme concerned the central building of the Christian faith. In 1505 he ordered the demolition of the ancient basilica of St Peter's and commissioned its replacement from Bramante. The saga of St Peter's, with which Raphael was soon to become involved, became interminable, and for decades the most important church of the Christian world seemed doomed to remain unfinished, its plans undergoing many changes. It was finally completed only in the seventeenth century. But Julius's boldness in taking the initial step and demolishing so much of the old church ensured that the project rapidly passed the point of no return. In the Vatican he began another major project, also planned by Bramante: the Belvedere courtyard, flanked by two long wings running up the *Mons Vaticanus* to connect the Vatican Palace with the Villa Belvedere, which became a museum of classical sculpture housing, among many other statues and reliefs, works such as *The Apollo Belvedere* and *The Laocoön*, which Julius had acquired.

When the tomb project was postponed, Julius recruited Michelangelo – who returned to Rome only a few months before Raphael arrived – to fresco the ceiling of the Sistine Chapel. And Julius's decision, late in 1507 – in part prompted by his detestation of his predecessor, Alexander VI – to transfer the papal apartments to the second floor of the Vatican provided the great opportunity for Raphael.

When Julius discovered outstanding talent, as with Bramante or the unruly Michelangelo, he backed it and allowed such men considerable leeway: impatient, decisive, his taste geared to the heroic in all areas, Julius was not a man for committees, and from this Raphael would profit. Julius and Raphael, and Raphael and Rome, were to prove ideal partnerships.

II

We know nothing precise about the terms of Raphael's employment, but he joined a team of painters engaged in decorating the three Stanze. They were probably selected by Bramante, who, before devoting himself to architecture, had been an innovative and powerful painter leaving important work in Milan. He no doubt supervised the project, which comprised the pope's private library, his audience chamber and, probably, his dining room, plus a private apartment that extended to the floor above. Following common practice, which favoured rapidity, the decoration of the rooms and the different parts of those rooms was divided among several

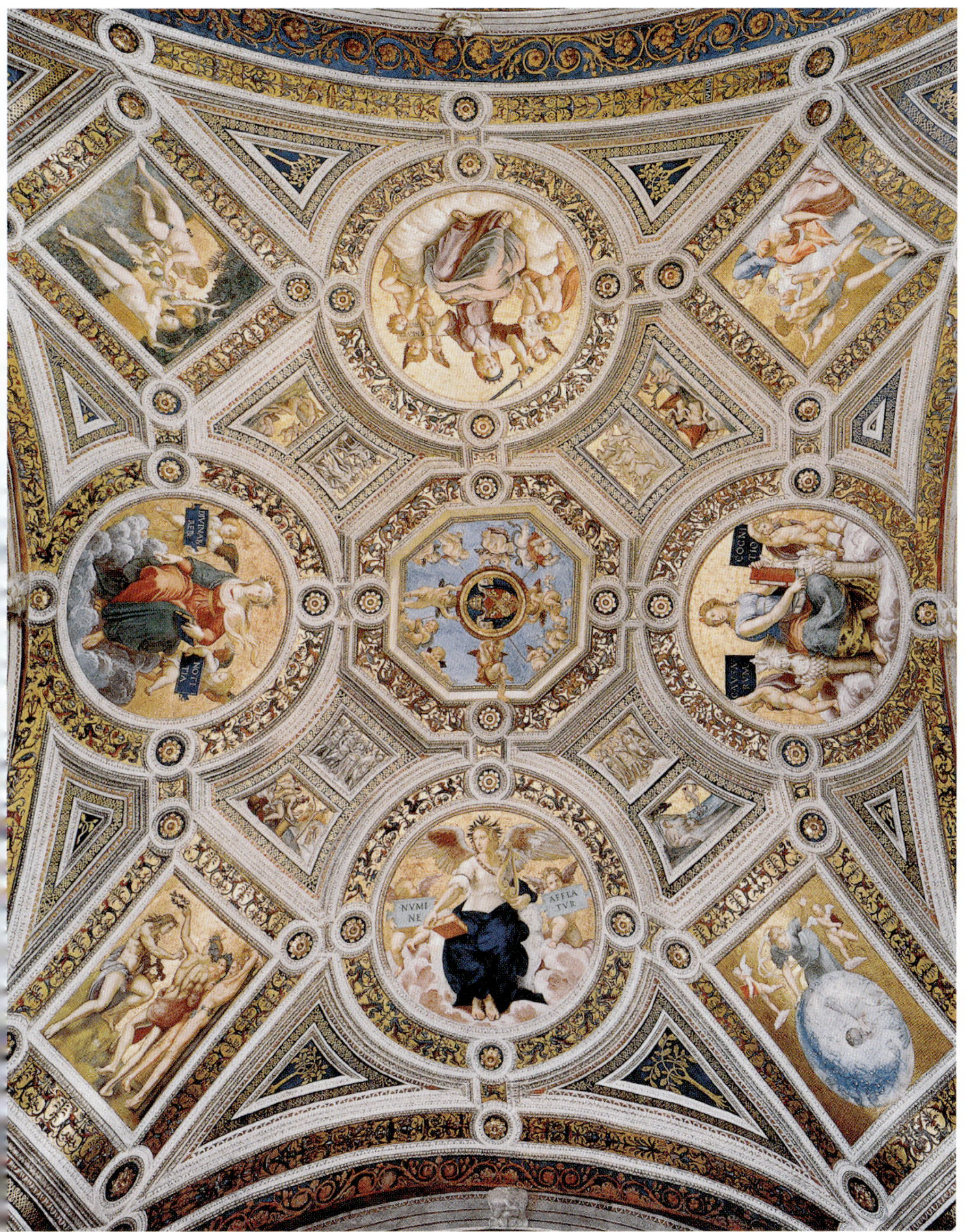

74 The Vault, Stanza della Segnatura, 1510

artists and probably further subdivided according to different competences. Among the painters involved were Giovanni Bazzi, called Il Sodoma (1477–1549), born in Piedmont but Sienese by adoption; the German Johannes Ruysch (*c.* 1460–1533), a decorative expert; Lorenzo Lotto (1477–1549), from the Veneto; and, from Milan, both Bramantino (*c.* 1456–1530) and Leonardo's follower Cesare da Sesto (1473–1523). The last demonstrably had access to some of Raphael's drawings. All are mentioned in payment documents, but it is rarely clear which parts of which scheme were assigned to which painters. In addition, some of the Stanze contained pre-existing frescoes – including two by no less than Piero della Francesca – that Julius may initially have intended to preserve.

Two of the painters who had worked in the Sistine Chapel in the 1480s were recalled to Rome for the Stanze – Perugino, whose vault in the Stanza dell'Incendio remains intact, and Luca Signorelli, a small part of whose work in the Stanza di Eliodoro survives – but neither is mentioned in surviving payment records, which are manifestly incomplete. Both men, of course, were well known to Raphael, as was Sodoma, who had used one of Raphael's discarded Piccolomini Library designs for a fresco at Monteoliveto. When Raphael arrived in Rome, parts of the scheme had no doubt already been allocated, and painting was probably under way on the vaults of all three Stanze.

Raphael began work in the Stanza della Segnatura, but we do not know precisely when. The vault was a collaboration between Ruysch, responsible for the framework, and Sodoma for the figurative parts; payments to both were made in October 1508. But Raphael, who by October was probably already working on the walls, seems to have contributed to its design.

The original vault form common to the three Stanze remains only in the Stanze dell'Incendio, where its corners are supported by clumsy corbels. These were eliminated in both the Segnatura and the Eliodoro, where the vaults were transformed by the extension of the corners into pendentives. But in the Segnatura – and *not* in the Eliodoro – these extensions are homogeneous, and the framing elements are consistent throughout. And that the vault design was changed when the painting was in its early stages is implied by the centrepiece, in which *putti* seen in steep foreshortening seem to raise the papal arms, which are in relief. During execution, the original roundel was transformed into an octagon, which is significant because, while a circle is not directional, an octagon is: it encourages a '+' reading towards the walls and an 'X' reading into the pendentives, tying together the four roundels and the four *quadri* (rectangles). It is likely that this change was instigated by Raphael – the new element in the equation – which would in turn imply that he was thinking of the room as a totality. The revised vault would be his earliest known architectural design. According to Vasari, Sodoma did complete the figurative parts of the vault, but of his work only the octagon and eight small scenes in simulated relief survive: the roundels and the *quadri* were redone a year or so later by Raphael.

If the revision of the Segnatura's vault was Raphael's idea, it would support Vasari's account: that his superiority to all the other artists working in the Stanze soon became so evident that they were dismissed and much of their work destroyed and replaced. But the fictive arches framing the wall frescoes in the Eliodoro – three of which are by Signorelli – and *The Incendio* were retained. It seems, therefore, that the scheme of single-field arched wall frescoes was projected from the beginning, no doubt by Bramante. The latest record of any other painter working in the Stanze is of 18 September 1509, when a payment of 50 ducats was made to Lorenzo Lotto, but it is not clear for what.

The Segnatura was frescoed between 1508 and 1511: identical inscriptions in the window embrasures below *Parnassus* and *Justice* give the (presumably completion) date of 1511 and the eighth year of Julius's pontificate, that is to say, before 26 November 1511. The internal chronology of the four wall frescoes is disputed, as is the date of Raphael's replacement of Sodoma's roundels and *quadri*, but it is certain that, with his innate spatial awareness, Raphael planned the room as an ensemble, and that the broad idea that the frescoes on the uninterrupted walls and those on the two window walls should respond to one another was a foundational decision, but not a rigid one. Raphael certainly made changes to his frescoes while they were under way, and even later: thus he inserted the figure of Heraclitus into *The School of Athens* after it had been completed, and the seated figures either side of the window in *Parnassus* were added late in that fresco's development. Careful planning did not preclude improvisation.

73–78 The room is organised according to the four faculties of Theology, Poetry (or Literature), Philosophy and Jurisprudence (or Justice), and each wall fresco is governed – or labelled – by a personification in the vault roundel above it. The themes of the *quadri* in the pendentives – as Vasari remarked – are carefully chosen to relate to those of the frescoes at each side: *The Fall* is placed between Justice and Theology, for instance. For these thematic linkages, as well as for the disposition and cast list of the wall frescoes, Raphael must have had specialist advice, but he was able to synthesise what he was told and to embody it in

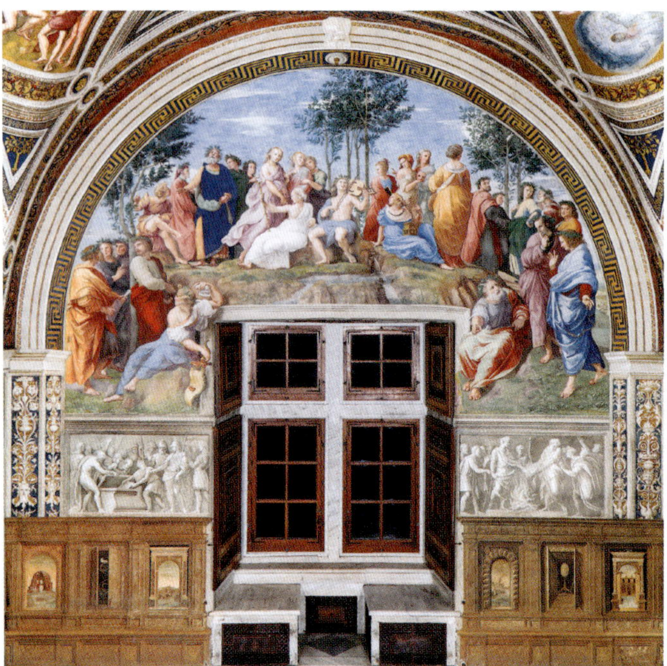

75 LEFT Parnassus,
Stanza della Segnatura,
1509–10
76 BELOW The Disputa,
Stanza della Segnatura,
1508–09

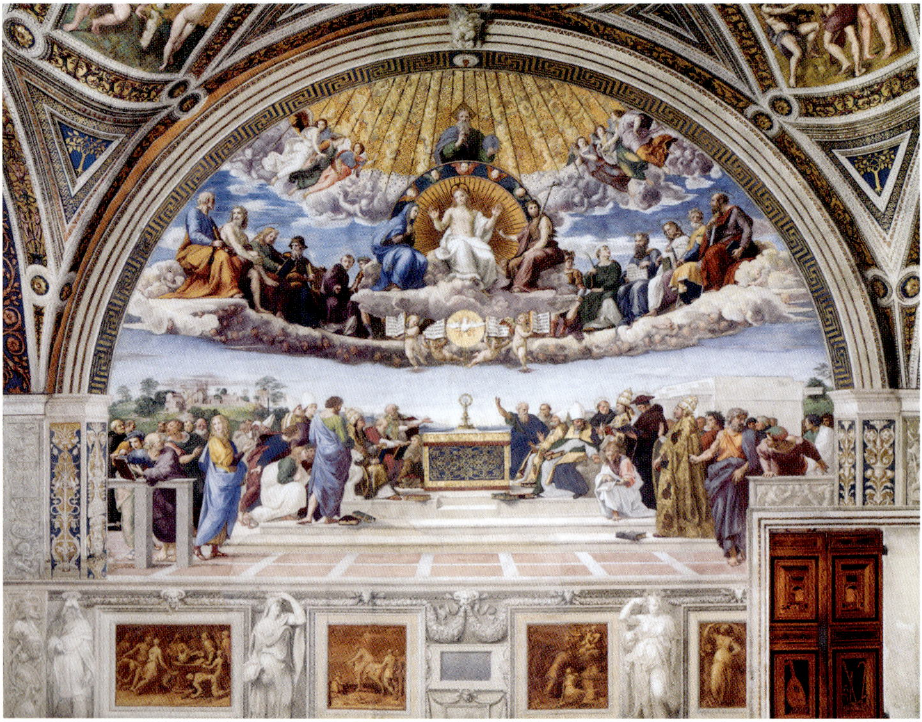

77 RIGHT *Justice,* Stanza
della Segnatura, 1511
78 BELOW *The School
of Athens,* Stanza della
Segnatura, 1509–10

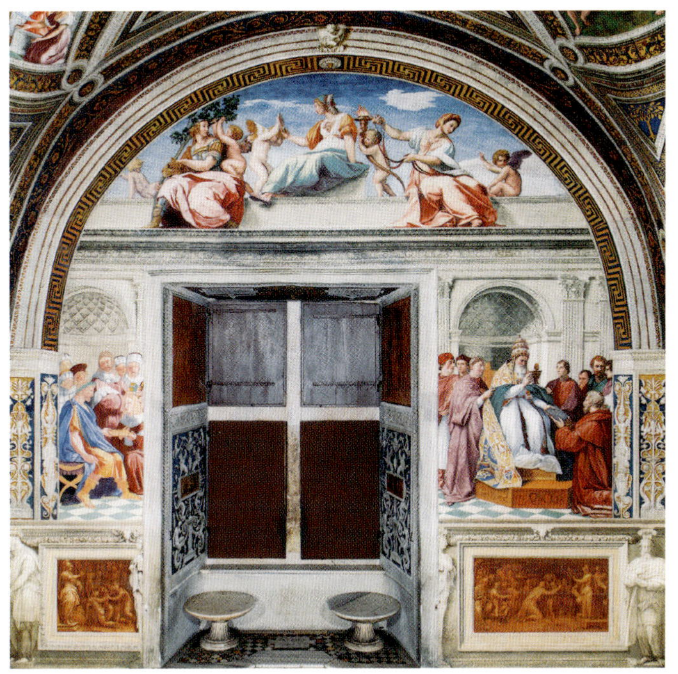

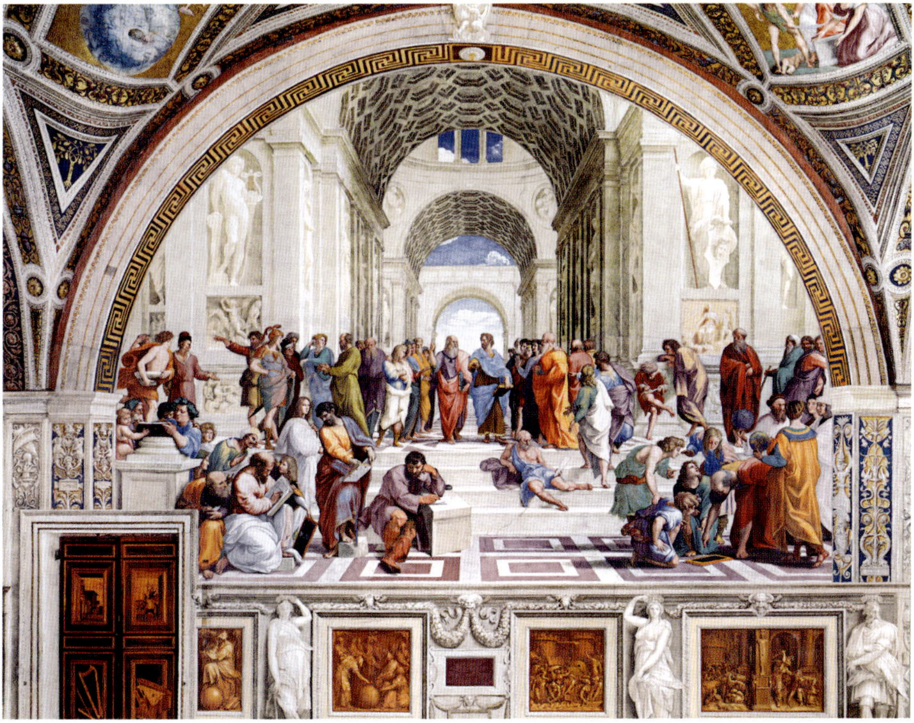

his own terms: there is no sense in the Segnatura of a painter following a programme that he does not fully understand.

The four faculties spring from a divinity, a person or a symbolic presence, and they are embodied in, and given a human dimension by, their most illustrious representatives, engaged with one another in synchronic colloquy. But each faculty required different treatment. *The Disputa* (Theology), for example, centres on the physical manifestation of the numinous in the Host on the altar, around which are grouped the four Doctors of the Church, amplified by later theologians and prelates, including Sixtus IV. Poetry is embodied in the god Apollo, accompanied by the Nine Muses, around whom the preeminent representatives of poetry's different forms are arranged: Homer at the top left, Virgil immediately behind him, and many others – including, of course, Dante and Petrarch, and even contemporaries such as the poet Antonio Tebaldeo. Philosophy, or *The School of Athens* – a later sobriquet but an appropriate one, for it was in Athens that the two main schools of philosophy originated – is divided into two sections. Idealist philosophy is represented by the flame-like figure of the upward-pointing Plato, whose principles extend to harmonic ratios. Empirical philosophy and the sciences spring from the earthbound figure of Aristotle, whose principles encompass geometry. Unlike Poetry and Theology, whose divine origins are embodied by Apollo and the Trinity, Philosophy has no single source. Raphael therefore placed the simulated statues of two divinities – Athena (or Minerva), goddess of wisdom, and Apollo, bringer of light and enlightenment – on, respectively, the right and left of the façade of his imaginary building, which they identify as, effectively, a cathedral of the mind. Raphael created the illusion of a vast vaulted space, obviously inspired in scale and in some details by the great project of St Peter's that Bramante and Julius had under way, but not recording it. It suggests the immeasurable scope of human thought and to an extent reifies it: few later artists could escape Raphael's solution.

The wall devoted to Justice – the only scheme among the four that does not present a unified field – offers a different solution. If it replaced an earlier, unrecorded design, it is likely that the change occurred late in Raphael's work in the room, for it includes elements datable to 1511. *Justice* with sword and scales is personified in the vault roundel but, according to Plato, Justice is not a single quality but a portmanteau concept comprised of Fortitude, Prudence and Charity: the three Cardinal Virtues. It is these that are embodied by the majestic women in the lunette, arranged on a notional platform that incorporates the top of

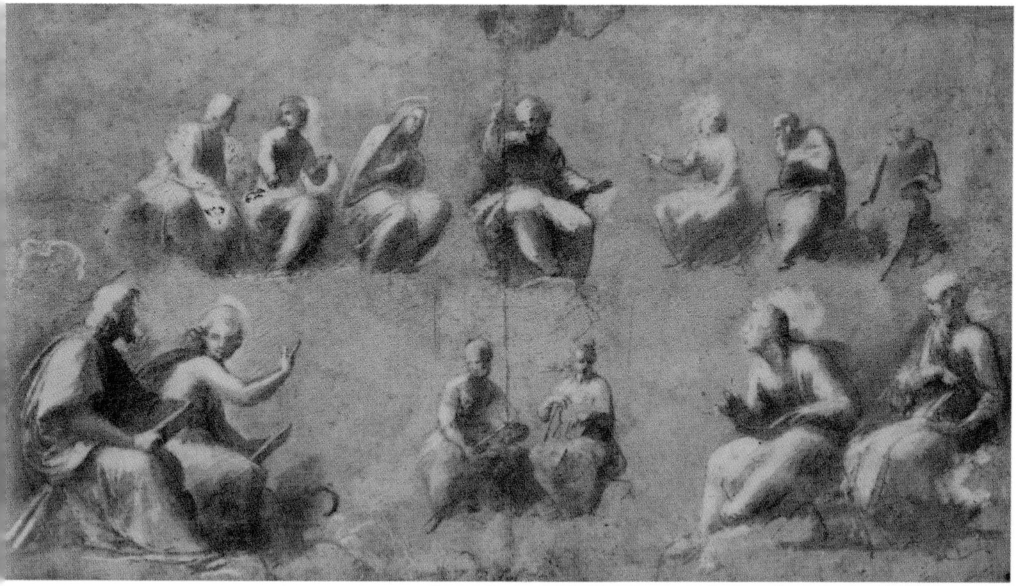

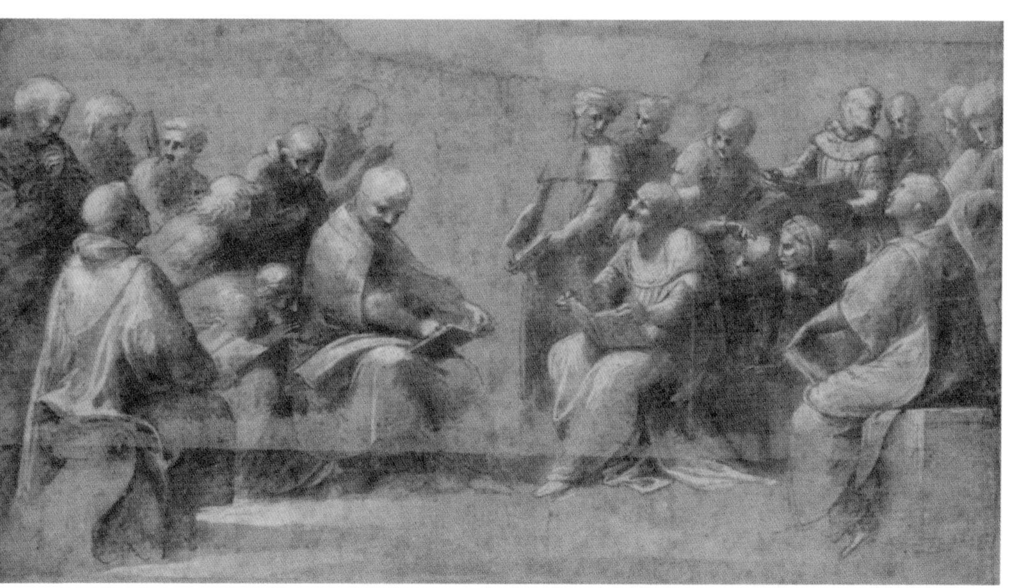

79 TOP Compositional study for the upper part of *The Disputa*, probably 1508
80 ABOVE Compositional study for the lower part of *The Disputa*, c. 1508.
These two drawings were originally halves of the same large *modello*, which
was divided at an unknown date. Taken together they illustrate Raphael's
scheme for *The Disputa* before he decided to extend the figural groups to
the edges of the picture field

The Stanza della Segnatura

the window. The lower sections of the wall, either side of the
window, are divided into civil and canon law. In the narrower
field, at the left, the Byzantine emperor Justinian receives the
codex of civil law, the Pandects, from the jurist Trebonianus.
At the right, Gregory the Great accepts the volume of canon law
from Raimond de Peñaforte, who has codified his instructions.
Both frescoes evoke frontispieces, illuminated and printed, and
the allusion is surely intentional. Gregory is impersonated by
Julius II, in the first of his appearances in the Stanze; his pose
recalls the image of his uncle, Sixtus IV, by Justus van Ghent
in the Urbino *studiolo*. Since Raphael would have known Julius
clean-shaven until his reappearance in Rome, bearded, in late
June 1511, the wall, at least in its present form, cannot have been
painted before July. Julius is accompanied by members of his
court. Three of them – Giovanni de' Medici, Alessandro Farnese
(of whom Raphael had painted an innovative independent
portrait a couple of years earlier) and Giulio de' Medici, not
then a cardinal – were to become popes.

The wall frescoes went through one or more changes of
plan, although this can be demonstrated for only two of them.
A series of drawings – more numerous than for any other work
by Raphael but still very incomplete – survives for *The Disputa*,
which show that the initial conception was quite different from
the final fresco. For *Parnassus* (or Poetry) there is an engraving
by Marcantonio after a lost *modello* that includes winged
genii in the sky and with the figures couched in antique garb,
whereas their garments are largely modernised in the fresco –
which, *inter alia*, demonstrates that Raphael was not rigidly
committed to the antique.

The sequence of drawings for *The Disputa* allows us to
follow several of its stages of development. The earliest is
a lightly sketched compositional draught in wash; it shows
the left half of an evidently symmetrical composition in which
all the figures, seated or standing, are on one level (Windsor,
Royal Collection). At the side, a pair of columns supports an
open entablature, rather flimsy and without obvious purpose.
At this moment Raphael felt constrained by the door that
enters the picture field at the right and decided to acknowledge
it at both sides of his composition. However, this solution
confined his figures to the central part of the field, leaving the
edges unoccupied. This sketch was clarified and amplified in
a large and fairly detailed drawing, now divided horizontally
into two, that shows the central section of the field in some
detail. The upper level is now composed of two heavenly layers
that stretch across the field, apparently parallel to the picture
plane. But the arrangement is static and lacks energy and focus.

The final organisation was the product of two choices. Raphael decided to dominate the door, not submit to it, and did so by espousing dynamic rather than static symmetry. At the right, the real door morphs into a low painted parapet that is matched at the left by an open balustrade. This solution allowed Raphael to extend his figure composition to the edges of the field. The other decision was fundamentally an iconographic one, for which Raphael no doubt had advice. He placed an altar in the centre of his composition and divided the ground plane into two levels, setting the altar on the higher one, at the top of a short flight of steps, as it would be in a church, with the seated Doctors of the Church arranged at either side of it. This gave his composition a central focus. And the replacement of one level with two opened the steps as a site of movement on which Raphael created varied poses for the prelates and acolytes who press towards the altar. The altar supports a monstrance displaying the sacred Host on which the orthogonals of the pavement – and frame – converge, giving the composition a powerful symbolic centre.

This geometrical structure also controlled the congregation of heavenly presences who sit side by side in an apparent semi-circle that, extending into depth, simulates an apse. It contains intercalated Old and New Testament figures, fronted at left and right by Sts Peter and Paul. Christ, lifting his arms to display his wounds, and flanked by the Virgin and St John the Baptist, is seated on a higher – mezzanine – platform, corresponding in width with the altar below; above him is a half-length figure of God the Father, the keystone, so to speak, of the apse. The apse is further established by radiating lines that act as scaffolding for a host of angels. The effect is of an architecture created without architecture: of a notional apse constructed only by size, shape and diminution.

The different levels of the composition are joined by gesture and gaze: one of the saints, Stephen, points down from the heavenly conference at the discussion groups below, and Lawrence looks upwards at the angels who hover at the apex of the space. But most important is Raphael's use of full and partial circles. In the upper centre, Christ sits before a circular glory, whose interrupted lower section is restored in the smaller glory that frames the Holy Ghost. This, in turn, is echoed in the circular monstrance, which is echoed once more in the circular Host, the gleaming focus of the composition. The presence of Christ's body in the Host could hardly be visualised more effectively.

Within so powerful a framework Raphael could allow himself latitude in the movements and poses of his cast;

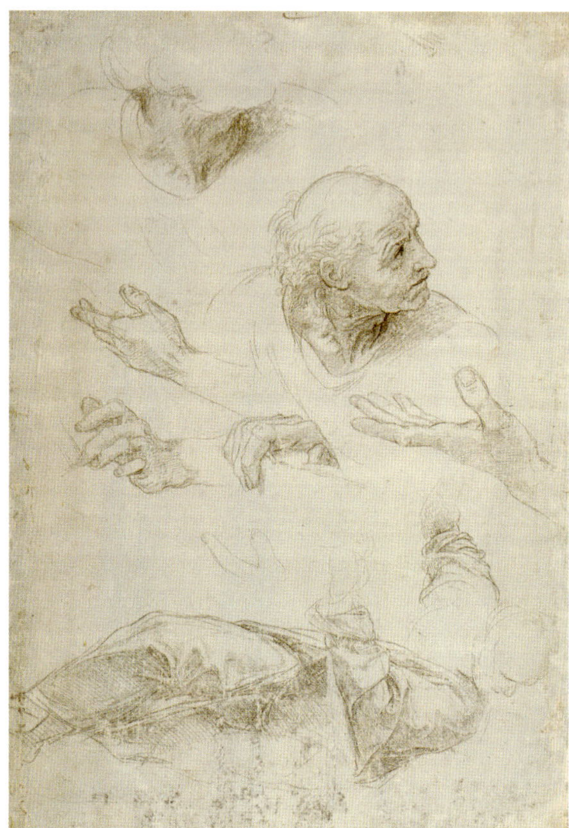

81

figures are seen from many angles and in many positions. At the edges, Raphael used the low wall and the open balustrade as prompts and pivots for lively forward-facing and turning figures, allowing himself further diversity in this grand unity. One potent figure, prepared in a particularly beautiful metalpoint drawing, is a balding man – perhaps Bramante – who gestures impatiently at a book, at which another man peers, only to have his attention returned to the Host by a smiling angelic youth. *The Disputa* is rife with felicities of this kind, which allude simultaneously to character, intellectual orientation, dogma and revelation. *The Disputa* is probably the most unified and yet diverse, most constructed but freest constellation of figures – over sixty in number – in the entirety of Western art, and it and *The School of Athens* have been inescapable reference points for any later attempt to create ideal assemblies.

But *The Disputa* is not entirely without precedent. Raphael
had tried the idea of a heavenly apse in the San Severo *Trinity*,
and he obviously thought again of *The Last Judgment* of Fra
Bartolommeo and Albertinelli in San Marco, and the upper
part of Ghirlandaio's vision of heaven in Santa Maria Novella.
And Melozzo da Forlì, whom Giovanni Santi had admired, had
created something of a precedent in the now destroyed apse
of Santi Apostoli in Rome. In the earthly section Raphael was
inspired in general terms by Leonardo's *Adoration of the Magi*,
and there are some direct borrowings, such as the bearded
figure who leans forward in a secretarial function, who appears
even in Raphael's earliest drawings. But whereas Leonardo's
composition, although worked out perspectivally, is put
together symbolically – by carpentry, as it were – Raphael's
conception is precision visual engineering.

To conceive, let alone to execute, a unified composition
that comprehends such complexity and such variety must
have taken a mental effort of superhuman intensity. That this
was achieved by a man in his mid-20s, who had not previously
attempted anything of this richness, seems barely possible.

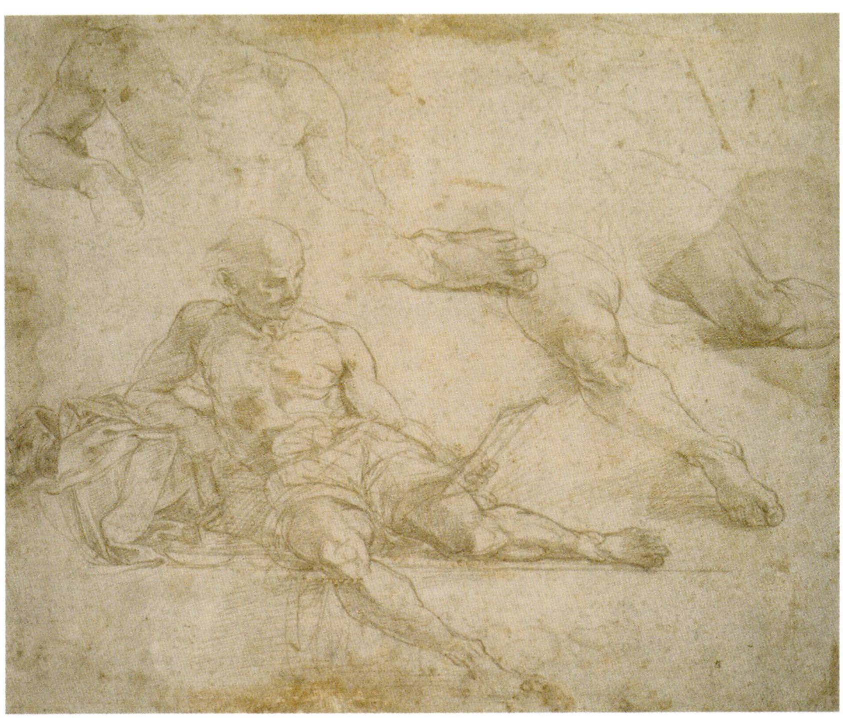

Once the cartoon had been prepared, it would have been obvious that no living artist could match Raphael in organising a multi-figure composition, quite apart from his command of individual character and movement. It is not hard to understand why Julius assigned all the Stanze to Raphael, even though he knew that this would delay the project's completion.

We cannot trace the internal development of *The School of Athens.* Some scholars believe it to have been the first fresco to be painted, but stylistically, and taking account of the supreme accomplishment of its figural structuring, this revision is hard to accept. Several studies of the highest quality exist for individual figures and groups, plus the full-size cartoon employed for the fresco – a unique and magnificent survival – but no compositional drawings. The studies are almost all in metalpoint on coated paper, mostly pink but occasionally green, unlike the studies for *The Disputa*, in which all the media at Raphael's disposal were used. The high proportion of metalpoint drawings must in part be due to accident of survival, but Raphael's choice of medium does correspond to the specific demands posed by *The School of Athens*, in which orthogonal unity is less commanding and which is made up of semi-independent groups or clusters of figures. It was natural that Raphael should employ a medium suitable for individualising forms with clarity and in sharp relief. The preparation stimulated some of his most beautiful and virtuosic drawings, but they come from a stage in the composition's realisation in which figures and poses had been fixed: there are few differences between the drawn and the painted figures.

Like *The Disputa*, *The School of Athens* could be analysed endlessly, but a couple of examples must suffice. The group of Euclid instructing a group of youths at lower right was singled out by Vasari and is justly famous for its portrayal of the students' different levels of comprehension: Raphael's ability to express the motions of the mind through gesture and movement equals, if not surpasses, that of Leonardo. And the concept of the two men debating on the steps is breathtaking. One ascends, the other descends, but they nevertheless engage in debate as their paths cross: the ascending man gestures downwards towards Diogenes, sprawled on the steps at his left, while the descending man looks and gestures backwards towards Plato and Aristotle, as if to say that they are the sources of true knowledge rather than the inactive and self-absorbed Cynic. But although their allegiances and gestures diverge, they are simultaneously united: their two forms compose a diamond,

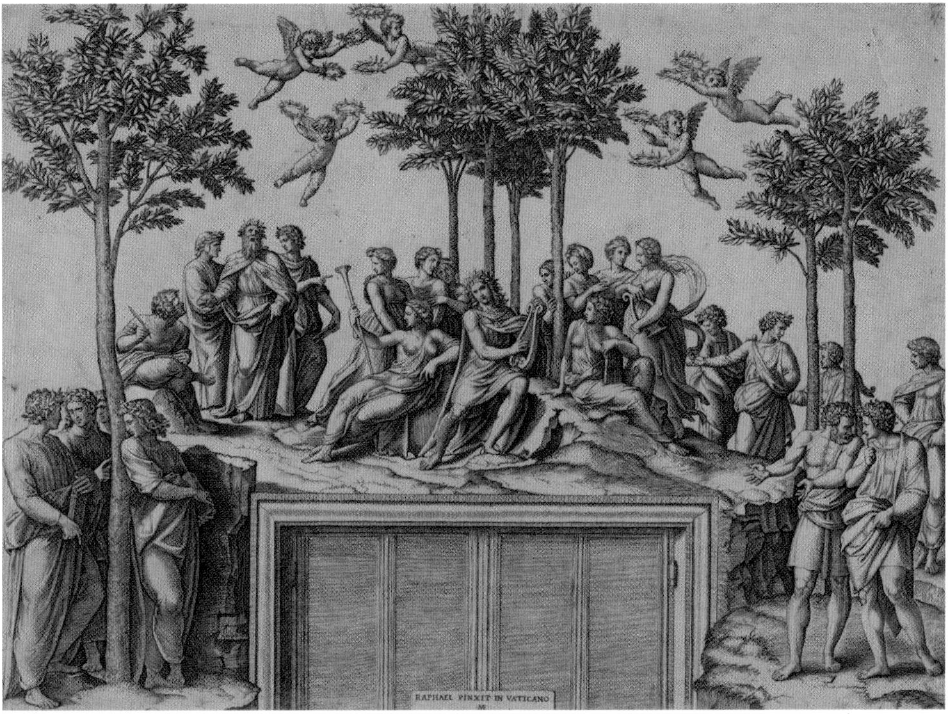

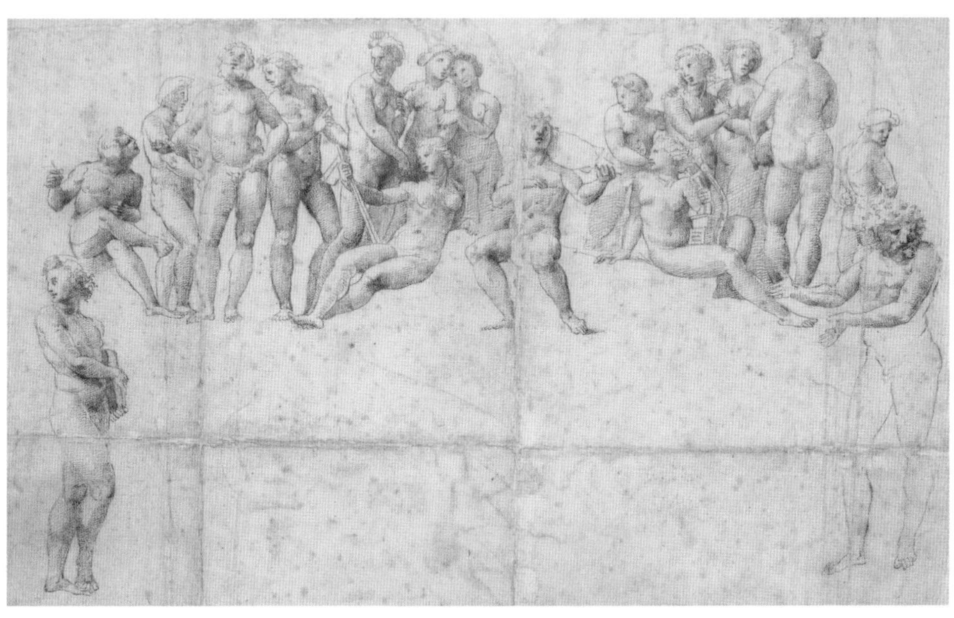

83 TOP Marcantonio Raimondi, after Raphael, *Parnassus*, c. 1513
84 ABOVE Unidentified draughtsman, *Parnassus*, copy after a lost drawing by Raphael, probably of 1509

and their drapery folds connect one with the other. Diversity
is contained within a common search for truth.

The development of *Parnassus* is a little clearer. In addition
to the 'antiquising' engraved *modello*, there is a copy of a lost
compositional drawing in pen in which all the figures are
studied nude – although not in the detail of the nude study
for *The Disputa* (Vienna, Albertina). There is also a metalpoint
drawing for the entire left-hand side (London, British Museum),
but it differs minimally from the fresco. Most of the others are
in hard pen, which Raphael would have chosen to create grand
and dynamic forms. Among them are some of Raphael's most
vigorous drawings; they consist of individual figure studies and
a few details, including head studies for Dante, Petrarch and
Homer, the last adapted from the head of *The Laocoön*. The line
throughout is firm and decisive, emphasising the plasticity of
the forms.

The cast list of *Parnassus* is smaller than those of *The
Disputa* and *The School of Athens*, and it is not controlled by
a perspectival structure – a fact that favoured the deployment

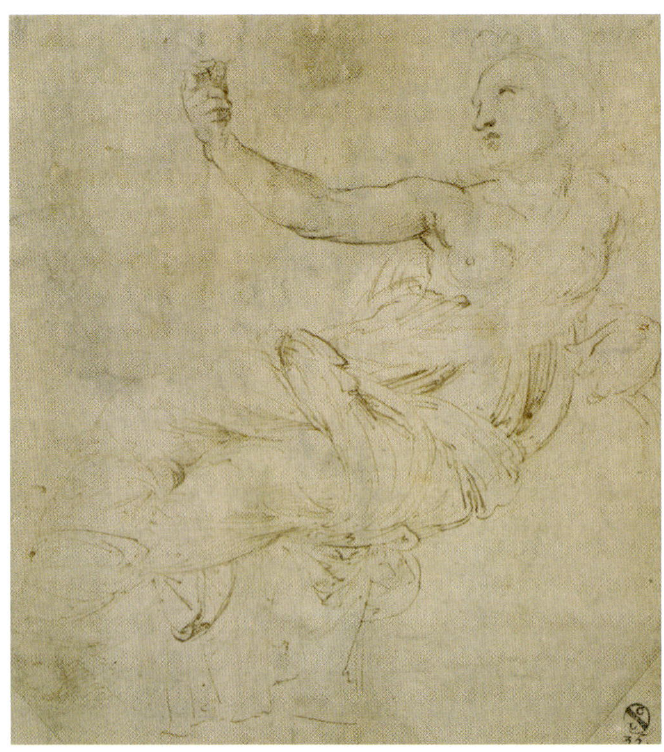

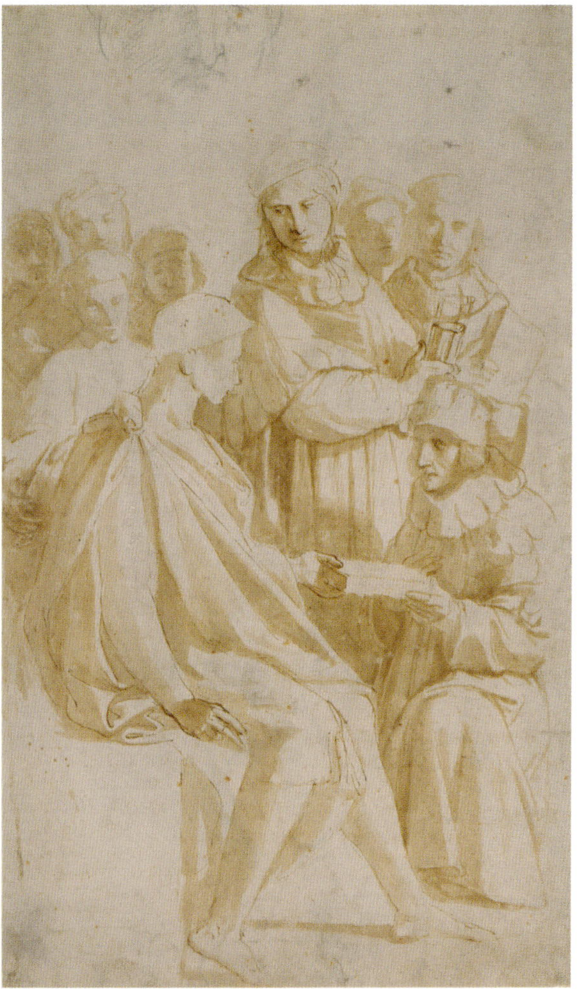

of larger figures. The composition rides up the surface,
and different layers of depth are signalled by figure scale,
not perspective. Furthermore, a perspectival structure would
have clashed with the view through the window towards the
Belvedere, a site traditionally associated with Apollo.

Raphael continued to change his mind as he finalised
the design. He had made a drawing for a standing figure to
be placed at the right of the window (London, British Museum)
but at the last moment eliminated him and replaced him with
a seated poet, probably Horace, who breaks from the surface of
the fresco and points directly into the room. His forms have a

Michelangelesque energy, and in the *Parnassus* we see Raphael
for the first time beginning to address the Sistine ceiling,
of which Bramante had afforded him a preview. A drawing for
the Muse seated next to Apollo clearly refers to Michelangelo's
Creation of Adam, a reference somewhat diluted in the fresco.
And Sappho, absent both from the engraved *modello* and the
nude design, was also a late addition: she is based on the
ignudo seated next to the *Adam*, and her raised right arm
recalls that of the Virgin in the Doni Tondo. It may have been
at this time that Raphael added to *The School of Athens* the
seated Heraclitus. He has the brooding power of Michelangelo
and may – as has often been suggested – be a symbolic portrait
of him.

No studies are known for the lunette zone of the Justice wall,
although the personifications must have elicited magnificent
ones. In these figures Raphael's turn to Michelangelo is
still more evident: the Prudence is as grand as one of the
Sistine Ancestors, and Fortitude is unmistakably quoted
from Michelangelo's statue of *Moses*, of which Raphael
presumably knew a wax or clay model.

The Virtues are in complete contrast with *Justinian Receiving
the Pandects* and *Gregory and the Decretals*, for both of which
compositional drawings survive (Frankfurt, Städelsches
Kunstinstitut). Neither contained complex figures and,
although their preparation no doubt required more drawings
than survive, they would have been many fewer than for the
other frescoes. *The Decretals* must have been particularly
meaningful for Julius, for it looks back to a fresco by Melozzo
da Forlì of the early 1480s celebrating Sixtus IV's foundation
of the Vatican library, in which Sixtus is accompanied by
his nephew, Julius, in his earlier incarnation as cardinal.

It was probably between work on *Parnassus* and *Justice*
that Raphael replaced the vault frescoes. Among the *quadri*,
there are pen drawings for *Astronomy* and *The Judgment of
Solomon*, and a metalpoint sketch for the latter (Oxford,
Ashmolean); and among the roundels a pen sketch for
Theology (Oxford, Ashmolean), plus a particularly beautiful
black chalk drawing (Windsor, Royal Collection) for *Poetry*.
Her head, like that of *Galatea* a little later, takes up that of
the *St Catherine*. The drawings for *The Judgment of Solomon*
fed into Raphael's designs for *The Massacre of the Innocents*,
the ambitious design engraved by Marcantonio, and suggest
that this was being prepared in 1510–11.

Although Raphael may have employed assistants in the
Segnatura, the overall level of execution could hardly be higher,
and the room is, to all intents and purposes, entirely autograph.

But *Justinian Receiving the Pandects*, while it follows Raphael's drawing closely, lacks modelling in some areas and seems raw. It might have been intended to be finished with a now lost layer *a secco*, but it is sometimes thought to be by another artist. Among the various candidates Lorenzo Lotto has had some favour; however, when it is compared with fresco work certainly by Lotto, plausible connections are few. Furthermore, it stretches credulity that so individual – not to say eccentric – a painter as Lotto could have disciplined himself to follow Raphael's design undeviatingly. If an associate is to be sought, the most likely is Timoteo Viti, who was collaborating – or about to collaborate – with Raphael on the chapel of Agostino Chigi in Santa Maria della Pace, and whose loyalty to Raphael's designs was uncompromised by individuality.

The Segnatura was prepared in hundreds of drawings, now mostly lost, but those that survive are in the full range of available techniques and include some of Raphael's most beautiful and vibrant sheets. It is unlikely that Raphael ever again made so many drawings for a single scheme. The Segnatura is probably the most famous and admired achievement in Raphael's oeuvre. It is often seen as the embedment of the High Renaissance in its majestic fusion of space and figures. The room is wonderfully grand and airy, and seems to open onto and summarise the entire range of Western thought. Yet despite the range of movement with which Raphael imbues all of them, the compositions are essentially static, and the lighting is even. The Stanza di Eliodoro, which Raphael began planning even before the final touches were applied to the Segnatura, was to be vastly different.

There was a brief aftermath. The original arrangement of the shelving and panelling of Julius's library is not known: the woodwork in the *basamento* below the frescoes was damaged in the Sack of Rome, removed *c.* 1540 and replaced by frescoes by Perino del Vaga. But the *Parnassus* wall underwent some changes soon after Leo's accession in 1513. It is probable that shelving extending up to the base of the *Parnassus* was removed, and in its place, either side of the window, were added *trompe l'oeil* reliefs, designed by Raphael but probably executed by an assistant. One depicts *Augustus Forestalling the Burning of the Aeneid*, the other *Alexander preserving the Books of Homer,* subjects eminently suitable for a library; below these, simulated intarsias were added, probably designed and painted by a decorative expert.

Chapter 5
Schemes outside the Vatican and the Beginnings of Engraving

I

Projects for Julius II in the Vatican occupied most of
Raphael's attention during the pontiff's lifetime, and that
pattern continued under his successor, Cardinal Giovanni
de' Medici, who became Pope Leo X on 9 March 1513. But
Raphael also worked for other patrons. One of his paintings,
a small fresco but significant conceptually and stylistically,
is the *Isaiah* in the Roman church of Sant'Agostino. It was
painted for the Apostolic protonotary Johannes Goritz, from
Luxembourg, who obtained permission to construct an altar
in December 1510. The ensemble was unveiled in October 1512,
concurrently with the Sistine ceiling.

The seated *Isaiah* is painted on a pillar above Andrea
Sansovino's niched group of *The Virgin and Child with St Anne*,
which is dated 1512. We know nothing about relations between
Raphael and Andrea Sansovino, but they were probably cordial,
and that there may have been some reciprocal influence is
suggested by similarities between Andrea's *Virtues* on the
twinned tombs in Santa Maria del Popolo and Raphael's
Muses in *Parnassus*. But the *Isaiah* looks to another sculptor.
According to Vasari, the fresco, which would have been
executed in the space of a few days, was completed but
then redone after Raphael saw the Sistine ceiling. The *putti*
at either side of Isaiah recall those in the arms of the thrones
of Michelangelo's prophets and sibyls, and Isaiah's outward
address and dominant presence are clearly Michelangelesque.
But the specific source for the retracted left leg and the right
forearm carried across the chest is Michelangelo's *Moses*,
intended for the tomb of Julius II. Raphael employed the same
model for *Fortitude* on the Justice wall of the Segnatura. It is

improbable that Michelangelo had begun carving the *Moses* at this date, but he would have prepared it in models. A pleasant, if unattested, anecdote attaches to the *Isaiah*. Goritz was reportedly shocked at the sum that Raphael demanded, and Michelangelo was asked to evaluate the fresco. He upheld Raphael's fee emphatically, stating that *Isaiah*'s knee alone justified the price.

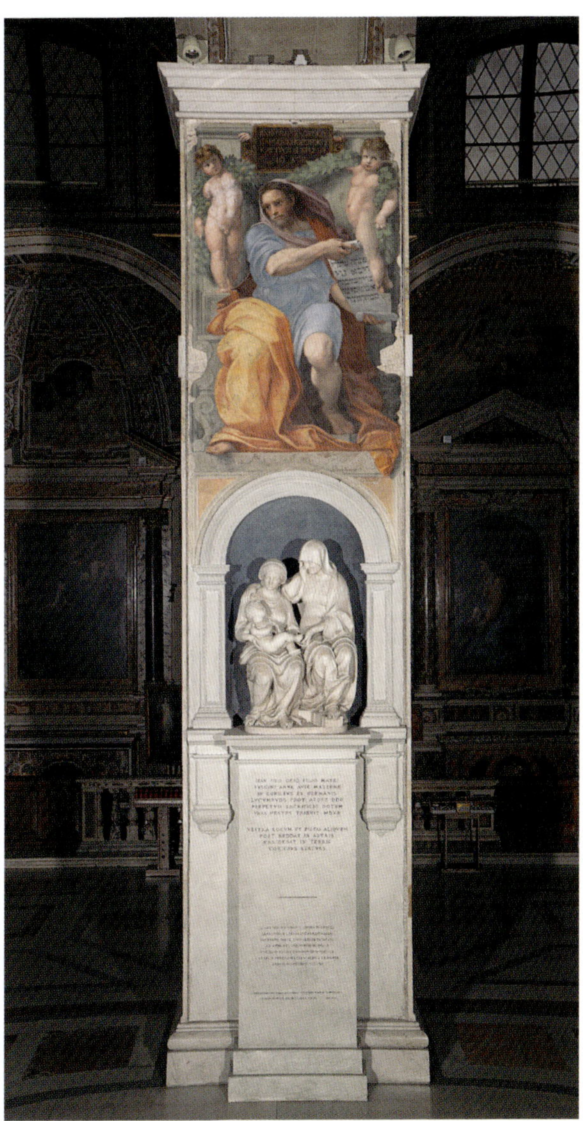

87 *The Prophet Isaiah*, 1512. Fresco, in Sant'Agostino in Rome. Andrea Sansovino's group of the Virgin, Child and St Anne, which was for centuries displayed elsewhere in the church, now stands again in its original position

Raphael's Michelangelism was developed further in his prophets and sibyls in Santa Maria della Pace. Second only to the popes in Raphael's life, his most important patron was the enormously wealthy and exceptionally cultivated Sienese banker Agostino Chigi (1466–1520). Chigi's monopoly on the alum mines at Tolfa made him the richest man in Rome and, indeed, Italy. He moved in the highest circles of power: a close ally of and financier to Julius II, he also acted as a diplomat, spending six months in Venice during 1511 to secure a loan from Venetian bankers for the pope. These activities began to diminish under Leo X (r. 1513–21), with whom, however, Agostino was on the friendliest terms. An avid antiquarian with unlimited means, Chigi formed an important collection of classical sculpture, long underestimated and now gradually being reconstituted. This included major and influential statues such as the so-called *Arrotino* (Knife Grinder), a standing Venus, a figure interpreted as Psyche, and many precious small-scale works. Chigi proved to be an outstandingly imaginative and stimulating patron, and gave Raphael opportunities that he would not have had elsewhere.

In 1502 Agostino's father, Mariano (1439–1504), had commissioned for the Sienese church of Sant'Agostino a large *Crucifixion with Saints* by Perugino, and Agostino seems to have overseen its progress. He may have heard of Raphael from Perugino, but he would, in any case, have known of Raphael's design participation in the Piccolomini Library and would have learnt much more about him after his arrival in Rome. Soon after 1505 Chigi commissioned the design and construction of a suburban villa from his fellow Sienese Baldassare Peruzzi (1481–1536), one of the most innovative painters and architects in Siena in the early sixteenth century and nearly as precocious as Raphael. More palace than villa, the large and immensely luxurious Farnesina (a name it acquired later) lay between the Via della Lungara and the banks of the Tiber, little over a kilometre from the Vatican. The building was constructed quite rapidly, and by 1510 it seems that Agostino began to develop its decoration. Simultaneously, he commissioned religious schemes in his private chapels in two prominent Roman churches, both founded by Sixtus IV and both favoured by Julius.

Raphael and the banker had certainly met by November 1510, when Raphael was contracted to furnish Agostino with designs for two roundels in bronze, about 4 *palmi* (90 cm, or 35 in.) in diameter, to be executed by Raphael's Perugian friend the goldsmith and sculptor Cesarino. The contract – known

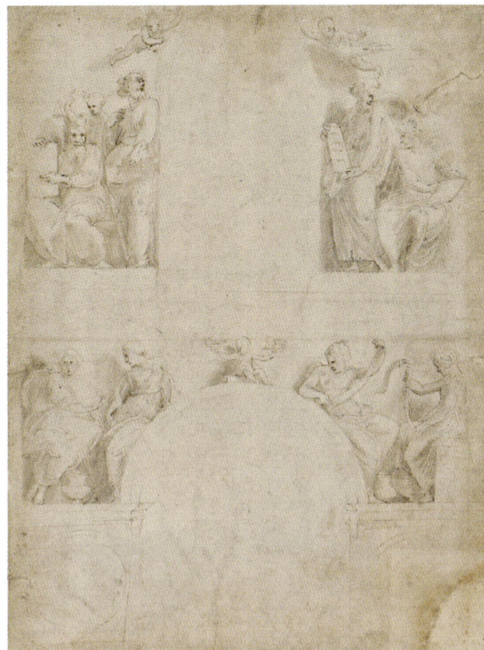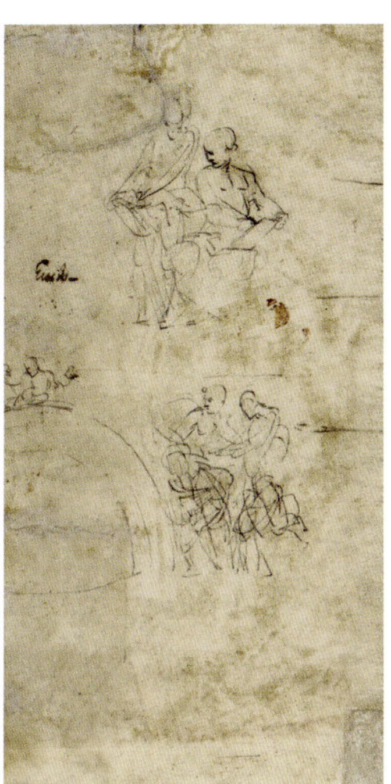

88 ABOVE LEFT Gianfrancesco Penni, compositional study for the Chapel of Agostino Chigi in Santa Maria della Pace, Rome, probably 1510
89 ABOVE RIGHT Compositional sketch for the Chapel of Agostino Chigi in Santa Maria della Pace, probably 1510

only in later transcriptions – describes the roundels as containing flowers ('floribus'), but this is likely a misreading of 'figuribus' (figures). If so, they were certainly intended for Agostino's chapel in Santa Maria della Pace, whose planning and programme must by then have been well advanced. The chapel was presumably the first scheme that Agostino commissioned from Raphael.

It may be that Raphael paused his work in the Segnatura, as Michelangelo interrupted his in the Sistine Chapel, while Julius was on campaign. A pen sketch establishing the chapel scheme in outline is found on the verso of a study for a group in *The School of Athens*, and a chalk sketch for part of the lunette is on the verso of a study for *The Expulsion of Heliodorus*; it may be inferred that the chapel was frescoed in 1510–11. The pen sketch was succeeded by a lay-out drawing pen and wash for the whole scheme, executed by Gianfrancesco Penni (*c.* 1494?–1528?) (Stockholm, Nationalmuseum). This is one of the earliest recognisable and approximately datable appearances in

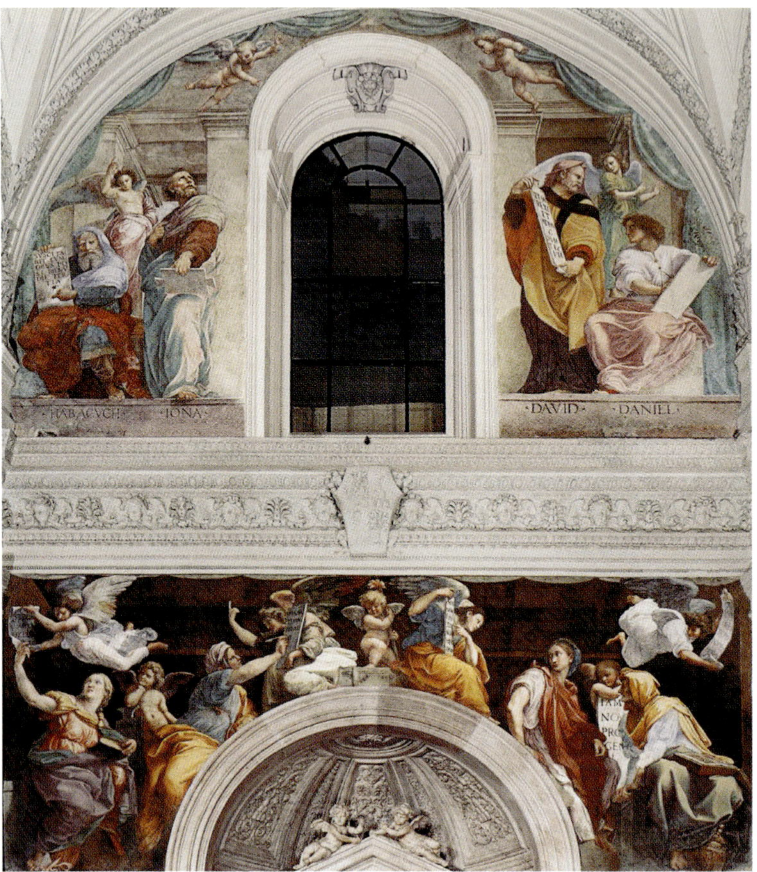

90 The Chapel of Agostino Chigi, 1510–12 in Santa Maria della Pace; unfinished. The lunette zone, containing the four Prophets, was executed from Raphael's cartoons by Timoteo Viti

Raphael's entourage of his Florentine-born assistant, here performing the secretarial role that would be one of his main functions.

Agostino's chapel, the first on the right in Santa Maria della Pace, is illuminated from the right. Work would have begun in the lunette zone, the realm of the prophets. According to Vasari, it was frescoed by Raphael's friend Timoteo Viti, who was absent from Urbino between the spring of 1510 and the summer of 1511, a period of fourteen or fifteen months in which he could have accomplished a great deal. The lunette is visible only at a steep angle, with viewing made more difficult by the central window: it was the obvious area to delegate. Timoteo's frescoes, although not in good condition, are competent performances, and he must have followed Raphael's cartoons loyally, without personal inflection. One of the prophets, probably Habakkuk (the veracity of the inscriptions is disputed), is again based on *Moses*. Raphael's reliance on Timoteo implies that in 1510–11 he had not yet recruited his own Roman team; perhaps, too, he wished to avoid painters brought to Rome by Julius, choosing to rely on an old friend from his native town. According to Vasari, who saw letters begging Timoteo to remain in Rome, his insistence on returning to Urbino discomforted Raphael. The loss of Timoteo may account in part for Raphael's evident difficulties with assistants in the following years.

On the main level of the chapel is a sequence of four sibyls attended by angels. The combination of prophets and sibyls of course recalls the Sistine ceiling, and the sibyls are redolent with Michelangelism: that at the left is clearly inspired by the upward-reaching Eve in the Sistine *Fall*, and the movement of the sibyl at the far right could also find a place in Michelangelo's vault. (The winged genius in the keystone of the arch, on the other hand, is yet another recollection of the Child in the Doni Tondo.) But Raphael wove the women together in a chain of intercommunication, whereas Michelangelo's figures are isolated.

A pen *modello* survives for the left-hand group at the upper level (Washington, National Gallery of Art), but all the figure studies are in red chalk, perhaps a response to Michelangelo's use of red chalk in his drawings for the later parts of the Sistine ceiling.

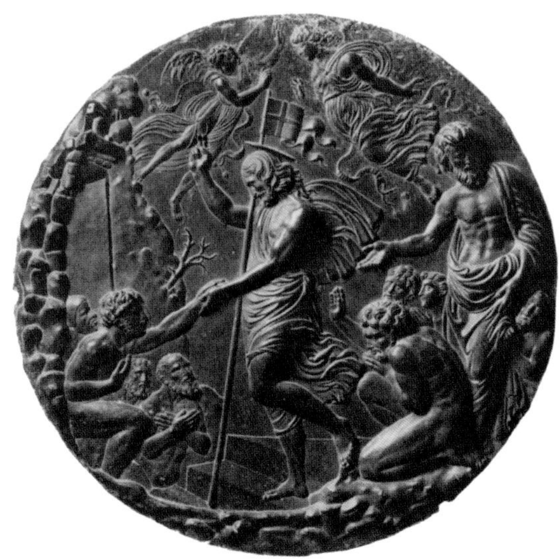

91 Cesare (Cesarino) Rossetti to Raphael's design, *Christ's Descent into Limbo*, 1510–11. One of the two roundels (its companion shows St Thomas verifying Christ's wounds), to be placed at either side of the (unexecuted) altarpiece. It is not known why they were never installed

Vasari claims that the Pace chapel was frescoed by Raphael under the direct impress of the Sistine ceiling, which would date it after the ceiling's full exposure, in October 1512. But he also says – and Raphael's citations of Michelangelo in the Segnatura would bear it out – that he gained access to the chapel considerably earlier, probably late in 1509 or early in 1510. So the Michelangelism of the Pace chapel does not entail a date after the vault's completion. And in this context, it should be noted that Raphael's quotations from the Sistine ceiling concern only the first two-thirds of the cycle. There is no trace in Raphael's work in the Segnatura or here of the powerfully dynamic forms of the latter part of the ceiling: the first three days of *Creation*, or the two double pendentives of *Haman* and *The Brazen Serpent*. Raphael came to these a little later: in 1512–13 he adapted Michelangelo's *Jeremiah* for a seated Virgin in a Holy Family drawing (private collection) that Giulio Romano later used as the basis for his Spinola *Holy Family* (Los Angeles, J. Paul Getty Museum).

The sibyls interact across the arch of the chapel's central niche, which is flanked by two piers. The layout of the niche in 1510 is not certain and it was later remodelled, but it presumably mirrored – or was mirrored by – that of the Ponzetti Chapel immediately opposite, frescoed by Peruzzi in 1516, which has a rectangular altarpiece. In Penni's Stockholm drawing the piers carry roundels, and it is virtually certain that these were intended to contain two bronze roundels ordered in November 1510, now in the abbey of Chiaravalle: one depicts *Christ's Descent into Limbo*, the other *Doubting Thomas*. Autograph drawings by Raphael survive for both: two in pen for the former (Lille, Musée des Beaux-Arts, and Florence, Uffizi), and two – one in pen, the other in metalpoint (Cambridge, Fitzwilliam Museum; Frankfurt, Städelsches Kunstinstitut) – for the latter. The media are appropriate for translation into bronze.

Such subjects imply that the never executed altarpiece – no doubt in fresco – was to represent an episode of Christ's Passion. We lack hard information, but two possibilities have been suggested. One is that the altarpiece was to be a *Pietà*, with the standing Virgin mourning over the body of her son; there exist two variants of this subject by Raphael of about 1511–12, one known in an autograph drawing and the second in a drawing by Penni (Windsor, Royal Collection). The other suggested theme is the Resurrection of Christ, for which there is a dynamic multi-figure compositional study and six masterly and highly Michelangelesque black chalk figure studies in various collections (although two of them – London, British

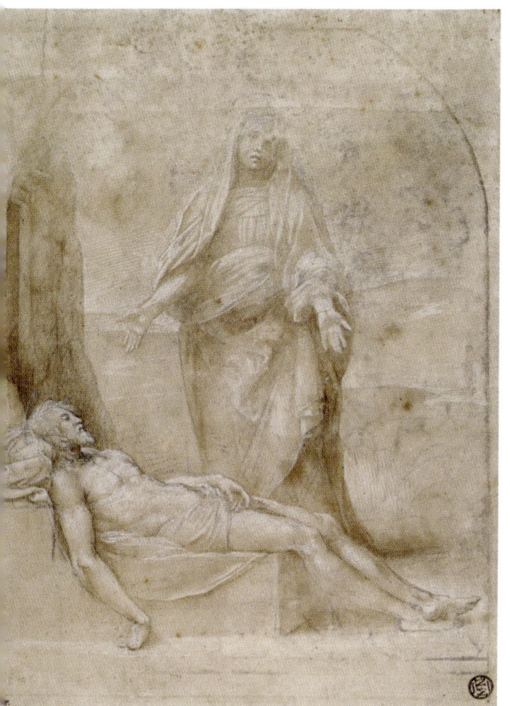
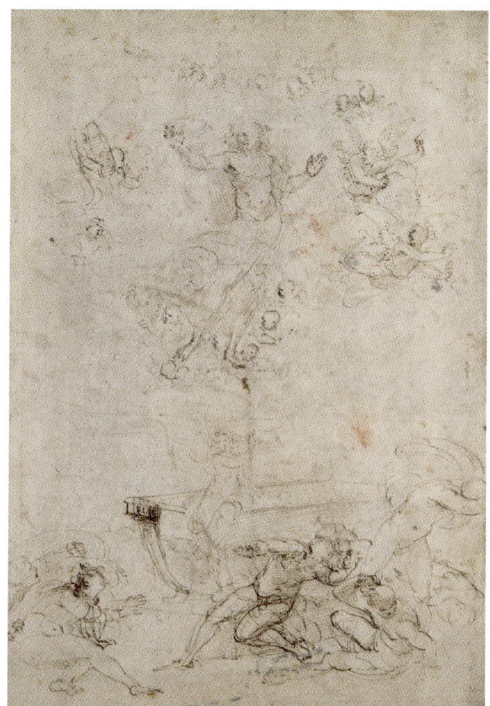

92 ABOVE LEFT   *Pietà*, probably 1511
93 ABOVE RIGHT   *The Resurrection*, probably 1511–12

Museum, and Chatsworth, Devonshire Collection – cannot
be linked to its compositional drawing).

92   The *Pietà* designs are proportionally appropriate to the field,
and the cast is confined to two figures; but the Louvre drawing
is round-topped and, although that at Windsor is rectangular,
both are illuminated from the left, which counts against them.
The Resurrection is accepted by most scholars as the subject
of the altarpiece, and this is supported by the stipulation of a
Resurrection in the contract drawn up in 1530 with Sebastiano
del Piombo for the chapel's completion. The date of Raphael's
93   *Resurrection* drawings, all of which are lit from the right, must
be *c.* 1511–12, appropriate for the chapel, so iconography and
date would seem to fit. But there are two caveats. One is that
the space available in for the altarpiece is no more than about
200 × 145 cm (79 × 57 in.), meaning that the figures would have
been only 40–50 cm (16–20 in.) high. This would have been
congruent with the bronze roundels, but so complicated an
altarpiece on such a small scale would have been overpowered

by the sibyls above it. Second, the Bayonne drawing seems
to have been made for a round-topped field, not a rectangle.

Alternatively, it has been suggested that Raphael's
Resurrection was designed for Agostino Chigi's other
ecclesiastical project, his funerary chapel in Santa Maria del
Popolo. This was a new construction built to Raphael's design,
on which work must have begun at about the same time. We
know little of the internal chronology of the Popolo chapel,
which also remained unfinished, but it was completed
structurally by 1516, the date of the mosaics in the dome,
executed and signed by the Venetian Luigi da Pace. Unlike
the Pace scheme, which consisted of frescoes plus two bronze
reliefs, the Popolo chapel was an immensely lavish and costly
gesamtkunstwerk in which many elements were planned to
cohere. It was richly pictorial: rare marbles of various colours
were used for the walls and floor, white marble served for
the statuary, and bronze was employed for various fittings;
and mosaic work, never executed, was to be extended to the
drum and the roundels in the pendentives.

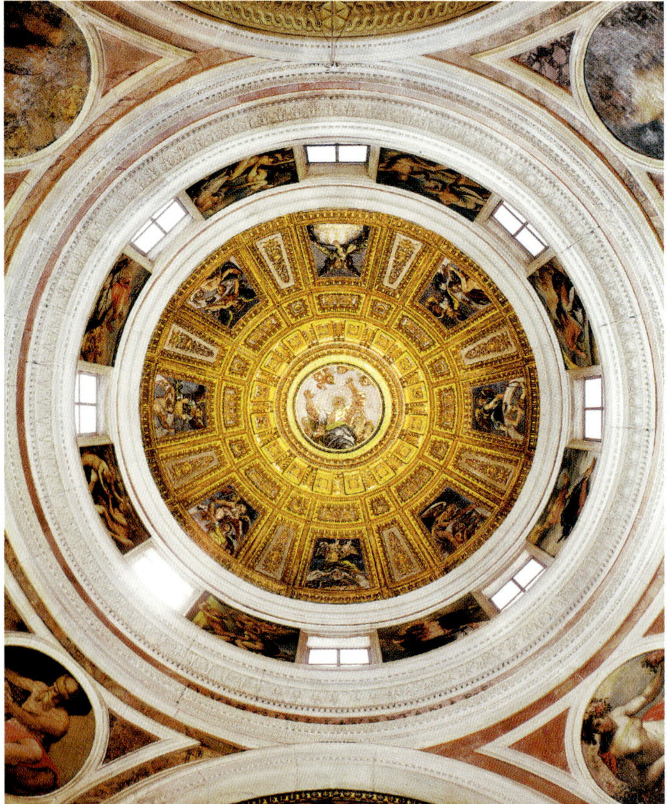

94 The Sepulchral
Chapel of Agostino
Chigi, the dome was
monogrammed by
the mosaicist Luigi
da Pace and dated
1516

As was customary in Rome, the altarpiece was to be a mural, not a moveable painting. Apart from the mosaic, the only surviving figurative elements designed by Raphael are the two sculptures, half of the planned four, and neither finished at the time of Raphael's death. Executed from about 1516 onwards by the young Florentine sculptor Lorenzo Lotti, known as Lorenzetto (1490–1541), they represent Jonah and Elijah, both of whom are antetypes of Christ with specific reference to his resurrection: Elijah transported to heaven in a fiery chariot, and Jonah emerging unharmed from the belly of the whale. In the 1650s Bernini added Daniel and Habakkuk: whether these were the prophets planned by Raphael is an open question.

The altarpiece field is huge, nearly 6 m (20 ft) tall and some 3.5 m (11½ ft) wide, and if Raphael's *Resurrection* were intended for this space it would explain the lavishness of his graphic preparation. A Resurrection would also fit with the God the Father in the centre of the dome, whose arms are spread in welcome. But the hypothesis that Raphael's *Resurrection* was planned for the Popolo chapel also presents problems. The subject of the altarpiece in the immediate aftermath of Raphael's death, when Sebastiano prepared a drawing for it (Amsterdam, Rijksmuseum), was to be an *Assumption of the Virgin*. Since a *concetto* by Raphael datable to *c*. 1510 (it is on the verso of a sketch for *Theology* on the Segnatura vault) shows *The Assumption*, it has been assumed that this was the subject of the Popolo's altarpiece from the beginning – a contention that can be supported by the chapel's dedication to the Madonna of Loreto. But dedications do not invariably determine the subjects of altarpieces, and it seems more likely that the choice of a Marian subject was made by Agostino's widow, Francesca, after his death. The ambient iconography of the chapel can be made to fit an altarpiece depicting the Virgin's Assumption only with difficulty, and Raphael's sketch is inappropriate in aspect ratio for the field in the Popolo. The altarpiece finally painted, incidentally, is lit from the right, whereas Raphael's *Assumption* sketch seems to be – and his developed study for the upper part (Stockholm, Nationalmuseum) certainly is – lit from the left. Raphael's *Assumption* drawings were presumably were made for some other, unrecorded project and may have morphed, some years later, into what became the lower part of the Monteluce *Coronation*, which will be discussed later. Raphael's Bayonne *Resurrection* design would fit the altar field of the Popolo chapel neatly, and the subject, obviously, is ideal for a funerary chapel. But if a large *Resurrection* was indeed planned as the altarpiece of the Popolo (it may be that another, smaller *Resurrection* was intended for the Pace), the project may soon have been shelved, for Raphael reused one of the guards shortly thereafter in his *Release of St Peter*. Agostino, however, favoured the subject of Christ's Resurrection, and probably in the middle of the decade commissioned from Girolamo Genga a very large panel on the theme for the high altar of the Roman church of St Catherine of Siena. This opens a further possibility: that Raphael's design was in fact made for that project, which, distracted by other work, he handed to Genga, whose *Resurrection* is also illuminated from the right.

As in other cases, the issue remains open. But it is worth underlining that Raphael's *Resurrection*, as we know it from the Bayonne drawing and the figure studies, was a project of extraordinary ambition. Whatever site it was planned for, had it been executed as a painting it would have been outstanding, infusing drama and physical vitality into a subject that had hitherto been treated statically. It would have transported the energy of the most dramatic scenes on the Sistine ceiling to an altarpiece and would have had a massive effect. As it happened, the design was a product of a particular, Michelangelesque phase of Raphael's art that he was not to pursue further. Some of its drama was carried into *The Transfiguration*, but that picture

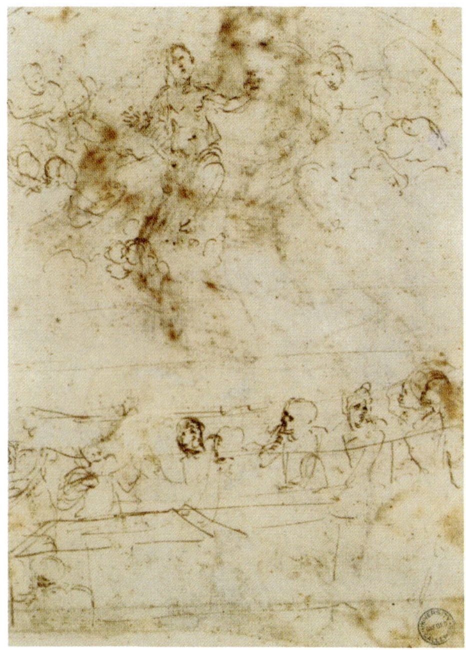

95 Compositional study for an *Assumption*, probably 1510

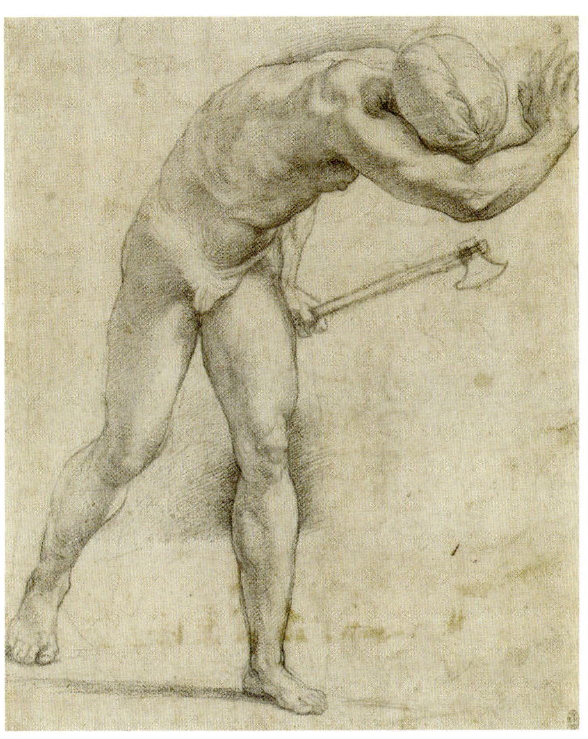

is divided into two episodes: it is not a unified scene. *The Resurrection*'s true heir is Titian's *Assumption of the Virgin* of 1516–18, although whether – and how – Titian could have learnt of Raphael's design is a matter for speculation.

III

Raphael also worked in Agostino Chigi's villa. The Farnesina was innovative in several ways: it had two loggias, both opening onto the garden, which creates a continuity between interior and exterior and was to affect the decoration of both. Exterior decoration was pioneered at the Farnesina. Peruzzi populated the walls with *grisaille* representations of mythological scenes; of these little remains, but a few copies have been identified, one of which, representing Mars and Venus, foreshadows the erotic orientation of much of the interior.

An autobiographical thread runs through Agostino's secular choices. The vault of the Loggia di Galatea, the first of the major spaces of the interior to be frescoed, was painted by Peruzzi, probably in 1511, with representations of the classical gods arranged to form Agostino's horoscope. But Peruzzi,

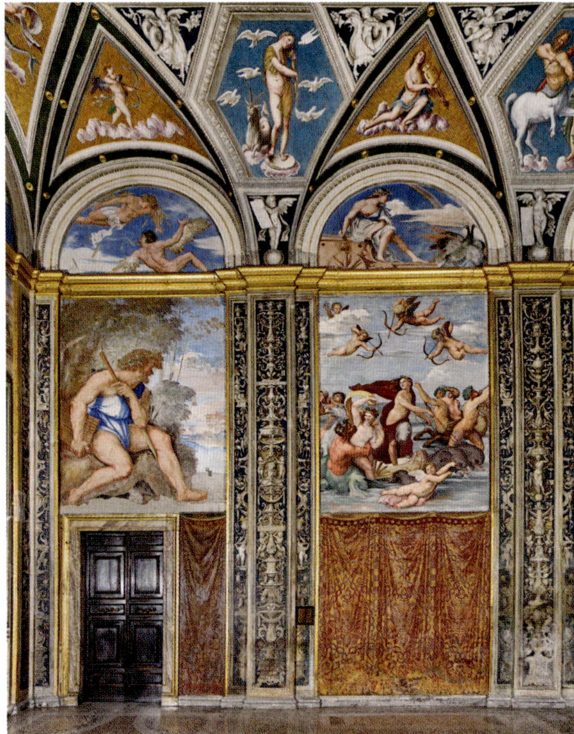

although he later worked in other rooms of the villa including, most impressively, the Sala delle Prospettive on the *piano nobile*, continued no further in this room. Perhaps Agostino envisaged from the start that it should be a gallery of many talents, like the studio of Isabella d'Este. Peruzzi's immediate successor in the Loggia di Galatea was the Venetian painter Sebastiano Luciani (*c.* 1485–1547), who later acquired the sobriquet 'del Piombo'. Sebastiano had met Chigi during his Venetian embassy and probably accompanied him on his return to Rome in September 1511. He promptly frescoed the lunettes with, mostly, Ovidian themes related to love and loss, and then moved to the wall proper, where he painted – in a different, softer style – the bulky *Polyphemus*, ardently gazing at his unattainable love, the nymph Galatea. Sebastiano probably completed *Polyphemus* in late 1511, and it is likely that Raphael frescoed the companion *Galatea* in 1512, although its date has been disputed, and it has even been placed among Raphael's earliest works in Rome. It does indeed show a reminiscence of Florence in the resemblance of Galatea's head to that of

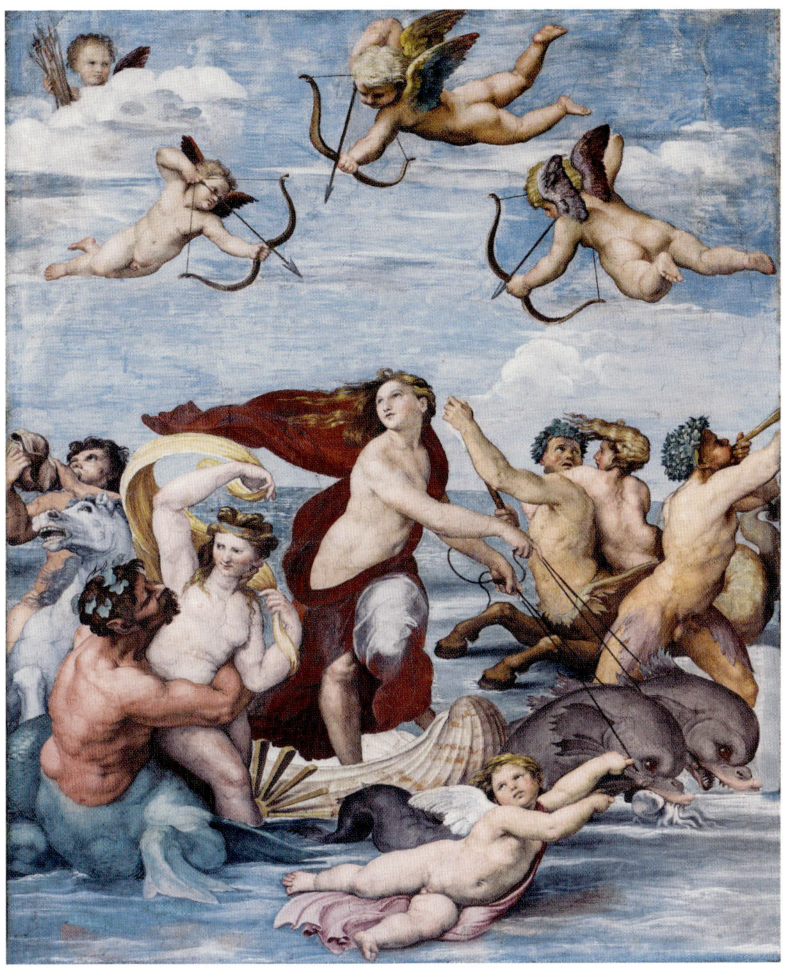

St Catherine, but the extreme complexity of the design, with
seven figures in spiralling poses performing complex actions
disposed without congestion in a small space, implies the
experience of multi-angle figure design in *The School of Athens*.
And it also seems more likely to be a riposte to the newcomer
Sebastiano than the reverse.

The Galatea is an experiment in a mode new to Raphael:
painting as three-dimensional sculpture. Although the figures
are fully coloured and their forms are flesh, not marble, their
solidity and their slightly frozen action suggest a complex
statuary group. This stylisation is made obvious in the sea,
which is conceived not as water but as a membrane against

which the sea centaurs' hooves drum. The fresco is virtuosic
in design, at the same time as evoking an aspect of classical
antiquity unusual in the period. Despite Galatea's unfortunate
end, killed alongside her lover Acis by a rock hurled by the
rejected Polyphemus, the fresco breathes joy and vitality.
It was engraved by Marcantonio Raimondi (*c.* 1480–*c.* 1534)
directly from a copy of the fresco, not from a preparatory
study, a rarity in his work.

The long wall has three further compartments, and the
windowless short wall has two. In the seventeenth century
these were filled by landscape frescoes, but for them Chigi
and Raphael no doubt planned complementary scenes.
Two wide drawings by Penni, combining the amorous and
the aquatic, probably recycle designs made by Raphael for
those compartments (Oxford, Ashmolean; Lille, Musée des
Beaux-Arts). At this time Agostino was attempting to secure
a marriage with one of the major ruling families of Italy,
even though he had a live-in mistress in Francesca Ordeaschi,
but his attempts failed, and it may be that the room reflects,
ironically, upon his aspirations.

IV

It was probably in 1510 that Raphael made his first forays
in engraving, in collaboration with Marcantonio Raimondi.
Marcantonio had trained in Bologna with Francesco Francia,
the same master who had taught Timoteo Viti, and had
engraved some of Francia's compositions. After a period in
Venice, during which he made pirated engravings of Dürer's
woodcuts and cut a couple of plates after Sebastiano and
Titian, he worked briefly in Florence, where he reproduced
some figures from *The Battle of Cascina*. He probably reached
Rome in 1510. According to Vasari, Marcantonio perceived that
compositions by Raphael would be suitable for engraving and
approached him. Raphael gave him a drawing made for some
other purpose, and Marcantonio cut from it the famous print
of *The Suicide of Lucretia*. Vasari's account is plausible: a large
pen drawing by Raphael of a *Gesturing Woman* (New York,
Metropolitan Museum), close in style to those for the *Parnassus*,
fills the bill. And it obviously was adapted, not created, for *The
Lucretia* and was probably made for a frieze of dancing women
or as a pendentive figure in a secular scheme. The pose is
not one immediately associable with Lucretia, and it took a
stroke of brilliance to see how it could serve as such. A knife
was clumsily added to the figure's right hand, and in the print
her head was turned into profile to increase the energy of her
movement – and her modesty.

99

The *Lucretia*'s success alerted Raphael to the potential of engraving. Still according to Vasari, he then designed for Marcantonio a large multi-figure print of *The Massacre of the Innocents*, which immediately became famous and, indeed, remains one of the most appreciated of all Renaissance engravings. The date is likely to be 1511: some of the drawings made for the *Massacre* overlap with ones preparing the Segnatura's *Judgment of Solomon*. In conceiving a group of nude executioners murdering children before their terrified mothers, Raphael saw the subject balletically, not realistically, as an exercise in form and movement that intentionally drains from the print much of the subject's horror: violence to women and children did not fall into Raphael's range. He was creating a vision of nudes in action that would compete with Pollaiuolo's *Battle of Nudes* and Michelangelo's *Cascina*. But there are no borrowings from Michelangelo in *The Massacre of the Innocents*, so Raphael may deliberately have wished to propagate an alternative, graceful mode. The concepts of symmetry, duplication and reversal, and the fluent interactions of figures, are characteristic of the Segnatura, and the simulated relief

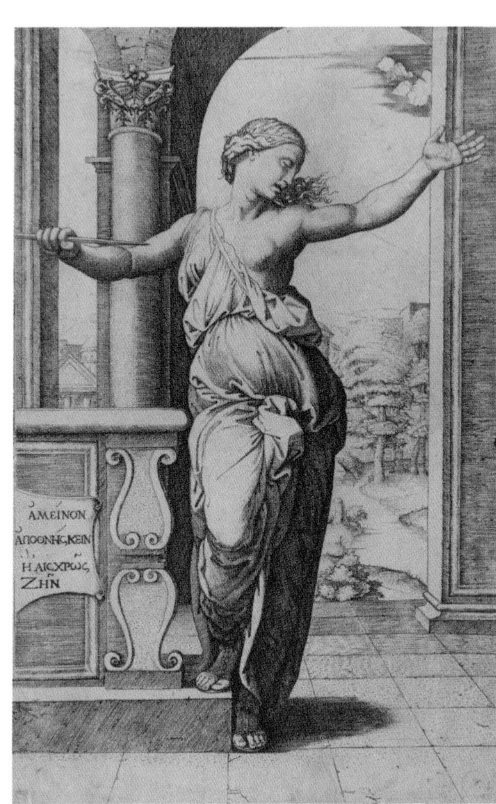

99 Marcantonio Raimondi after Raphael, *The Suicide of Lucretia*, probably 1510

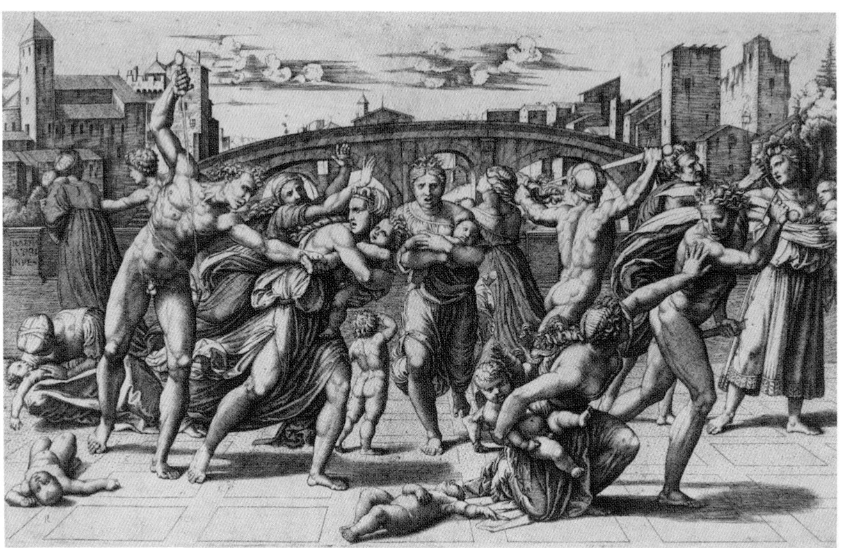

100 Marcantonio Raimondi after Raphael, *The Massacre of the Innocents*, 1511

below the statue of Apollo in *The School of Athens* might be taken as a model for the figure types in the *Massacre*.

It is surprising that Raphael should have taken so much trouble and made so many drawings for a print, and it may be that the *Massacre* was prepared for an aborted painted project and recycled for Marcantonio. But the *modello* itself (Budapest, Museum of Fine Arts) was probably made with the print specifically in mind, for it is uniquely precise, as though Raphael wished to determine all the movements of Marcantonio's burin. However, the next major engraving made by Marcantonio from a Raphael composition, *The Last Supper*, certainly was the by-product of a failed ecclesiastical commission. The *modello* is by Penni (Windsor, Royal Collection), and it is conjectural whether it was made for the painted project or the print; in either case Raphael no doubt wished to delegate the time-consuming task.

Raphael then seems to have realised that such elaborate effort was unnecessary. When drawings made for engravings can be identified, they are always made by Raphael's associates, increasingly by Giulio Romano rather than Penni. Raphael saw that providing drawings intended to anticipate the engraver's line work was counter-productive, since the incisions created by a steel burin differ from those of even the finest pen. Brush and wash drawings, which established the transitions of light

and shade, were sufficiently informative to allow the engraver
to create the desired contrasts and transitions, and red chalk
was better still, because it offered great flexibility, whether
sharpened to obtain thin contours or used broadly to obtain
different densities of shadow.

Most of the engravings cut between 1510 and Raphael's
death by Marcantonio and his associates, Agostino Veneziano
(*c.* 1490–*c.* 1540) from Venice and Marco Dente da Ravenna
(1493–1527), were not made from specifically prepared drawings.
The drawings they engraved were generally made for other
purposes and recycled in the form of prints. But there was an
intermediary category: in a few cases it is clear that a design
made by Raphael for a painted project was copied in a modified
form expressly for engraving – thus a drawing by Giulio after
The Venus, Juno and Ceres pendentive in the Psyche Loggia
(Vienna, Albertina), which extends that composition into a
rectangle, was engraved by Marco Dente. And occasionally,
as with *The Galatea*, a completed painting was copied and then
engraved. But most engravings seemingly after paintings by
Raphael show significant differences from the final paintings
and record preparatory stages rather than the completed
works. And since some of these engravings were printed
before the paintings that they record were completed, they
acted as advertisements of 'works in progress' – which may
have added excitement to their marketing. Raphael was perhaps
the first artist who wished to make the public aware of his
creative processes.

The choice of subjects and compositions that were engraved
follows no discernible logic. None of Raphael's Umbrian
compositions were engraved, and only a couple of the designs
that he produced in Florence. Of these, surprisingly, the
Ashmolean's loose preparatory drawing for *The Entombment*
was engraved, not the larger, more highly finished and more
impressive Louvre *modello*. None of Raphael's Florentine
Madonnas were engraved, and only one, now lost, that he
probably painted soon after his move to Rome. Neither were
Raphael's wall frescoes in the Vatican engraved in his lifetime,
save for the first unexecuted design for *Parnassus*, but *Poetry*
from the Segnatura vault, enlarged to a rectangle, was issued
as an engraving. Innovatively, a few details from frescoes
were printed – notably the simulated statue of Apollo from *The
School of Athens*. The reasoning that underpinned publication
is also hard to understand. For example, the prints cut from
the small mythological scenes in the bathroom of Cardinal
Bibbiena do not maintain a constant size and therefore –
unlike the frescoes they reproduce – do not cohere as a set.

68

Chapter 6
The Stanza di Eliodoro

We have no documentation about the Stanza di Eliodoro, which served as Julius's audience chamber, but the inscription below *The Miracle of Bolsena* refers to the eighth year of Julius's pontificate, that is, before 26 November 1512, while that below *The Release of St Peter* refers to year two of Leo's, so after 19 March 1514. The earlier date must apply to a section of the room, and the later one to the completion of the whole.

There is a significant structural difference between the decoration of the Segnatura and the Eliodoro: the height of the woodwork in the Segnatura required Raphael to take into account the doors that intrude into *The Disputa* and *The School of Athens*. In the Eliodoro, and in *The Incendio*, the lower level of the frescoes coincides with the tops of the doors, which leaves the fields uninterrupted.

The Eliodoro is comprised not of static compositions like the Segnatura, but of dramatic ones, illustrating the direct intervention of God in the affairs and history of the Church at four periods: those of the Old Testament (the Apocrypha, to be precise) and the New, and two later moments. The choice of episodes relates to preoccupations current in Julius's reign, and then Leo's, but they are connected by God's constant and continuing concern with the prosperity of his Church. It is, in contrast to the Segnatura, an eschatological chamber, and avatars of the divinity are present throughout.

In historical order, the earliest scene represented is *The Expulsion of Heliodorus*, an event of *c.* 178 BC during which the sun-worshipping Heliodorus, a minister of the Hellenistic ruler Seleucus, attempted to loot the Temple of Jerusalem (2 Maccabees 3: 21–28). In response to the high priest's prayers, three angels appear, one of them mounted, who chastise Heliodorus and eject him and his followers. Obviously

the subject, for which there was virtually no representative
tradition, was an admonition to any ruler who aimed to abuse
the Church's possessions, but it was probably chosen by Julius
more specifically as a defence of the territories that fell under
the Church's rule, which his pontificate was dedicated to
recovering and retaining. It must also refer to incursions,
for Heliodorus, standing in for French invaders, is a foreigner
bent on plunder, not an example of internal dissent.

The next episode chronologically, in which Raphael employed,
perhaps for the first time, the device of continuous narration,
describes St Peter's miraculous release from imprisonment
in Jerusalem (Acts 12: 3–19). He is freed by an angel, whose
radiance stuns and blinds the guards and eclipses torchlight
and moonlight, and who leads Peter to safety. This episode
was not to be included in Raphael's tapestry cartoons, perhaps

103

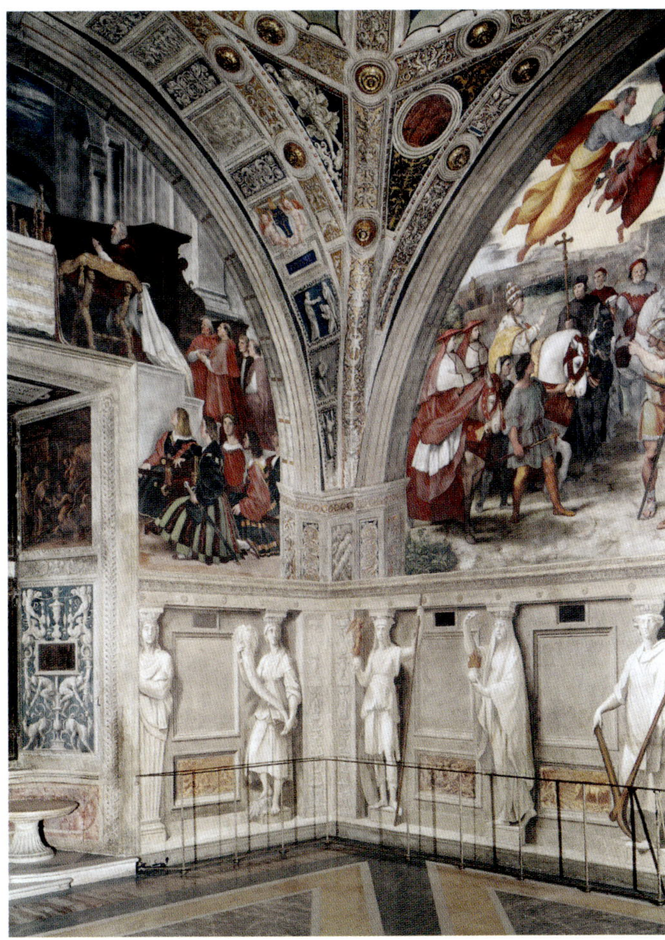

101 The Stanza
di Eliodoro,
1511–14

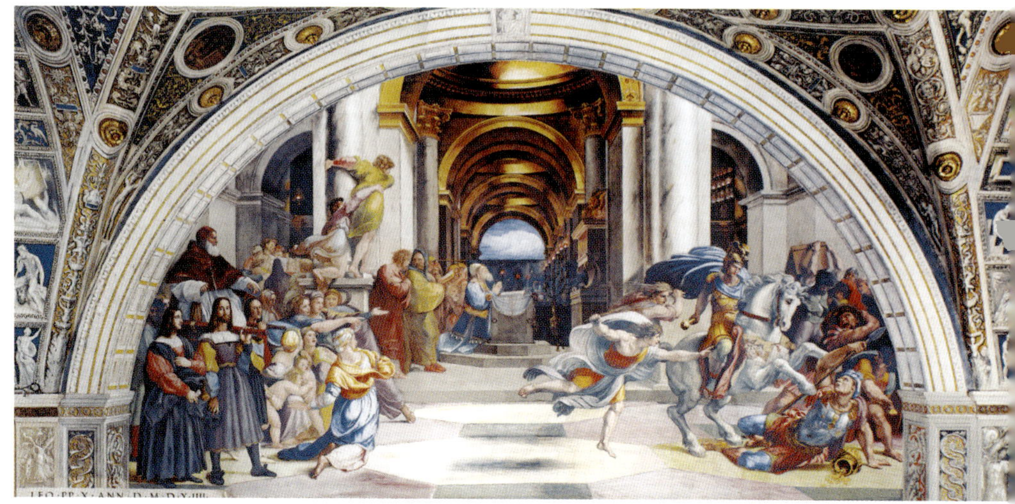

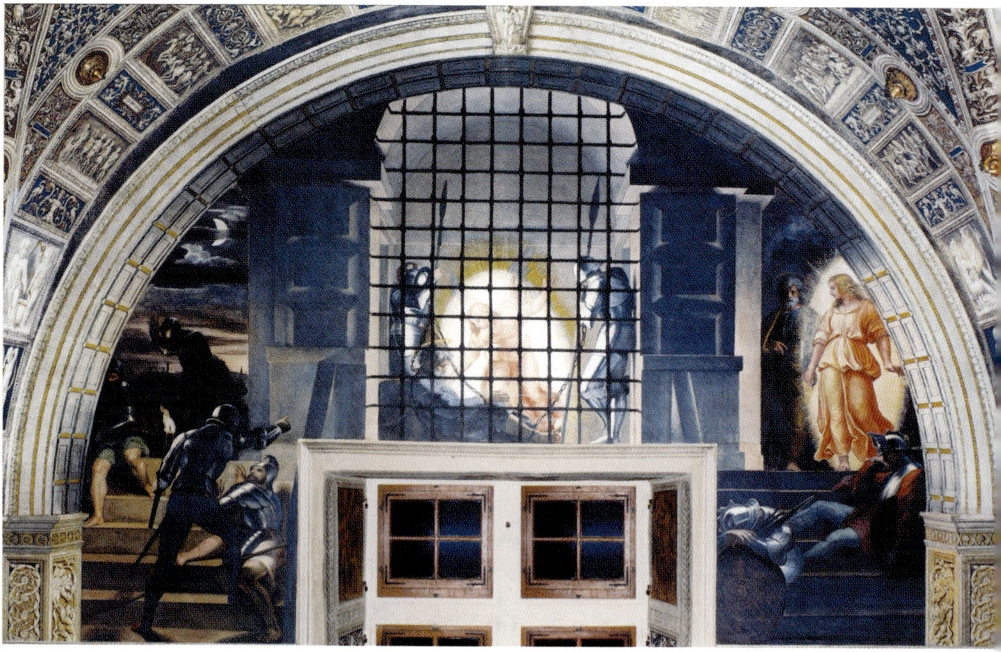

102 TOP *The Expulsion of Heliodorus*, 1511–12
103 ABOVE *The Release of St Peter*, 1512–13

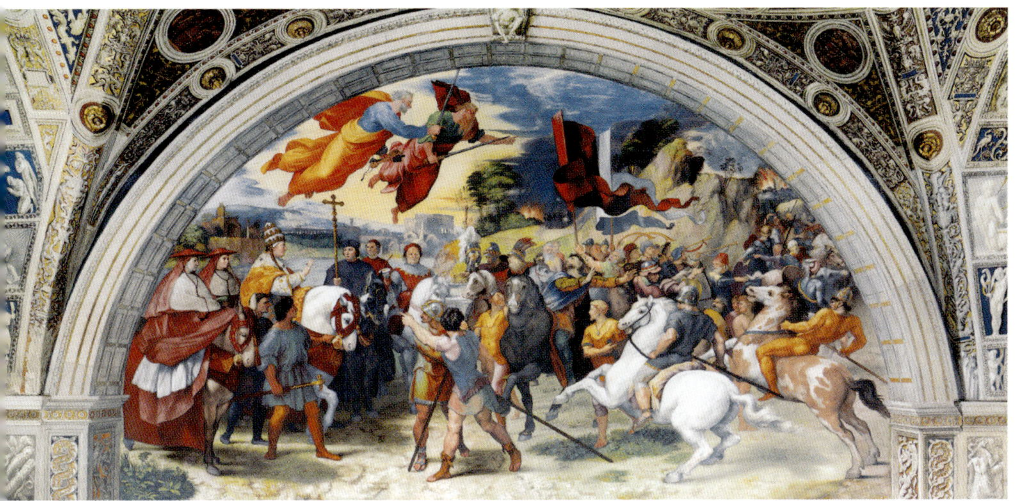

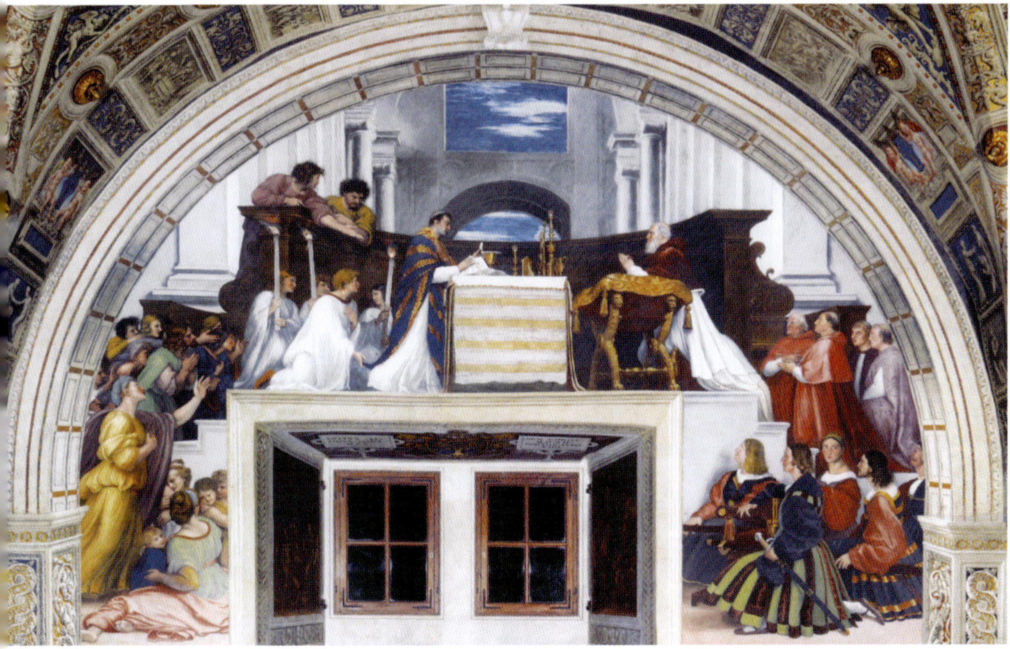

104 TOP Raphael and assistants, *The Repulse of Attila*, 1513–14
105 ABOVE *The Miracle of Bolsena*, 1512

The Stanza di Eliodoro

because it is so memorably treated in the fresco. St Peter, of course, was the first pope and Julius's lineal forebear, and the scene thus registers divine protection of the papacy. But it had a special relevance for Julius: his titular church as cardinal was San Pietro in Vincoli (St Peter in Chains), whose most significant relics were, and are, the chains that traditionally bound Peter. *The Release* is also a pictorial thank-offering for the liberation of the Papal States from French occupation earlier in 1512. According to Vasari, *The Release* and *The Miracle of Bolsena* replaced frescoes by Piero della Francesca. Their subjects are unrecorded but, given the appearance of Piero's *Dream of Constantine*, they might have included dramatic lighting and, if so, provided stimuli for Raphael.

The third episode depicts an event of AD 452, during the pontificate of Leo I, when the unarmed pope rode out from Rome to confront the armies of Attila the Hun, which are halted by the miraculous and threatening manifestation of Sts Peter and Paul. This subject, of course, also has a role as a warning to any invader of Italy or, more specifically, the lands of the Church.

The last episode dates from 1263. A German priest, preparing mass in the church at Bolsena, is suddenly struck with doubt whether the body of Christ is truly present in the Host. But he is answered by the sacramental wafer, which begins to bleed. As well as affirming the doctrine of the real presence, a particular concern of Julius, the priest's nationality may also be significant, as a response to agitation for doctrinal reform coming from Germany, for which Luther was to be the standard-bearer (his theses were nailed to the door of Wittenberg Cathedral only four years later, in 1517).

After the completion of the first three wall frescoes – *The Repulse* followed later – Raphael revised the vault. When he began work in the chamber, the vault, which was finished, was divided into eight fields; they probably contained figures, but narrow triangles would have been unfavourable to narratives. Raphael reduced the fields to four and, as in the Segnatura, extended downwards the corners of the vault. Unlike in the Segnatura, however, there is a clear break between old and new in the pendentives. One of the new pendentive compartments contains a *putto* in simulated stone bearing the Medici ring and feathers – for which there survives a beautiful autograph drawing (Haarlem, Teylers Museum) – indicating that the revision was undertaken after Leo's accession.

All four episodes on the vault are taken from the Old Testament. They comprise *Moses' Vision of God in the Burning*

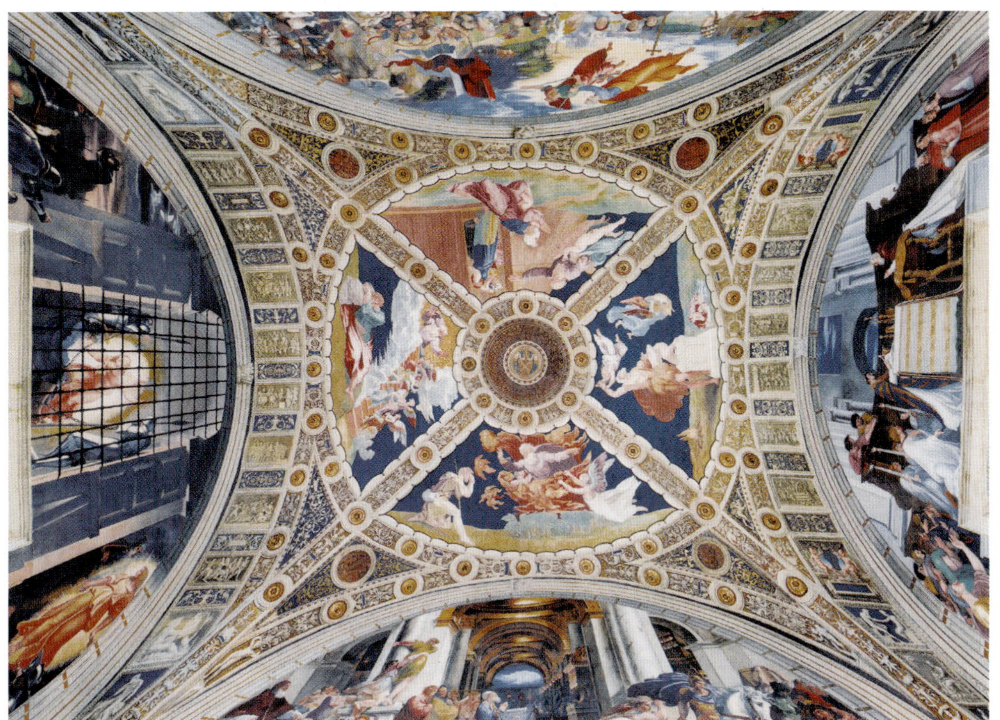

106 The vault, 1514

Bush (for which two preparatory drawings by Raphael – both of which reflect interest in Dürer's work – and a fragment of his cartoon survive), *The Sacrifice of Isaac*, *Jacob's Dream* and *God Appearing to Abraham*, the last prepared in one of Raphael's most dashing pen drawings (Stockholm, Nationalmuseum). The clarification of the vault was achieved seamlessly, and Raphael employed a novel device: the four scenes are treated as though painted in tempera on canvases notionally stretched between the ribs, thus transforming the vault into a temporary structure from which the canvases could, in principle, be peeled back. The conceit may allude to the tent of the Lord, which protected and concealed the Ark of the Covenant during the Israelites' peregrinations in the wilderness. The device offers Raphael a further opportunity to simulate the effects of another art form: the shapes are deliberately flattened and the colours simplified to create the effect of decorations carried out in the dry medium of tempera, with flat gold additions. It avoids any competition with the walls and counteracts the fussy remains of the original vault.

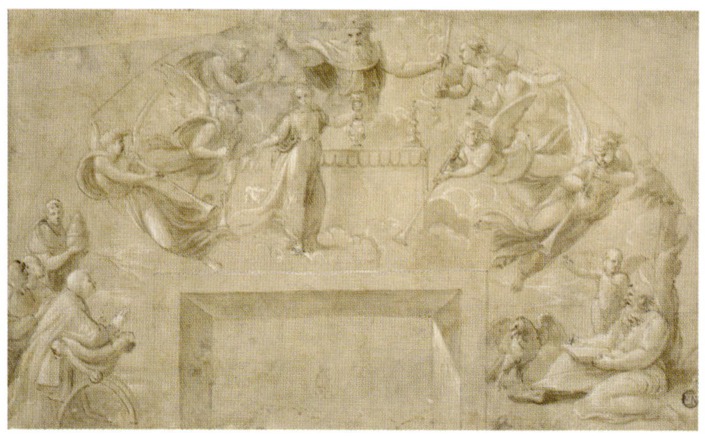

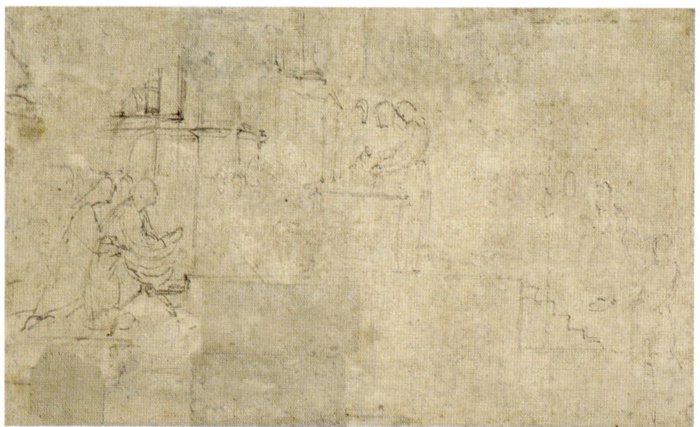

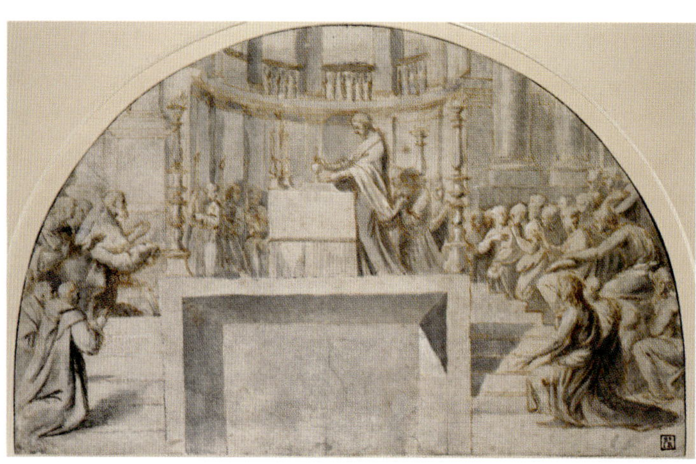

107 TOP Gianfrancesco Penni after Raphael, *The Vision of St John, modello*
for a discarded scheme for the Bolsena wall of the Stanza di Eliodoro
108 MIDDLE Sketch for *The Miracle of Bolsena*
109 BOTTOM Unidentified draughtsman after Gianfrancesco Penni after Raphael,
modello for *The Miracle of Bolsena*, original 1511

Like the other two Stanze, the execution of the Stanza di Eliodoro took around three years, but three of the wall scenes were completed either before Julius died or very shortly thereafter. The order of execution is usually accepted as: *The Expulsion of Heliodorus*, *The Miracle of Bolsena* (both of which contain portraits of Julius), *The Release of St Peter* and *The Repulse of Attila*, which was first planned to include Julius but, as painted, substitutes Leo – appropriately, since the event took place during the reign of his namesake, who was also its protagonist. There seems to be no doubt about the order of *The Release* and *The Repulse*, but that of the other two is contested, with *The Bolsena* sometimes placed before *The Heliodorus*. On balance the traditional view seems more plausible, but the debate remains open.

Compared with the graphic preparation of the Stanza della Segnatura, that of the Eliodoro would have been less extensive. But some parts of *The Expulsion of Heliodorus* are formally complicated, and it is evident that there have been severe losses among Raphael's drawings; furthermore, what survives is not necessarily representative.

Either in the original or in copies, compositional studies of different degrees of finish survive for all four frescoes and, for two of them, studies showing different solutions. Probably from the earliest stages of preparation is a drawing by Penni illustrating the opening of the seals as recounted by St John the Evangelist in the Book of Revelation. It contains powerful and rather Michelangelesque trumpeting angels who swoop around the Father. St John is seated at the right; at the left, Julius, kneeling before a faldstool, witnesses his vision. This drawing, sufficiently finished to be considered a *modello*, has sometimes been considered a first idea for the Segnatura's Justice wall, which has the same shape; and that Julius is beardless implies a date before late June 1511. But the episode can be made to fit the theme of Justice only by the most tortured argument; nor does the composition relate formally to any other part of the Segnatura. Its theme, energy and unified composition, plus the dramatic light effects invited by John's revelation, place it firmly on the Bolsena wall. This location is confirmed by the rapid pen sketch on its verso, which unequivocally prepares *Bolsena* and must represent Raphael's starting point for the scheme as painted. That Julius is beardless may indicate that Raphael was already planning the Stanza di Eliodoro before Julius returned to Rome. In fact, Julius shaved off his beard in April 1512, but throughout Raphael's Vatican imagery he retains it.

The pen drawing links directly with a lost *modello* for *Bolsena*, which survives in several copies. Whether the

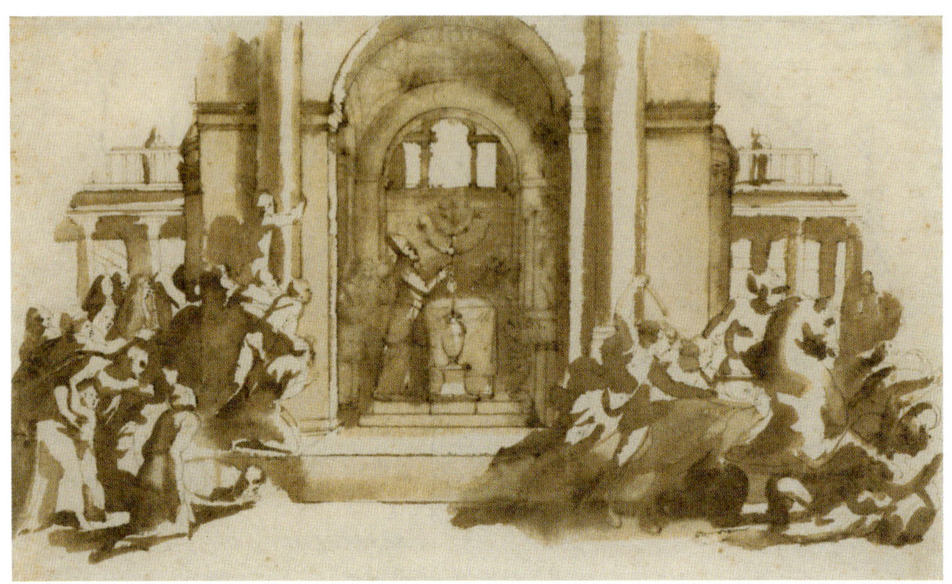

110 Circle of Nicolas Poussin after Raphael, compositional study for *The Expulsion of Heliodoros,* original 1511. Note the serliana in the rear wall

original was by Raphael or Penni is moot, but Penni certainly knew it, for he borrowed a figure from it in another, unrelated composition. Although differing in many ways from the fresco as executed, it marks a clear step towards it. One feature is worth noting. The window in this wall (like that in the Segnatura) is not centred, and Raphael had to choose whether to situate the central axis of his scene on the central axis of the wall, displacing it in relation to the central axis of the window, or to place it on the central axis of the window, displacing it from the central axis of the wall. In the drawing the first option is chosen; in the fresco, the second. Raphael made the dramatic focus coincide with the centre line of the window. He disguised this sleight of hand by extending the upper frame of the window to the right, deceiving the eye into accepting that the window is indeed central in the wall. In tandem he reduced spatial recession by concealing the background building – inspired by Roman thermal architecture – behind a wooden screen and flattening the lower part of the fresco. In short, Raphael sacrificed coherent illusion for pictorial effect.

Graphic survivals are more plentiful for *The Expulsion.* A seventeenth-century copy of a lost brush and wash sketch stages the action in front of the temple rather than within it. The transformation from this preliminary account of the subject to the final one is as least as great as for *The Bolsena,*

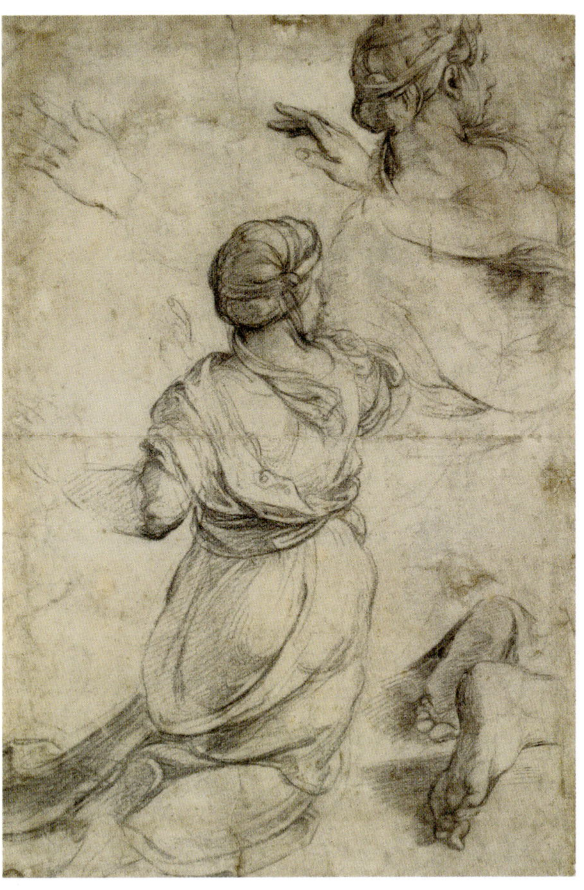

111 Studies of a kneeling woman for The *Expulsion of Heliodoros,* 1511–12

but we have no further compositional studies, only a later copy of a *modello* that comes very close to the fresco (Paris, Louvre) but in which, interestingly, Julius is beardless. There are, however, two magnificent sheets of figure studies that prepare the recoiling women in the foreground: one (Zurich, Kunsthaus), single-sided, shows a woman half stooping, as in the *modello* copy; the other prepares directly the two women as painted, one each on recto and verso. These two sheets, among Raphael's most energetic, are identical in style and imply that Raphael changed the *modello*'s scheme very soon after he conceived it. The verso of the Oxford sheet contains at the lower right a *concetto* for the prophets upper right in the Pace chapel, confirming that the final phase of the Segnatura and the beginnings of the Eliodoro overlapped with that project. Three fragments of Raphael's cartoon for *The Expulsion* survive

(Oxford, Ashmolean, and Paris, Louvre), comprising the heads of the three angels. All show a development of the cartoon style of the Segnatura towards breadth and surface continuity, and serve as a control for later cartoons or auxiliary cartoons.

The graphic survival for *The Release of St Peter* consists of a single broad brush and wash sketch laying out the distribution of light and dark that Raphael envisaged (Florence, Uffizi). It is notable that the grille fronting Peter's cell is absent: the decision to insert it, which dramatically accentuates the angelic radiance, came at a later stage. None of the figural poses is developed, but the drawings for *The Resurrection* project exemplify those that Raphael must have made. The relation between the two projects is thematically close, and one of the guards planned for *The Resurrection* – for which Raphael made a nude study – was re-employed as the guard shielding his eyes from the angelic blaze.

For *The Repulse of Attila*, the situation is different again. We have records of two variant schemes. One drawing, clearly a copy, shows a bearded pope, obviously Julius, carried on a litter confronting Attila. He serves as a visual barrier beyond which Attila's armies cannot pass, and the airborne figures of Peter and Paul are prominent. Had this arrangement been executed, Raphael would probably have employed the chromatic possibilities of the papal robes, the throne and the costumes of the attendants to accentuate the majesty of Pope Leo. But nothing of this carried into the final fresco.

The next stage is illustrated in a drawing by Penni, widely attributed to Raphael. Although often called a *modello*, it must in fact expand on a lost one. It is made on the expensive support of vellum, which would be unique for a *modello* – and inappropriate, for ink and wash cling poorly to vellum, as can be seen from the flaking. Furthermore, while the curve of the lunette is acknowledged, the composition is extended at the corners by groups of angels to turn it into a rectangle. It was probably made as an independent illumination, but its evidential value, as a record of a scheme by Raphael that probably postdated Julius's death is considerable. Attila and his forces are arrested by the heavenly appearance of saints Peter and Paul, who throw them into disorder. The pope is unidentifiable, seen only in the far distance. Although he instigates the divine apparition, like the high priest in the fresco opposite, he is not directly involved with it. The conception is innovative: Raphael boldly, and perhaps for the first time, plays on the expressive and narrational value of confusion (which he would refine in the lower part of *The Transfiguration*) and on a foreground reaction to a distant

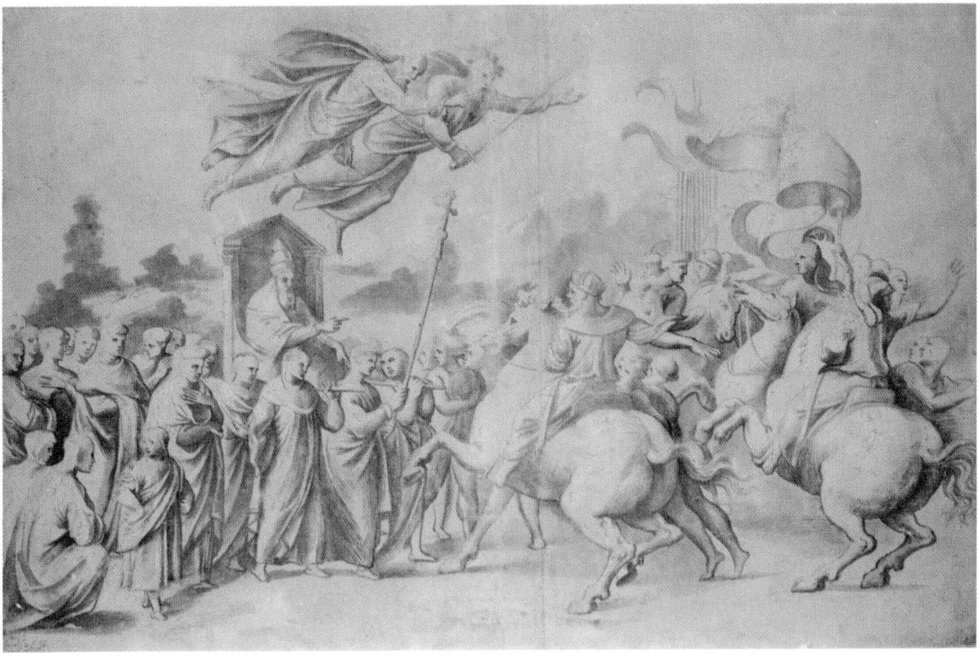

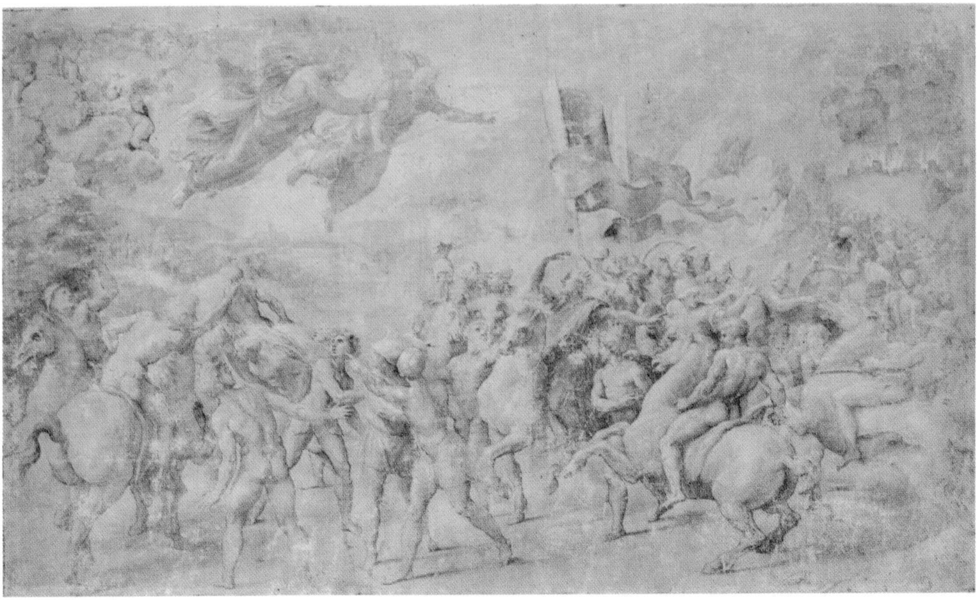

112 TOP Unidentified draughtsman after Gianfrancesco Penni after Raphael, *modello* for *The Repulse of Attila,* original 1513
113 ABOVE Gianfrancesco Penni after Raphael *The Repulse of Attila,* probably 1513

stimulus, seen obliquely. This was the design followed in the right two-thirds of the fresco; if we did not have it, what is on the wall would be difficult to understand.

Two detailed studies survive for the project, both in metalpoint and white bodycolour on grey preparation. One is of the head of a horse (private collection) that appears in the first design but was then dropped; the other (Frankfurt, Städelsches Kunstinstitut) is a rider who appears in the second but was modified in the fresco. The employment of a hard medium – the polar opposite of the black chalk used for *The Expulsion* – signals a change in, or the diversity of, Raphael's approaches. He is now thinking of accentuating the sculptural individuality of his figures, anticipating an aspect of the preparation of the tapestry cartoons.

But *The Repulse of Attila* is an equivocal painting. The attempt to combine the second design with a large papal group comprising Leo and two cardinals, advancing in the left foreground, is clumsy: body language, gesture and gaze are not coordinated, nor are the scales of the figures. The papal group was probably inserted while the fresco was under way, and was painted quickly: much of its execution seems worthy of Raphael, although below his best. But a significant part of the remainder is of poor quality: while the foreground horseman and his mount are solidly modelled and display convincing physical effort, the others are coarsely drawn, weakly and implausibly modelled and sourly coloured. Attila himself, whose awed response to the miraculous warning should be a powerful dramatic focus, is lost amid the crowd, and some figures, such as the man calmly working forward, are entirely inappropriate in pose and mood. Parts of the fresco may be by the same otherwise unidentifiable painter who worked on *The Battle of Ostia* in the next Stanza. The effects of fire and the vegetation in the background are more effective and are often given to Raphael himself, but they are probably by Penni who, Vasari says, was a specialist in landscape and whose independent paintings sometimes display attractive landscape inventions. In sum, *The Repulse* introduces a fault line that runs through the Stanza dell'Incendio and other areas of Raphael's production for the next four years: the problems of his workshop, control of design and glaring internal discrepancies in the finished works.

The *basamento* was certainly executed after the wall frescoes and may have succeeded the adjustment of the vault. It consists of twelve simulated stone statues of allegorical figures, some of whom carry attributes in simulated gilded bronze. In so far as they are identifiable, they embody virtues, but they form no immediately recognisable ensemble, and the reason for their choice remains to be discovered. They seem to exist as a self-contained series and have no obvious relation to the narratives above them.

The Stanza di Eliodoro is one of Raphael's most exalted achievements and a wholly unexpected one. As an ensemble and in all but one of its wall frescoes, it is masterly: extraordinarily inventive in design and execution and varied in its areas of simulation, of great dramatic and spiritual intensity, and of unsurpassed pictorialism, creating effects not seen elsewhere in fresco. To move from the Segnatura to the Eliodoro is to move from one world to another. Were it not certain that both were painted by Raphael, we would assume them to be by different artists: in every respect – lighting, colour, figure design, internal illumination – they are radically different. The only substantive similarity is that the name-piece, *The Expulsion*, is based on a perspectival scheme with a central vanishing point, but the other frescoes effectively eschew measurable space. In this chamber all is subordinated to drama, whether of violent action (in *The Expulsion*), spiritual manifestation (in *The Bolsena*) or the overwhelming force of the numinous (in *The Release*). And much of the drama and excitement is conveyed by colour, tone and handling of paint. In *The Expulsion* the temple is dark, illuminated in part by candles, but unevenly, which creates an aura of mystery. It is richly built, corresponding to Raphael's architectural aspirations, with coloured marble flooring and shallow mosaic-filled domes, which create a play of flickering light. Against these, in stronger relief, the chastising angels emerge powerfully. Raphael uses the perspectival structure to create an in–out movement: as the frightened women at the left appeal to the high priest, so his prayers initiate the action that thrusts Heliodorus and his terrified henchmen out of the picture. Effectively Raphael varies the focus and relief of his figures: some elements are enhanced, others reduced. The relatively even emphasis and lighting of the Segnatura are abandoned: had *The Expulsion* been uniformly lit, the drama would not have succeeded.

Raphael exploited a wide range of possibilities and transfers. Thus in *The Expulsion* he included a cavalier angel – a celestial St George – and flying, but unwinged, warrior angels. The horse is borrowed from Leonardo's *Battle of Anghiari*, and the overturned Heliodorus, in a modified river-god pose, is taken from the same source as it is known in an extended copy. Raphael's return to Leonardo was prescient, for his Florentine mentor was to arrive in Rome later that year and affect him once more. And, of course, Heliodorus and his henchmen in their dramatically contorted poses grow from the guards in *The Resurrection* and, in turn, from Michelangelo.

The frightened women on the left develop some of the ideas tried in *The Massacre of the Innocents*, and the most dramatic figure, her arms thrust out, may respond to Michelangelo's *Libyan Sibyl*. But Raphael makes use not of classical models or Michelangelo's fantasy drapery but of a costume that he might have thought was that of ancient Israel, but that has in its colours and textures much of the feel of contemporary popular or, perhaps, gypsy dress. The variety of colour enlivens the figures: they become individual presences, not simply extras, absorbed into a reacting crowd.

The group of Pope Julius on a litter is, as has recently been established, an insertion into a completed fresco. It has been proposed that the insertion was undertaken early in Leo's reign, but this is unlikely, for Leo was concerned to put himself forward rapidly after his election. A group very like that as painted was planned from the start of the second design phase, as the copy of the lost 'beardless' *modello* indicates. It may be that, as painted, this section proved unsatisfactory in some respect and was replaced.

In the left foreground Raphael placed a portrait of a member of the papal court. He was a minor papal secretary, but the reason for his inclusion is unknown. Another portrait is more surprising: in contrast to his earlier self-presentation as a young scholar, Raphael here shows himself wispily bearded as a litter-bearer, an apparently servile role, incommensurate with the kind of dignity he must by now have acquired. Perhaps it was a private joke, a humorous expression of his loyalty to Julius. Vasari identifies the tall, bearded man beside him as Marcantonio Raimondi (of whom a slightly later bust portrait, by or after Raphael, is known; private collection). Marcantonio had, it would seem, no connection with the pope and cut only one engraving from a composition in this room: *God Appearing to Abraham*. Perhaps he was included for his role in promoting the art of engraving.

The papal group differs in execution from the rest of the fresco, supporting the view that it is a revision. The costume of the standing man is executed with a richness of surface not seen elsewhere, and Julius's velvet robe, with its thick pile and fur lining, is treated with the succulence of advanced oil painting. And this introduces the topic of Raphael's technical prowess, which is more prominent still in *The Bolsena*.

The Bolsena contains different kinds of painting, corresponding roughly to its four quadrants, but overriding local differences is the fact that the whole fresco is conceived in colour, texture and tone. It is a painterly achievement that seems to come from nowhere, and that has long bemused scholars. So much of the emphasis depends on colour and touch rather than graphic definition: the flames of the candles that flicker as awareness of a miracle they only half understand rustles through the acolytes; the repeated outlines of the bleeding Host manifesting themselves on the corporal that stimulate the priest's astonished recoil; the thick pile of Julius's *mozzetta*; and, perhaps, the supreme piece of painting: the construction of the faldstool in perfectly coordinated dabs

116

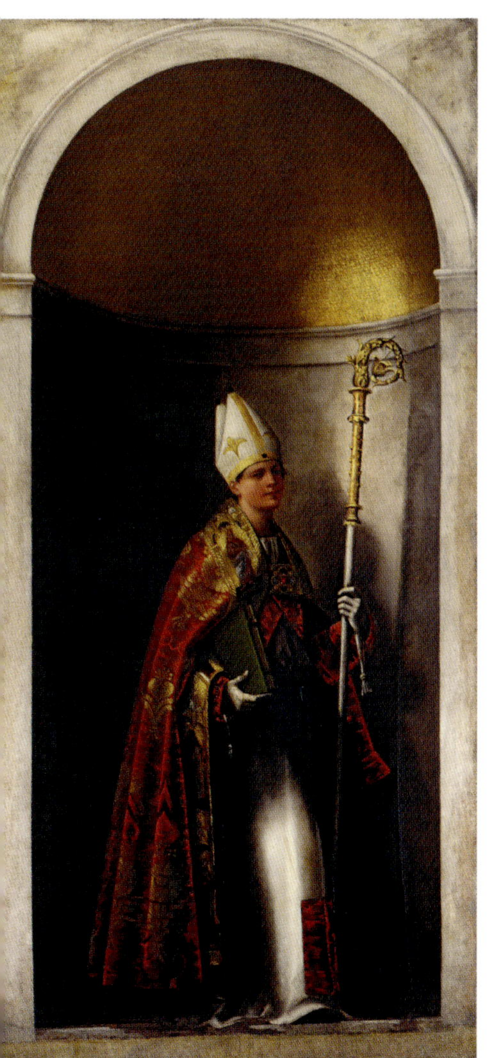

114 LEFT Sebastiano del Piombo,
St Louis of Toulouse, 1511
115 BELOW Julius II from *The Miracle of Bolsena*, 1512

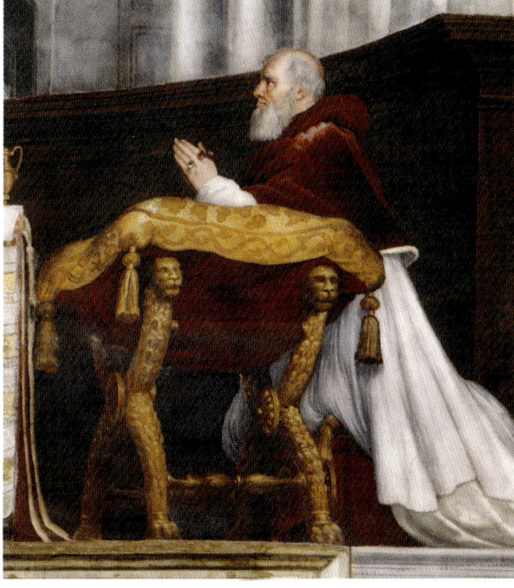

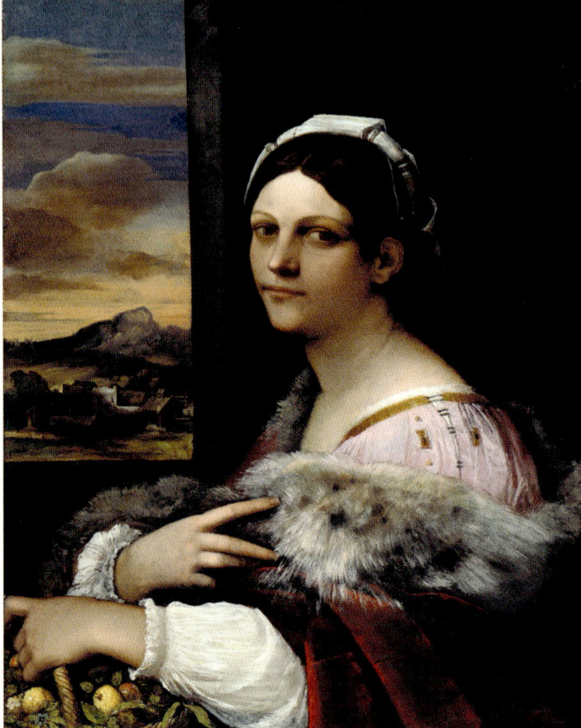

of paint, so that it becomes present in its full materiality.
The form does not possess colour and texture: it is created
by them.

How did Raphael achieve this painterly brilliance, of a
richness seemingly inconceivable in fresco? It surely cannot
be wholly an internal development, for nothing he painted
previously leads to it, whereas there is a reasonable congruence
between other parts of *Bolsena*, such as the shimmering
contemporary group of Cardinal Riario and his entourage
and, for example, the Madrid *Cardinal*. But for the pope and
the attendants there are no antecedents and no clear parallels.
It has been natural for critics to cite influence from Venice.
Thus Lorenzo Lotto would be an obvious candidate for the
introduction of a painterly style, but nothing by him resembles
The Bolsena. It has even been proposed, boldly, that at this
time Raphael travelled to Padua and Venice. But there 'is no
documentary confirmation of any such trip, neither is one
mentioned by contemporaries, or Vasari. Furthermore, Titian
himself had not yet reached this level of richness. His frescoes

164

in the Santo in Padua, of mid-1511, although in parts richly textured, do not resemble *The Bolsena* in handling.

The most likely transmitter of Venetian modes is also the most obvious: Sebastiano, whose arrival in Rome coincided with the beginning of the Stanza di Eliodoro and who became – or had become – Raphael's rival. Nothing in Sebastiano's frescoes in the Sala di Galatea resembles Raphael's richly toned and structural paint application, but when his moveable work is considered a relation can be seen. But this presents a problem. One of the peaks of Sebastiano's 'painterly phase' is his *St Louis* on the interior of the San Bartolomeo al Rialto organ shutters, his final work in Venice. The treatment of St Louis's drapery, with broken strokes of different reds to evoke the depth and texture of velvet pile, comes close to the Julius of *The Bolsena*, and the painting of Louis's staff, in apparent chunks of golden-yellow pigment, is the only conceivable precedent for Julius's faldstool. Something of the same approach – although not quite to the same level – can be seen in Sebastiano's female portrait of *c.* 1511, certainly Roman, the so-called '*Dorothea*', and it is, of course, possible that he painted more pictures in this manner, on canvas or wood, on his arrival in Rome, or brought more with him, than we currently know.

But if it is accepted that Raphael benefited from Sebastiano's moveable work, the problem remains that nothing else that survives by Sebastiano in Rome – including *The Death of Adonis* painted *c.* 1513 for Agostino Chigi – really resembles *The Bolsena*. And it also must contend with the fact that Sebastiano's subsequent work in Rome relinquishes rich, painterly handling for fused, smooth, dense surfaces. In short, in the present state of knowledge, Raphael's achievement in parts of *Bolsena* and *Heliodorus* cannot fully be explained.

Bolsena contains other miracles. The portraits of the Swiss guards are entirely new – and hardly equalled – in their directness, immediacy and conviction. They seem real presences viewed impartially and without idealisation. Their names are unknown, but each one is rendered with convincing physiognomy and personal integrity. In their definition, in their skin colours, in the objectivity with which they are seen, and in the pliable materiality of their costumes these figures were not surpassed, even by Velázquez.

As counterparts, Raphael placed participants in the mass in the narrower space on the left. We see four women – two full-length – three of them with children, and one who stands with a raised arm to acknowledge the miracle. Behind them their menfolk lean forward to see it. These figures occupy the thirteenth-century space of the fresco – even if they are

in modern dress – whereas Julius, Riario and the guards
occupy 'modern' space. But Raphael's sense of drama, form
and colour means that we read the juxtaposed periods as
simultaneous rather than as an historical event and its
modern contemplation.

The women have an amplitude otherwise seen only in the
Pace sibyls, and the child types are new: fuller-fleshed, more
animated and more charmingly naturalistic than before. They
recur in *The Madonna della Sedia* and *The Madonna della Tenda*
(Munich, Alte Pinakothek) as well as in two contemporary
metalpoint drawings (Chatsworth, Devonshire Collection)
of seated women in interiors holding children, which are
poised between depictions of the Virgin and observed reality.

The twelve allegorical figures – underrated and often ignored
– are potent in conception and of a high level of execution,
convincingly and solidly formed. Although they were not
painted by Raphael himself, their quality approaches his work,
and their executant was evidently accomplished (his presence,
however, has not been identified elsewhere in Raphael's
production). The allegorical figures show that Raphael could
produce simulated life-size sculptures even more effectively
than in *The School of Athens*. Raphael was clearly emulating
antique caryatids, but he visualised them in a new way. The
costumes are not, in most cases, those of Roman types, nor
are the poses closely based on the antique. He devised figures
to express certain qualities. All are conceived, as was Raphael's
wont, in the round and could have served as models for real
sculpture (it may be that they were prepared in wax figurines).
It is surprising that Marcantonio or his followers did not cut
engravings from them, for they issued other single-figure
series; but an unidentified engraver, probably active in the
1530s, did issue a set comprising six of them. Only two drawings
survive related to these figures. One, in metalpoint (Oxford,
Ashmolean), was not used and was recycled as a simulated
statue in *The Conversion of the Proconsul* (see p. 169); the other,
in red chalk (Paris, Louvre), is usually taken to be a preparatory
study for the figure that represents *Commerce*, but its flaccid
facture and poorly modelled draperies suggest that it is a
studio copy of such a drawing.

Chapter 7
The Stanza dell'Incendio

In his letter to his maternal uncle Simone Ciarla of 1 July 1514, Raphael announced that he was soon to begin another room in the Vatican, for which he was to be paid 1,200 gold ducats. This came to be called the Stanza dell'Incendio, after the most important of its four narrative frescoes. According to the inscription it was completed in 1517, in the fourth year of Leo's pontificate, thus before 19 March, but it seems that additional, probably minor, work continued until June. It apparently served as the pope's private dining room, and the choice of scenes to be represented hinges on his name. All four record events in the pontificates of his predecessors, two each from the reigns of Leo III and Leo IV. Leo's features serve for those of his predecessors, and the historical choices reflect events or preoccupations of his own pontificate.

The fenestration of the Stanza dell'Incendio is irregular. There is a window in the north wall but none in the south. The second window, which is large and reaches down nearly to the floor, is at the left side of the west wall, overlooking a courtyard. Of course, such irregularity was not an insurmountable barrier to symmetry of form, especially to a composer of Raphael's ingenuity, but it may have encouraged him, following *The Repulse of Attila*, further to experiment with instability.

The internal chronology of the room is still under discussion. Until recently it was assumed that the first fresco to be executed, in 1514–15, was *The Battle of Ostia*. This illustrates the defeat of a Saracen invasion of AD 849 by Leo IV and may have been inspired by a recent skirmish, of type frequent in the early sixteenth century, with Moorish raiding parties. The dating

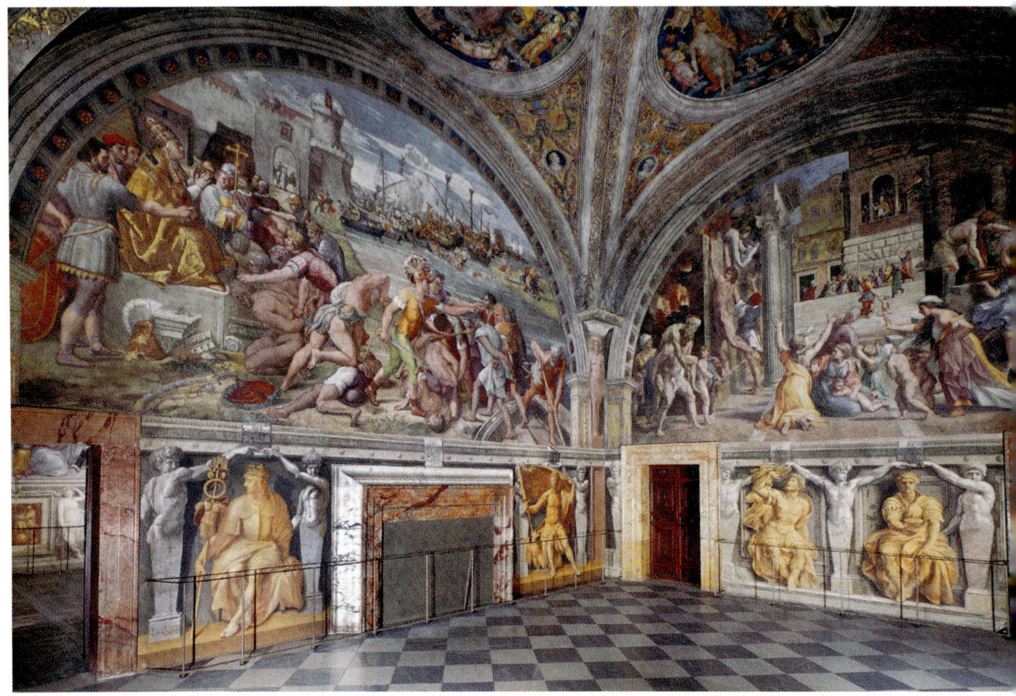

117 Stanza dell'Incendio, 1514–17, general view including the *basamento* by Giulio Romano

134

had been supported by the '1515' inscribed by Dürer on a drawing of two standing nudes, studied from the same model, sent to him by Raphael. That the drawing was a starting point for the two armoured men on the left of *The Ostia* is unquestionable; but that it was *made* for them is much less so, for the painted figures are clumsy transcriptions that hardly suggest the careful elaboration of forms in the drawing. The drawing was more likely made in preparation for Sts Paul and Barnabas at the left of *The Conversion of the Proconsul*, and the two figures simply borrowed by the painter of *The Ostia*. It has recently been argued that *The Ostia* is, in fact, of 1517: if so, it would be either the last or the penultimate fresco in the Stanza.

119

The Coronation of Charlemagne as Holy Roman Emperor by Pope Leo III illustrates the ceremony that took place in St Peter's in AD 800, but it is deliberately modernised to refer to the alliance concluded by Leo with the young French king, Francis I – whose features are identifiable – in Bologna in October 1515, an event Raphael may have witnessed. Several contemporaries can be identified: interestingly, according to Vasari, Ottaviano de' Medici, one of his first patrons, is the child before the throne. *The Coronation* can hardly have been begun before the first months of 1516.

The north wall, with *The Oath of Leo III*, depicts a second event of 800, when the pope swore an oath before Charlemagne; but it also refers to a rule promulgated in December 1516 declaring that ecclesiastics could be judged only according to canon law. Presumably *The Oath* was devised after this date. Of course, it is possible that *The Coronation* and *The Oath*, and even *The Ostia*, were adaptations or replacements of different scenes initially planned by Raphael for these walls and discarded as events took over, but there is no evidence to support this hypothesis.

The fresco on the south wall, which gives the chamber its name, depicts a major fire that occurred in Rome in AD 847 and was miraculously quenched by Leo IV. The subject has no direct counterpart in Leo X's reign, but it is probably to be understood emblematically, as the pope extinguishing the flames of war or civil conflagration, one of the express aims

of Leo's election promises. *The Incendio* (or *The Fire in the Borgo*) is by universal consent by far the best fresco in the room and is generally considered to have been the first to be executed, in 1514–15. But the figure style of the foreground actors is more developed physically and rhetorically than those of any of the other frescoes and corresponds to a stage at which Raphael seems to have arrived in 1517 rather than 1514. The same is true of the preparatory drawings.

The *basamento* now consists of six seated figures, in simulated gilded bronze, of the Christian monarchs who supported the Church, from Constantine to Ferdinand the Catholic. A seventh, later destroyed, probably occupied the space furthest left below *The Incendio*. They are accompanied by herms, in simulated stone. Vasari tells us that these figures were the first (significant) paintings made by Giulio Pippi (called Giulio Romano; 1492/5–1546) for Raphael, and it is likely that he executed the entire *basamento* during the first half of 1517. Giulio's birth date is famously uncertain: when he died, his age was recorded as 47, which places his birth in 1499 – which would make him more precocious than Raphael himself. Vasari – although often unreliable in such matters – gives it more plausibly as 1492. In any case it has recently been noted that Giulio seems to have attained legal majority (25 years of age) by 1520.

It is not known when Giulio joined Raphael's workshop but it was probably in 1515. He would have trained previously with another master, and the most likely candidate is Baldassare Peruzzi, who had many stylistic traits in common with those

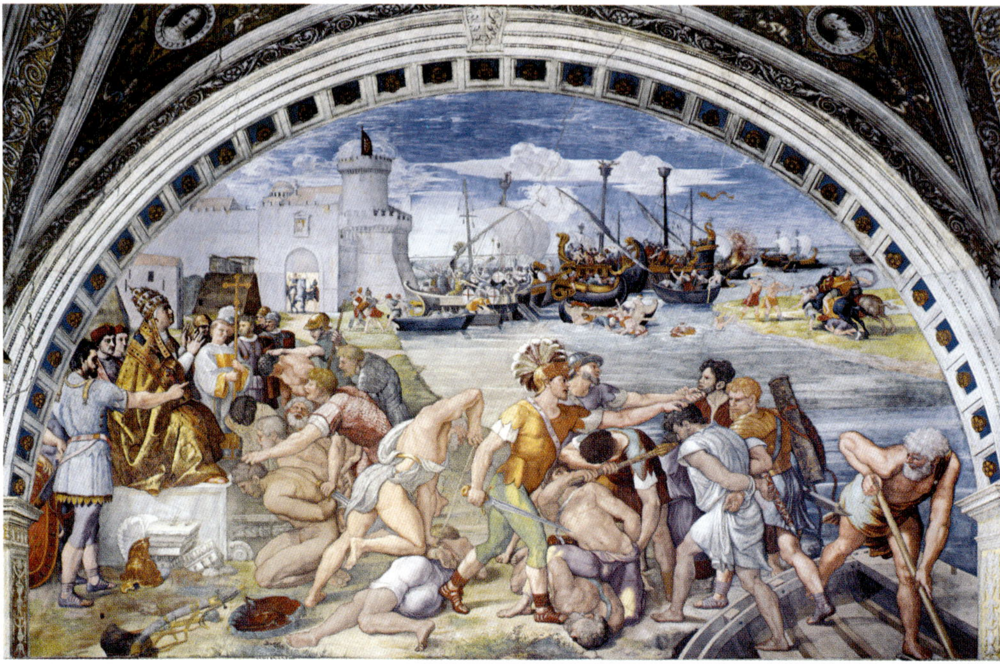

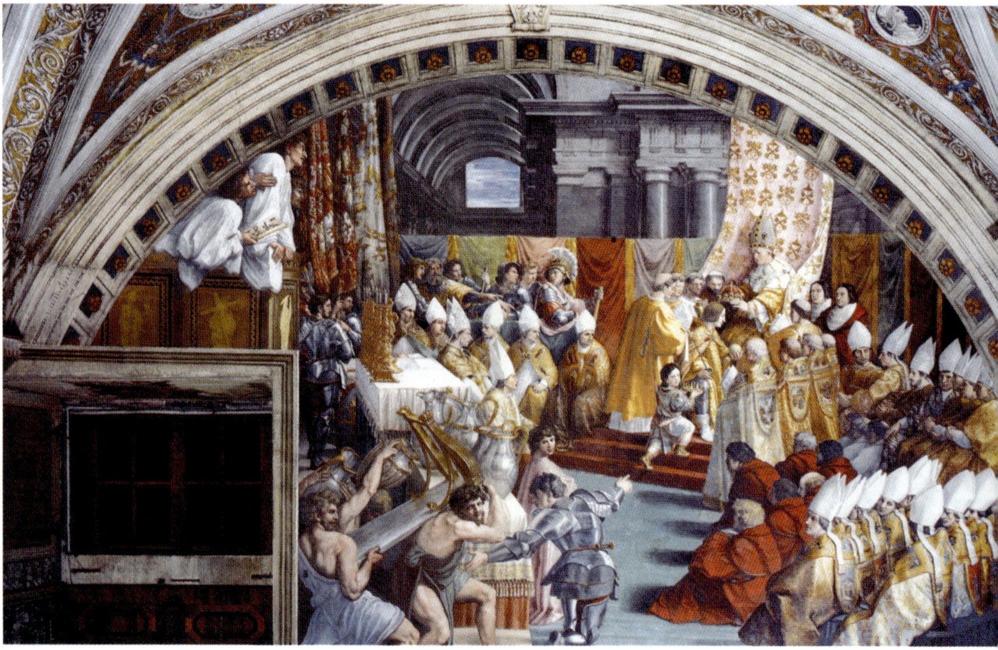

118 TOP Associate of Raphael, *The Battle of Ostia*, 1515
119 ABOVE Giulio Romano, Gianfrancesco Penni and others, *The Coronation of Charlemagne*, 1516

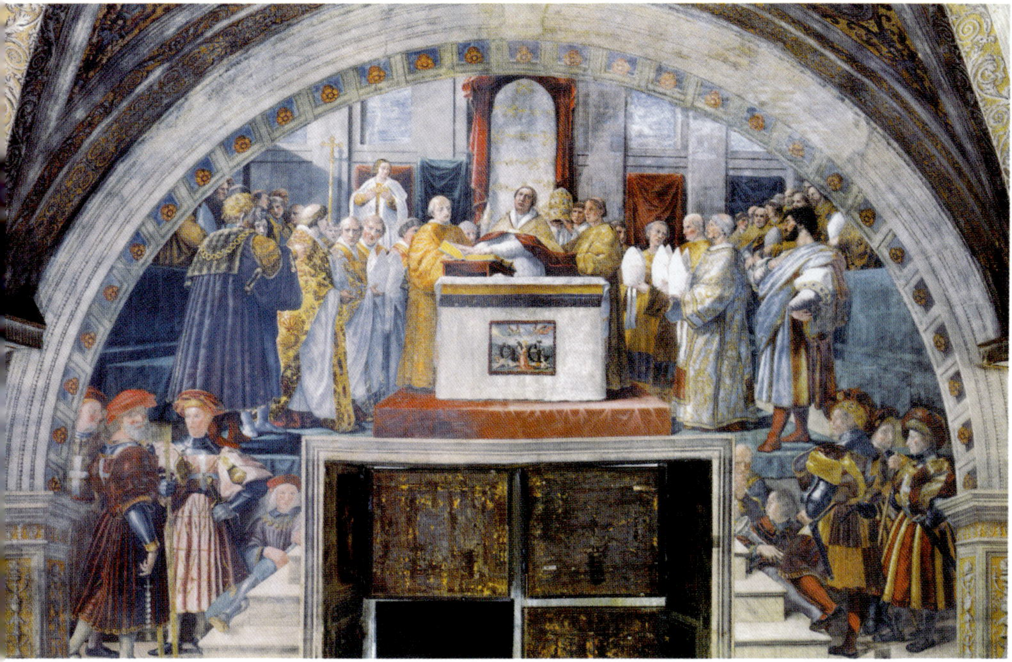

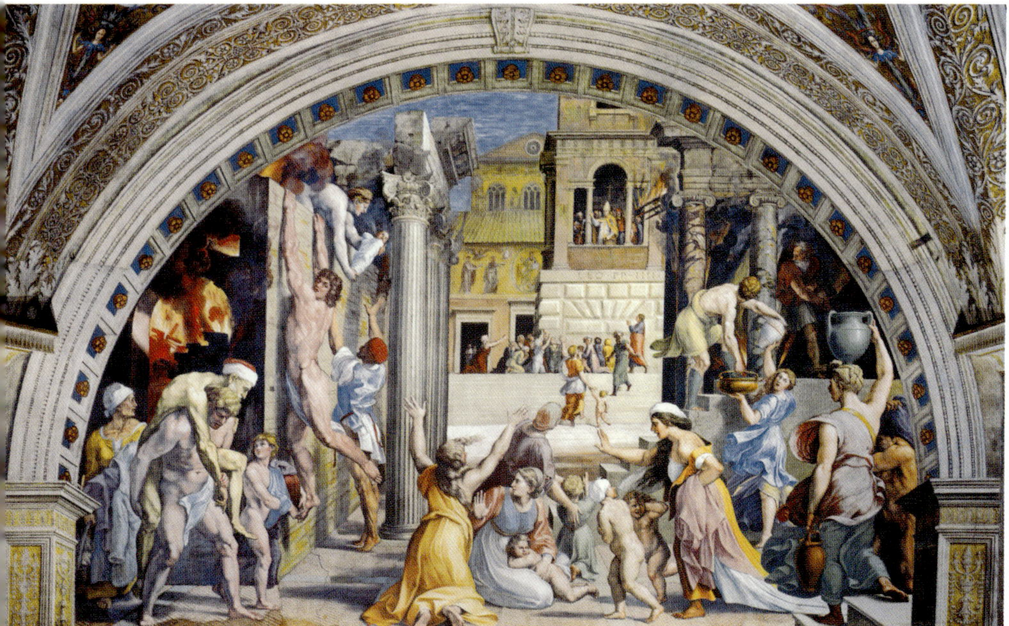

120 TOP Gianfrancesco Penni, *The Oath of Leo III*, 1516–17
121 ABOVE Raphael and Giulio Romano, *The Fire in the Borgo*, 1517

of the Raphael workshop. Giulio certainly played a subsidiary role in *The Coronation* and a larger one in *The Incendio*, but the *basamento* is effectively an independent work. The only drawing to survive for a king, a nude study for *Lothaire*, is by Giulio, and of the two drawings for the herms that flank the monarchs one is by Giulio while the other, much livelier and physically alert, is by Raphael (both Haarlem, Teylers Museum), which implies that he oversaw what Giulio was doing. All three are in red chalk.

The Stanza dell'Incendio is the most anomalous project in Raphael's oeuvre. Even the most positive critics have acknowledged the inferiority of its frescoes to those of the first two rooms and, one might add, to the schemes that succeeded it. It was criticised as early as 1517–18 by Michelangelo's friend and correspondent Leonardo Sellaio – admittedly, hardly an impartial judge; and Vasari, who made every effort to praise Raphael's work, was forced to bite his authorial lip. The room obviously caused Raphael problems, and it may be that they

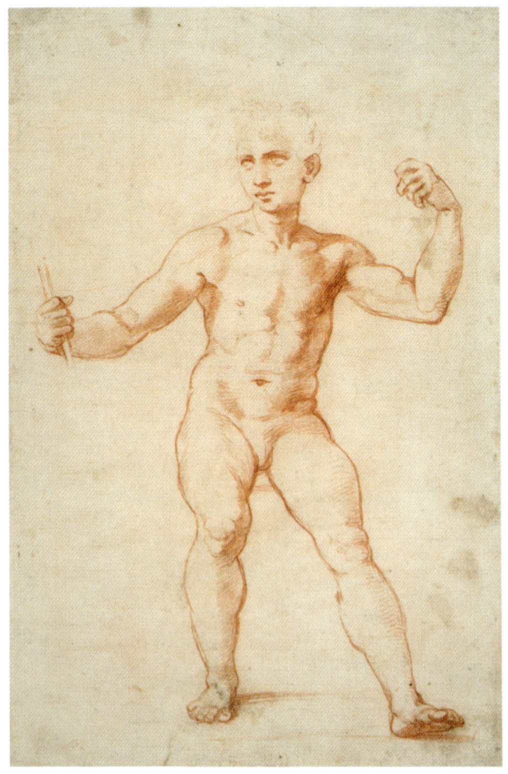

122 Giulio Romano, nude study for *King Lothaire*, 1516–17. As painted the figure is armoured

were of a personal kind (fatigue, perhaps a nervous breakdown produced by over-work?) rather than artistic ones. But any such explanation would have to address the fact that the cartoons for the Sistine tapestries were painted by Raphael in 1515–16, concurrent with work on the Stanza. Of course, the pressures of this, the more magnificent and more prestigious project, not to mention Raphael's duties as architect of St Peter's, might explain weaknesses in the room's execution – Raphael, pressed for time, over-delegating work – but its faults are not only of execution: they are faults of conception, of local design and of focus.

The vault is the single one in the Stanze to retain its original form. It was executed *c.* 1508–09 by Perugino, together with assistants probably including Giovanni Battista Caporali (1476–1560), who later became an expert on Vitruvius and who recorded dining with Perugino, Pinturicchio and Bramante *c.* 1509. Perugino probably arrived in Rome at about the same time as Raphael and left shortly thereafter, never to return. The four roundels show Christ in different manifestations and presumably were intended to relate to whatever subjects were then planned for the wall frescoes whose framing arches were painted at this time. Vasari says that Raphael did not touch the vault out of respect for his master, but that he left the unsightly corbels in place and did not extend the vault in the corners, which could have been done without affecting Perugino's scheme, suggests that he wished to minimise work.

The problems in the Stanza dell'Incendio continue those seen in *The Repulse of Attila*: discrepancies of scale, coarseness of characterisation, clumsiness of gesture, weakness of pose and modelling, and another, more fundamental issue: a lack of coordination colouristically and compositionally among the frescoes, save that in both axes an open-air scene faces an enclosed one. Whereas in the *Eliodoro* three of the four frescoes correspond well in colour, composition and figural complement, in *The Incendio* all four differ radically from one another, and the room possesses neither spatial nor compositional coherence.

Since *The Coronation* and *The Oath* must post-date October 1515 and December 1516 respectively, it makes sense to start with *The Battle of Ostia*. As a whole the composition is confused: there are glaring disparities of scale among the figures, and weaknesses of foreshortening, figure construction and placing. There is an evenness of executive emphasis that does not aid the viewer in understanding the action, and the emotional expressions are unfocused. But the basic idea of prisoners being brought before an enthroned potentate and

118

the contrasted attitudes of vanquished and victors had
potential, and *Ostia* became a model for the fresco of *The
Martyrdom of the 10,000*, projected by Raphael's pupil and
follower Perino del Vaga (1501–47) for the Compagnia de' Martiri
in Camaldoli in 1522 but never executed. And the awkwardness
of the composition was seen in a positive light by some Central
Italian artists of the 1530s and 1540s, who experimented with
disruptive and disjunctive arrangements: areas of Francesco
Salviati's work are of this kind. But in *The Ostia* it was arrived
at unintentionally.

Within the scheme, there are some exceptional – if clumsily
realised – inventions for refreshing a relief composition by
punctuating it with display figures, a familiar expedient
for designers of battle scenes. Among the grandest is the
nearly nude man binding a sprawling prisoner. His heroic
and complex pose is obviously inspired by *The Laocoön*,
but it does not follow any known model. The extended right
leg, the powerful shoulders and the energetic arrangement
make the figure a demonstration piece, but it is vitiated by the
wholly inadequate foreshortening, especially of the prisoner.
It is difficult not to believe that this group rests on a sketch
by Raphael, but it can hardly follow a developed study.

Another figure, potentially of great expressiveness, is the
ferryman on the right. He has great power and energy, but
his figure is inadequately realised, with implausible jointing
of his limbs and unconvincingly realised body volumes.
A figure that should combine suppleness and powerful
musculature, like one of the guards in *The Resurrection*,
seems without substance. But the conception – not always
correctly interpreted – is an interesting example of visual
wit. The boatman secures his barge against the bank so that
the prisoners can be dragged onto land and humbled; but in
order to do so he pushes his pole not on the sea bed, like a
punt pole, but against the inside of the *basamento* – a conceit
that acknowledges the illusory nature of the setting and that
is in line with Raphael's playful treatment of different levels of
reality. This figure too probably derives from a Raphael sketch.

Who might have painted *The Ostia*? Historically it
has generally been given to Giulio, and certain features –
such as the antique fragments grouped around Leo's throne
– are ones found in his independent work. But the figure style,
technique and colouring are quite unlike his, as can be seen
by comparison with the *basamento*. *The Ostia* is evidently not
by Penni, although a copy of what may be a lost *modello* by
him (London, British Museum) might suggest that he helped
assemble the composition. So it was presumably delegated

by Raphael to some painter whom he mistakenly trusted,
and for whom he did not make a full design, still less a cartoon.
This painter, whoever he was, may already have worked on *The
Repulse of Attila*, but he does not seem to reappear in any of
Raphael's later schemes.

119 *The Coronation* too presents problems, but of a different
kind. It is loosely coordinated with *The Ostia* by mirroring,
thus the two images of the pope sit opposite one another and
the boatman in *The Ostia* finds a counterpart in the foremost
man lifting the table up into the picture field at the left side
of *The Coronation* – an idea that accommodates the intrusive
window and was perhaps inspired by Ghirlandaio's Sassetti
Chapel fresco of *The Confirmation of the Franciscan Rule*.
But otherwise the two schemes are very different. *The Ostia*
is a relief composition, whereas *The Coronation* is disposed
diagonally in depth, but the spaces that comprise the great
hall are uncoordinated, and the perspective of the tunnel-
vaulted passage, articulated and supported by transverse bands,
in the rear is skewed. This problem is already evident in Penni's
modello (Venice, Querini Stampalia), in which the vault clashes
with the obliquely viewed hall in which the coronation takes
place; and while this is partly disguised in execution by a
screen running across the left third of the fresco, the clash
remains. It is amplified by the placement of the altar in the left
middle ground, whose vanishing point is not coordinated with
any other in the fresco. The disturbances in *The Coronation*
are multiple, and the spatial confusion they create is further
increased by the disposition of the figures, by their abrupt
changes of scale, by the different modes of painting evident
within the fresco, and by the poverty of much of the figure
construction: the awkwardness and stiffness of the armoured
man who gestures inwards to show the porters where to place
the table, for instance, and the insubstantiality of those porters.

Once more, some of what is found in *The Coronation* was
fertile for later artists. The idea of situating the main theme
in the background – with which Raphael experimented
elsewhere – was used by, for example, Salviati and Taddeo
Zuccaro, who often placed trivial episodes in the foreground,
in part to establish a circumstantial realism for ceremonies or
significant events. But in the other instances in which Raphael
experimented with this kind of arrangement, the events in the
foreground are relevant to the narrative.

It would seem that Raphael wished to combine a comparatively
'realistic' account of a ceremonial occasion, as viewed by a
spectator placed to one side, with a novel mode of narration,
but the results – which differ little from the *modello* in

structure – are hard to explain. That Raphael had some involvement is demonstrated by two sheets of drawings. There is a bold pen study for the three choir boys in the cantoria high on the left (Vienna, Albertina), which extends the window upwards; and a double-sided sheet in red chalk contains studies for the row of bishops at the lower right, drawn from models in the studio – one of whom is compressed out of existence – while on the verso is a sketch for the deacon beside three figures flanking the pope, probably taken from life during some ceremony. In addition to these drawings there is a developed red chalk study from a model for the foremost porter, but its weaknesses of structure and blandness of surface modelling forbid an attribution to Raphael. Additionally, an auxiliary cartoon for the head of a bishop (Paris, Louvre) has recently been given to Raphael himself, but it is flabby in structure and over-emotive in characterisation, and is probably by Penni.

It is uncertain how many hands were involved in the fresco. Giulio likely executed the metallic forms on the altar, and in the surrounding figures the armour of the standing man is appropriate to his still-life skills. The softer forms on the right are probably by Penni, but other painters must also have been present. In sum, *The Coronation* is a deeply confusing fresco whose internal contradictions resist satisfactory explanation. But it does contain, in embryo, significant visual inventions, and the architecture, with Doric half-columns supporting a powerful cornice, is grand and solid.

If *The Coronation* is clumsily and unresolvedly forward-looking, *The Oath of Leo* is dully retrospective. It is simple and symmetrical in arrangement, seen frontally, with Pope Leo placed centrally behind the altar and gesturing ineffectually, and groups of stiffly posed figures, roughly mirroring one another, at either side. Some bystanders are recognisable, among them Leo's nephew Lorenzo, duke of Urbino, at the right. The arrangement loosely recalls that of the preliminary *modello* for *Bolsena*. The execution throughout is not overtly disparate but it is uninspired, with little made of the variety of costumes. There is no inventive characterisation and little figural coordination. It is generally accepted that the fresco is entirely by Penni, and this is probably correct. The two drawings that survive for it, a layout for the upper left quadrant (Florence, Horne Museum) and a facial study for the bishop to the viewer's left of the pope (Haarlem, Teyler Museum), are his. So symmetrical a composition with so little opportunity for figural movement or expression would not have required extensive graphic preparation. The overall tone is dark, as

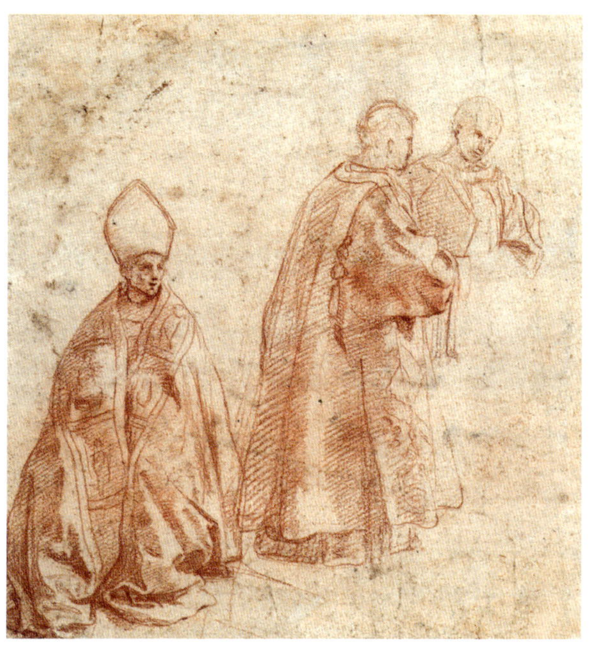

revealed by cleaning, and corresponds reasonably to what
might be expected of Penni in 1516–17, about the time he
began work on the panel that became the lower half of the
Monteluce *Coronation*. But there, of course, he was following
closely Raphael's design (Berlin, Kupferstichkabinett) and, in
any case, Penni's abilities were not particularly fitted for the
decisiveness that fresco painting demands: he worked better
with the slower and more relaxed methods of oil painting.

The Stanza's name-piece differs vastly from, and is infinitely
more successful than, the other frescoes: some aspects of it
count among Raphael's highest achievements. And we have
external evidence that what we see on the wall was fully
designed by him. In November 1517 he sent the cartoon for
a story of Leo IV to Alfonso d'Este, part compensation for his
delays with Alfonso's commission of *The Triumph of Bacchus*.
This cartoon must have been for *The Fire*, both because it
is inconceivable that *The Ostia* – the other story of Leo IV –
was painted from a cartoon by Raphael, and because *The
Fire* left traces in Ferrarese and Venetian art. This was the
first of three cartoons sent by Raphael to Alfonso, and they
seem consistently to have been for his most recent work.

Broadly speaking, the composition is centralised, but the
orthogonals of pavement and cornices converge on a point to

the viewer's left of Leo IV and not, as might have been expected,
on the pope himself. Why he was offset is an open question.
The scene is staged in the Borgo, the area before St Peter's,
and the façade of the Constantinian basilica is seen at the
left: an imaginative reconstruction of its appearance in the
ninth century. The building at the right, to which the Serlian
window was added in execution, has been shown by technical
examination to have been begun as a modern palace similar
in type to Bramante's Palazzo Caprini, with workshops below
a powerful *piano nobile*; but it was altered during painting to
assume a greater severity, as though it were part of the Vatican.

The Fire is conceived theatrically rather than historically
or realistically. It was suggested long ago that the division

124 BELOW LEFT Gianfrancesco Penni (?), study for a man carrying a table
in *The Coronation of Charlemagne*, 1516
125 BELOW RIGHT Study for the 'Aeneas' group in *The Fire in the Borgo*, 1517

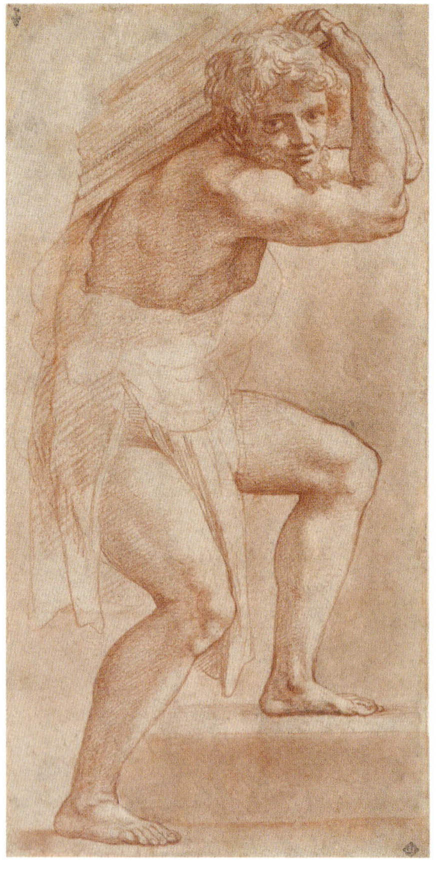

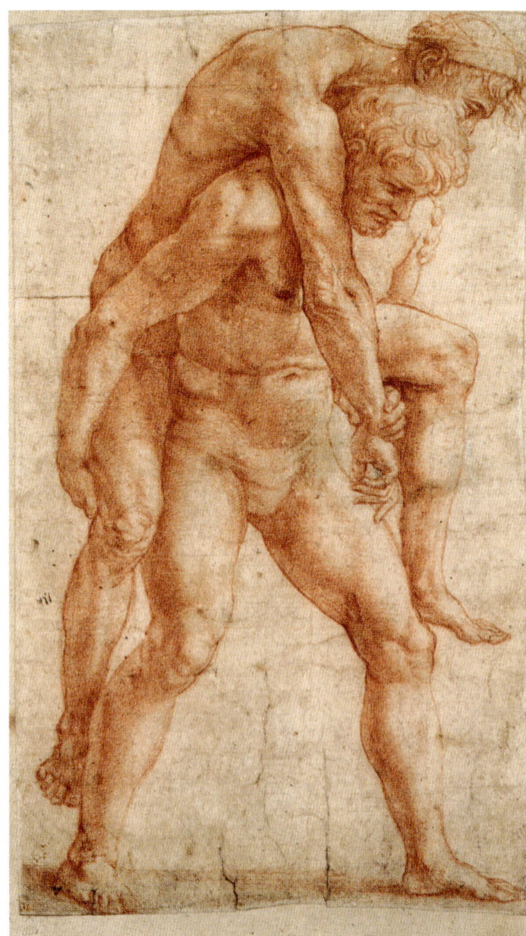

of the narrative into three parts – the initial flight from the
fire, the active response to it, and its resolution by Leo IV – is
inspired by the principle of beginning, middle and conclusion
inherent in Aristotelian drama. While the temporal division is
porous, support for the view that the conceptions' antecedents
derive from the theatre is provided by the foreground buildings,
set-like rather than real, and by the nude figure whose
distance from the pavement does not justify his terrified
expression. Raphael populated his fresco with emblematic
figures and groups, not 'documentary' ones. The narrative
is frozen into a representative tableau.

To convey this effect – and affect – Raphael developed some
of his most memorable figures. The young man carrying his
father, followed by his mother, embodies filial piety, based
on the Virgilian narrative of Aeneas saving his father, Anchises,
from the flames of Troy. The young man clinging to the cornice
represents fear – even if exaggeratedly. The woman kneeling
on the ground with a child in her lap, calling to her husband,
embodies protectiveness and family unity, while the woman
emerging half-dressed, with a crying child holding his ear –
has he just been slapped? – embodies maternal care. Finally,
the magnificent figure of the young woman carrying a water
jar, helping to fight the fire, is an extraordinary invention that
fuses fortitude, resilience and beauty as her drapery is moulded
onto her body by the suction of a firestorm. The draught is felt
too by the woman who hands bowls of water to the firefighters,
but the figures in the centre are relatively unaffected, implying
either a time-lapse or unconcern with atmospheric consistency.

There is widespread agreement that Raphael himself
executed the main figures: the 'Aeneas' group, the kneeling
mother and the young woman at the right are of the highest
quality in modelling, expression and drapery painting. No
drawing by Raphael survives for the water-carrier, but one of
his greatest was made for the 'Aeneas' group: it has the three-
dimensional solidity of sculpture and an unsurpassed richness
of surface modelling. It is unsurprising that Jacopo Caraglio
made an engraving after it around 1523, since it is perhaps
Raphael's finest rendering of male anatomy, and comparison
with the Chantilly drawing for *The Coronation*, taken from the
same model, makes it evident that they are by different hands.
The group contains an allusion to the Medici: the profile of
'Anchises' is taken from a medallic portrait of Cosimo il
Vecchio. Maybe it evokes Leo X as the saviour of the dynasty.

The arrangement of the foreground is in part the result of a
change of mind, but it is uncertain when this change occurred.
Raphael's drawing for the crouching woman shows her with her

right arm held out to 'Aeneas'. In the fresco, her right arm is
awkwardly retracted, but her pose is not otherwise adjusted.
Her gesture is now interrupted by the kneeling woman clad
in yellow, seen from the back, who raises her arms in appeal
to the pope. She performs a valuable function since she alone
links the foreground to Leo IV and his salvific intervention.
But while dramatically conceived, as painted the figure lacks
substance and articulation. This is true too of the preparatory
drawing, made like the others in red chalk, but differing in the
weak foreshortening of the legs, the slat-like realisation of the
drapery, the insecure hinging of the arms, and the absence of
neck between shoulders and head. These features identify the
hand of Giulio Romano, who also frescoed the figure. Whether
the insertion was made at cartoon stage or later is unclear. If
this attribution is correct, it would imply that Giulio worked
side by side with Raphael on this fresco before he began the
basamento. This, in turn, would support the view that *The Fire*
was the latest of the narrative frescoes in the room and would
make sense of the drawings. The bright ridges of the kneeling
mother's drapery recall drawings made by Raphael for the
Chigi Chapel's mosaics (Oxford, Ashmolean) and for the St Paul

126 BELOW LEFT Giulio Romano, study for the Appealing Woman in *The Fire
in the Borgo*, 1517
127 BELOW RIGHT Study for the Protective Mother in *The Fire in the Borgo*, 1517

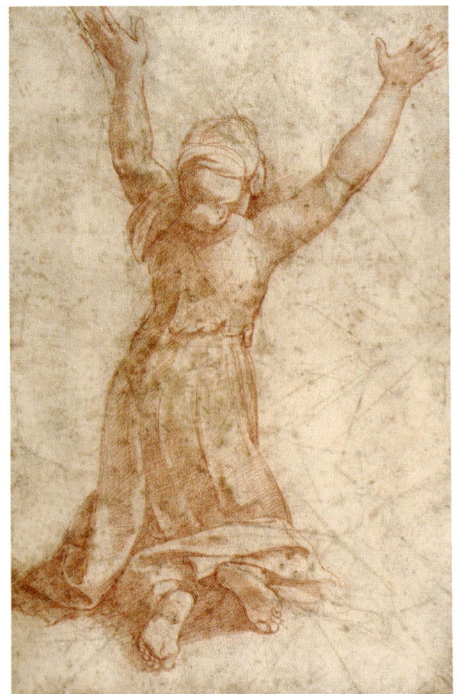

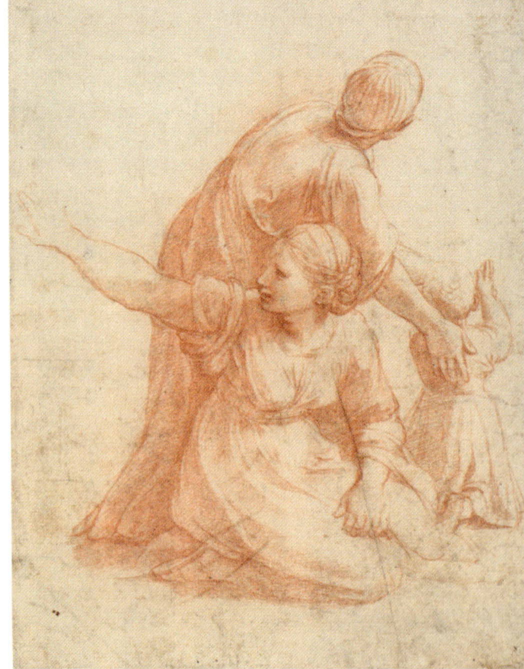

(Haarlem, Teyler Museum) in the *St Cecilia*; while the 'Aeneas and Anchises' drawing comes closest to the nude studies made for *The Transfiguration*.

The Stanza dell'Incendio remains a puzzle: the significant figures in *The Fire* are so resonant emotionally and so strongly constructed that they throw all the others in the room into the shade. One can only speculate why Raphael's part in the design of the other narratives was so limited, and why he exercised so little quality control.

In 1516–17 Raphael seems to have undergone a form of crisis. He must have been exhausted, physically and mentally, by his other responsibilities. He could hardly have been unaware that the Stanza dell'Incendio was a failure, even though it contained some fertile inventions. He would have realised that he needed to reassert design control and also construct a reliable and disciplined team to execute his wishes. The painter of *Ostia* was no doubt dismissed; the involvement of several hands – apparently not coordinated – in *The Coronation* created confusion and was not repeated; and while Penni's authorship of *The Oath* showed that he might serve as a collaborator, it revealed that his talents for design were limited and, for fresco-painting, mediocre. But Raphael would also have seen that the chamber's most effective and coherent section was Giulio's *basamento*. Giulio was to play an ever-expanding role in Raphael's organisation, while concurrently developing a semi-independent practice in portable work. In the schemes to come, Raphael seems to have reserved work that required inventiveness and energy for Giulio, and assigned routine and secretarial functions to Penni, who executed most of the fair copies of Raphael's designs.

The year 1517 is a key moment in the ascent of Giulio Romano. Giulio, although he gradually came to diverge from Raphael's aims and ideals, was able to produce more effective approximations of what Raphael would himself have done than any other artist. Raphael would also have had confirmation that Penni, although a limited painter, was an effective supervisor of others. It is surely significant that, following his limited participation in *The Fire*, Raphael – among the greatest of all fresco painters – executed rather little work in fresco, instead turning his personal attention to moveable paintings of different kinds. This led to, or was the product of, a conceptual reorientation.

Chapter 8
The Sistine Tapestries

 To understand the Sistine tapestries, it is necessary to
consider their context. Medieval in origin, the Sistine Chapel
was reconstructed and secured in the 1470s, during the papacy
of Sixtus IV, hence its name. In 1480–83 it was entirely frescoed
by a number of painters who worked autonomously but were
probably coordinated, perhaps supervised, by Perugino. The
project director was Cardinal Giuliano della Rovere, later Pope
Julius II, Sixtus's nephew and right-hand man.

The decoration of the vault comprised a simulated blue
heaven studded with golden stars, painted by Piermatteo
d'Amelia (*c.* 1445–1508), and presumably included abstract
decoration in the severies and lunettes. On the level below,
between the chapel's windows, the institutional lineage of the
Saviour was frescoed. Starting chronologically from the altar

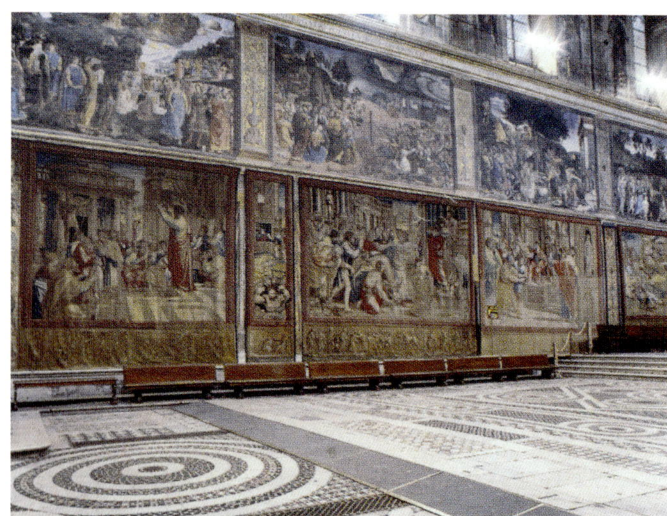

128 General
view of the
Sistine Chapel,
with a selection
of Raphael's
tapestries as
displayed in
1983

wall (whose Quattrocento decoration was wholly destroyed
by Michelangelo in 1534 in preparation for *The Last Judgment*),
Christ appeared in the central axis of the wall, flanked by
Sts Peter and Paul, and was followed by the chronological
procession of pontiffs who had shepherded the Church
during its years of persecution until the Emperor Constantine
proclaimed Christianity as the state religion in 313. The niched
popes were probably shared between Sandro Botticelli and
Domenico Ghirlandaio. Below them, also proceeding from
altar to entrance wall, are two facing historical cycles, each
comprising eight episodes, paralleling the lives and missions of
Moses (on the north wall) and of Christ (on the south), probably
painted concurrently. The opening scenes – *The Finding of
Moses* and *Christ's Nativity* – were destroyed by Michelangelo,
and the closing scenes of both cycles, *The Death of Moses* and
Calvary, damaged by a fall of masonry in 1522, were replaced
with frescoes of the same subjects in the 1570s. The Moses
cycle represented the world *sub lege* (under law), that of Christ
sub gratia (under divine grace), and the mirrored themes
of the cycles were explicated via inscriptions – effectively
surtitles – in the frieze. The cycles were painted by Perugino,
in partial collaboration with Signorelli and Pinturicchio, and
by the Florentines Ghirlandaio, Botticelli and Cosimo Rosselli.
Raphael, of course, knew the Umbrians personally and was
familiar with their work, and in Florence certainly studied
Ghirlandaio and probably met Botticelli. On the lowest level
are simulated hangings interwoven with gold thread, but
silver in every third bay.

The iconography of the chapel was massively amplified,
and reoriented, between 1508 and 1512 by Michelangelo, who,
to Julius's commission, destroyed the star-studded sky painted
by Piermatteo and frescoed on the vault nine episodes from
Genesis, starting with *The Creation* and ending with stories of
Noah, again moving chronologically from altar wall to entrance
wall (there is one anomaly: *The Sacrifice of Noah* precedes
rather than follows *The Flood*). Four large scenes alternate
with five small ones: each of the latter is framed by four nude
youths, twenty in all, probably unwinged angels, who support
ten simulated bronze medallions, perhaps symbolising the
Ten Commandments. The severies and lunettes were frescoed
with individuals and groups representing the ancestors of
Christ, again proceeding chronologically from altar to entrance
wall. According to Michelangelo's own account, he was initially
commissioned to paint the Apostles in the twelve pendentives
and to fill the rest of the vault with geometrical patterns,
and it was at his initiative that his remit was expanded.

Michelangelo's scheme extended sacred history back to
the Creation, established Christ's bloodline, and divided the
twelve pendentives between seven Old Testament prophets
and five sibyls – representatives of the Gentiles – who were
granted foreknowledge of the Virgin Birth and the advent
of the Messiah.

The Apostles eliminated from the first scheme for the vault
appear instead in the tapestries, which are collectively known
as *The Acts of the Apostles*. But they do not in fact deal with
all the Apostles: the narratives, in common with the biblical
books, are focused on the two who were most important to the
papacy: Sts Peter and Paul. The tapestries were to hang at the
lowest level of the chapel, covering the simulated hangings
painted thirty years earlier, and they parallel the ministries
of Peter, apostle to the Jews, and Paul, a Roman citizen, apostle
to the Gentiles. Although Paul had no direct connection with
Christ and persecuted Christians before becoming one by
miraculous conversion, he was considered joint founder of the
papacy, whose first official pope was Peter. The tapestries took
sacred history forward into the era following the Crucifixion
and linked directly with the pre-Constantinian popes. Thus
Raphael's scheme further modified the chapel's iconography,
but coherently.

The earliest recorded payment to Raphael for the cartoons
is of 15 June 1515, but the project had probably been under way
since the beginning of the year. It is likely to have concluded
late in 1516, when another payment was made, but payment
records are scant, and many must be lost. There is no
obvious stylistic development in the cartoons, which are,
of course, in reverse to the tapestries, and their internal
chronology is conjectural. They were probably designed
over a relatively short period and in tranches of perhaps
three or four, executed concurrently and sent to Flanders
to be woven.

Six of the ten tapestries are devoted to St Paul, four
to St Peter. The Pauline cycle comprises *The Stoning of
St Stephen*, *The Conversion of St Paul on the Road to Damascus*,
The Conversion of the Proconsul, Sergius Paulus (often known as
The Blinding of Elymas), *The Sacrifice at Lystra*, *Paul's Miraculous
Release from Prison* (in a narrow field that certainly responds to
a structural element in the chapel) and *Paul Preaching at Athens*.
The Petrine cycle comprises *The Calling of Peter and his Brothers*,
The Charge of the Risen Christ to St Peter (establishing him as
the first of the Apostles, a subject already treated in Perugino's
fresco), *The Healing of the Lame Man at the Golden Gate of the
Temple*, and *The Death of Ananias*.

Was the commission always confined to ten episodes?
Or were there to be sixteen, the number of spaces available in
the chapel? It would seem natural for the cycles to have depicted
later events in the Apostles' missions, culminating in their joint
martyrdoms in Rome – Paul beheaded, Peter crucified head
down – supposedly on the same day, 29 June AD 64. When, on
30 July 1517, Cardinal de Beatis saw the tapestries being woven
in the workshop of Pieter van Aelst, as well as recording the
subject of *The Charge of the Risen Christ to St Peter* he mentions
sixteen tapestries. But no confirmation of this number can be
found in any other account or document, and no drawings by
Raphael or his assistants are known that might be pertinent
to other scenes. Nor can it be argued that the scheme was
truncated on grounds of cost, since other tapestry series were
soon commissioned. The issue of number must remain open.

There is a second problem. The two sequences began on
the altar wall, flanking Perugino's frescoed altarpiece of
The Assumption of the Virgin, but the placement of the cycles is
disputed. It was long accepted that the Petrine cycle ran below
the cycle of Christ, and the Pauline below the cycle of Moses,
but this option entailed accepting that the marble screen that
did, and does, divide the chapel into clerical and lay sections
had later been moved. When in 1984 a selection of tapestries
was hung in the chapel according to this scheme, some
difficulties arose fitting them in their supposed positions.
More recently, it has been argued that the screen and cantoria
have not been modified, and that the Petrine cycle originally
ran below the cycle of Moses and the Pauline below the cycle
of Christ. This alternative layout was tried in 2020. There can
be no objection to the exchange on iconographic grounds and,
as far as can be judged, it is more congenial to the dimensions
of the individual tapestries. But their new position requires
accepting that they were to be lit in opposition to the pre-
existing decoration of the chapel, which elsewhere consistently
follows the illumination established by the windows present in
the altar wall until 1534. It would be exceedingly rare, perhaps
unique, for a narrative cycle within a fully painted space
to be illuminated in opposition to the rest of the decoration
and, if for no other reason, the traditional arrangement
seems preferable.

The execution of the ten cartoons must have occupied most
of Raphael's intellectual and physical energies for two years.
In area they would have totalled (very roughly) nearly 150 sq. m
(1,615 sq. ft; the total area of the tapestries is about 250 sq. m,
or 2,691 sq. ft) – broadly equivalent to the walls of the Stanza
della Segnatura. Although Raphael worked rapidly, the design

129

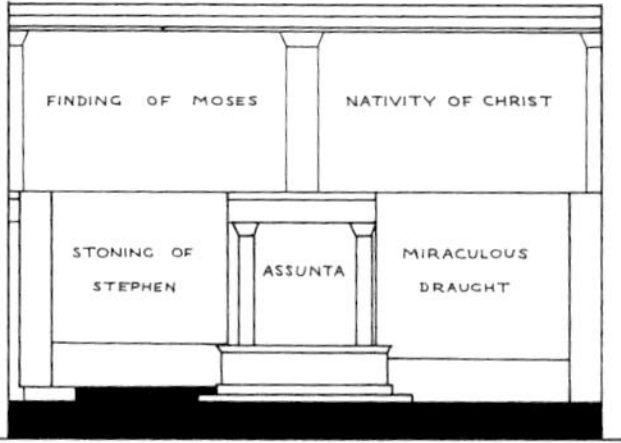

129 The Sistine Chapel: reconstruction of the original hanging order of the tapestries from John Shearman, *Raphael's Cartoons in the Collection of Her Majesty the Queen, and the Tapestries for the Sistine Chapel*, 1972

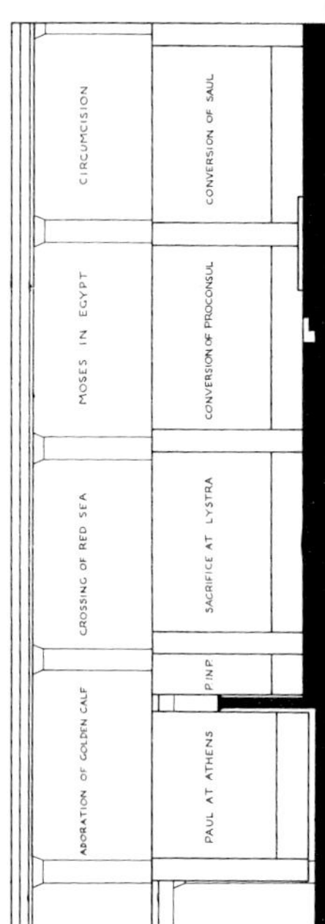

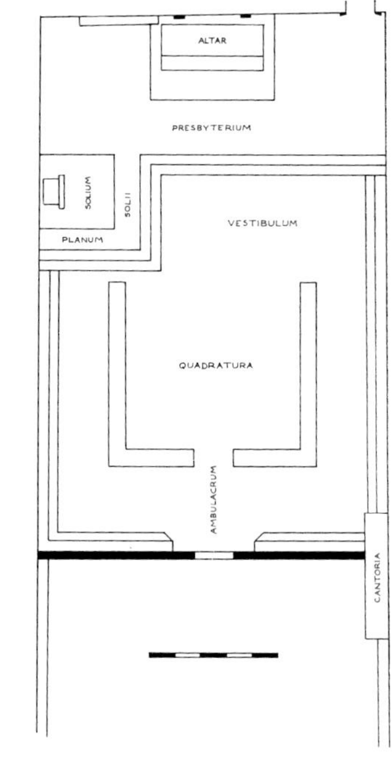

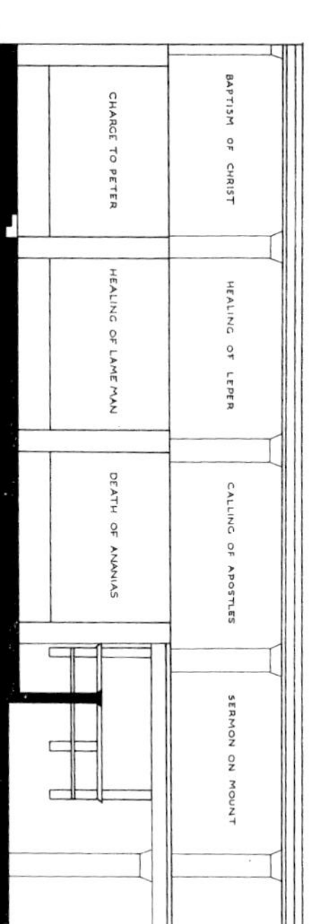

and colouring demanded careful planning, quite apart from the complexities of accommodating the tapestries visually to the frescoes above them.

It is likely that several cartoons had arrived in Flanders by 1516. Agostino Veneziano's engraving of the final scene in the Pauline cycle, *The Preaching at Athens*, no doubt cut from a lost *modello*, was probably produced as a pendent to *The Death of Ananias*, the last of the Petrine scenes. Neither is dated but the latter was copied in a chiaroscuro woodcut by Ugo da Carpi dated 1518. *The Conversion of the Proconsul*, which bears the date 1516, and differs slightly in dimensions, was cut from Raphael's surviving *modello*. In sum, three of Raphael's compositions were reproduced in prints between the dispatch of the cartoons and the arrival of the tapestries; they must be

130

131

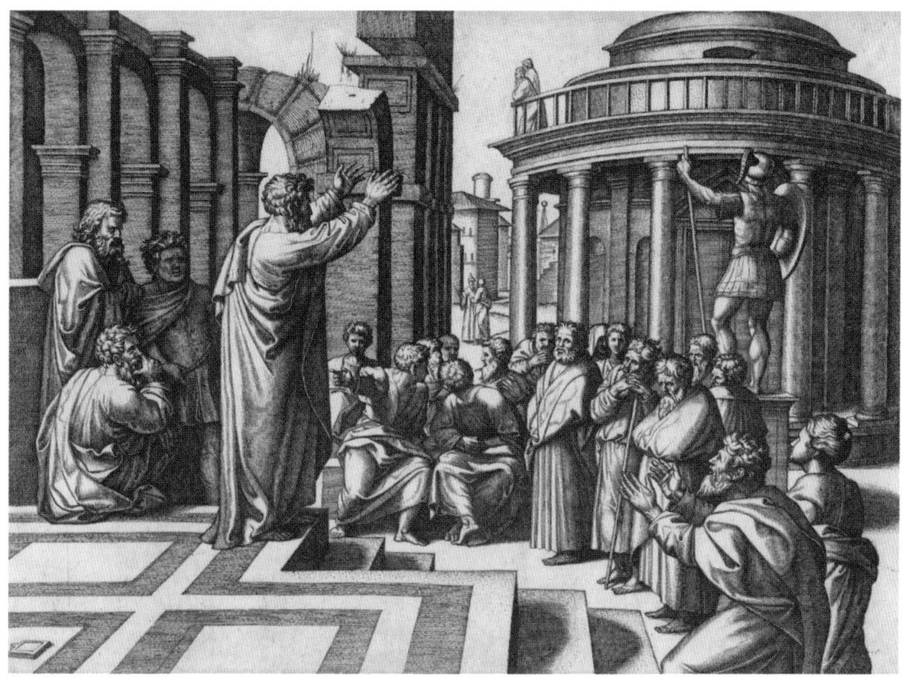

130 Marcantonio Raimondi after Raphael, *St Paul Preaching at Athens*, 1516

seen as advertisements for work in progress, one of Raphael's
strategies for self-promotion. The delivery schedules of the
tapestries are unknown, but seven were displayed in the
Sistine Chapel in December 1519. The remainder probably
reached Rome before Raphael died, but no further engravings
of them were made.

The cartoons are in remarkably good condition for large
works on the fragile and vulnerable support of paper. This
puzzled scholars when it was thought that they had been
divided into strips and used directly by the weavers. But
it is now clear that, on their arrival in Flanders, they were
copied, and that these copies – some fragments of which
survive – were the tapestries' immediate source. It seems
certain that the elevated quality of the cartoons, both as a
whole and individually, was part of their purpose. From the
outset it must have been intended that they should return
to Italy to be mounted on canvas and displayed as paintings.
Thus in *The Conversion of the Proconsul*, the inscription on
the throne is the right way round, appropriate to its display
as a painting: Raphael knew that the weavers or the authors

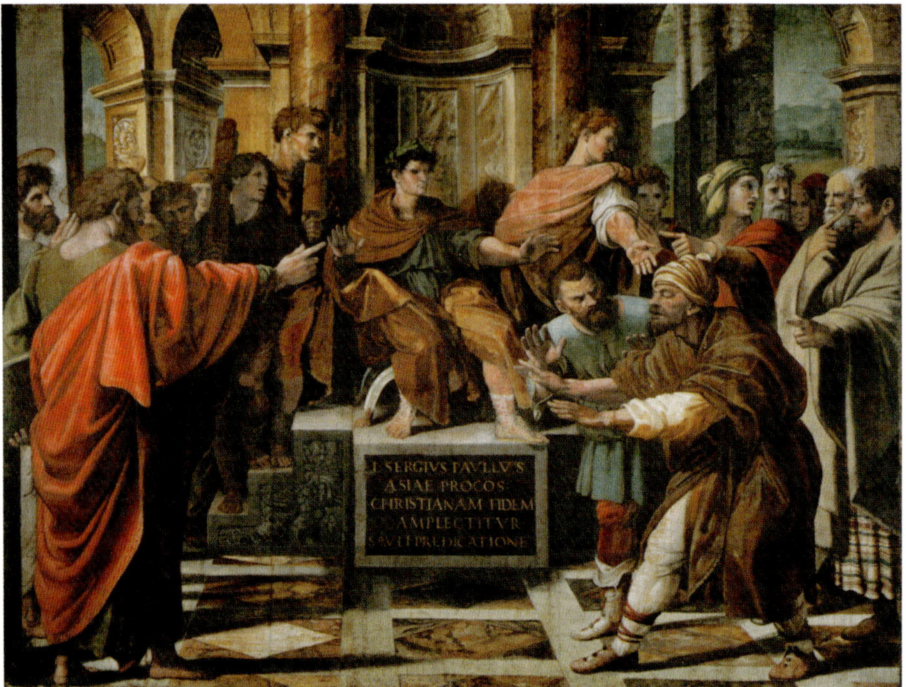

131 *The Conversion of the Proconsul, c. 1515–16*

of the intermediary cartoons could readily reverse lettering, and he did not want to have to revise his work when it returned to Rome.

The cartoon of *The Conversion of St Paul* is recorded in Venice in 1521, in the collection of Cardinal Grimani (presumably it was a gift from Leo X). But otherwise the cartoons' whereabouts are obscure until seven reappeared in Genoa, where Charles I purchased them in 1623, perhaps on Rubens's advice. Charles intended the cartoons to serve at the recently founded Mortlake Factory, which from 1630 onwards produced several sets. The Mortlake tapestries are more faithful to the cartoons than those woven by van Aelst, and Mortlake's best sets are the equal of any tapestries produced in the seventeenth century. Charles was able to acquire only seven cartoons; two others – *The Stoning of St Stephen* and *The Conversion of St Paul* – were owned by Ferdinando de' Medici at that point but were subsequently lost. *Paul's Miraculous Release from Prison*, tall and narrow and meaningless outside the original context of the Sistine Chapel, was probably lost at an early date.

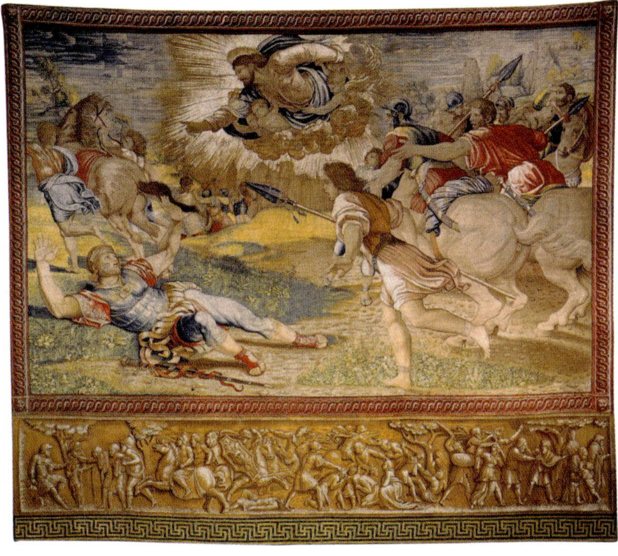

132 *The Conversion of St Paul*, tapestry from the *Acts of the Apostles*, designed by Raphael 1515–16, woven in Brussels under the supervision of Pieter van Aelst, 1516–19

In the cartoons, which partake both of paintings on canvas and of fresco, Raphael developed a grand style of unwavering seriousness. They are effectively autograph paintings but, executed *alla prima* in a water-based medium with little opportunity for revision, resemble frescoes in technique. The quality of the cartoons is such that they belie any notion of extensive studio collaboration, but Raphael did not work unaided. Vasari says that Penni painted much of the architecture, and that he also made the cartoons – all lost – for the tapestries' borders, a claim that the few surviving drawings for them support. The borders include frames in simulated porphyry and historical episodes from the life of Leo in simulated bronze, providing a material and textural contrast to the scenes they surround.

Raphael had to construct multi-figure narratives that were clear, forceful and solemn. Action is elevated and aggrandised. There is a resolute rejection of confusion and a broad alignment of forms within a grid of vertical and horizontals – particularly in scenes that do not involve violent action. Where they do, geometrical frameworks are less evident, but the figural design is clear and the gestures large. Raphael deliberately played against one of his strengths, eschewing fluency and rhythmical knitting for declamatory clarity. Thus *The Conversion of St Paul* is conceived more rhetorically and more stiffly than, for example, *The Expulsion of Heliodorus*, which also includes a rearing horse and a fallen man. Raphael

132

exploited disjunction rather than conjunction, stasis rather than mobility, and largeness and simplicity rather than sharply focused characterisation. Even in the most dramatic scenes, his actors tend to geological impassivity, and their slow movements, as in *The Conversion of the Proconsul* or *The Healing of the Lame Man*, become all the more compelling. Gestures are intensified to carry in the competitive arena of the chapel. The Apostles display minimal individual volition: vehicles of divine will, they perform preordained rituals. They interact relatively little. Colours are plain and simple and, for the most part, high-keyed, although now much dimmed (they are recoverable in the unfaded reverses of the tapestries). Brighter tones and colours tend to be more prominent in the earlier episodes of the cycles: Raphael makes greater use of earth colours as the narratives progress.

Raphael aimed to recreate the dawn of Christianity, an era of simple, dedicated, determined and robust men undertaking a sacred task in an indifferent world. They follow an indwelling spirit and respond to an inner voice: direct celestial intervention is limited to the first two episodes of the Pauline cycle. Michelangelo had memorably – and stingingly – rejected Pope Julius's request to add gilding to the vault because the Prophets were poor men and dressed poorly: Raphael shared this credo. He enhanced the Apostles' autonomy and strength by shortening them and thickening their forms, although not uniformly (the figures in *The Sacrifice at Lystra* are elongated for dramatic effect). There is nothing graceful about these rugged men: powerful, with the physiques of manual workers, they can support weight and suffering like primitive columns – indeed, there is a columnar quality about many of the groupings, as befits those men who formed the foundations of the Church. The Christianity embodied in Raphael's scheme precedes and transcends confessions. In 1542, a decade after the break with Rome, Henry VIII acquired a set of the *Acts*; and following the execution of Charles in 1649, the cartoons he had acquired were excluded from the Commonwealth sales and retained by Oliver Cromwell.

It was recognised even in the eighteenth century that Raphael's primary model in form and mood was Masaccio's Brancacci Chapel. Commentators pointed to the resemblance between Paul in *The Preaching at Athens* and *Paul Visiting Peter in Gaol* in the Carmine, even though that fresco was executed by Filippino Lippi in the 1480s, probably over Masaccio's sinopia. But specific borrowings are minimal. It is Masaccio's direct and heroic style most obviously in *The Tribute Money*, described by Cristoforo Landino as 'pure, without embellishment', that

Raphael absorbed. Masaccio, furthermore, was an appropriate model for a painter working in the Sistine Chapel, for Masaccio was also Michelangelo's own most important pictorial model. Raphael took a deep draught from the same well.

In the cartoons Raphael avoids evoking the antique in the manner of Mantegna, which might have been a temptation given the erudite antiquarian culture in which he participated. There are, of course, many references to the antique – a Roman relief was the main source of *The Sacrifice at Lystra* – but allusions to Roman monuments and architecture are fewer in the cartoons than in the Sistine's Quattrocento cycles. And when Raphael included a statue of Mars in *The Preaching at Athens*, it is shown from the rear, thus avoiding explicit citation of ancient art. Of course, Raphael alludes loosely to antique or neo-antique buildings, but his landscapes are mostly populated by the same Northern structures that are found in his pre-Roman work, and his townscapes here have the look of building sites. There are no grand sets, unlike the one he designed for a performance of Ludovico Ariosto's *I Suppositi* in 1519.

Raphael could not escape comparison with Michelangelo's ceiling, where homely types are employed for the Ancestors of Christ, and which also used bright and pure colour. There are a few direct borrowings – the woman starting back in alarm

133 *Christ's Charge to Peter*, probably 1515

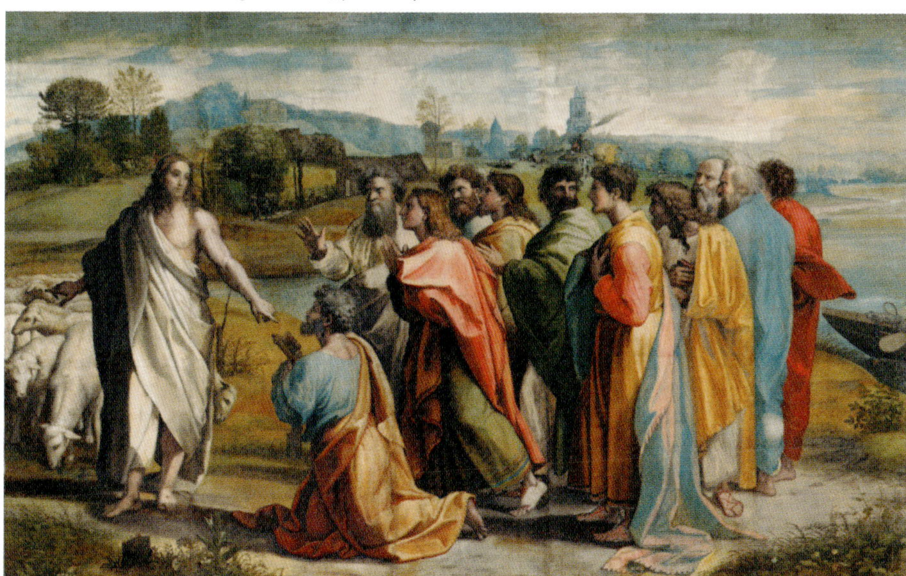

in *The Death of Ananias* is taken from Esther in *The Crucifixion of Haman*, for example – but for the most part Raphael avoided reference to his great rival. Sobriety, restraint, solidity and clarity are the watchwords of the cartoons' style.

For the ten pieces around fourteen preparatory drawings survive (the number is disputed), of which eleven are by Raphael. There are compositional sketches in pen, for *The Miraculous Draught of Fishes*; in metalpoint, for *The Sacrifice at Lystra* (Paris, Louvre); and in red chalk for *Christ's Charge to Peter* (Windsor, Royal Collection; a counterproof to show the composition in the final direction). The last two, demonstrating Raphael's reliance on life study, were made from assistants posed in the studio, whom he instructed, while he was working,

136

133

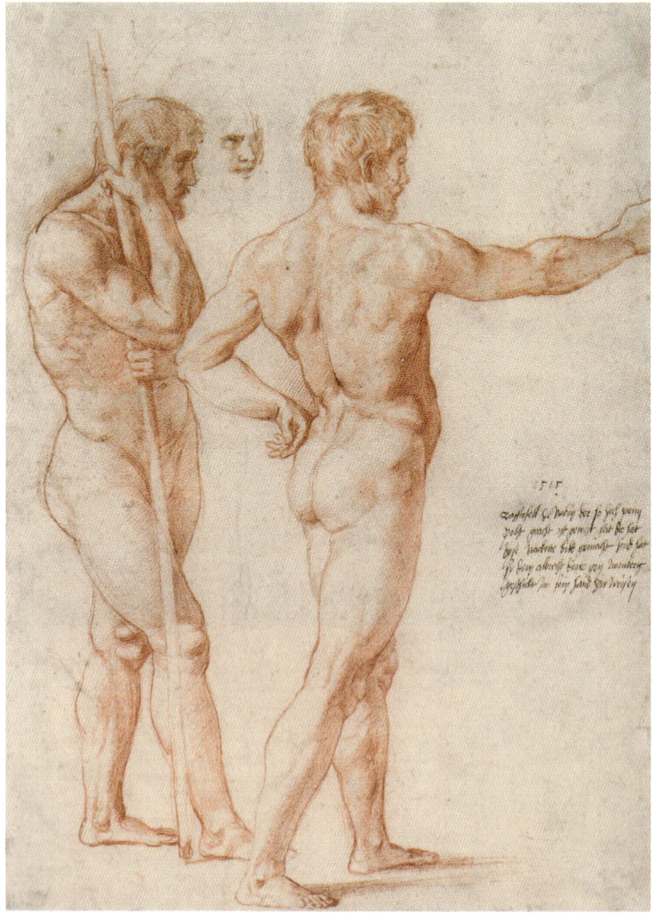

134 Two studies of a *Male Nude*, inscribed by Dürer and dated by him 1515. This is the single securely identifiable survival from the gifts that Raphael exchanged with Dürer

to change places and roles. There is a compositional draught in red chalk for *Paul Preaching at Athens*, establishing the anchor figures. There are four multi-media *modelli* in total; two of them – an experimental version of *The Calling* and the same scene in broadly its final design – are by Penni (fig. 135, and Windsor, Royal Collection). One of the two autograph *modelli* by Raphael, for *The Conversion of the Proconsul* (Windsor, Royal Collection), is, unusually, in metalpoint; but the other, for *The Charge* (Paris, Louvre), in nearly its final form, is in wash and bodycolour over black chalk underdrawing. In its strength and solidity it is a benchmark for a multi-media *modello* by Raphael against which those by Penni may be measured. There survive also several figure studies, in both metalpoint and red chalk: one of the latter, the study of two nudes sent to Dürer, prepared saints Paul and Barnabas in *The Conversion*.

Only one drawing offers any insight into possible changes of plan: the *modello* by Penni that shows *The Calling* in the background and a screen of Apostles in the foreground. Perhaps Raphael considered placing – at least in some scenes – the central event in depth, as in his second idea for *The Repulse of Attila*. If so, he soon abandoned it and – as with Penni's *modello* of *The Vision of St John*, for the *Bolsena* wall – made a rapid pen sketch on the verso that anticipates the final layout and was the basis of Penni's second *modello* (which, incidentally, also served Ugo da Carpi for a chiaroscuro woodcut). One metalpoint drawing that deserves attention is a study for a *Caryatid* (Oxford, Ashmolean), intended for the *basamento* of the Eliodoro but used instead for the simulated niched statue in the pier at the right of the tapestry – but not the cartoon – of *The Conversion of the Proconsul*.

Such grand compositions would have required extensive graphic preparation, and the survival of drawings is evidently exiguous. No doubt Raphael followed the procedure he had most fully explored in *The Disputa*: initial sketches, studies of groups, individuals within those groups, and then *modelli* to be squared up and transferred to the cartoons proper by assistants.

A high proportion of the surviving drawings for the cartoons – studies of both individuals and groups – are in metalpoint, the last time, it seems, that Raphael used that demanding medium so extensively: it was eminently suitable for sharp definition and to create the effect of rugged plasticity. There are no drawings for the cartoons in black chalk. For four or five years after *c.* 1514, Raphael preferred red chalk, and his most elaborate study in that medium for the cartoons, for *Paul Preaching*, simplified and, as it were, calcified the folds

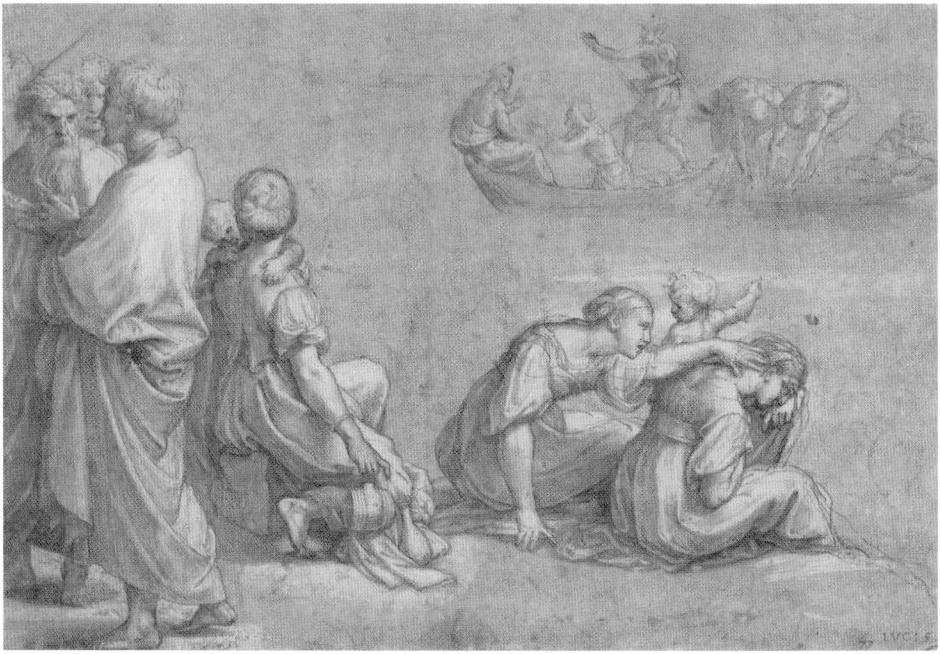

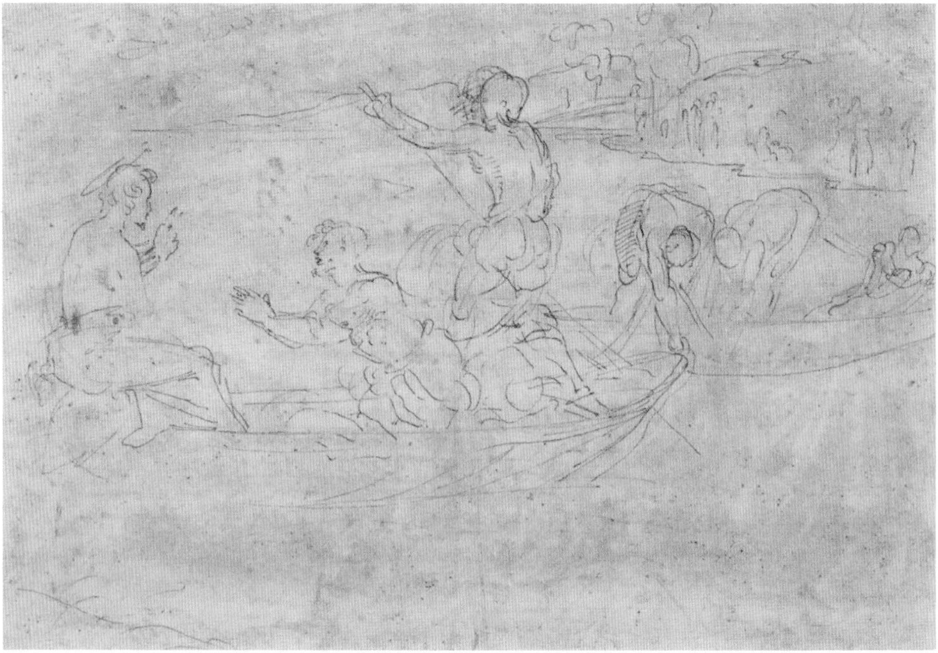

in Paul's garment by employing an uninterrupted ridge of
spared paper as the highlight, as though the form were carved
rather than modelled. This device is seen in other drawings of
1516–17, such as those for the mosaics in the dome of Agostino's
Chigi's Popolo chapel, completed in 1516. The spared ridge
was particularly appropriate for works to be executed in a
simplifying medium. But it also carried an emotional and
spiritual charge – severity, simplicity and rigour – and is
used too in the drawing for St Paul in the *St Cecilia*.

The tapestries woven in Flanders follow the cartoons
closely, but they prettify and sometimes over-decorate
Raphael's austere surfaces. The most flagrant example
is the robe of Christ in *The Charge*, to which the weavers
or the painters of the intermediary cartoon added stars.
The insertion weakens the majesty of Christ's pose and
exemplifies van Aelst's incomprehension of Raphael's
ideals. But there are many other minor infringements,
and the lavish use of gold and silver thread, while probably
responding to the demands of the pope (whose taste tended

135 OPPOSITE ABOVE Gianfrancesco Penni, *modello* for an alternative scheme
for *The Miraculous Draught of Fishes*
136 OPPOSITE BELOW Sketch for *The Miraculous Draught of Fishes*
137 BELOW Compositional study for *St Paul Preaching at Athens*, 1515–16

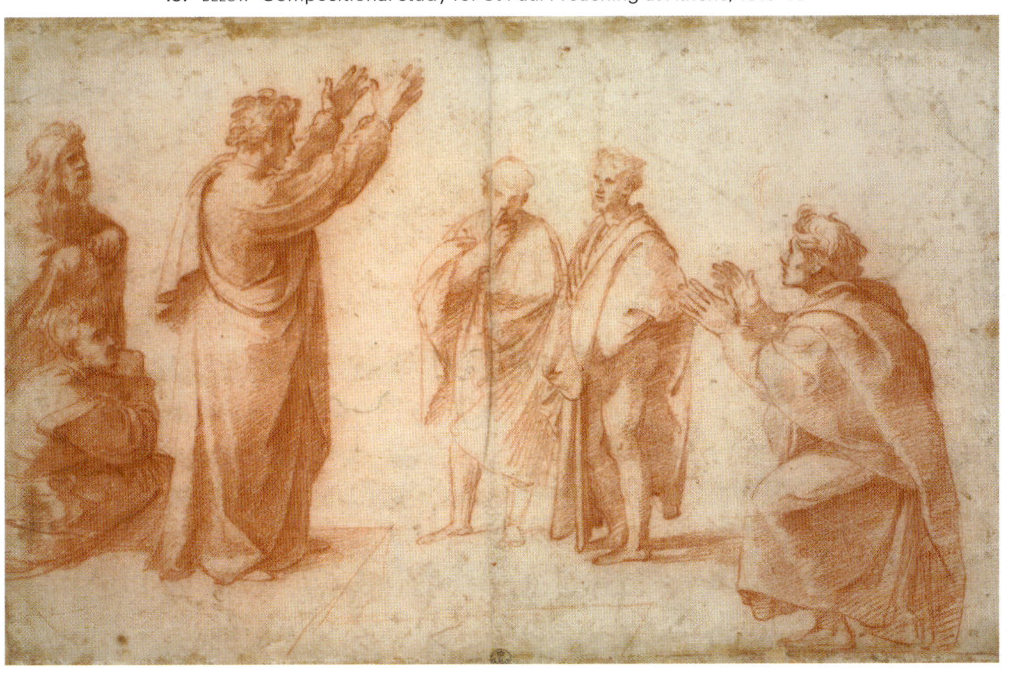

to opulence) militates against the cartoons' austerity, which the Mortlake weavings respect.

The cartoons have the simplification and compression of classical drama but also of their Gothic forebears: the fishing boats in *The Calling* are miniaturised in the manner of Pietro Cavallini: Raphael desired no distractions from the action of the figures. The cartoons' true heir and only equal is Poussin's Chantelou *Sacraments*.

The cartoons' austere manner and the relatively squat proportions of the actors were pursued in two other Apostolic schemes. One of these, which dates from 1516–17, was the Sala dei Palafrenieri, which connects the Stanza dell'Incendio and the Sala di Costantino. This large room, Leo's robing chamber, frescoed with simulated niched statues of Evangelists and Apostles, was destroyed and remodelled under Paul IV in the second half of the 1550s, but several of the original figures survive. Raphael extends to the main level of his scheme the simulated statuary in the *basamento* of the Eliodoro.

138 Gianfrancesco Penni, Giovanni da Udine and others, the Sala dei Palafrenieri, 1516. Most of the decoration of the Sala dei Palafrenieri was destroyed in the later 1570s, but Sts John, Luke and Stephen from the original cycle were preserved

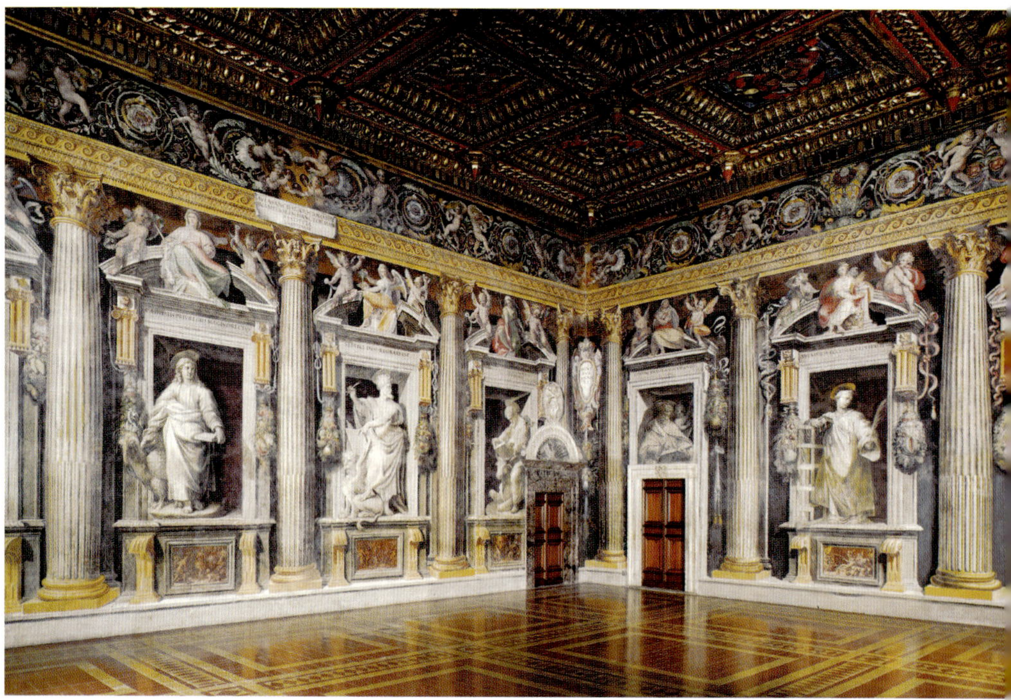

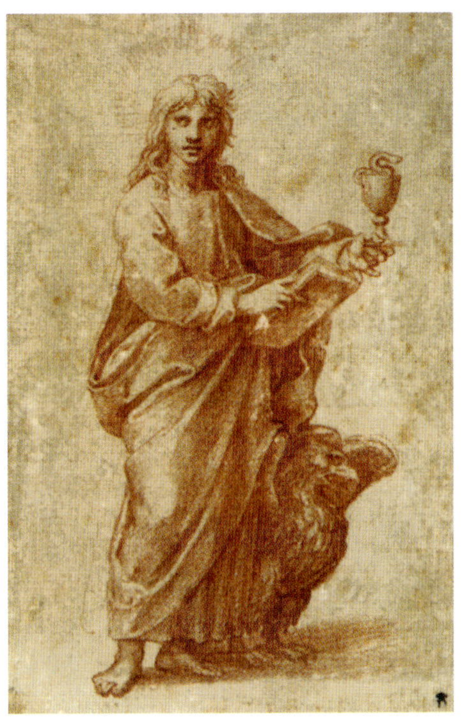

139 Giulio Romano, *St John the Evangelist*, from the suite of *Christ and the Twelve Apostles*, probably 1516. Giulio's drawings, which presumably depend from sketches by Raphael, were reproduced in two different suites of engravings, by Marcantonio and Marco Dente da Ravenna

The room was completed by lost frescoes of vines and birds by Giovanni da Udine. The execution of the simulated statues was by Penni, and the surviving *modelli* are all by him: their soft forms, imprecise contours and lack of plastic force contrast with Raphael's solidity. But they no doubt rest on the master's sketches.

The Palafrenieri figures have sometimes been connected, mistakenly, with a series of thirteen designs, issued in slightly varied sets of engravings by Marcantonio Raimondi and by Marco Dente da Ravenna. Both series must be of 1516–17. They were prepared in densely modelled red chalk drawings by Giulio (Chatsworth, Devonshire Collection), but it is hard to believe that these were made solely for engraving, and they may have served a double function: *modelli* for painting *and* engraving – a sensible economy. The prints were influential and were frequently quoted in later fresco schemes such as the pillar figures in San Paolo alle Tre Fontane, but the project for which they were made remains unknown; perhaps it was aborted.

138

139

Chapter 9
The *Loggetta* of Cardinal Bibbiena and the Loggia of Leo X

I

Next to Leo X (1475–1521) himself, the most important member of the Vatican hierarchy was Bernardo Dovizi (1470–1520), called Il Bibbiena after his hometown. He had been a loyal Medici supporter during Leo's years of exile from Florence, and an astute advisor. Bernardo was in the first group of cardinals to be created by Leo, on 23 September 1513, and was his right-hand man in the following years, although he gradually lost ground to Leo's cousin Cardinal Giulio towards the end of the decade. Politician, diplomat, scholar and antiquarian, with a passionate interest in classical remains, Bibbiena was also a playwright and wit; his comedy *La Calandria* was staged in Urbino in 1513 with a set by Girolamo Genga, and at the Vatican in 1514 with one by Peruzzi.

Whether Bibbiena and Raphael were already friends during before Leo's accession is unknown, but their common link with Urbino makes it likely. They were certainly on close terms within a few months of Bibbiena's elevation, for Bibbiena, as we learn from Raphael's letter to his uncle of 1 July 1514, offered his niece Maria to Raphael in marriage. Raphael temporised, and in the event the marriage did not take place; Maria shortly predeceased him. But that the betrothal was serious is implied by her interment beside Raphael in the Pantheon. That a cardinal should wish to marry his niece to an artist was probably without precedent and it is confirmation of Raphael's uniquely high social status.

Unlike most cardinals, Bibbiena did not rent a palace; his familiarity with Leo favoured residence in the Vatican. It was therefore decided, probably in 1515, to fashion for him an apartment, situated on the floor below Leo's. It consisted of a loggia (known as the *loggetta*); a small, heated bathroom,

the *stufetta*; and a private chapel, the last now demolished.
The construction is undocumented, but Raphael was with virtual
certainty the architect, and the loggia is elegantly formed,
employing three linked triumphal arches in an example of
motivic elision rather than simple repetition. The apartment
was ready for decoration by early 1516. On 19 April Pietro Bembo,
writing to Bibbiena, then absent from Rome on a diplomatic
mission, says, teasingly, that he is enjoying his friend's new
apartment, which is nearly finished; he adds that Raphael has
just put his head round the door to ask what further subjects
Bibbiena wants painted in his bathroom. This is unique
testimony of what must have been a common situation. It
confirms that the *stufetta*'s programme was not fully planned
in advance and offers an insight into the relatively casual way
that such a project might be managed. Within a closely knit
court, contracts were not as necessary as they would have
been in, say, a public commission for a town hall or a church.

The *loggetta* and the *stufetta* were painted primarily by
Giovanni da Udine (1487–1564). They embody a revival of
different aspects of antique decoration, inspired by the
recently uncovered Golden House of Nero. Exhibiting a
new archaeological precision in the reproduction of Roman

140 BELOW LEFT Giovanni da Udine, the *loggetta* of Cardinal Bibbiena, interior, general view, 1516
141 BELOW RIGHT Giovanni da Udine and Giulio Romano, the *Stufetta* (bathroom) of Cardinal Bibbiena, general view

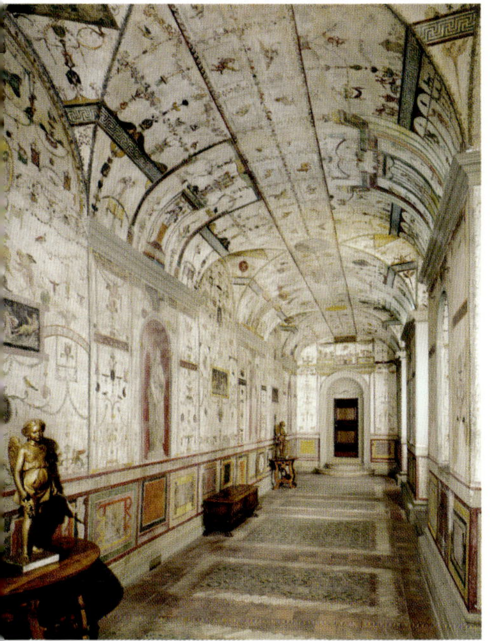

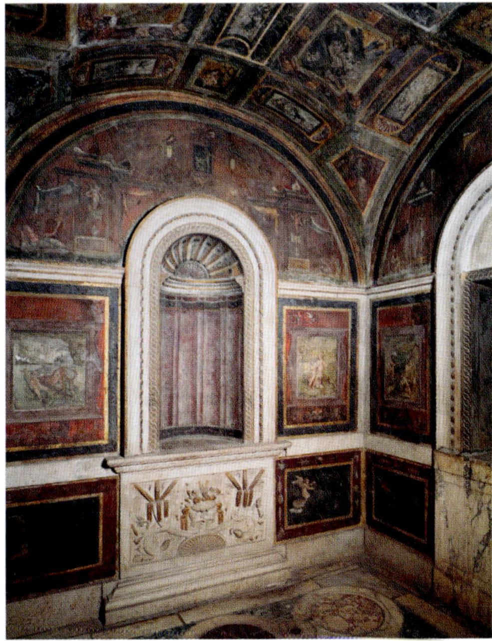

decorative painting, the two spaces were the forerunners of vast
campaigns of grotesque decoration in Italy and elsewhere. They
differ in type. The *loggetta* frescoes are in openwork, deploying
thin columns and small decorative forms, and the space is
bright and refreshing. It is convincing as a re-creation of parts
of the Golden House, which Giovanni studied assiduously, and
it looks like a work produced in antiquity rather than a revival.
The scheme also includes three simulated female statues: that
of *Ceres* was repeated in the cover of *The Small Holy Family*,
painted by Giulio for Bibbiena *c.* 1518 (Paris, Louvre).

The contrast between the lightness of the *loggetta* and
the areas of intense colour in the *stufetta* shows Raphael's

142 Giulio Romano, *Venus and Cupid*, 1516

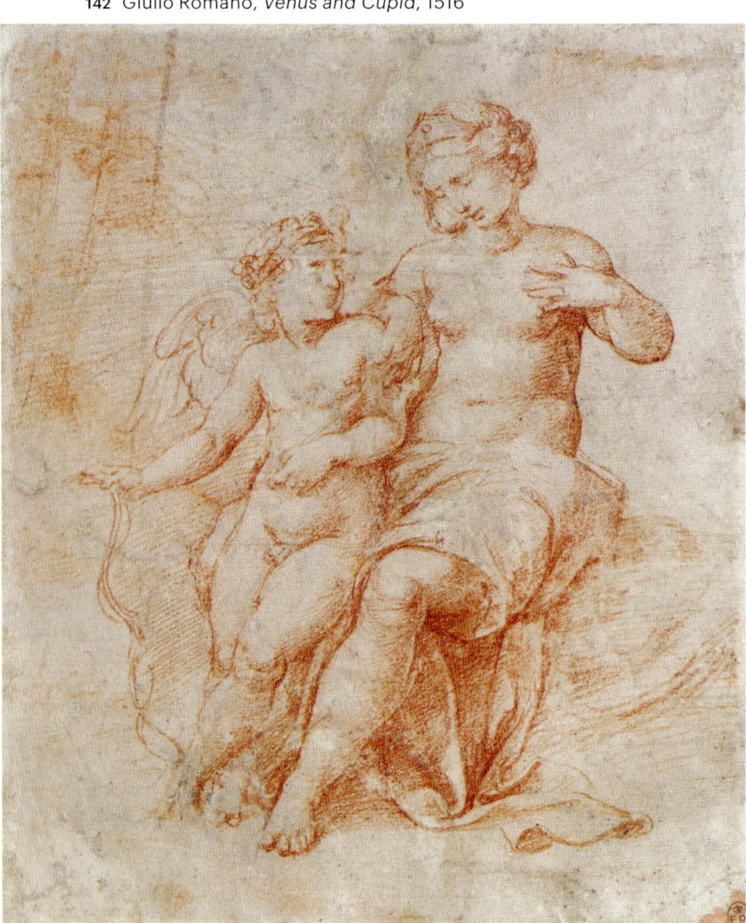

deployment of style and space for contrast rather than continuity. The airiness of the loggia contrasts with the warmth of the bathroom, which is largely painted in what is known as the 'Third Pompeian Style', with large areas of solid colour and strongly planar in effect. As well as a stucco relief of wheatsheaves – Bibbiena's emblem, which also appears on *The Small Holy Family*'s cover – it includes eight small stories of Venus executed by Giulio Romano, who also made the preparatory drawings, all in red chalk (other examples at Vienna, Albertina; Paris, Louvre). They provide a rather clear insight into one area of Giulio's graphic style in spring 1516. Dense and rather heavy in modelling, it is distinctively different from Raphael's, as are his more compact physical types. Bibbiena, naturally, would have known who was painting his bathroom, and it is likely that he befriended Giulio too. Probably a year or two before his death he commissioned from Giulio a powerful interpretation of Christ's *Flagellation* for the Roman church of Santa Prassede, a panel that recent scholarship has shown to be influential, especially in the early seventeenth century – indeed, it has even been connected with Caravaggio.

Some of the *stufetta*'s scenes were engraved – from Giulio's drawings, not the frescoes – by Agostino Veneziano and Marco Dente da Ravenna; surprisingly, the engravings vary in size and were not planned as a set. Giulio's *stufetta* drawings, like his *Apostle* series at Chatsworth, probably had a double purpose from the outset, functioning as guides for the frescoes – which were executed freehand, without cartoons – and, simultaneously, as templates for printmaking. Via the prints, small mythological compositions in an inaccessible private bathroom in a restricted area of the Vatican came to be widely known.

It is generally assumed that Giulio's designs followed sketches by Raphael although none have yet been found. In any case, the *stufetta*'s paintings seem to have been regarded by Giulio as his own property, for *c.* 1522 they were reproduced on a larger scale, and without modifications, in the loggia of the villa of Cristoforo Stati (later known as the Villa Mattei) on the Palatine, which he oversaw. The detached frescoes are now mostly in the Hermitage, and a fragment of Giulio's cartoon for *The Venus and Adonis* is in the Albertina. It was for Stati that Giulio at the same period designed a substantial and impressive palace adjacent to Piazza Navona: now known as the Palazzo Maccarani, it is one of Giulio's earliest architectural successes.

II

Work on the great Loggia of Leo X probably began in 1516. Level with the Stanze, it is the middle storey of the bank of three superimposed loggias rising above a solid basement on the west wing of the palace. The construction had been begun by Bramante and, after his death, the second and third storeys were continued under Raphael's supervision; he was less alert to statics than Bramante, for Antonio da Sangallo had to shore up Raphael's parts after 1520.

The pope's Loggia was a hugely ambitious and complicated undertaking. Thirteen bays long, it is decorated from the vault to the floor – which was itself also a component of the scheme, paved with tiles from the della Robbia workshop in Florence. The execution of all the decorative parts seems to have been subcontracted by Raphael to Giovanni da Udine, but Raphael certainly intervened in the overall design and acted as a quality controller: nothing that Giovanni subsequently executed on his own account approaches the Loggia either in conceptual sophistication or executive richness.

The vaults are treated as fictive architecture, but of different kinds. One bay has faux latticework filled with angels, another a view to open sky through unroofed cornices. All bear witness to Raphael's freedom and fertility in devising painted architecture. The architectural and framing element of the vaults repeat each other from end to end. Thus the first bay is identical to the thirteenth, the second to the twelfth, and so on. Only the central seventh bay is unique: it is structured as a stucco canopy set with figures in relief.

All thirteen vaults are divided into four sections, each containing a rectangular narrative scene, whose formats likewise match each other from end to end. Some have low arched tops, and the first and thirteenth are extended lozenges. The narratives were not under Giovanni's control, although he may have overseen their execution: their design remained Raphael's responsibility – inevitably, for no other artist was so effective a storyteller. Of the fifty-two narratives, forty-eight are dedicated to subjects from the books of Genesis, Exodus, Samuel and others, supplemented by the Psalms and other sources. The first bay illustrates *The Creation*, the second the story of Adam and Eve. There follow stories of Noah (Bay 3), Abraham (Bay 4), Isaac (Bay 5), Jacob (Bay 6), Joseph (Bay 7), Moses (who occupies Bays 8 and 9), Joshua (Bay 10), David (Bay 11) and Solomon (Bay 12). The cycle is the most extensive devoted to the Old Testament in the Renaissance. Only four frescoes treat New Testament scenes (Bay 13).

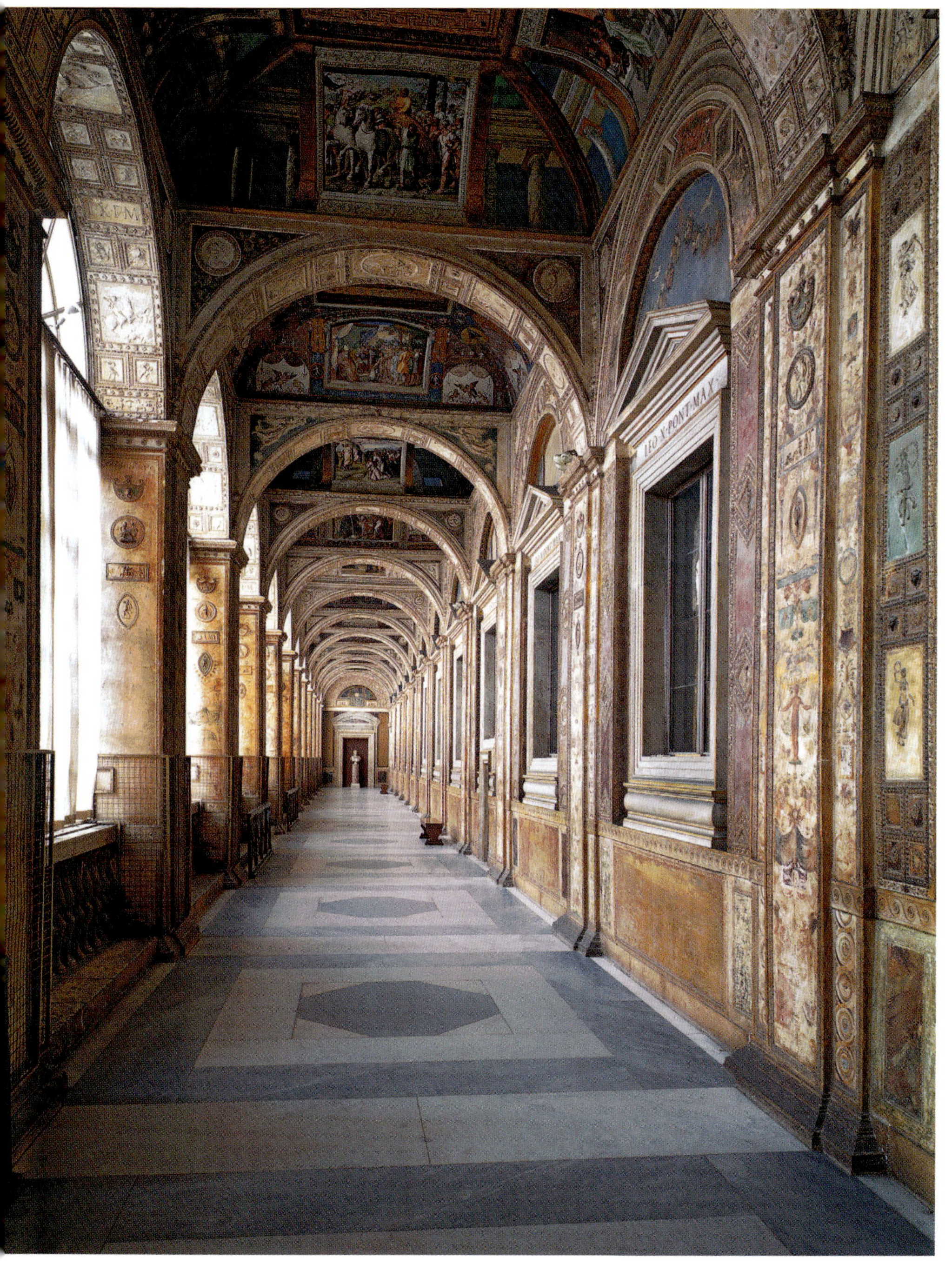

143 Giovanni da Udine, Gianfrancesco Penni and others, to Raphael's design, the Loggia of Leo X, 1516–19

The narratives are not designed in foreshortening to be viewed from below but as *quadri riportati*, i.e. easel paintings made for viewing at eye level but lifted to the vault. They are clearly composed and in general easy to read, as befits paintings to be viewed at some distance (one wonders how the notoriously short-sighted Leo X managed). They are effectively glorified book illustrations, and the sequence has become known as 'Raphael's Bible'.

Treatments vary according to the events depicted and the number of figures to be included, but in most the narratives occupy between one-third and one-half of the height of the field. Unlike the vault frescoes in the Stanze, the narratives are not set against simulated fields of mosaic or canvas: they are placed within contexts, built structures or landscapes, as one would expect from normal narrative paintings.

The logic governing the choice of episodes is not fully clear. One might have expected Old and New Testament episodes to

144 Assistant of Raphael (Perino del Vaga?) after a *modello* by Gianfrancesco Penni, *David and Bathsheba*, probably 1517

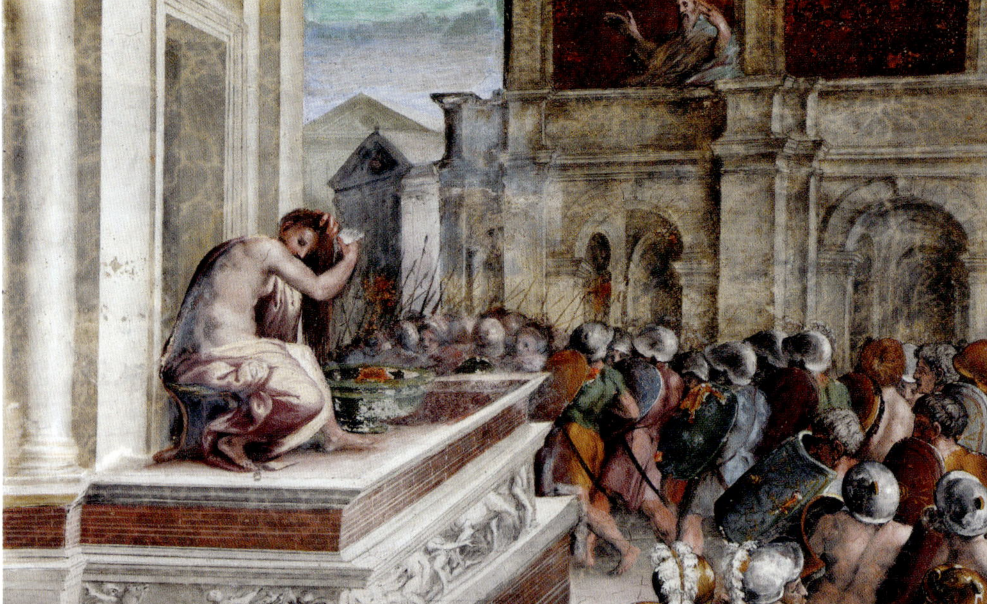

be set in conjunction as antetypes and fulfilments, as in the
Sistine Chapel, but the narratives are overwhelmingly from
the Old Testament. Many of the episodes are conventional and
inescapable: the foundational episodes of *The Creation* and *Fall*
in the first two bays selected themselves, and it is hard to see in
them any specific tendency. The choice is an expansion and
glossing of the episodes frescoed by Michelangelo and earlier
painters: *The Expulsion of Adam and Eve*, for example, refers
directly to Masaccio.

Raphael had previously included three of the scenes of divine
intervention – a running theme of the Loggia frescoes – on the
vault of the Stanza di Eliodoro (and he repeats the composition
of *Jacob's Dream* verbatim). But the principles of selection in
less frequently represented scenes such as *Jacob and Laban*,
for example, or *The Triumph of David* are harder to elucidate.
Of course, all the scenes, to a greater or lesser extent, follow the
history of the chosen people under its successive leaders, and
in general the emphasis is historical rather than eschatological.
The episodes were no doubt selected with a purpose or purposes,
and the themes that recur most frequently are battles won
over the Israelites' enemies, and political events such as *The
Anointing of David*, with its evocation of the roles of Church
and state, and *Solomon and Sheba*, which treats of diplomacy –
in short, the public lives of the major Old Testament figures.
But episodes in their private lives, sometime discreditable,
are occasionally included – notably, perhaps, in episodes
of *David and Bathsheba* and *The Death of Uriah the Hittite*.

The four New Testament scenes in Bay 13 comprise *The
Nativity*, with shepherds; *The Adoration of the Magi*; Christ's
Baptism; and *The Last Supper*. Once more it is hard to see any
direction in this choice, but it may reflect passing concerns
now irrecoverable.

The scenes on the vault are complemented by twelve (the
central bay contains the door) elongated narratives, treated
as reliefs in *brunaille* in the *basamento* of the wall side of the
Loggia. Eleven of them treat Old Testament subjects, while
the twelfth, in the thirteenth bay, shows *The Resurrection of
Christ*. These are now largely lost, but they were among the most
accessible parts of the Loggia and many drawings record them.
They were memorable: Pietro Aretino recalled one composition
in the 1540s, at least a decade and a half after he had last seen it.

The layout of the Loggia had some influence in the sixteenth
century. The loggia on the floor above was decorated in
imitation of Raphael's Loggia in the 1580s, and variants on
the *quadro riportato* system were employed widely in schemes
in the Vatican and elsewhere, an obvious choice for extended

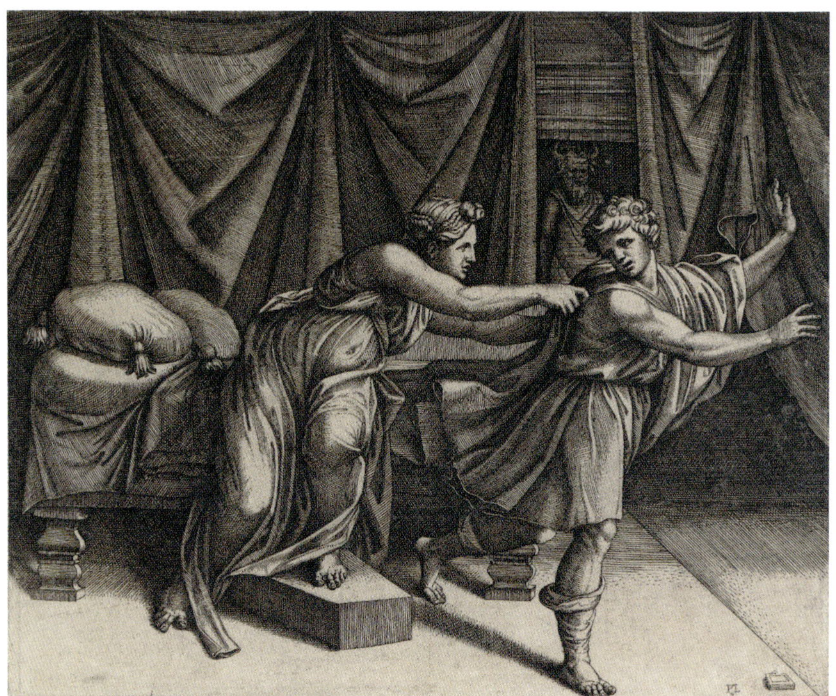

145

narrow spaces such as corridors and staircases. Some episodes – among them *Joseph Fleeing from Potiphar's Wife* – were engraved, by Marcantonio and others; but few of Raphael's individual compositions had much immediate impact. Only after 1620, when all fifty-two were published in etchings executed under the supervision of Giovanni Lanfranco, did they have widespread resonance. They were among the most important models for the religious and secular canvases of Nicolas Poussin, who appreciated their clear exposition of divine actions, moral decisions and historical events, notably battles. Indeed, Raphael's 'Bible' became a valuable reservoir for much later narrative painting and book illustration.

It seems likely that painting and stuccoing began in the vault and upper parts of the Loggia, as would normally be the case, and then moved downwards. It would have been executed from platforms erected on light and moveable scaffoldings (there might have been more than one). Stylistic analysis is not precise enough to determine the Loggia's internal chronology, but it is likely that it was painted mostly in 1517 and finished in 1518, but not fully opened until 1519. The *basamento* would have been the last area to be painted, and floor tiles would not have been laid until painting and stuccoing was complete.

The decoration of the Loggia required the collaboration of several painters and stuccoists and their management. Raphael and Giovanni assembled a team, and Vasari names several of its members. They, or some of them, probably worked on the fictive architecture of the vaults as well as the narratives; the non-figurative parts might in principle have been reserved for Giovanni da Udine, but he seems to have been happier with organic rather than architectural forms.

In his biography of Raphael, Vasari says that Raphael turned the organisation of the figurative parts over to Giulio Romano, but that Giulio did little on them – and, indeed, no drawings are known by Giulio that relate to the Loggia. Perhaps the conflict between Giulio and Giovanni da Udine, which boiled over only weeks after Raphael's death, was already simmering and he was assigned to other tasks. However, in his life of Giulio, Vasari specifically attributes to him *The Creation of Eve* in Bay 2, *The Building of the Ark* and *The Sacrifice of Noah* in Bay 3, and *The Finding of Moses* in Bay 8. But since drawings exist by Penni for all except *The Building of the Ark*, even if Giulio painted them he is unlikely to have designed them.

It seems, in fact, that Raphael delegated the graphic preparation of the narratives not to Giulio but to Penni, about whom Vasari, despite his efforts, was unable to gather much information, although he does name Penni in connection with the Loggia. But Vasari is more informative about the painters who actually executed the narratives, and there is no reason to doubt him: he names Tommaso Vincidor (Il Bologna, 1493–1536?), Vincenzo Tamagni (1492–1529), Perino del Vaga, Polidoro da Caravaggio (*c.* 1499–1543) and the much older Pellegrino da Modena (*c.* 1460–1523). None was based in Rome, which suggests that Raphael preferred to employ painters without local roots, more dependent on his favour and more conformable to his wishes. Vincidor, a native of Bologna who may have been introduced to Raphael by Marcantonio, was to work further for Raphael on tapestry projects.

Pellegrino seems to have had a more tenuous relation with Raphael and worked more loosely under his aegis. But he made prompt use of Raphael's (and Giulio's) ideas in his *Dormition and Coronation of the Virgin* in the church of Santa Maria Assunta in Trevignano and in the chapel of St James in San Giacomo degli Spagnuoli, Rome. Raphael especially liked to encourage beginners, however, and his gifts as a talent-spotter are evident in his employment of Perino and Polidoro, who were still teenagers. Both were to become prominent in Rome in the period between Raphael's death and the Sack of 1527.

Vasari's attributions to Giulio may not be reliable, but his information about Perino, whom he knew well, is probably solid. Vasari ascribes to him three of the four scenes in Bay 10, and all four in Bay 13, plus much of the *basamento*. Perino also seems to have been responsible for some figurative painting in the pilasters and certainly executed stuccos – indeed, he later became a famed stuccoist and no doubt learnt this art from Giovanni. Some of the forms in the pilasters reveal awareness of the latest trends in Florentine painting, which Perino would have seen before he moved to Rome and whose forms do not recur elsewhere in the productions of Raphael's shop.

Polidoro also had a part to play, but Vasari provides no clear guide to what he did. The physically powerful figure types seen in the magniloquent simulated reliefs of his façade frescoes – and the contrasting interest in homely realism seen in his drawings – are both hard to find in the Loggia, although a few compositions, such as *The Flood*, have conjecturally been attributed to him. But his style at this stage of his career, if we remember that he was untrained as a painter and that his initial steps would have been directed by Penni, is conjectural. Whether others not named by Vasari were employed is speculative: the Spaniards Pedro Machuca (1490–1560) and Alonso Berruguete have both been suggested as possible participants in the decoration of the Loggia, but the latter at least does not seem a likely candidate since he was close to Michelangelo. A relevant sidelight on Raphael's recruitment policies and rare testimony to a lack of generosity on his part are provided by a letter of 1519, postdating the Loggia project, that describes the efforts of a young Florentine painter, a follower of Michelangelo, to obtain employment in Rome. But since Raphael disliked his work, he was compelled to move away. The incident reveals something of Raphael's power in Rome.

The *loggetta* does not contain stucco work and the *stufetta* only a little. That the extensive employment of stucco, imitated from Roman models, was first tried in the Loggia is possible, but it is likely that Giovanni had already experimented with stucco previously, perhaps in private palaces, for he worked with confidence and elegance. It enriches the arches separating the bays and the frames of some of the *quadri riportati*; on the pilasters the variety of different shapes match those on the inner sides of the pillars across the width of the Loggia. The stuccos cite many different sources, including figures by Raphael himself, one of Michelangelo's Ancestors of Christ,

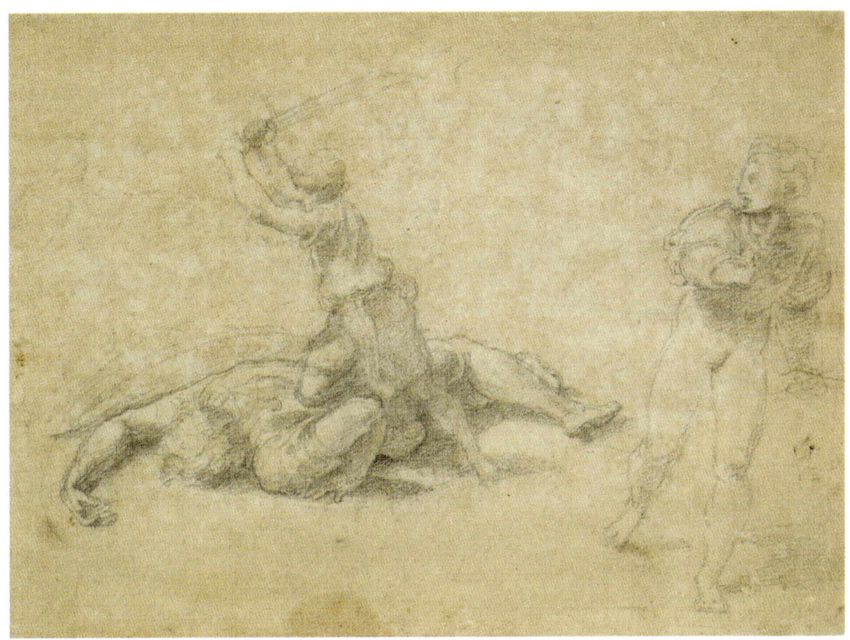

146 *David Beheading Goliath*, 1516–17

and figures that look to have been invented by Rosso Fiorentino or Berruguete, whose work Perino would have known. They are of great accomplishment and some wit (a view of Giovanni's studio is included). They seem to be ludic marginalia, designed to elicit pleasure rather than to play a part in a coherent thematic scheme. It may be that Raphael felt that, to get the best out of Giovanni, whose intellectual attainments were lightweight, it was worth allowing him and his assistants a fairly free rein.

A watercolour exists by Giovanni that obviously prepares a pilaster (Dresden, Kupferstichkabinett), and he no doubt made many studies of the fruits and vegetables that are so prominent in the decoration. He infused Roman models with nature study, just as he was to load the simulated arbour of the Psyche Loggia with flowers, fruits and vegetables. This was a way of enriching what he had inherited from the antique and returning it to life.

It is generally – perhaps universally – accepted that Raphael himself painted nothing in the Loggia, but the extent and reach of his involvement in planning the narratives is disputed. Only one preparatory drawing can be credited securely to Raphael's own hand: a swift and soft black chalk sketch, made from models in studio dress, of *David Beheading Goliath*. The forms are evoked with precision and economy, and Raphael tried two

positions of David's head; in one he looks down at the neck
that he is about to sever (the more energetic of the two), and
in the other his head is lifted to imply that he is acting without
effort; the latter is adopted in the fresco, in Marcantonio's
engraving after it, and in Ugo da Carpi's chiaroscuro woodcut
made after that.

The drawing has implications for Raphael's working
method. It includes the scene's three anchor figures – the
stunned and sprawling Goliath, the energetic David, and
(serving a choric function) a Philistine soldier fleeing in
horror – but excludes the other figures that inhabit the fresco.
Did Raphael cease preparation at that point or did he take it
further? The argument is open, but if this was as far as his
preparation went, then he presumably allowed his assistant(s)
space to invent other figures. Only the *David Beheading Goliath*
can properly be called a sketch, but we have nearly thirty
modelli (the precise number is disputed) for the narratives

147 *Modello* for *Moses Receiving the Tables of the Law*, 1516–17

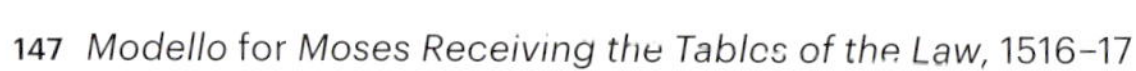

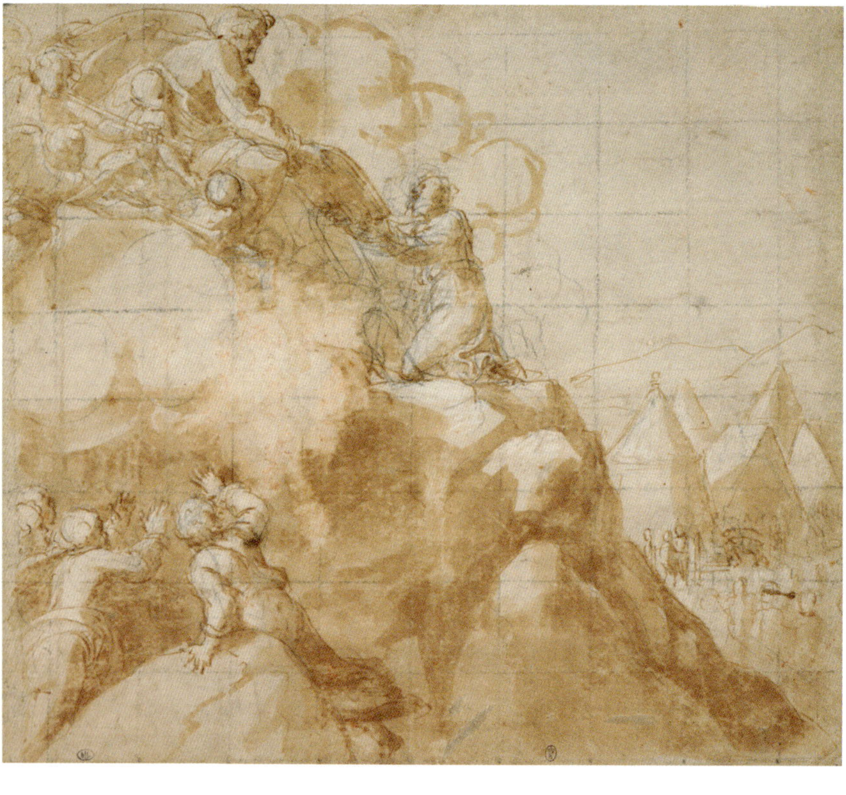

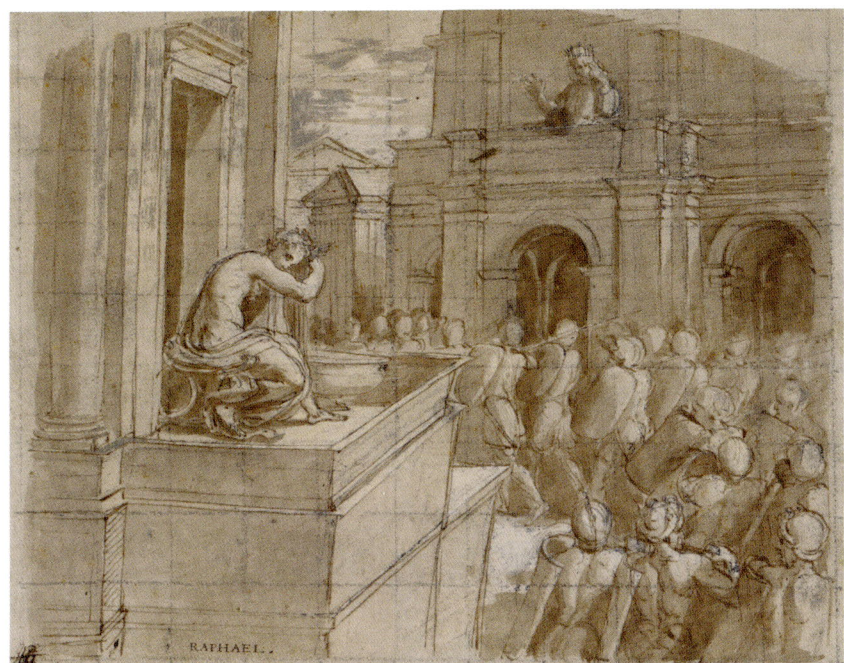

148 Gianfrancesco Penni after Raphael, *modello* for *David and Bathsheba*, 1516–17

in the vaults. They are of a relatively constant size and many
are squared for enlargement. The majority are in brush and
wash with bodycolour over black chalk outlining, although
there are several others – also similar in size – in pen. Leaving
aside the latter, the question imposes itself: what is the status
of these drawings? There would be general agreement about
their function but their authorship is disputed.

Traditionally, they have been attributed to one of Raphael's
assistants, and the weight of opinion has – or had – fallen on
Penni. The handling of wash, although efficient, is simplified,
and the same is true of the application of bodycolour. The black
chalk underdrawing is minimally inventive and demonstrates
few *pentimenti* of any significance. The modelling of figures
is generally competent, but they are rarely convincingly three-
dimensional. There is one exception, however. In *Moses
Receiving the Tables of the Law*, successive positions of the
tablets, the energy with which Moses and the Eternal are
sketched, the astonishment of the onlookers, and the fluency
and evocative atmospherics of the wash strongly suggest
the mind and the hand of Raphael. But none of the other
modelli displays such verve. This begs the question, are they

all by the same hand, with different intensities of realisation acknowledged, or is *The Moses* a special case, with all the others to be allocated to a different (and implicitly lesser) artistic mind and hand? In recent years there has been a strong move to give all the *modelli en bloc* to Raphael. And since their style, handling and technique are indissolubly linked with those of many other *modelli*, these too have drifted towards Raphael, even when they fall well below his inventiveness and focus. But once a drawing such as *The David and Bathsheba* is given to Raphael, the rest inevitably follow, and the critic is forced to accept as autograph drawings manifestly clumsy in arrangement and pedestrian in execution.

In this writer's view, the drawings in question, save *The Moses*, are all by Penni and show constant characteristics. This style and hand can be seen as far back as the compositional studies for the Stanza di Eliodoro and the Chigi Chapel in Santa Maria della Pace and define one of Penni's key functions: a secretary and fair-copyist who brought his master's sketches to usable form. In the Loggia his drawings served as the intermediary between the ideator, Raphael, and the various executants. It was not for nothing that Penni was nicknamed 'Il Fattore', that is, 'the Factor', or organiser and administrator.

A few of the *modelli* for vault scenes are in pen: most also seem to be by Penni, whose pen drawings related to the Loggia reflect the rougher pen style practised by Raphael at the end of his Florentine period, when Penni no doubt joined him – a style that Penni also carried into other drawings. But the pen *modello* for *The Triumph of David* (Budapest, Museum of Fine Arts) is more precise, with tighter hatching, and lyrical in its line; since this is a fresco that Vasari gave expressly to Perino del Vaga, that drawing may be by him. The fluency and decorative integration of figures, the subtlety of the pen work, and the delicacy with which white bodycolour has been applied, in individual strokes rather than in patches with a loaded brush, are distinctive of Perino. The matter is open, but some overlap between Penni and Perino is to be expected: Perino subsequently married Penni's sister, and it seems that the two were beginning to form a subgroup within Raphael's studio. The surviving *modelli* for the scenes in the *basamento* show a comparable situation, with both brush and wash and pen employed. One of the former – by Penni, for *The Resurrection* (Chatsworth, Devonshire Collection) – was reproduced by Ugo da Carpi in a same-size chiaroscuro woodcut.

After he completed his share of the Loggia, it is likely that Perino worked outside the Vatican, perhaps with Raphael's recommendation, and painted schemes in various palaces and churches. His frescoes in the Palazzo Baldassini are probably of 1519, like those in the chapel in San Marcello al Corso, now destroyed. But he did make designs for the Cappella degli Svizzeri in Santa Maria della Pietà, in the Vatican, which was executed largely by Polidoro. However, Polidoro soon formed a partnership with the Florentine Maturino, and until 1527 – interrupted by a sojourn in Naples in 1524 – they and, inevitably, their team decorated the façades of nearly fifty Roman palaces with powerful and dramatic frescoes. Polidoro, Maturino and their teams made publicly available the Roman relief style that Raphael had developed in his last years, although it is only by a stretch that Polidoro's façades could be called Raphaelesque. Their vigour and drama made a considerable impression on Rubens. Polidoro also pioneered a kind of genre realism that had little to do with Raphael, which played a larger part in his art when, after the Sack of Rome, he moved to Naples and then to Sicily.

Following his own part in the Loggia, or perhaps overlapping with it, Giovanni da Udine would have executed the framework of the Psyche Loggia. Still in 1519, he frescoed the lowest loggia of the Vatican entirely to his own design, which comprised foliage without figures. He had completed it by December and then began work in the great Loggia of the Villa Madama where, perhaps, Perino may have assisted him. At the completion of his work there, probably in 1520 or early 1521, Giovanni was rejoined by Perino, and the two collaborated on the Sala dei Pontefici, a large room on the floor below the Sala di Costantino.

Chapter 10
The Psyche Loggia

Raphael, in common with his contemporaries, had relatively few opportunities to create paintings of mythical subjects or moralising narratives from ancient history. But when he did so, he seems to have felt that a relief format was most appropriate. This allowed him to evoke the most familiar kind of antique survival and to create compositions in which spatial depth was not an issue and in which forms could be arranged, rhythmically or not, across a surface. And within such a sculptural format he could create semi-independent figures, sometimes of great beauty, often based on classical statues.

In the two simulated reliefs added below the *Parnassus*, following Leo's accession, Raphael painted subjects evoking the respect of kings and emperors for poetry: Alexander preserves the books of Homer, and Augustus prevents the burning of Virgil's *Aeneid*. But both subjects were virtually without precedent, and Raphael's fluent and graceful designs do not allude directly to antique prototypes. A year or two later, however, in an exercise at once archaeological and experimental, Raphael reconstructed a complex multi-figure Roman relief of *The Judgment of Paris*, sharpening its narrative and adding further figures. *The Judgment* is known only in one of Marcantonio's most elaborate and widely influential engravings, and we have no preparatory drawings. Whether *The Judgment* was planned for realisation in painting is conjectural. But in its format and the elaboration of its design it could serve as a pendent to an ill-fated painting projected for the court of Ferrara.

Raphael's *Indian Triumph of Bacchus* was to be one of a suite of canvases of mythological subjects commissioned by Alfonso d'Este (1476–1534) for his *studiolo* in the Castello Estense in Ferrara. Alfonso, following the lead of his sister, Isabella d'Este

149

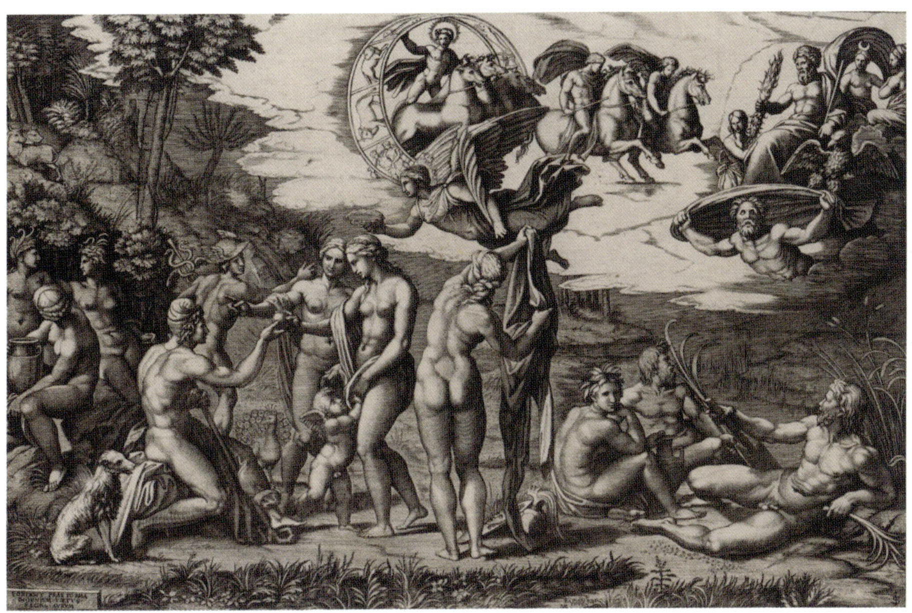

149 Marcantonio Raimondi after Raphael, *The Judgment of Paris*, c. 1514–15

(1474–1539), marchioness of Mantua, wanted to have a gallery of diverse talents and ordered paintings from the most prestigious artists: Giovanni Bellini, Dosso Dossi, Fra Bartolommeo and Michelangelo, as well as Raphael. But in the event only Bellini (in 1514) and Dosso delivered their paintings, and Dosso's is lost. The history of the commission was fraught. Fra Bartolommeo died in 1517, leaving only preparatory drawings for his scene, and Michelangelo failed to deliver a painting, although he did make some drawings for a Bacchanal, whose purpose went unrecognised until recently. The scheme was finally completed by Titian, who had not been part of the original commission but who painted variants of the subjects commissioned from the Frate, Raphael and Michelangelo.

Raphael seems to have become involved in the project late in 1514: he received an advance of 50 ducats in December and may already have sent a *modello* to Ferrara for approval. However, he failed to follow it with a painting, to the increasing ire of Alfonso who, probably out of frustration, commissioned in 1517 a version of Raphael's design from Pellegrino da San Daniele. Pellegrino's painting, which is lost, was not intended to substitute Raphael's in the *studiolo*, but Alfonso's faux pas allowed Raphael to temporise further. He decided to prepare an alternative, *The Hunt of Meleager*; but if this reached *modello*

stage, we have no record of it. The radical change of subject
implies that the commission was iconographically flexible.
After Raphael's death Alfonso was adamant in recovering
his advance.

150   Raphael's *Indian Triumph* is known from an eighteenth-
century print after a now lost *modello* by Penni. Numerous
sixteenth-century echoes, drawn and painted, including
a large and magnificent adaptation by Garofalo in Dresden,
testify to its effect. It is an elaborate composition with a large
cast, synthesising several antique Bacchic reliefs although
following none directly. The individual figures are given a
statuary independence and display a great variety of poses.
Raphael adroitly included many incidents and elements. As
a collector of antique sculpture, Agostino Chigi would have
been receptive to this neo-antique manner, and knowledge
of Raphael's design may have prompted him to commission
further decoration of the Farnesina in a related style.

Neglecting the unfinished Loggia di Galatea, which probably
reflected his unsuccessful pursuit of elevated marriage alliances,

150 Conrad Martin Metz after Gianfrancesco Penni after Raphael,
The Indian Triumph of Bacchus, 1798

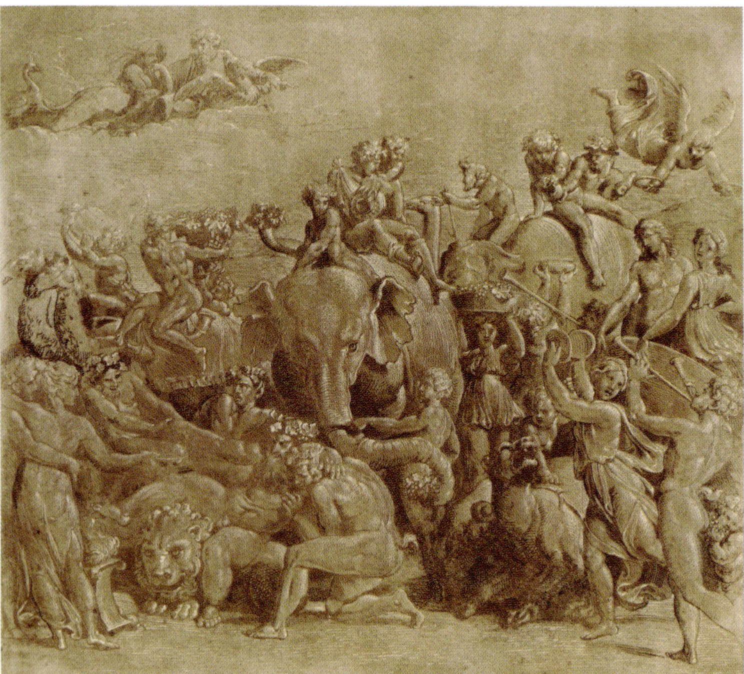

Agostino's creation of the Psyche Loggia sprang from his decision to marry his humbly born long-term mistress and the mother of his sons, Francesca Ordeaschi. Her social elevation was allegorised in the story of Psyche – or the soul – who, while earning the enmity of Venus for her beauty and the adoration that she receives, also earns the love of Venus's son, Cupid. After performing a series of tasks and penances imposed upon her by Venus, Psyche finally marries Cupid. The story is found in Apuleius's *Golden Ass* and could have been known to Raphael from the first modern edition, published in 1469, or from a poor translation published in 1478, but the salient episodes in the narrative could have been distilled for him by any competent scholar. There were also numerous adaptations, including one by Niccolò Machiavelli of 1517.

Agostino's forthcoming marriage occasioned a second scheme. Agostino's bedroom was frescoed by Sodoma with two episodes from the life of one of his heroes, Alexander the Great: *Alexander at the Tent of Darius* and *The Marriage of Alexander and Roxana*, which obviously refers to Agostino and Francesca. The central section is based, probably via an intermediary *modello*, on a drawing that, unusually, seems to be a joint work by Raphael and Giulio Romano. This includes the anchor figures of Alexander and Roxana, surrounded by playful *amorini*, and was in part drawn from models, whose forms Giulio simplified. Whether Raphael furnished the design out of friendship – either to Sodoma or Chigi – or whether he himself planned to execute the fresco but, pressed for time, handed it to Sodoma is an open question. Sodoma added the right-hand section, in which Alexander (alias Chigi), enamoured of Roxana, rejects the homosexuality represented by the nude youth. The left-hand section quotes the water-carrier from Raphael's *Incendio*.

The Psyche Loggia was probably begun in mid-1518. The vault was uncovered, seemingly in its present form, in late December and was promptly derided by Leonardo Sellaio, the common friend of Sebastiano and Michelangelo. He wrote to Michelangelo on New Year's Day 1519 that it was even worse than the Stanza dell'Incendio. According to Vasari, who was probably informed by Pietro Aretino, Agostino's protégé at the time and a member of his household, Raphael had been distracted by his love for a young woman (presumably the Fornarina) and was dilatory in fulfilling the commission. Only once she had been installed in the Farnesina did he set to work. But while this might account for slow progress before December 1518, it does not explain why work did not proceed in 1519 on the lunettes and walls. The unfinished lunettes are seen

151

152

153–55

151 BELOW Sodoma, *The Marriage of Alexander and Roxana*, 1517–18
152 BOTTOM Raphael and Giulio Romano, study for the *Marriage of Alexander and Roxana*, probably 1517
153 OPPOSITE Raphael and assistants, the Psyche Loggia, 1518

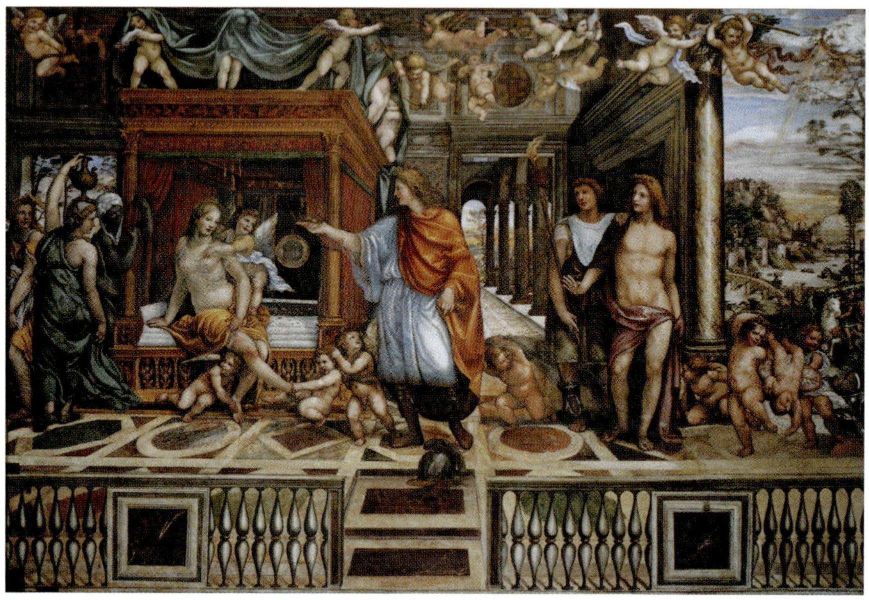

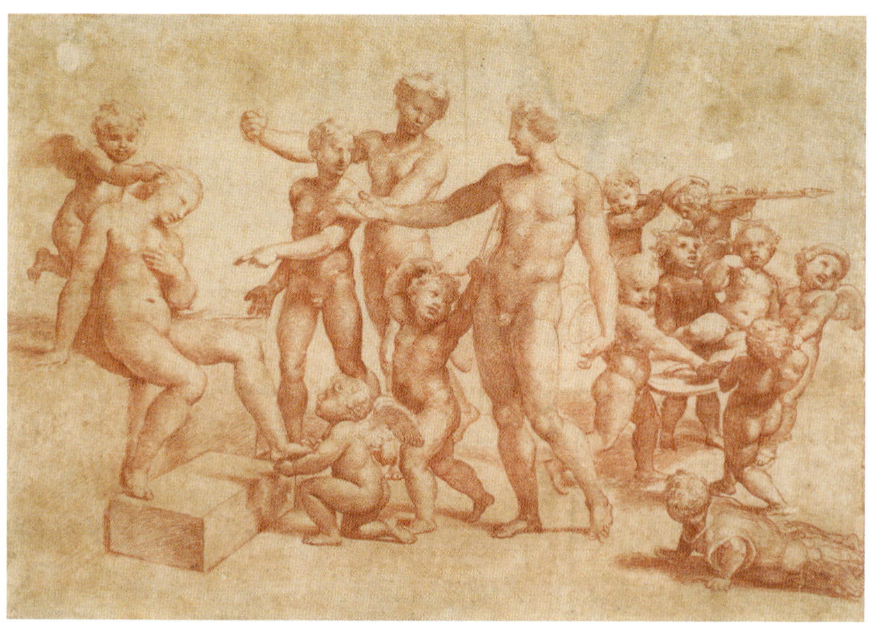

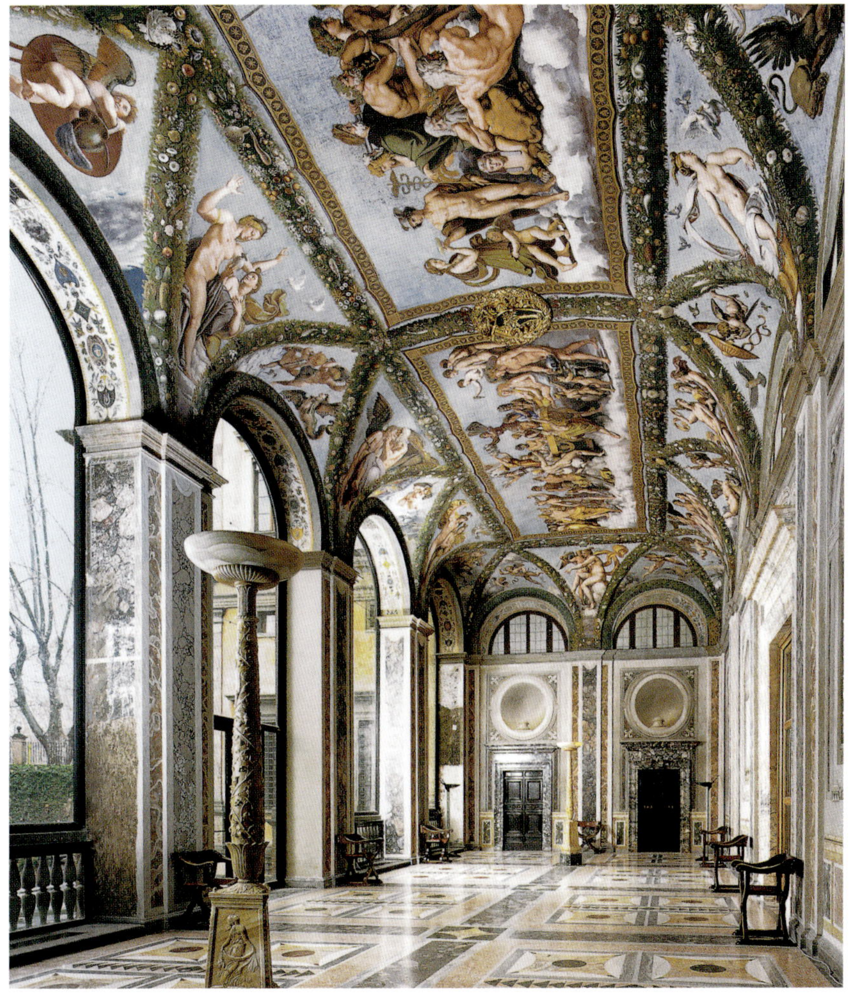

in three engravings of pendentive compositions cut by
Marcantonio, most likely in 1519, which show raw brickwork,
evidently – and deliberately – documenting work arrested. The
unfinished parts were probably concealed by hangings when
the marriage of Agostino and Francesca was celebrated on
28 August 1519. A wedding banquet accompanied by festivities
was held in the loggia, attended by Leo X and several cardinals.

Raphael's scheme is sophisticated. The loggia was the main
entrance to the villa and was open to the garden, and Raphael
took this as a starting point. The decoration links interior and
exterior: the vegetation of the garden enters the loggia and

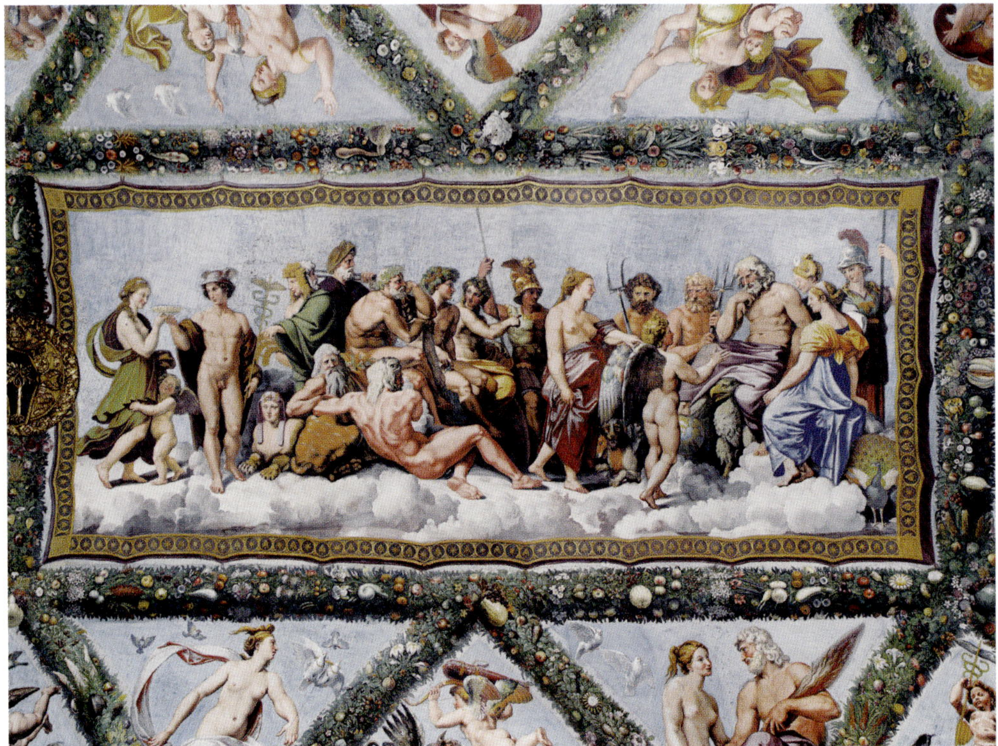

154 Raphael and assistants, the Psyche Loggia, Ceiling Narratives: *The Council of the Gods*

transforms a permanent space into a temporary one. And the bucolic air is appropriate to a loggia that contains the most extensive display of female nudes up to that time in Central Italy. One can only speculate whether Raphael was prompted by report of the nudes on the Fondaco dei Tedeschi in Venice, painted in 1508–09 by Giorgione and Titian, which Agostino Chigi would have seen during his stay in Venice in 1511.

Two large scenes occupy the central area of the vault: *Mercury Presenting Psyche with the Cup of Immortality* before introducing her to the gods; and *The Wedding Feast of Cupid and Psyche*. The figural assemblages are represented as if made up of freestanding sculpture arranged in extended reliefs; they include some direct citations of Roman statuary and others invented in a Roman mode. But the figures do not simulate sculpture: they are human forms in statuary poses. Paradoxically, these statuesque forms are presented as if painted on canvases stretched across a framework replicating an arbour adorned with vegetables

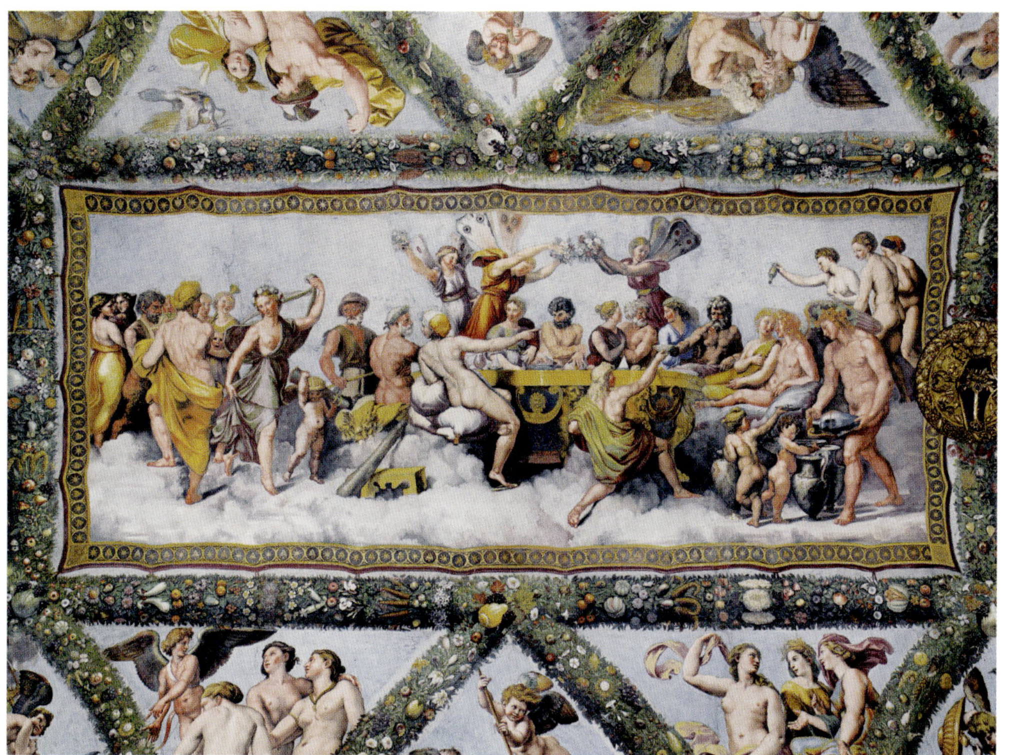

155 Raphael and assistants, the Psyche Loggia, Ceiling Narratives: *Marriage of Cupid and Psyche*

and fruits. This structure was painted by Giovanni da Udine, who presumably compiled his own herbarium, for his vegetation contains many botanically accurate forms. In employing the conceit of an arbour with awnings, Raphael was once more making play with different levels of reality, reprising his invention of 1514 in the Stanza di Eliodoro with the difference that here the effect is that of a temporary marquee.

At the arbour's sides, in the severies, Raphael shows open sky in which *putti* gambol, adding to the festive atmosphere: he was perhaps recalling those included in the first project for *Parnassus* but omitted from the fresco. They either hold attributes of the gods or playfully interact with creatures associated with them. They are among the most vivacious and best-executed elements of the scheme, and their treatment is comedic and light-hearted: indeed, although much of the painting in the Psyche Loggia is substandard, there is a consistent level of wit. The heaviness of the forms is

156

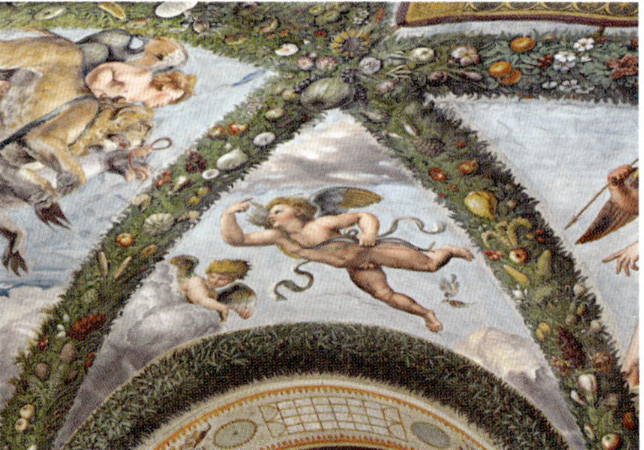

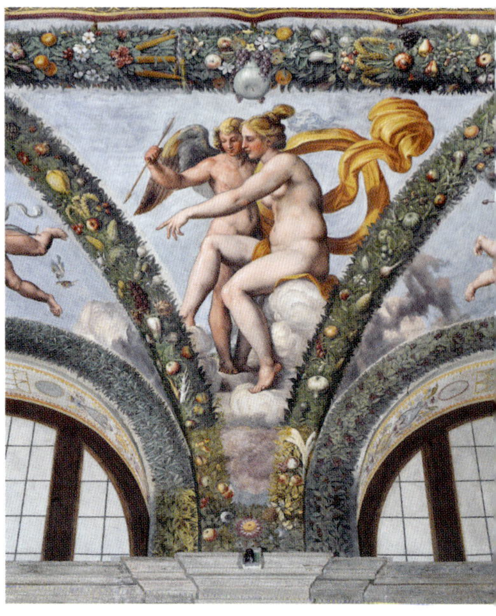

156 ABOVE Compartment with a *putto* carrying the arms of Cupid
157 RIGHT Assistant of Raphael (Giulio Romano?), pendentive with Venus pointing downwards
158 OPPOSITE LEFT Giulio Romano, *Psyche carried by Mercury to Olympus*
159 OPPOSITE RIGHT Marcantonio Raimondi after Raphael, *Mercury Introducing the Story of Cupid and Psyche*

counterbalanced by a suffusing lightness of tone, and at times one can be reminded of the French Rococo.

The figure style of the ten pendentives too is based on Roman sculpture, but less directly than the vault scenes, and their setting is indeterminate: neither open sky nor fictive tapestry. The pendentives, separated from the severies by garlands (also by Giovanni), contain episodes that take place in the heavens. Only two treat Psyche herself: her presentation of the ointment pot to Venus, and her ascent to Olympus in the arms of Mercury. The others show either the gods' reactions to Psyche or related aspects of Apuleius's narrative. Chronologically, the story proceeds clockwise from the pendentive on the east wall, in which Venus points downwards in annoyance to what is happening on earth, through to Psyche's elevation. The sequence is interrupted by the extraordinary figure of Mercury in the pendentive on the west wall, where he acts as a herald or master of ceremonies and gestures towards a symbolic representation of sexual intercourse, half-concealed in foliage.

The scenes in the pendentives would have been coordinated with those in the six lunettes. We know Raphael's intentions for only one of them: a counterproof of a drawing at Chatsworth shows a nude woman, presumably Psyche, carried by the winds, framed within a lunette. She occupies the entire field and is

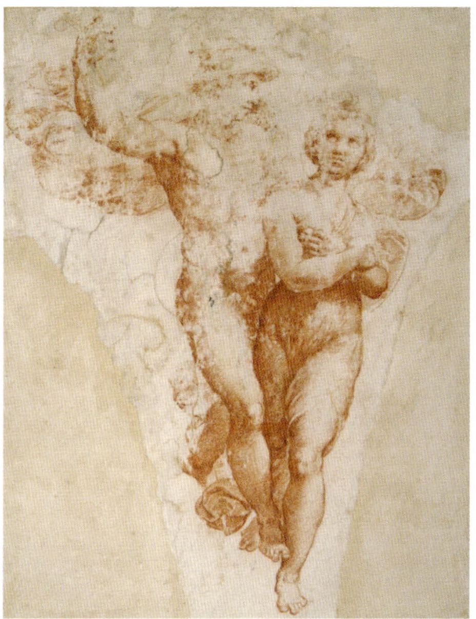

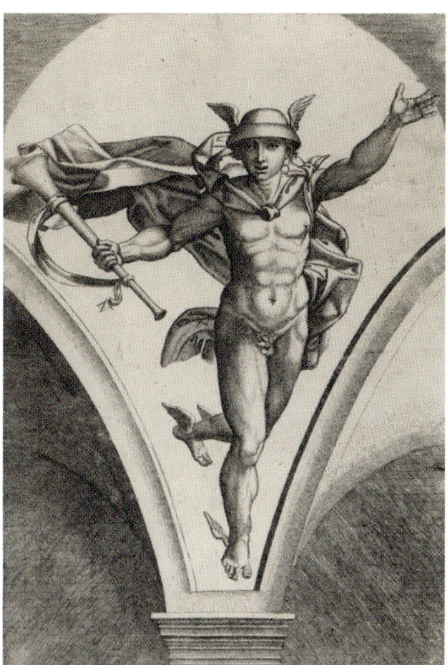

on a scale equivalent to the pendentive figures; it is unlikely
that any of the lunettes were intended to contain more than
two figures.

Finally, there are eight rectangular fields on the walls:
four, nearly square, above the doors at east and west; and
four tall rectangles, two either side of the entrance door,
on the long south wall that faces the garden. These would
have been frescoed with episodes taking place on the earth
or in Cupid's palace, in which Psyche is installed. Only one
episode is recorded: a poor, later engraving shows Psyche
at her toilet with her maidservants, but two nude studies
for this composition, one by Raphael) and one after him
(Paris, Louvre), establish its reliability. The proportions of
the engraving, which was probably made from a lost *modello*,
match those of the tall compartments.

Other than a small pen sketch that lays out a first idea
of Psyche presenting the vase to Venus (Oxford, Ashmolean),
there are no secure compositional sketches, and all the drawings
for the project known either in the original or in counterproof
(one in both) are in red chalk. The majority are of single figures
or small groups of between one and three figures, but one
drawing, surviving only in part (Paris, Fondation Custodia) but
known complete in an early copy, originally showed the whole
figural complement of *Psyche's Introduction to the Gods*. Another

160
161

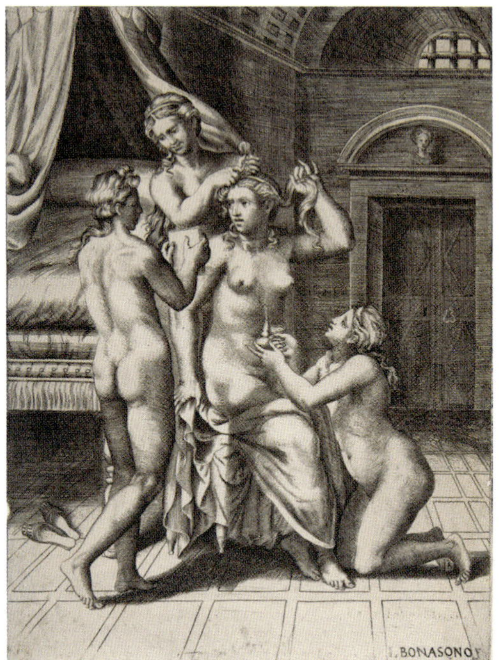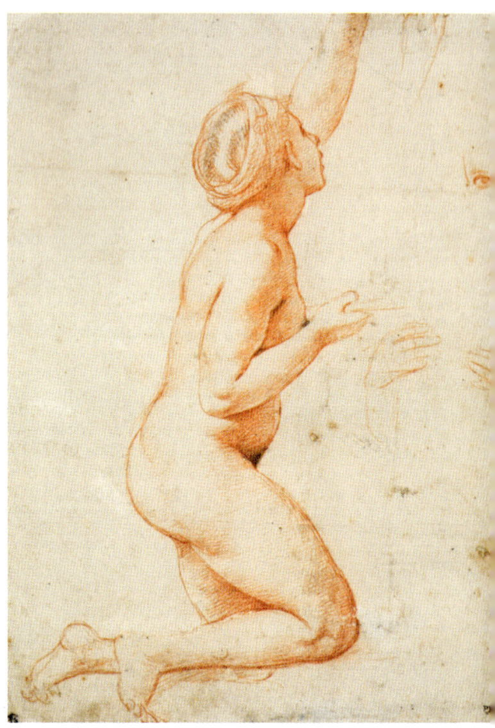

160 ABOVE LEFT Giulio Bonasone after Raphael, *The Toilet of Psyche*, c. 1540
161 ABOVE RIGHT Study for a *Kneeling Maidservant for The Toilet of Psyche*, 1518

is known for the left-most group, whose relatively stony surfaces, lack of fluency in formal relations and limited range of facial expressions indicate Giulio's authorship (Munich, Graphische Sammlung). Giulio made most of the other drawings: one of Omphale seen from the rear in *The Wedding Feast* shows him at his most accomplished, but his insecure command of anatomy is obvious in the position of her head and neck. Passages of sensitive and undulating hatching on her back effectively conjure up flesh textures, but the exterior hatchings that establish the contour of her right leg are awkward and reveal a lesser draughtsman, technically and emotionally, than Raphael. It should be compared with Raphael's study of the kneeling maidservant.

The figures in the Psyche Loggia – particularly those in the pendentives – haunted later artists. They present a series of fluent and graceful inventions that perfectly fill the spaces, and borrowings from them recur constantly in later Western art. But it was their design rather than their

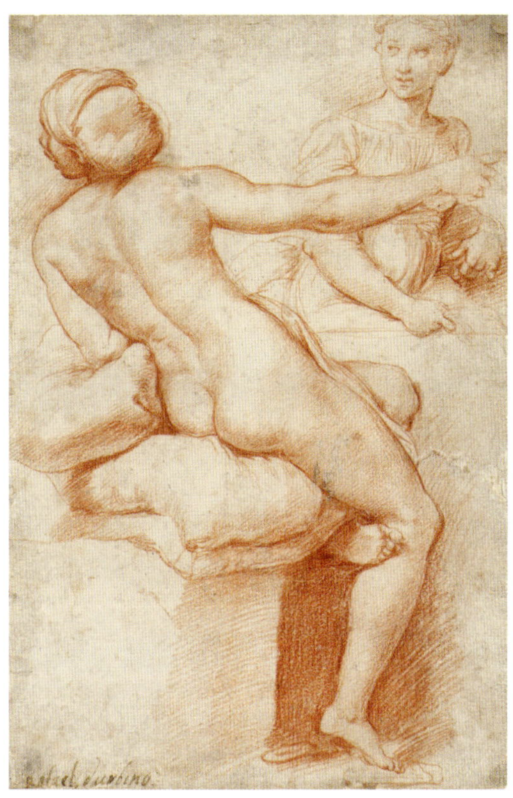

execution that impressed, for rather little of the Psyche
Loggia shows Raphael's hand. Leonardo Sellaio's remark
might be shrugged off as jealous animadversions, but Vasari,
who made every effort to see the best in what Raphael did,
criticised the frescoes strongly. He attributed their weaknesses
to Raphael's employment of pupils but did not know, it seems,
that pupil collaboration was extensive in the design stages.

Raphael had learnt lessons from the failure of the Stanza
dell'Incendio and ensured an overall stylistic and formal
coherence, working side by side with Giulio – and to a lesser
extent with Penni – in the preparatory stages. But he did
not control, still less correct, either their drawings or their
cartoons; and even allowing for the frescoes' condition it is
hard to accept that he worked more than fitfully on them, and
then mostly in the severies. The quality of what was executed,
plus the evident deferral – or abandonment – of the scheme,
further supports the contention that Raphael was losing
interest in *buon fresco*.

Chapter 11
Moveable Paintings I

I

From his arrival in Rome in 1508 until *c.* 1514, Raphael's primary preoccupation was mural painting; in 1515–16 the tapestry cartoons took precedence. Inevitably, his output of moveable paintings declined, and those that he executed, stylistically and conceptually, were adjuncts to, or local developments from, his work in fresco.

This was notably so with portraiture. Portraits were included liberally in Raphael's frescoes in the Segnatura and the Eliodoro, and he was obviously fluent in seizing likenesses. Independent portraits could be produced relatively quickly without disrupting Raphael's official work and, according to Vasari, he executed many: several among those that he mentions are lost or unidentified, as is a portrait of the young Federico Gonzaga (1500–40), in armour, mentioned by Castiglione in a letter of early 1521. This letter, incidentally, confirms that Raphael did paint Federico, for the correspondence about the commission in January–February 1513 implied that Raphael had put it aside.

Members of the papal court and associates of the pope were obvious candidates for portraiture, and one of the most famous and inventive portraits is that of the papal librarian, philosopher, actor and perhaps Raphael's iconographic advisor, Tommaso 'Fedra' Inghirami (1470–1516). Seated at his desk, Tommaso glances upwards, a pose that simultaneously disguises his wall eye and evokes his search for inspiration – an idea perhaps derived from Signorelli's frescoed portrait of Virgil at Orvieto, but also a by-product of *The School of Athens*, with its gallery of intellectual processes.

163

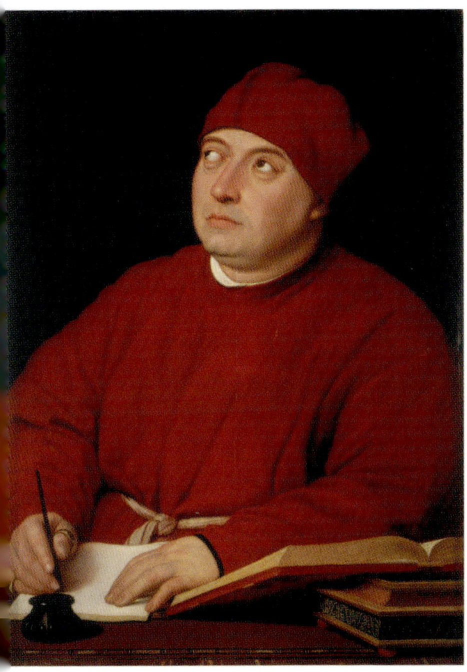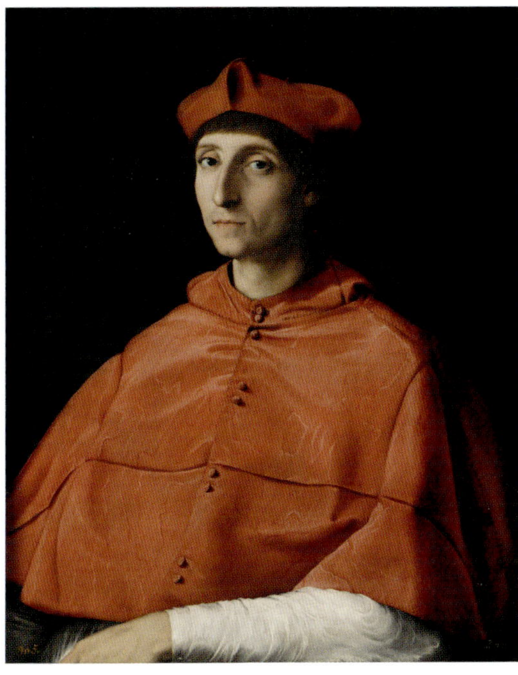

163 ABOVE LEFT *Tommaso Inghirami,* probably 1510
164 ABOVE RIGHT *Cardinal Francesco Alidosi (?),* 1510–11

164 More conventional is an unidentified *Cardinal,* which is probably a portrait of Julius's favourite, Francesco Alidosi (1455–1511), murdered in a fit of rage by the pope's nephew Francesco Maria della Rovere. He is arranged in a contained pyramid – a formula that proved very influential – which serves as a plinth for his refined features: pale, and with an aquiline nose. Here, Raphael's care went into the painting's exceptional surface refinement and the shimmering drapery, which evokes the sitter's intelligence as well as his status. Its execution probably coincided with that of *The Decretals* in the Segnatura.

165 166 Some of Raphael's independent portraits are connected to those that appear in the frescoes. Thus those of *Julius* himself and of *Cardinal Alessandro Farnese* (1468–1549), later to become Pope Paul III (1534–49), are both related to *The Decretals,* in which Alessandro stands beside Julius. Raphael invented for Alessandro a three-quarter-length format, the distant ancestor of the cinematic *plan américain.* Alessandro presents a letter – a motif found in Mantegna's Camera degli Sposi – directly to the viewer, who becomes a proxy for the recipient, perhaps Julius himself. It is tempting to think that Alessandro's portrait was

conceived to hang opposite one of the pope so that they would enact in painting their relation in life. But this would not have been the National Gallery's *Julius II*, which is of 1511, whereas the *Alessandro* was painted *c.* 1509–10.

The moveable portrait of Julius no doubt succeeds his frescoed portrait. That is a public statement, whereas the portrait is private, showing Julius isolated – even trapped – in the corner of a room, disconsolate and contemplative, closed in on himself. It is an astonishing picture that evokes a moment of despondency when Julius's plans seemed to be foundering. An absolute novelty as an image of a reigning pope in a private moment, without attendants, it is ground-breaking too as a representation of uncomfortable private emotion in portraiture. Raphael seems to have had the pope's pose firmly in mind from the beginning, but he made radical changes to the setting, eliminating a golden cloth of honour bearing papal arms and

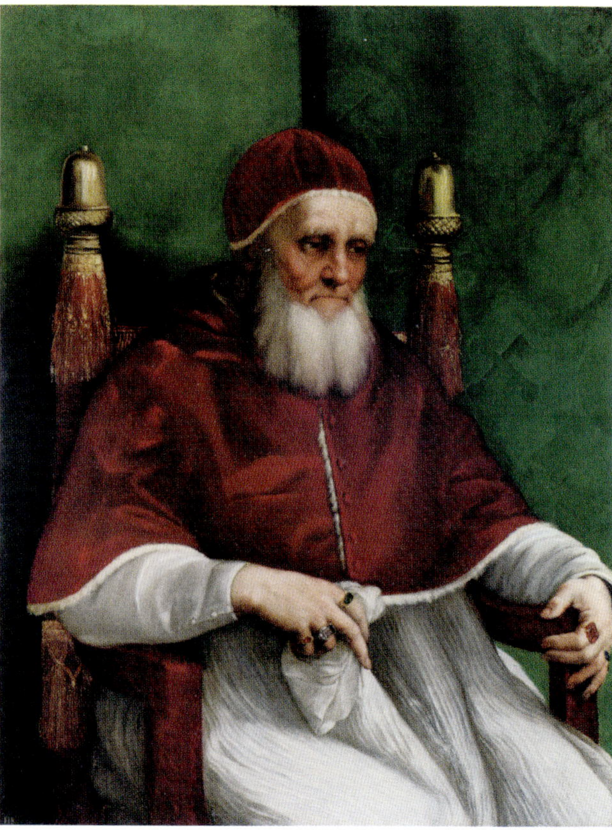

165 LEFT
Julius II, mid-1511
166 OPPOSITE
Cardinal Alessandro Farnese, 1509–10. Alessandro Farnese became Pope Paul III in 1534; see figure 222

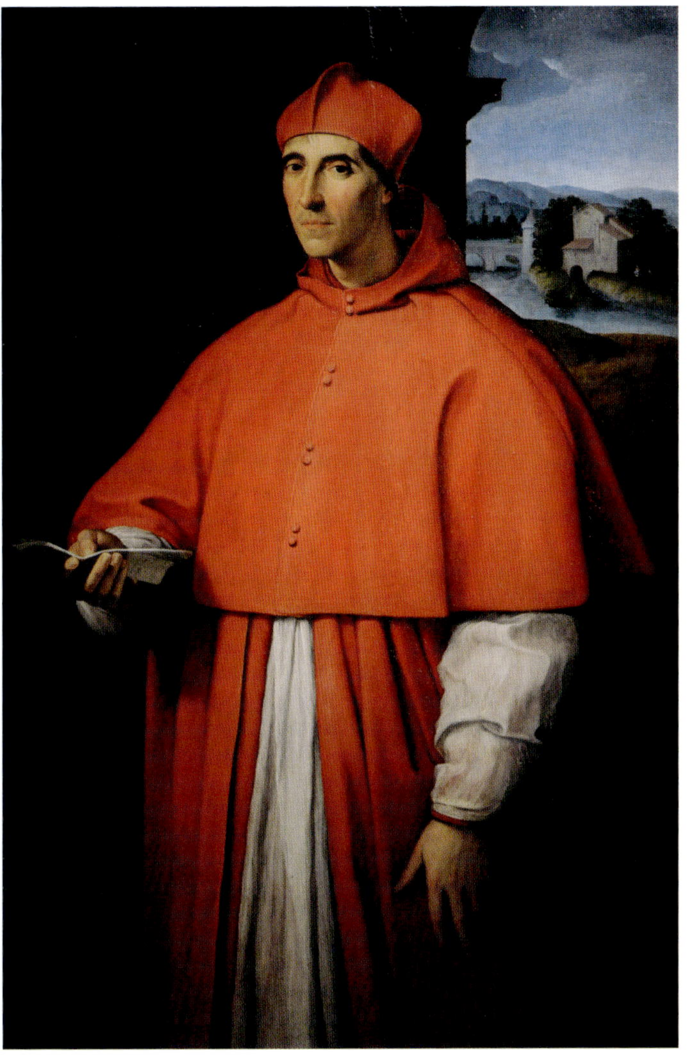

replacing it with the bright green hanging that intensifies
the reds of Julius's *camauro* and *mozzetta*. The portrait is first
mentioned in September 1513. At that time it was placed on the
high altar of Santa Maria del Popolo – apparently temporarily –
and reportedly commissioned by Julius. Whether or not it was
debatable, but it seems highly unlikely that it was intended for
a public place.

Between 1508 and 1513 Raphael executed a few small
devotional pictures, perhaps for powerful Roman families,

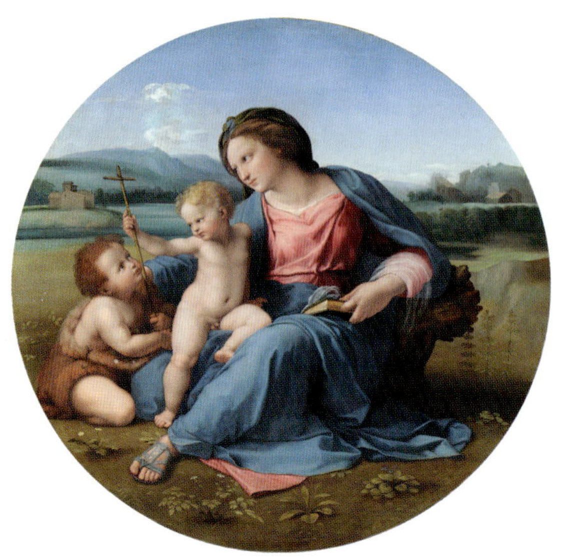

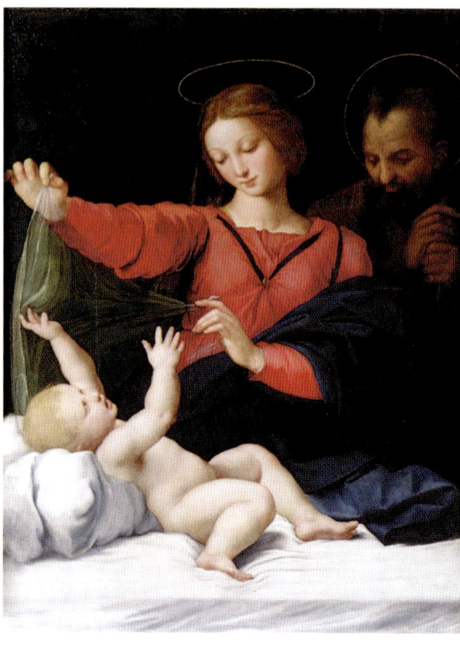

167 ABOVE *The Virgin and Child with St John*
(The Alba *Madonna*), probably 1509
168 RIGHT *The Holy Family (The Madonna
di Loreto)*, probably 1510

important members of the papal court and, possibly, friends.
But we do not know who commissioned or received such
paintings as the Aldobrandini *Madonna* (London, National
Gallery), the Alba *Madonna*, *The Madonna della Sedia* or
The Madonna della Tenda (Munich, Alte Pinakothek). The
first two, to judge from their colour and tone, were executed
contemporaneously – perhaps simultaneously – and probably
date from 1509. Both pictures continue preoccupations seen in
Raphael's later Florentine work – the Alba, for example, is set
in an open landscape like that of *St Catherine* – and both have
colouristic and formal links with the *Parnassus*. The Alba was
little known and may have been exported early from Rome,
but the Aldobrandini *Madonna*, seemingly set at twilight, in
a Roman suburb, probably remained in the metropolis, for its
composition was employed by Sebastiano in the Borgherini
Holy Family (London, National Gallery).

Distinctively different is *The Madonna di Loreto*, so called
because it hung in Santa Maria del Popolo adjacent to the
chapel of Agostino Chigi, which has that dedication. It may
be that Chigi commissioned it. On public view, it was widely
copied and, once again, its composition was reworked by
Sebastiano in two later Holy Families. In facial type and
costume the Virgin resembles the personification of *Justice*

in the vault of the Segnatura and may have been painted at the end of 1509, the date on an old copy. Like the Aldobrandini *Madonna*, it was prepared in a series of exquisite metalpoint drawings on pink paper, a support that Raphael used frequently between *c.* 1508–10 but not much thereafter. Set in a dark interior, sharply illuminated to attract the viewer's gaze, the iconography is bold and original: the Child propels himself upwards to greet his mother as she lifts the veil – perhaps proleptic of his shroud – from him with an outstretched right arm that protrudes strikingly into the viewer's space.

In Florence, Raphael had devised Madonnas in sequences, but each of Raphael's Roman Madonnas is different, and his next, of 1512–13, is radically unlike the paintings of 1509 and 1510. Among Raphael's supreme masterpieces, it is the *ne plus ultra* of tondo composition. *The Madonna della Sedia* incomparably fuses human and divine: the Virgin looks outward at the viewer, and the Child's expression seems apprehensive, as though a stranger had just entered the room. While not overtly Michelangelesque, it reflects his powerful compression and confident domination of the picture surface. Simultaneously it pursues a Florentine Quattrocento theme, taking up the outward-looking Virgin tried by Filippo Lippi in his *Madonna* in Munich – a painting that had earlier influenced Leonardo. But Raphael's vision has a new immediacy: it is easy to understand why he was thought to have seized upon a group, observed by chance, of a young woman and her child.

The full-figured Virgin's voluminous Roman costume and the domesticity implied by her rich chair (like that in the portrait of Julius) show that it comes from the same moment as two metalpoint drawings (fig. 169 and Chatsworth, Devonshire Collection) – both engraved by an associate of Marcantonio – of mothers and children in domestic interiors, with their poignant closeness of mother and child. There is also an obvious overlap of types with the women and children at the lower left of *The Bolsena*.

The Sedia probably left Raphael's studio immediately upon completion. Giulio Romano based two Madonnas of *c.* 1515 and *c.* 1517 on it (Paris, Louvre; London, Apsley House), but while he knew the design he probably did not know the painting, for his colours and textures differ radically. Vasari was unaware of *The Sedia*, and it is without recorded history before it appears in a Medici inventory in 1589. But early cloistering was more than compensated by *The Sedia*'s incalculable effect on later art, particularly in the eighteenth and nineteenth centuries, when it served as a reference point for the portraiture of mothers and children. It became an academic icon – Ingres, famously,

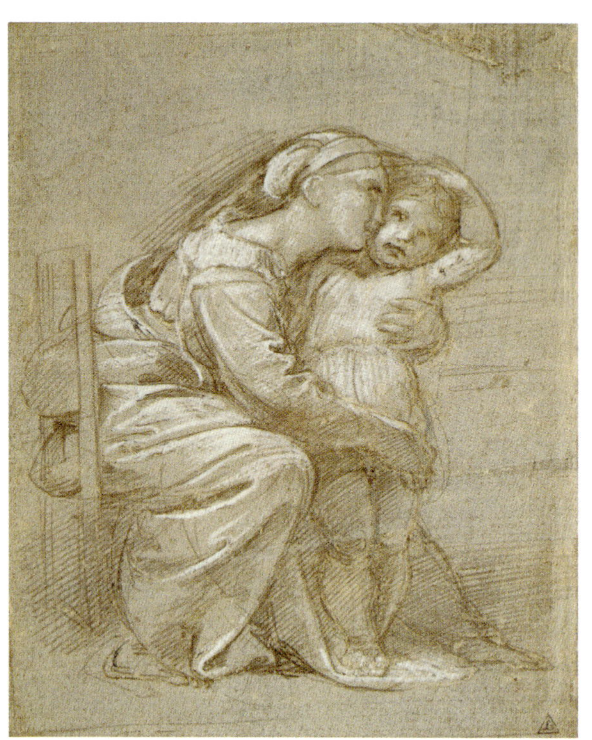

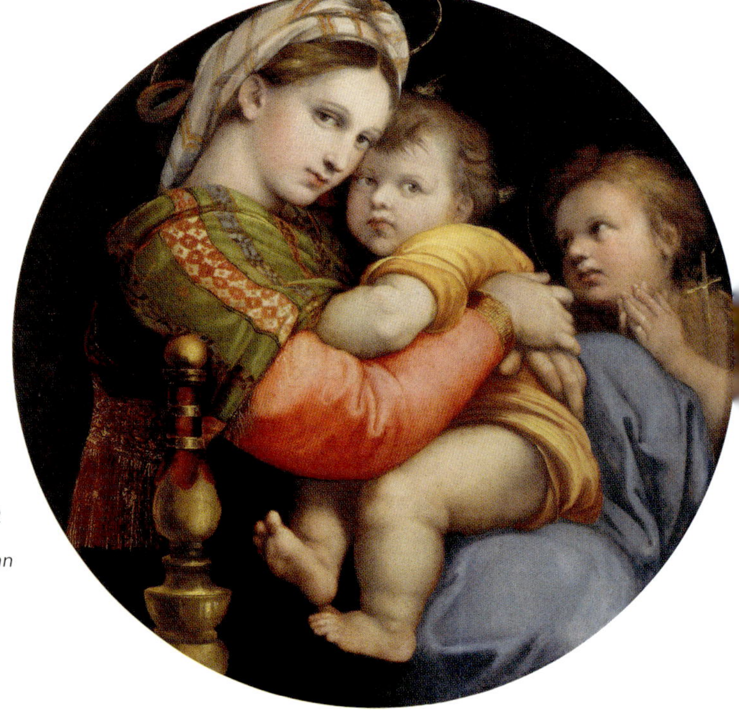

169 ABOVE *A Mother Embracing a Child (or The Virgin and Child)*, probably 1512
170 RIGHT *The Virgin and Child with St John (The Madonna della Sedia)*, 1512–13

revered it and quoted it frequently in his work – such that some artists reacted against it. Pierre-Auguste Renoir visited the Palazzo Pitti in 1881, expecting to find the *Madonna della Sedia* artificial and risible. Instead, he reports, he was startled to find the most straightforward and solid piece of painting imaginable, and the experience brought about a radical change in his art.

II

During this period Raphael executed two altarpieces. The larger and earlier, at least in design, is the so-called *Madonna di Foligno*, commissioned by the historian and papal official Sigismondo dei Conti (1432–1512) for the high altar of Santa Maria in Aracoeli. Most Roman altarpieces were in fresco, and Raphael's was unusual in being on panel (now transferred to canvas). Raphael's other moveable altarpieces were commissioned for sites outside Rome, and it is ironic that the single altarpiece planned and painted for a Roman church remained *in situ* only until 1565, when it was transferred to Foligno, dei Conti's native town.

The painting is specifically relevant to the Aracoeli. The Virgin and Child, set against a golden sun, allude to the mystical vision of the Virgin and Child revealed by the Tiburtine Sibyl (according to the *Golden Legend*) to the Emperor Augustus on the Capitoline Hill, where the church is located. Sigismondo, kneeling at the right, is recommended to the Virgin and Child by St Jerome, patron of scholars, while the Baptist, standing at the left, presents the heavenly vision to the viewer. Placed centrally, looking upwards, a child angel holds a blank tablet.

The composition suggests that the picture was conceived nearer the beginning than the end of the Segnatura: in 1511, its design was a little out of date. It employs for the last time the cup-and-ball structure familiar from Raphael's early work, and there is some relation to Ghirlandaio's painting of *The Virgin Appearing to Sts Dominic, Michael, John the Baptist and John the Evangelist*, the centrepiece of his majestic ensemble, then on the high altar of Santa Maria Novella and one of the most famous paintings in Florence (Munich, Alte Pinakothek). The Virgin's pose follows loosely that of the Virgin in Leonardo's *Adoration*, and that of the Child recurs both in the vault of the Segnatura and in Santa Maria della Pace: it is based on Michelangelo's Doni Tondo. Both figures modified Raphael's initial idea for the group, seen in a soft black chalk drawing (London, British Museum) of, probably, 1510.

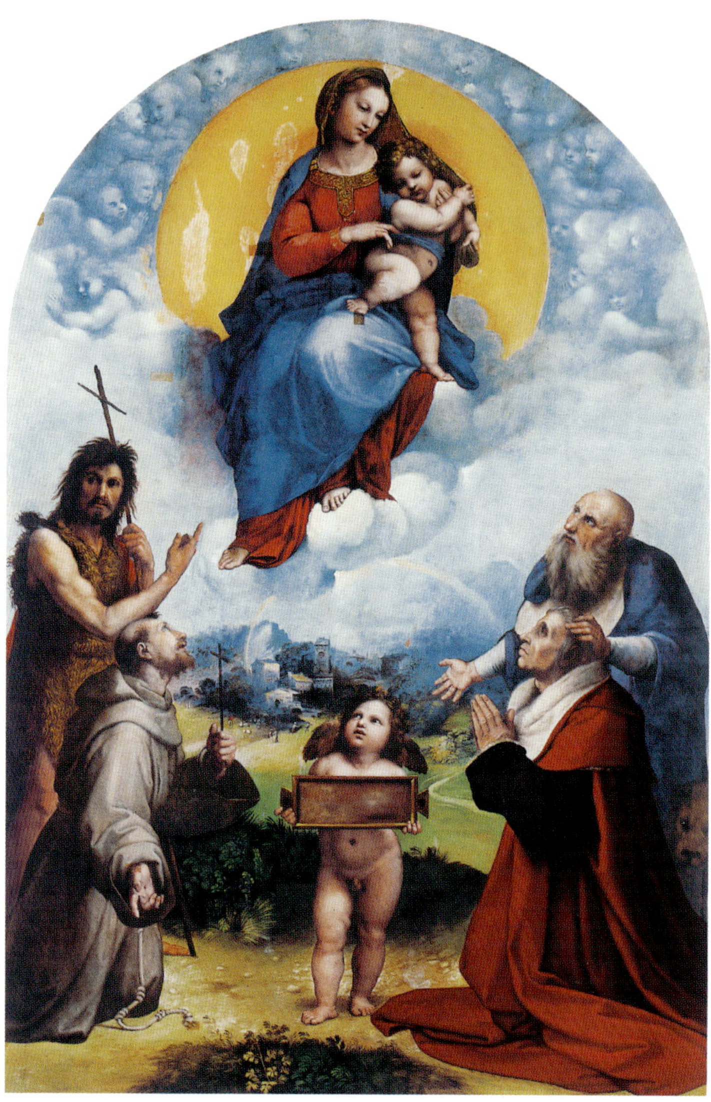

Various questions about *The Madonna di Foligno* remain unanswered. The Virgin and Child, as painted but in isolation, were reproduced in an engraving of exceptional refinement by Marcantonio that seems to be early. And the landscape has always intrigued scholars, for it resembles nothing by Raphael at any moment in its colours, its handling or the forms of the buildings, which immediately recall those found in paintings from the Veneto and those of Dosso Dossi (*c.* 1486–1542). Might

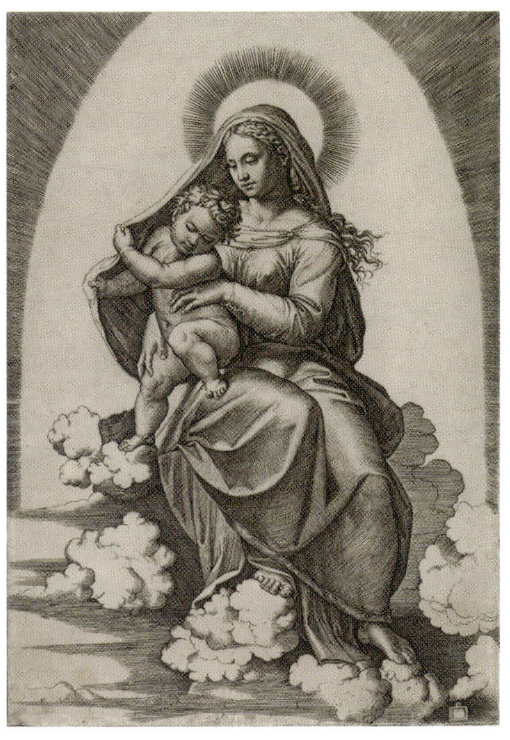

The Madonna di Foligno have been a work of collaboration? Dosso's less talented brother, Battista, was involved with the Raphael organisation, but his presence is not documented before 1518. Dosso too spent time in Rome, but it is not clear when. The landscape does not resemble Dosso's work of *c.* 1511–12, as far as that can be reconstructed, but rather the frieze of canvases that he painted for the *studiolo* of Alfonso d'Este from about 1515 onwards. Sigismondo's death in January 1512 invites the hypothesis that his altarpiece was set aside with only the upper part brought near completion – hence Marcantonio's engraving – and finished half a decade or so later by Dosso, during a Roman sojourn. Raphael had cast the picture in a 'painterly' mode, and Dosso was an appropriate artist to complete it. That the tablet lacks an inscription also implies that the painting was unfinished.

173   Raphael's other altarpiece of the Julian period is *The Sistine Madonna*, his single large painting on canvas. Although supporting documentation is lacking, it is universally accepted as a commission from the end of Julius's life, for the church of San Sisto in Piacenza, a town that had recently returned to the

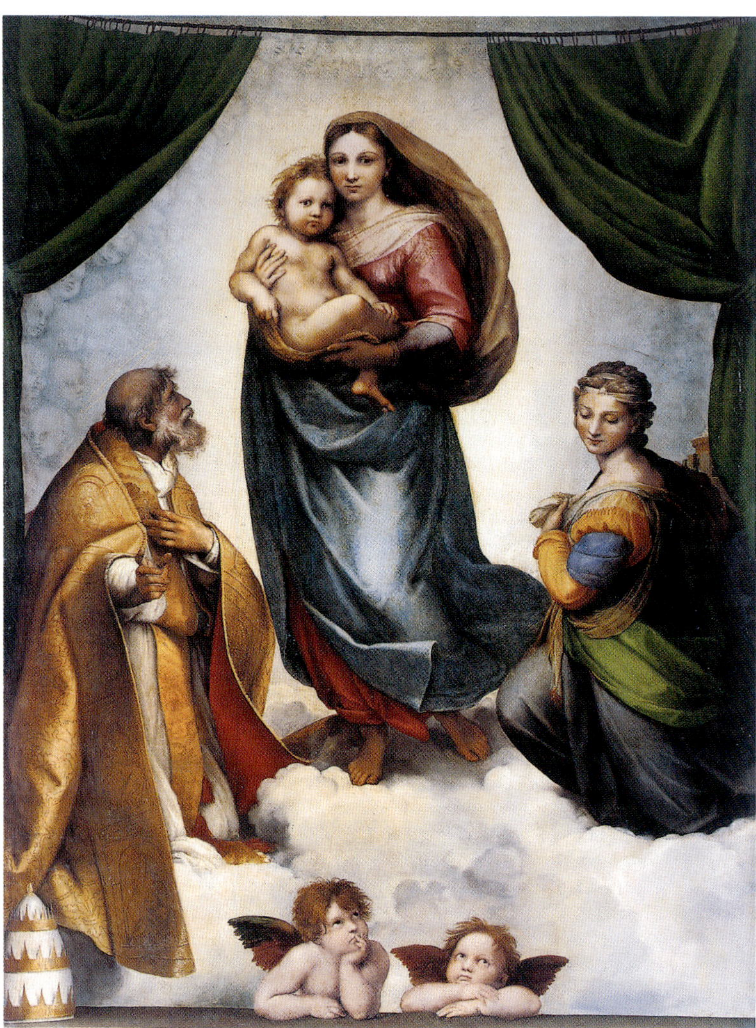

173 *The Virgin and Child with Sts Sixtus and Barbara* (*The Sistine Madonna*), 1512–13

papal fold. It was probably delivered before early March 1513, when the town was retaken by Milanese forces. The painting was unknown in Rome, and little noticed in Piacenza; Vasari mentions it but does not describe it, and its fame commenced only after its transfer to Dresden. The inclusion of Sixtus, the church's name saint, is also Julius's tribute to his uncle, Sixtus IV.

The physical types of the Virgin and the Child have clear links with those of *The Sedia*, and the forms, colours and soft-edged contours place its execution between *The Bolsena* and the *Release*. It is an experiment with the visionary, with the divine figures materialising from a mist comprised of an infinity of cherub heads. But notwithstanding its softness, *The Sistine Madonna* is redolent with Michelangelism. The 1513 scheme of the Julius Tomb showed the monument surmounted by a tall niche (a 'cappelletta' in contemporary documents) containing a standing, floating Virgin and Child group (Berlin, Kupferstichkabinett) that bears an obvious resemblance to Raphael's picture – which may have been intended to evoke Julius's monument. The colour range and physical types relate closely to those of the women and children at the lower left of *The Bolsena*, and the angels at the bottom of the canvas, added at the last minute, are the same children a few months older. And despite its visionary effect, the forms are as palpably human as those of *The Sedia*.

III

Most of the altarpieces that emerged from Raphael's studio after the election of Leo in March 1513 did not occupy his full attention and are interesting for their conception rather than their execution. The domestic theme is pursued in the compositional study for *The Madonna dell'Impannata* – named after the blind that covers the window – commissioned by the Florentine banker Bindo Altoviti (1491–1557) for his private chapel. In metalpoint and white bodycolour, it is datable *c.* 1512. St Elizabeth resembles the sibyl at the right of the Pace chapel, and the Virgin's costume conforms with those of the Virgin and Child drawings. Had the *Impannata* been painted in 1512, it would no doubt have resembled *The Sedia* in colour and texture. But the panel languished in Raphael's studio and around 1514–15 he modified the composition, cancelling St Joseph and inserting an adolescent St John, prepared in an energetic drawing (Berlin, Kupferstichkabinett), at the lower right. But completion was delayed further, and in the event the painting was executed largely by assistants – Penni for the Virgin and Giulio for the St John – with Raphael responsible for the Child and the head of St Elizabeth. The *Impannata* probably arrived in Florence in 1517. Its asymmetrical composition, situating the Holy Family in a domestic interior and furthering the idea of a family visit, was innovatory. Pontormo rapidly absorbed its lessons: his San Michele Visdomini altarpiece of 1518, which introduces skewed asymmetry into a large panel, is unthinkable without the *Impannata*. And Pontormo's new colouristic restraint and darkness of tone testify to its influence.

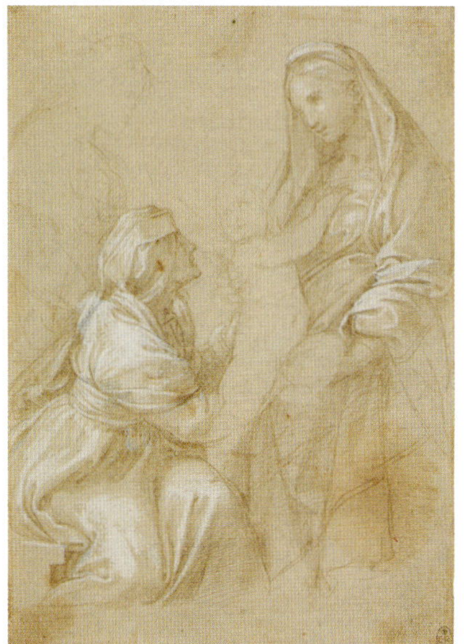

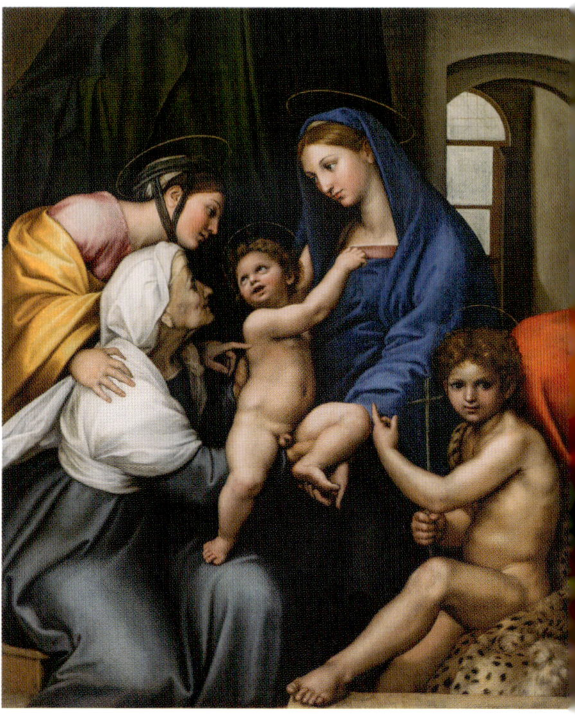

174 ABOVE Study for the *Madonna dell'Impannata*, probably 1512
175 RIGHT Raphael and assistants, *The Virgin and Child with Sts Catherine, Anne and John the Baptist* (*The Madonna dell'Impannata*), 1513–17

Consideration of the delay between inception and completion may clarify a scholarly disagreement over Raphael's famous portrait of the painting's commissioner. The style of *Bindo Altoviti* (Washington, National Gallery of Art) places it in late 1516 or 1517 – the sitter's head is inseparable from St John's in the *St Cecilia* altarpiece – but he seems younger than 25 or 26, which has led some scholars to date the portrait *c.* 1512. Raphael probably received the commissioned in conjunction with the altarpiece and made a portrait drawing of Altoviti *c.* 1512, but executed the painting only several years later, when it became retrospective.

Raphael's next altarpiece, intended for the church of San Domenico Maggiore in Naples, *The Madonna del Pesce*, is less innovatory. Two autograph drawings for it survive: a red chalk compositional sketch, made from models posed in the studio *c.* 1514 (Florence, Uffizi), and a broad brush and wash tonal study (Edinburgh, National Gallery of Scotland) that probably followed immediately; Raphael may not have made further drawings. The wash drawing was reproduced in an engraving by Marco Dente, probably issued before the painting was

176

finished – perhaps Raphael's first exploitation of 'work
in progress' advertising. Its links too are with the Stanza
di Eliodoro, but the level of execution is far from that of
The Sistine Madonna.

Raphael's design – which was adapted by Peruzzi in 1516
in the Ponzetti Chapel in Santa Maria della Pace – initiates a
tentative move away from biaxial symmetry in public altarpiece
design, justified by the entry of Tobias, to whom the Child
responds, at the left, introduced by the Archangel Raphael.
The *Pesce* was probably delivered to Naples in 1515. It is likely that
Penni was the main executant. Others may have been involved,
but probably not Giulio, who may not then have been active in
Raphael's organisation. Two areas of the painting are evidently
more felicitous texturally and emotionally than the rest:

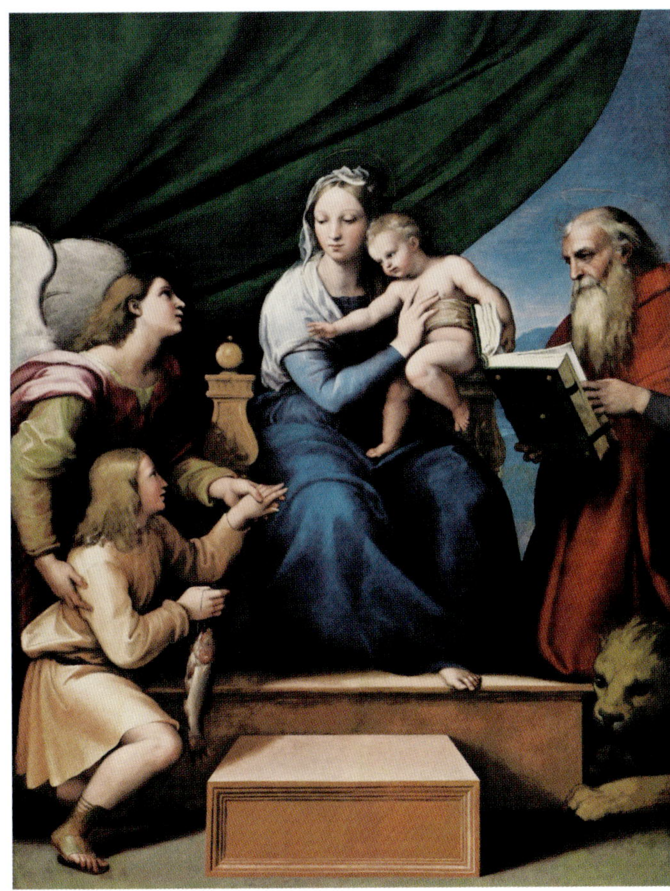

176 Assistants
of Raphael with
interventions
by Raphael, *The
Virgin and Child
with Tobias,
the Archangel
Raphael and
St Jerome (The
Madonna del
Pesce)*, 1513–15

St Jerome, seen at half length, seems to be entirely by Raphael, and his softly focused head and scarlet robe compare well with the upper right of *The Bolsena*. And the face of the Virgin, of a broader type – probably of a new model – is memorable.

This face, again painted by Raphael, was reused in the roundel of *The Virgin of the Host* (Baltimore, Walters Art Museum), executed largely by the studio; the flanking angels seem to be by Penni, who made a preparatory wash drawing for the Child (Oxford, Ashmolean). This was a harbinger of Raphael studio production of the coming years: devotional paintings of the Virgin and Holy Family were executed semi-independently by Giulio, Penni, and others still to be identified, but following broadly Raphael's designs. It was probably Raphael's way of fulfilling requests that he could not execute personally and of rewarding his associates. Thus Penni's *Holy Family* roundel at Cava dei Tirreni of *c.* 1512 and, slightly later, his repetition of the same composition in rectangular form in the Galleria

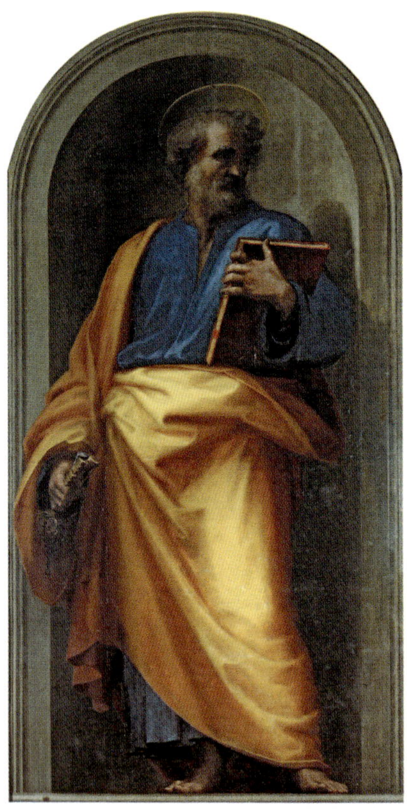

177 Fra Bartolommeo completed by Raphael, *St Peter*, 1514

Borghese derive, if rather timidly, from drawings by Raphael. In
contrast, Giulio's Spinola *Holy Family* (Los Angeles, J. Paul Getty
Museum) and his *Virgin and Child with St John* (Rome, Galleria
Borghese), of *c.* 1516–17, are more confident and forceful in
their rearrangements of designs by Raphael of about 1512.

Contemporary with the beginnings of the *Pesce* was a work
of friendship. According to Vasari, in 1513 Fra Bartolommeo,
intrigued by accounts of artistic developments in Rome, visited
the city where he undertook two over-life-size niched figures of
Sts Peter and Paul on wood, images so majestic that they are
kept in the Papal apartments. The panels reveal the Frate's
effort to aggrandise his style, but both develop Florentine
precedents rather than Roman ones: St Peter, for example, is
loosely inspired by Michelangelo's *David*. These paintings were
either commissioned by or given to the then keeper of the papal
seal, Fra Mariano Fetti (1460–1531), who had also been in the
Savonarolan convent of San Marco (surprisingly, for he was a
famous jester), and they are first recorded in his chapel at San
Silvestro al Quirinale. But, unwell or demoralised, Bartolommeo

177   left Rome before finalising the *St Peter*. Raphael's work, which
probably took him no more than a few days, greatly enlivens
the figure. The head is reconceived broadly in light and shade,
and the folds of Peter's garment are generalised and reduced in
relief to emphasise his head and the tense left hand holding the
book. Raphael accentuated the ruggedness of the Frate's design
and imbued Peter with an energy and latent movement that the
St Paul lacks. This figure was a step towards the style of the
tapestry cartoons, but it remains an offshoot of the Eliodoro,
most obviously *The Release of St Peter*.

178   The penultimate of the sequence of altarpieces produced
in the shadow of the fresco schemes is *Christ Fallen under the
Cross*, for the church of Santa Maria dello Spasimo (the 'Virgin
Swooning') in Palermo. We know nothing of the circumstances
of the commission, which probably dates to 1515, but it may
have been prompted by the arrival in Naples of the *Pesce*. More
obviously and directly than any other composition by Raphael,
The Spasimo di Sicilia (as it is known) is based on a transalpine
source. Raphael had long been intrigued by Dürer's work –
Vasari says he pinned prints by Dürer to the walls of his
studio for inspiration – and he would have discussed those
prints with Dürer's plagiarist Marcantonio. His exchange of
gifts with Dürer in 1515 would further have focused his mind.
Nevertheless, that *The Spasimo* is so overtly based on – is
effectively an Italianate version of – Dürer's large woodcut
of the same subject is surprising. Whether Raphael was
responding to a commissioner's stipulations or turned to

Dürer on his own initiative is conjectural. But it produced an ancillary benefit, for the finished picture – not a *modello* – was engraved by Agostino Veneziano in a monogrammed and dated sheet of 1517; close in size to Dürer's woodcut, it effectively competes with it.

The Spasimo was presumably dispatched to Palermo in 1517. According to Vasari, the vessel transporting it was wrecked but the picture was found to be undamaged when its case floated ashore near Genoa. No evidence has been found to confirm the story but, if there is any truth in it, it suggests that the painting acquired a miraculous status. Perhaps this prompted Bernardo Bibbiena to commission a half-size copy of the painting, in tapestry, for his private chapel (Vatican); tapestry is an unusual support for an altarpiece, and it may have been intended to accompany Bibbiena when he was on missions. This tapestry, of which a second version exists, introduces some improvements to the painting as finalised, and the cartoon for it was presumably drawn under Raphael's supervision.

The Spasimo was also painted under the influence of work in fresco. The disarticulated composition, the executive diversity from part to part, the disjunctions of scale, the counter-harmonies of form and the acidic colouring link with it the Stanza dell'Incendio, notably *The Ostia* and *The Coronation*, the preparatory drawings for which most closely resemble those for *The Spasimo*. But it is likely, too, that part of the disjunctive effect of *The Spasimo* – not inappropriate to the subject – comes from a change of design. Raphael conceived the man pulling the rope in a subtle and complex pose in which the tension and difficulty of the action are described convincingly (Florence, Uffizi). In the painting this tormentor is posed stiffly, conveying little tension or effort, and his pose repeats that of the executioner in *The Judgment of Solomon* on the Segnatura vault. One can only suppose that this insertion was made to establish a strong closing figure at the left, even at the cost of dramatic cohesion. The change may have been urged by Giulio: deliberate stiffness and disruptive insertions are traits that appear in the works that he executed both before and after Raphael's death, and he is a good candidate for the execution of the figure. But before the painting was dispatched to Sicily, Raphael intervened: the head of Christ – agonised, his tears falling not for himself but for the distress of his mother – and the noble head of Simon of Cyrene, who lifts the cross from the Saviour's shoulders, could come from one of the tapestry cartoons.

179   The last of the altarpieces is *The Visitation*, which is similar colouristically to *The Spasimo* and is probably of 1517. This

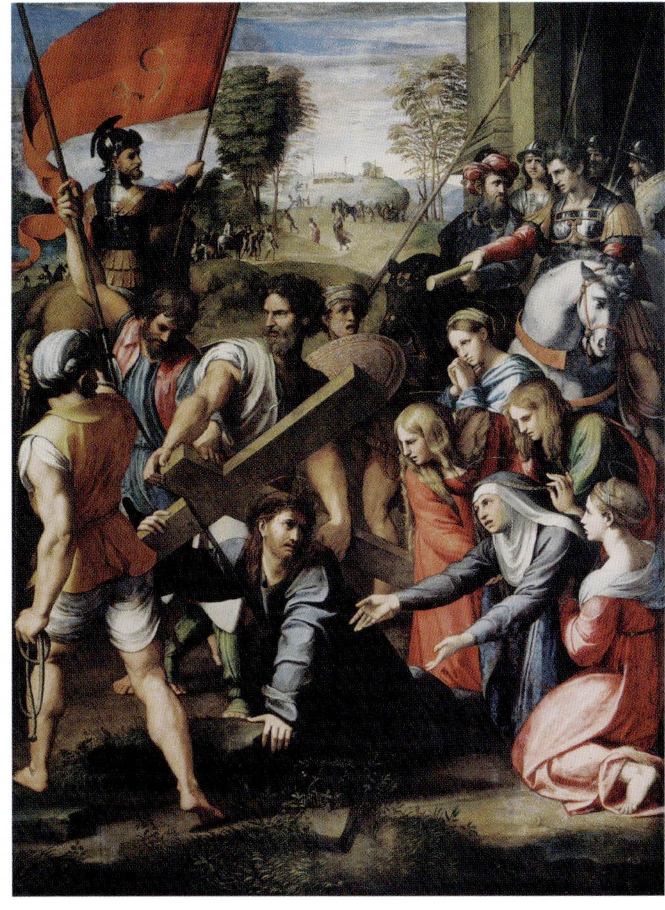

178 Giulio Romano and Gianfrancesco Penni to Raphael's design, with interventions by Raphael, *Christ Fallen under the Cross on the Road to Calvary being aided by Simon of Cyrene with the Virgin and other saints (The 'Spasimo di Sicilia')*, probably 1516–17

strange picture was painted for the family chapel in the cathedral of Aquila of Raphael's friend Giovanni Battista Branconio dell'Aquila, whose palace he designed. It is not known when it was delivered. Branconio is recorded as paying 300 ducats for the painting, which suggests that he accepted it as a studio production. The figures are conceived stiffly and without weight, and the costumes are treated as areas of shiny and somewhat acidic colour, without texture save for a few details such as the turban worn by St Elizabeth. The figures stand proud of the landscape; the Baptism taking place in the left background alludes to the patron's name. Whether Raphael himself even made sketches for *The Visitation* is doubtful; the design seems to be by Giulio and much of the execution by Penni, notably the landscape, which compares with many

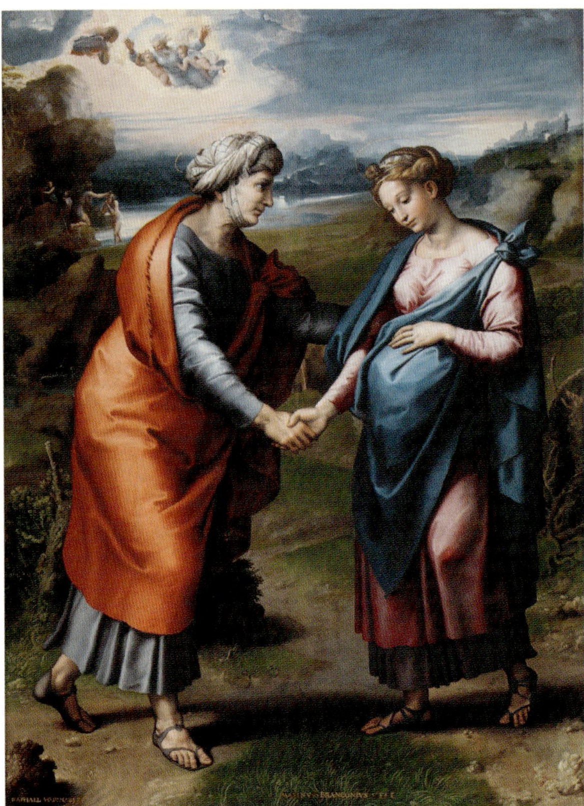

179 Giulio Romano and Gianfrancesco Penni, *The Visitation*, c. 1517. The inscriptions at the lower edge (RAPHAEL VRBINAS .P. MARINUS. BRANCONIUS. F.F) were probably added in the later 16th century or the early 17th century

in the Vatican Loggia. But it is worth remembering that Raphael's associates were not confined to Giulio and Penni, and that others may have been involved in some of his projects. Tommaso Vincidor, for instance, was a significant member of Raphael's organisation and entrusted with important design work, but we have very little idea of what his executive roles might have been or what he might have painted.

Chapter 12
Moveable Paintings II: A New Leonardism

I

For the last four years of his life, Raphael's attention as a painter was directed to moveable pictures of different types. Previously in his Roman work, fresco painting had governed that on panel. Now the priority was reversed. Raphael's involvement with fresco painting did not cease, but his role became that of planner and co-designer, and his executive presence dwindled.

The redirection of Raphael's creative energies was the consequence of, or coincided with, a change of aesthetic. And much of this conceptual reorientation, which concerned colour, tone and surface finish, was indebted to the presence in Rome of his old mentor. Between late 1513 and late 1516, when he left Italy for France, Leonardo da Vinci resided in an apartment in the Belvedere allocated to him by Leo X. Nothing is recorded of his relations with Raphael at this time, but relations there certainly were. Agostino Veneziano engraved one of Leonardo's early compositions in 1515, and at around the same time Marcantonio issued an amusingly pornographic print that was probably based on a drawing by Leonardo. Leonardo had occasional meetings with the pope, and Raphael surely met him with some frequency. The two men were friends and, given their respective ages and Raphael's commitments, there was no question of competition between them; they would have discussed their work freely. Raphael would have seen – or seen again – the paintings that accompanied Leonardo: the versions of *The Virgin Child and St Anne* (London, National Gallery; Paris, Louvre), the *Mona Lisa* and the half-length *St John* (both Paris, Louvre), *The Salvator Mundi* (private collection), and perhaps others, such as one or both versions of *The Madonna of the Yarwinder* (Buccleuch Collection and private collection), plus a host of drawings. Raphael would also have seen paintings by Leonardo's closest associates, Francesco Melzi (1491–1570) and Gian Giacomo Caprotto, called Salaì (1480–1524), which developed Leonardesque ideas that Leonardo himself had neither the application nor energy to paint. The full-length seated *St John* (Paris, Louvre), whose authorship remains uncertain, was surely among them.

Reacquaintance with Leonardo was a catalyst. Raphael was attracted by developments in illumination and finish in Leonardo's more recent work, such as the second version of *The Virgin of the Rocks* (London, National Gallery), which he would have known in copies, and in the *St John*. In part to obtain greater strength of relief and, correspondingly, emotional immediacy, Leonardo either reduced the colour range of his settings or suppressed them, so that the viewer concentrates solely on the forms displayed: in this, to some extent, he anticipated Caravaggio. But there was nothing rough in his approach. His flesh painting was brought to a pitch of refinement that virtually eliminates human accident and counters the 'realistic' emphasis seen in Raphael's work of the Eliodoro phase; and Leonardo's drapery painting was of unique subtlety and complexity.

The 'dark manner' was not the whole story, nor did Leonardo uniformly suppress context. The Louvre *Virgin and Child with St Anne*, on which he continued to work until his death, is suffused with daylight, and the figures are set within, not against, an incomparably panoramic landscape. This manner too influenced Raphael and his studio, especially Giulio Romano, increasingly Raphael's colleague rather than assistant. After about 1517 Raphael and Giulio worked through the range of possibilities to which they had been introduced – or reintroduced – by Leonardo, but it was the master's 'dark manner' that had the greatest and most immediate effect.

The adoption of Leonardism was qualified. Raphael rejects lyrical interrelation in favour of juxtaposition: forms are constructed individually, and rhythmical patterning is eschewed. The components of Leonardo's compositional structures are reimagined as separable units. Raphael's dark settings and polished surfaces were also in part designed to outdo his now bitter rival. Sebastiano had introduced the nocturne in his *Pietà* (Viterbo, Museo Civico) in, probably, 1514, and followed this in 1516 with the Vich *Entombment* (St Petersburg, Hermitage). And Raphael would have observed Sebastiano's own tendency, encouraged by Michelangelo, to separate and juxtapose rather than conjoin figures and would have been eager to outdo him. Admiration for Leonardo joined with the effort to surpass Sebastiano to favour Raphael's change of direction.

II

The first major manifestation of Raphael's new manner was the *St Cecilia*, a turning point in his art and one of his masterpieces, autograph save for the musical instruments painted, according to Vasari, by Giovanni da Udine. Although it was probably commissioned in 1514, a plausible date for Penni's *modello* (Paris, Petit Palais; it was engraved by Marcantonio as another

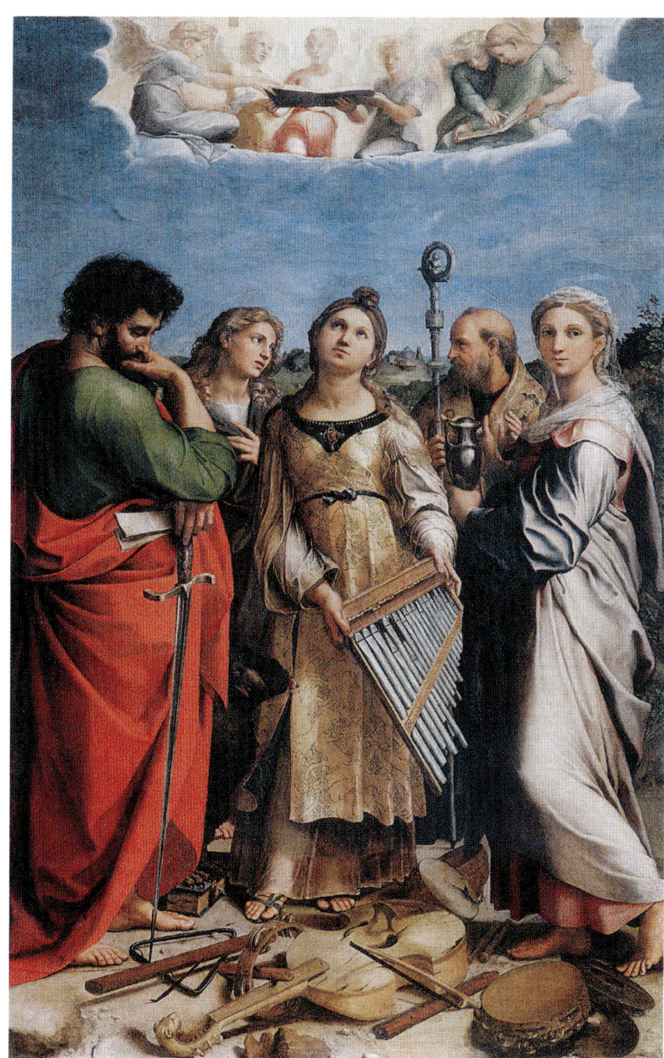

180 Raphael, with Giovanni da Udine for the still-life of musical instruments, *St Cecilia with Sts Paul, John the Evangelist, Augustine and Mary Magdalen*, 1516

advertisement for work in progress), its pictorial execution seems to have been deferred until 1516. Raphael's solid red chalk study for *St Paul* (Haarlem, Teylers Museum), drawn from the same model as the nude study sent to Dürer, shows the same spared-ridge highlights as the drawings for the Chigi Chapel mosaics of 1515–16. The accomplishment of the *St Cecilia*, which shows the new style completely mastered, might tempt one to date it later, but Vasari's account is circumstantial: he recounts that, on its arrival in Bologna, the elderly Francesco Francia, who had agreed to install it, was so shaken by its magnificence that he took ill and died shortly thereafter, reportedly in January 1517. Vasari's story may be metaphor rather than history, but it does register the innovative force of Raphael's painting.

The altarpiece evokes divinity in sound: terrestrial instruments are rendered impotent by the music of heaven. The five saints are ravished by angelic harmonies, each responding differently but collectively rapt. The musical life of the Leonine court was intense and, if not himself a musician, Raphael was certainly a lover of music and understood its effects. Cecilia, the patron saint of music, her portable organ lowered, some of its pipes sliding out, gazes upwards; she alone is vouchsafed direct vision of the angelic quintet. It is the compositional mode of the tapestry cartoons, adjusted to contemplation. Each of the three figures seen at full length is grand, and the busts of John and Augustine are densely realised: the painting looks forward a century in its fusion of rich description and stately form, and in different ways it was to haunt later Bolognese art, especially that of Guido Reni and Domenichino. The colour range is rich and the execution solid: the painting glows. The lustre of the organ pipes might well have been created by Raphael himself: they contrast greatly with Giulio's treatment of metal.

III

It is likely that the *Cecilia* and the so-called *Madonna of Divine Love*, which Vasari says was painted for Leonello Pio, the lord of Carpi (1477–1571), are contemporary. Raphael had begun to reconsider a genre that Leonardo had made his own: the complex Holy Family composition. It had attracted Raphael in his later years in Florence – supremely in the Canigiani *Holy Family* – but in Rome he had pursued it only in a few drawings. Raphael now began a second sequence of Holy Family compositions. The earliest is probably *The Madonna of Divine Love*, in which the Virgin is seen in profile, seated on the ground in an arrangement stressing her humility. It is compositional type with which Donatello had experimented

and of which Raphael had made drawings when he was in
Florence. The low tones, crepuscular mood and density of
colour in *Divine Love* resemble those of the *St Cecilia*, but much
of the execution is by associates: Giulio for the kneeling St John,
developed from a type by Raphael, while the Virgin is probably
by Penni. But the three-dimensional Child, and the aged
St Anne who guides his blessing hand, were contributed by
Raphael. The underdrawing is varied and shows many changes
of mind, but only a single drawing survives for the picture, a
red chalk study for the small St Joseph in the left background,
which is probably by Penni (Vienna, Albertina). Although
Raphael had included antique ruins in the backgrounds of
some earlier paintings, such as the Esterházy *Virgin and Child
with St John* (Budapest, Museum of Fine Arts), the Holy Family
is now encased by them, a transfer from the grottos of Leonardo.
Significantly – and despite its popularity, for it was widely

181 BELOW LEFT Raphael and assistants, *The Virgin and Child with Sts John and Anne?*
(The Madonna of Divine Love), probably 1516
182 BELOW RIGHT Marcantonio Raimondi after a lost design by Raphael, *The Holy Family
with St John (The Madonna of the Long Thigh)* (date of design probably 1516), c. 1520

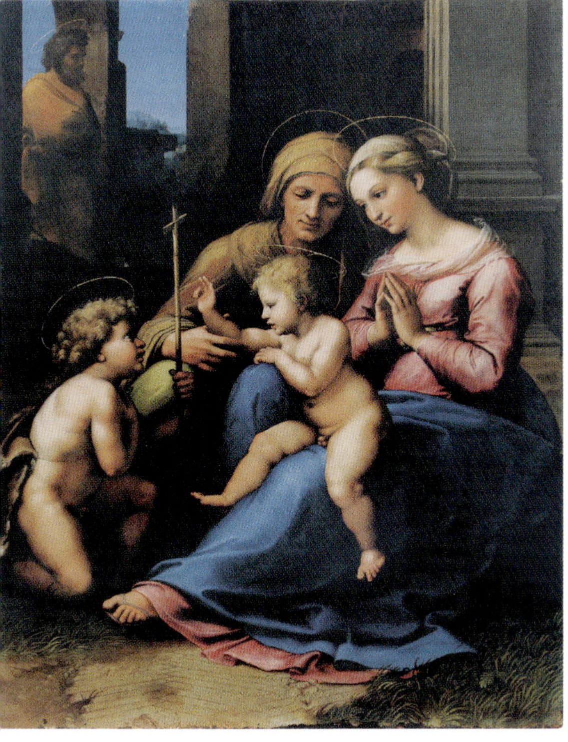

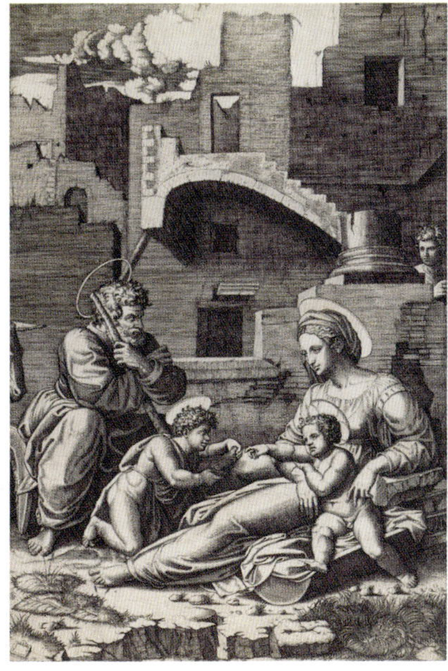

copied – when the painting was offered for sale as part of
the estate of Leonello's son Cardinal Rodolfo Pio da Carpi in
1564, it was obviously recognised as of questionable execution,
for it fetched much less than its asking price.

A variant of *The Madonna of Divine Love* is recorded in
an engraving that places the group, minimally modified,
under a palm tree. Perhaps Raphael or one of his associates
considered making a version with different illumination. The
composition corresponds to aspects of the underdrawing of
the Naples picture. It is not known if this version was executed
as a painting, but the design was reproduced in a tapestry
(Loreto, Palazzo Apostolico) whose colours ring true to the
Raphael School.

A more developed daylight treatment of the profiled Virgin
and the two children is a Holy Family, probably of a year or so
later: the so-called *Madonna of the Long Thigh*. It is documented
in variant engravings by Marcantonio and Marco Dente, but
we do not know whether they record a painting. The figures
are placed before a group of ruinous buildings, some of which
may be real, no doubt prompted by the topographical work on
which Raphael was engaged. It is the most emphatically urban
of Raphael's exteriors. The robust Joseph is now deeply involved
with the Virgin and Child, and the design conveys a strong
sense of family unity.

IV

Raphael's adoption of a Leonardesque aesthetic was deepened
by Leonardo's departure for France. In the paintings executed
in the winter and spring of 1517–18 for the French court,
Raphael was thinking precisely about Leonardo, by then
resident in the Loire Valley. He no doubt wished to produce
paintings in Leonardo's style because that is what the French
court would have valued. It would also have been an astute
calling card, to encourage further patronage from a monarch
eagerly recruiting Italian artists. Furthermore, that these
paintings would be seen by Leonardo and their stylistic origins
recognised would demonstrate Raphael's acceptance of his
ideas, and would reassure Leonardo that his style was alive
in Central Italy.

At least five panel paintings – four religious, one secular –
were sent to France. The most important were the *St Michael
Vanquishing the Devil*, *The Holy Family of Francis I* and the
St Margaret. Another picture, *St John in the Wilderness* (Paris,
Louvre), was painted for Cardinal Adrien Gouffier. All are
high-contrast paintings and all are, to a greater or lesser
extent, Leonardesque.

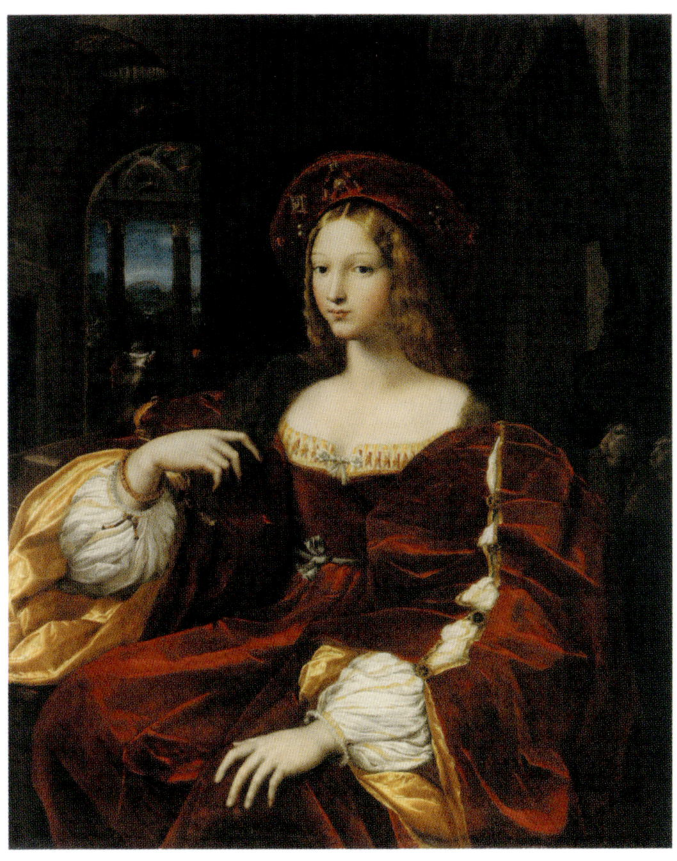

183   The secular picture – the portrait of *Doña Isabel de Requesens*,
the vicereine of Naples (1495/6–1532) – is less Leonardesque but,
ironically, was copied by a Leonardo follower whose version
was exported to Italy, probably for Alfonso d'Este, who had
seen and admired the *Isabel* in Paris at the end of 1518. The
portrait, which was commissioned by Bibbiena for Francis I,
is a little later than the other paintings intended for France,
and when it was painted Raphael was probably already at work
on the portrait of Leo X, for Isabel's velvet dress surely shows
awareness of Leo's robe in texture and handling. Raphael sent
the cartoon of the *Isabel* to Alfonso d'Este early in 1519 but made
clear to Alfonso's emissary that it was not his own work but that
of a 'garzone' sent by him to Naples. Vasari states that the *Isabel*
was by Giulio Romano, but adds that her face was by Raphael.
This is a division that many scholars accept, but it is hard to
see Raphael's hand in the detextured skin and marble-like eyes,

which seem entirely characteristic of Giulio. That a portrait of an important – and beautiful – sitter could be entirely delegated to a colleague is a further indication of Raphael's esteem for Giulio; it also implies that Giulio was favoured by Bibbiena. The *Isabel* is remarkable in many respects, but two features might be mentioned: one is the elaborately compartmented loggia in the left background; the other is the maidservant leaning over its parapet. The loggia shows Giulio's already burgeoning interest in richly decorated architecture, and the woman his penchant for casually posed but evocative figures set in depth. They are seen elsewhere in his early work, often

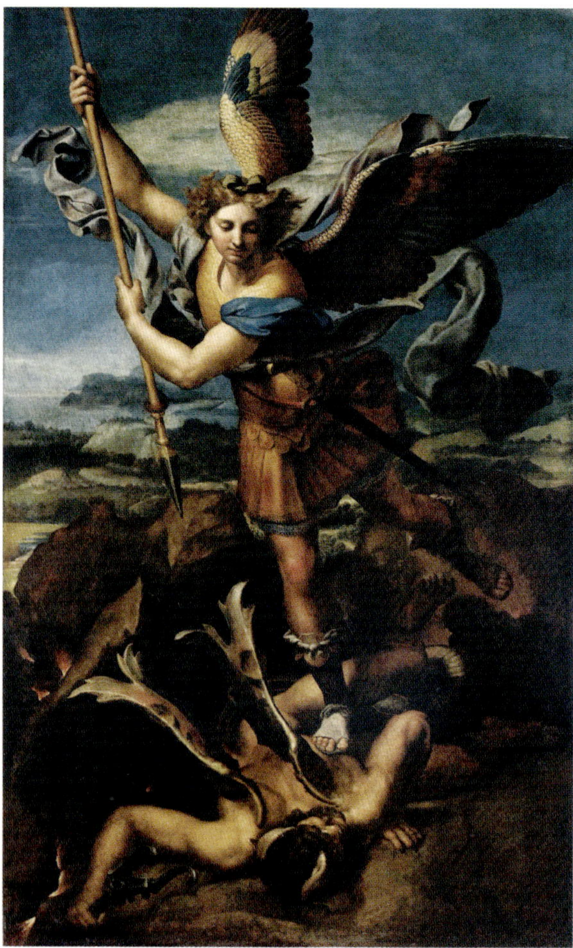

184 LEFT *St Michael Vanquishing the Devil*, signed RAPHAEL VRBINAS PINGEBAT and dated MDXVIII (1518)
185 OPPOSITE Raphael and Giulio Romano, *The Holy Family with Sts John, Elizabeth and two? Angels (The Holy Family of Francis I)*, signed RAPHAEL VRBINAS PINGEBAT and dated MDXVIII (1518)

entering foreground spaces from the rear, and they convey
a sense of ambient life.

The lustrous surfaces and vaporous shadows with which
Raphael played, especially in the *St Michael Vanquishing the Devil*
and *The Holy Family*, were perceived to be novel. The new style
was summed up derisively by Sebastiano, who had seen them in
Rome before their dispatch to France, in a letter to Michelangelo
of 2 July 1518: 'They seem to be figures that have been smoked or,
rather, of iron that shines, all bright and dark.' He adds that they
are in the style of Leonardo. This style animates, to a greater or
lesser extent, all the paintings in the group.

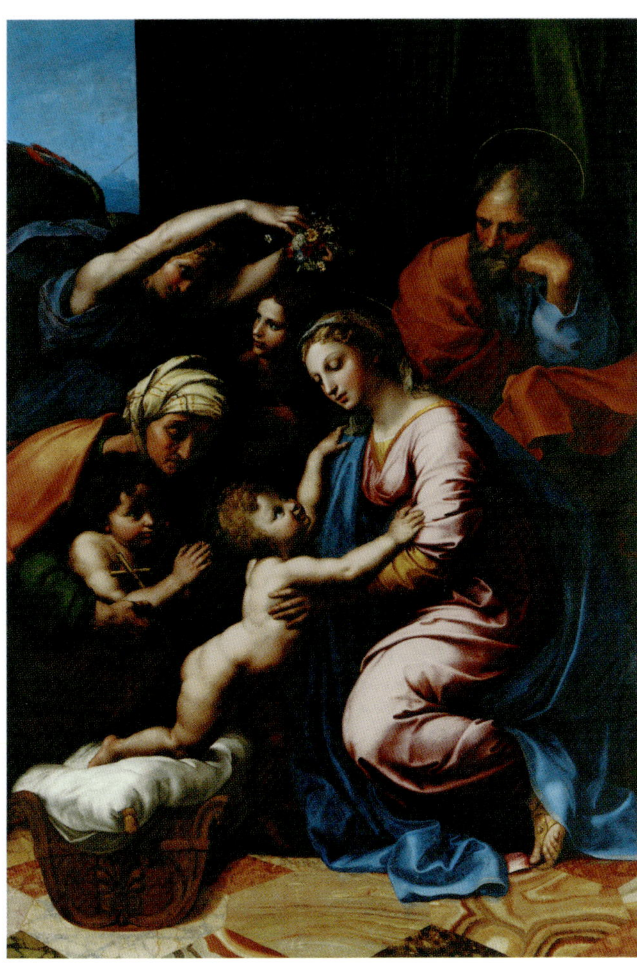

Vasari reports that *St Michael*, painted for Francis, was entirely autograph and, although it is severely damaged, its surface quality matches that of the *St Cecilia*. The archangel's lambent flesh, golden wings and spun-gold hair, set against a dark lapis sky, give the painting intense richness. Michael's pose is specifically Leonardesque: it recalls a spearman that Leonardo designed for the 'Fight for the Standard' in *The Battle of Anghiari*, known in a slight preparatory drawing and in a later copy that shows more of the figures around the central clash. In another effort to placate Alfonso d'Este, Raphael sent him the cartoon for the *St Michael* in October 1518.

185   The central motif of *The Holy Family of Francis I* is a double encounter: of St Elizabeth and St John with the Child, and of

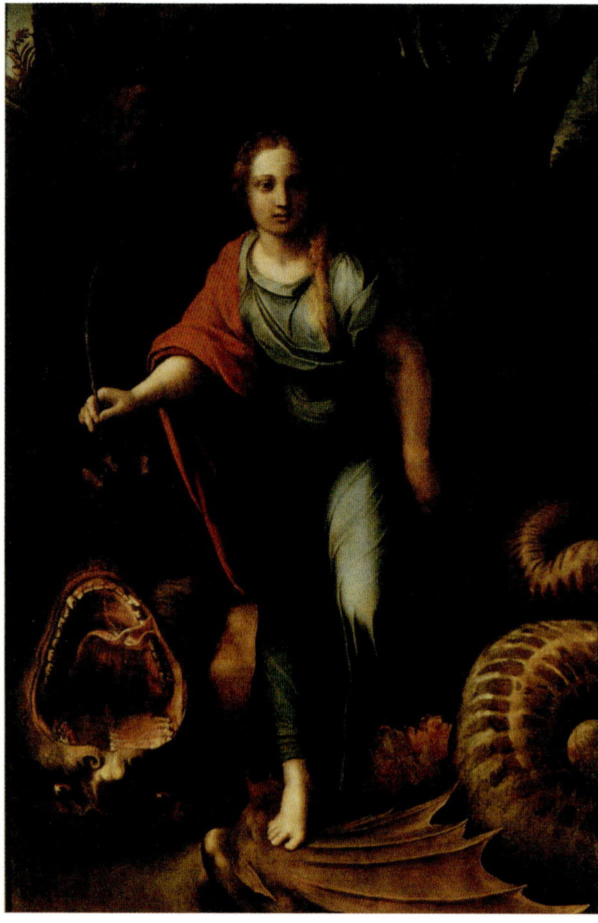

186 Giulio Romano to Raphael's design, *St Margaret*, 1518

the Child with the Virgin. The pensive Joseph, mature but
virile, whose pose had enormous resonance, is set to one side:
he becomes a prophet contemplating the significance of the
action, not a participant. The interior setting, with its coloured-
marble floors and a carved porphyry cradle, is of the stoniest
luxury, continuing in paint Raphael's experiments in the Popolo
chapel. Destined for Francis's queen, Claude of Brittany, who had
recently borne him a son – perhaps inspiring the celebratory
motif of the angel casting flowers – it is iconographically
poignant: Christ springs from the cradle to embrace his
mother (who perhaps also represents his Church) in an
anticipation of his resurrection and, perhaps, the future
of the French monarchy.

Vasari says that *The Holy Family of Francis I* was partly
painted by Giulio; he seems to have been responsible for
most of the left-hand side. Giulio also contributed a life study
to the painting's preparation (Paris, Louvre), and he and Raphael
probably worked out the design together. But the two developed
studies for the Child and the Virgin (Florence, Uffizi) are by
Raphael. The iridescence of the Virgin's drapery, created
by stylus lines that punctuate it with channels of light, also
shows a relation to Flemish painting – which was, of course,
one of the components of Leonardo's own style.

The third of the major panels for the French court, the
St Margaret, made for the king's sister, Margaret of Valois,
was, according to Vasari, painted entirely by Giulio to Raphael's
design. A miracle that in *The Golden Legend* takes place in
a prison is set in the open, at twilight. The destruction – or,
rather, self-destruction – of the dragon is a by-product of
Margaret's indifferent advance; she does not deign a glance
at the monster writhing at her feet. Raphael's conception is
undramatic, describing Margaret's serene passage through
the valley of death. The painting is poorly preserved and
its handling hard to judge, but it seems that, in colour, the
saint's cloak is most like that of Christ in the lunette of
the Monteluce *Coronation* and that of St Elizabeth in the
Aquila *Visitation*, a brown-orange. It offers a further insight
into Giulio's relations with Raphael that, having executed
the *St Margaret* on Raphael's behalf, he should have issued,
probably concurrently, a same-size reinterpretation. Giulio's
own *St Margaret* (Vienna, Kunsthistorisches Museum), first
recorded in Venice in 1528, in the house of Zuanantonio
Venier, who may have been the patron, is set in a *contrapposto*
pose, and the saint looks down at the dragon her passage
has destroyed. It foreshadows Giulio's bolder revisions of
Raphael's compositions in the following years.

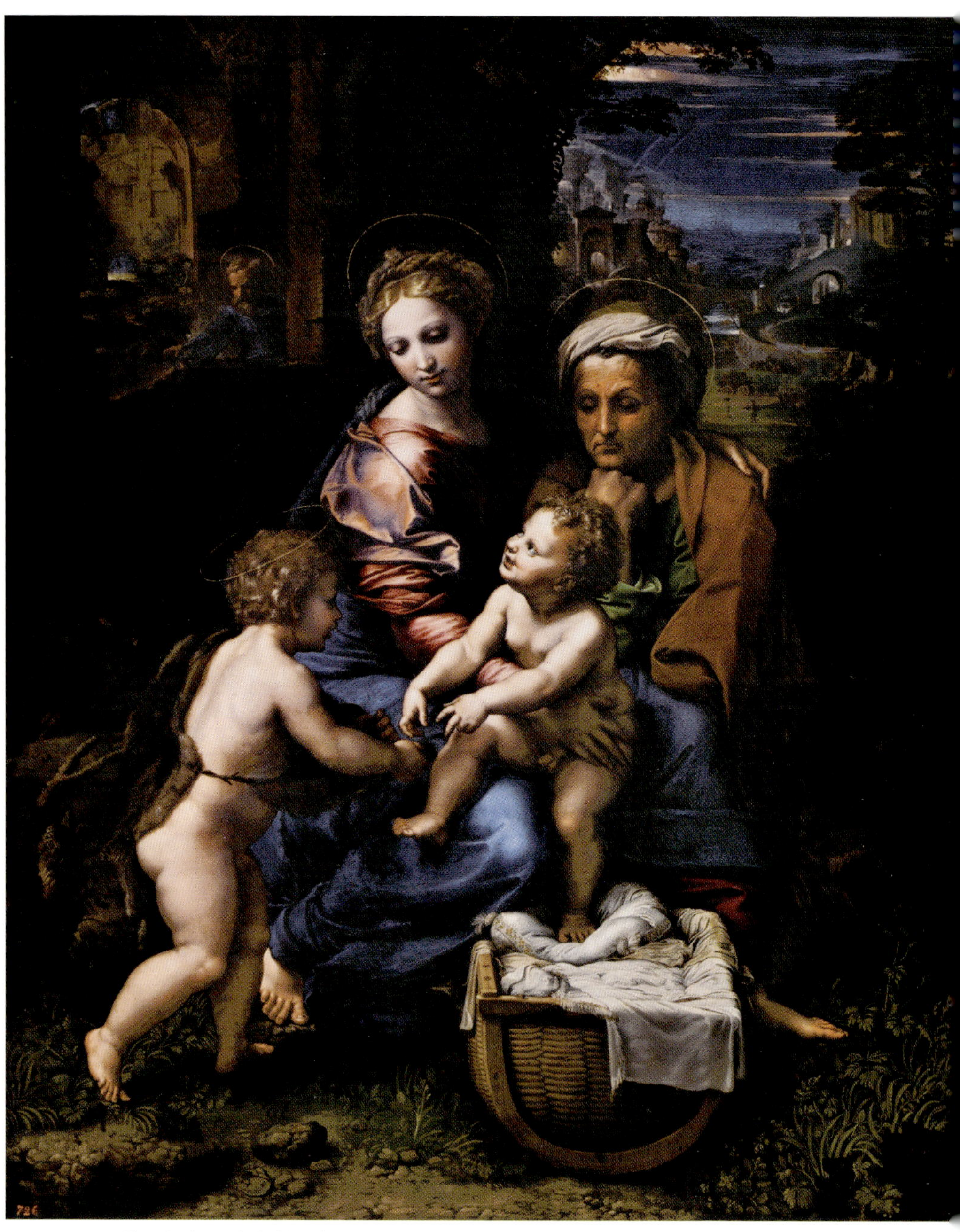

187 *The Virgin and Child with Sts John and Anne ('La Perla'),* probably 1519

V

Raphael's most complex and ambitious Holy Family, and perhaps his most profound homage to Leonardo, is his four-figure group *La Perla*, so called because Philip IV, who acquired it after Charles I's execution, considered it to be the pearl of his collection – a supreme compliment from the patron of Velázquez. Raphael painted it for Ludovico da Canossa (1476–1532), a familiar at the court of Urbino and among the interlocutors in Castiglione's *Cortegiano*. Ludovico was able to obtain from his friend Raphael a high degree of personal attention, and that he was vastly wealthy no doubt helped: according to an unverifiable remark of 1558, the *Perla* cost the enormous sum of 1,200 ducats, the equivalent of the Stanza dell'Incendio.

Raphael was obviously thinking of Leonardo's three- and four-figure versions of *The Virgin and Child with St Anne*, with and without St John. The Virgin is seated on an unseen support facing to the viewer's right, but with her head turned to the left to observe the young St John, who offers the Child a gift of cherries, symbolic of the Passion. Mary's left arm is placed around the shoulder of her mother, St Anne, who seems to be kneeling behind her, her right elbow on Mary's thigh, musing prophetically on the Child. St Joseph's role is once again reduced; it is that of a sentry, reclining in the ruins at the left background. The Virgin holds the Child protectively, but he looks at neither his cousin nor his mother: he gazes upwards, past her, towards his celestial Father, manifest in the light that flows over them and animates the countryside with its beneficence. The view at the left is of controlled complexity, incorporating a functioning town as well as a distant view of mountains; it looks through Leonardo to one of his own sources, van Eyck. Its geometrical organisation, which extends to the long clouds and the golden light on the horizon, conveys to the viewer an impression of pre-ordained order that is also a characteristic of the whole composition, held together with a series of upright and inverted arches stretching across the surface. Despite the variety and detail of the forms incorporated in it, the *Perla* is one of Raphael's most tightly orchestrated paintings, and its combination of richness and organisational clarity communicates subliminally a sense of the divine presence in the physical world. The Creator is not represented, but he is universally immanent.

VI

The final painting of Raphael's career – his largest altarpiece, *The Transfiguration* – is also a culmination. Raphael could not foresee his premature death, and he died with a host of projects

outstanding; but the painting has a testamentary air, like
a summary of achievements. It contains over twenty figures
who are individually characterised, many with portrait-like
depth and force, united in their response to the arrival of the
possessed boy but separated from one another as personalities
and differentiated by gesture and expression.

The painting is arranged in geometrically coherent
formations: an interrupted circle at the lower level, seen in
depth, surmounted by a flat triangle. The scheme is effectively
a deconstruction and reconstruction of Leonardo's *Adoration
of the Magi*, and Raphael acknowledged his debt by including
a quote: the heavily bearded Apostle at the lower centre – for
whose head an auxiliary cartoon survives (London, British
Museum) – is taken directly from the elderly Magus in
Leonardo's panel. Stylistically, the smooth finish and dense,
separated colours, coordinated by consistent tonality, develops
the system seen in the *St Cecilia* and other works, but costumes
are necessarily simpler and plainer, and textures are reduced:
the severity of the tapestry cartoons is still in play, but with
subdued tonalities.

The illumination of the lower section, which falls from
the left, models the figures with sculptural force. But this is
abandoned above, where the Saviour floats against a mandorla
of light, comparable in effect, if less dazzling, to the angel in
The Release of St Peter. But the two sections of the painting are
cunningly coordinated. Below, the Apostles react confusedly to
the arrival of the possessed boy with his mother and relatives;
they are unable to help him in the absence of Christ, and their
comparative disorganisation shows Raphael profiting from
the experiment with confusion in *The Repulse of Attila*. The
action takes place in a plausible if theatrically shallow space.
Above them rises the stage-set mount, on whose summit three
Apostles recline uneasily while Christ rises above them in a
celestial radiance. He is accompanied by Moses and Elijah,
stressing his fulfilment of Old Testament prophecy. The
airborne figures are much larger than the Apostles and
drift forward: their position in space cannot be ascertained.
The effect on the viewer is that everything in the painting
is happening simultaneously, an impression enhanced by a
linking device: the raised arms of the figures at the outer edges
connect with what is happening above and unite – if factitiously
– the picture's two parts. There is a massive contrast in method
with Titian's contemporary *Assumption of the Virgin*, in which
unity of time, place and action is reinforced by the structural
triangles of red drapery and the gestures of the Apostles. In *The
Transfiguration*, Raphael's double action and individualised

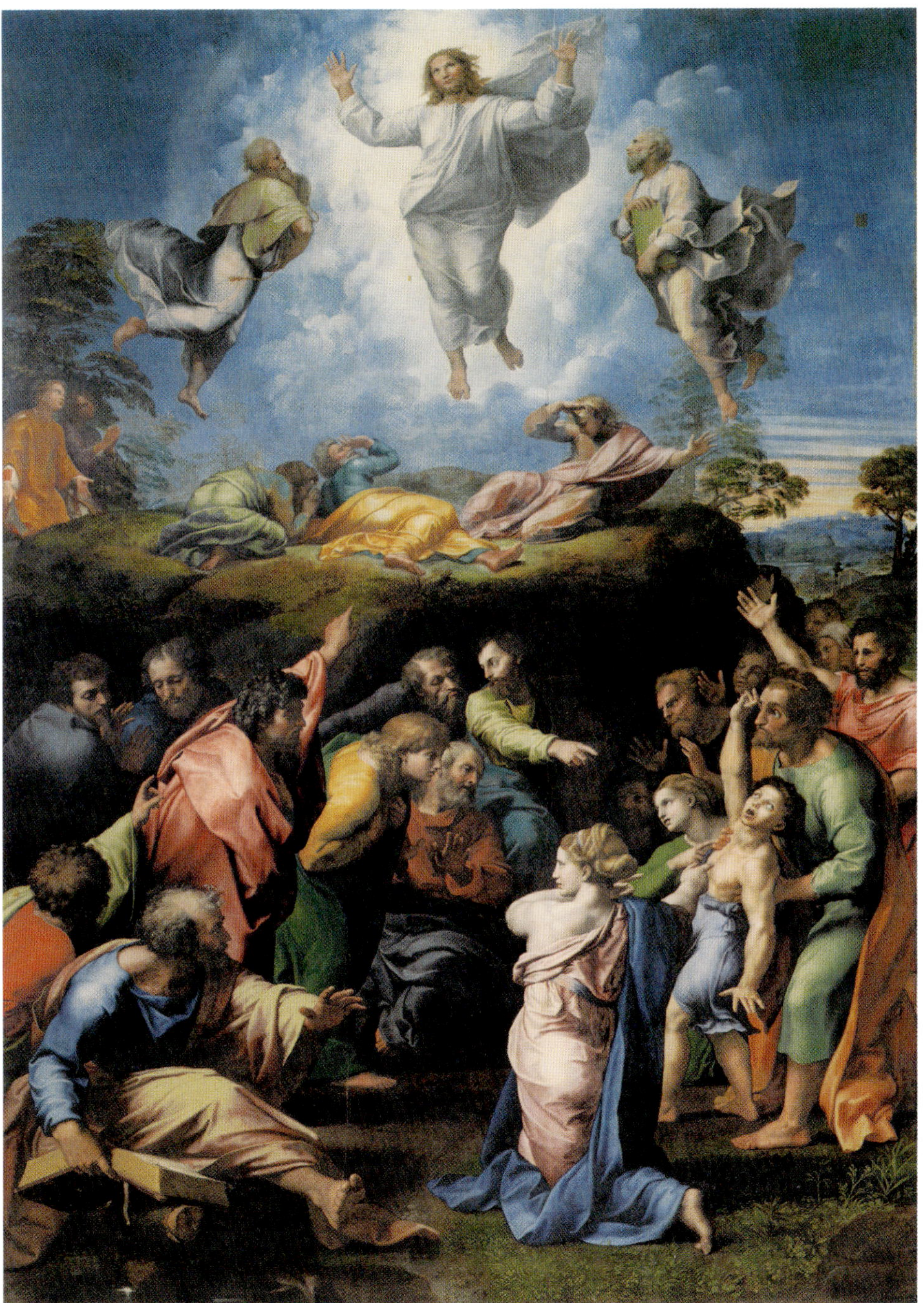

188 *The Transfiguration*, 1518–20

approach compelled him to coordinate many more elements.
But he was able to look back to his unexecuted *Resurrection*
project for the two-level composition and for the explosion
of light behind Christ. *The Transfiguration* is, to an extent,
a transposed *Resurrection* and absorbs some of its energies.

Raphael's use of Leonardesque chiaroscuro and smooth
modelling was also intended to outflank Sebastiano. By 1516
their rivalry had become so public that Cardinal Giulio de'
Medici set them in direct competition. He had acquired the
bishopric of Narbonne in 1515 and decided to endow the
cathedral with a pair of large altarpieces, to establish
his munificence, to illustrate his care of his diocese and
no doubt to introduce an up-to-date Roman manner in
southern France. Their subjects were *The Raising of Lazarus*
and *The Transfiguration*.

Sebastiano soon began the *Lazarus* – interrupting work on
the Borgherini Chapel at San Pietro in Montorio – and enlisted
Michelangelo's help with the group on the right-hand side.

189 BELOW LEFT Sebastiano del Piombo, *The Raising of Lazarus*, 1517–19
190 BELOW RIGHT Unidentified draughtsman after Raphael, *modello* for
the first? design of *The Transfiguration*, 1516

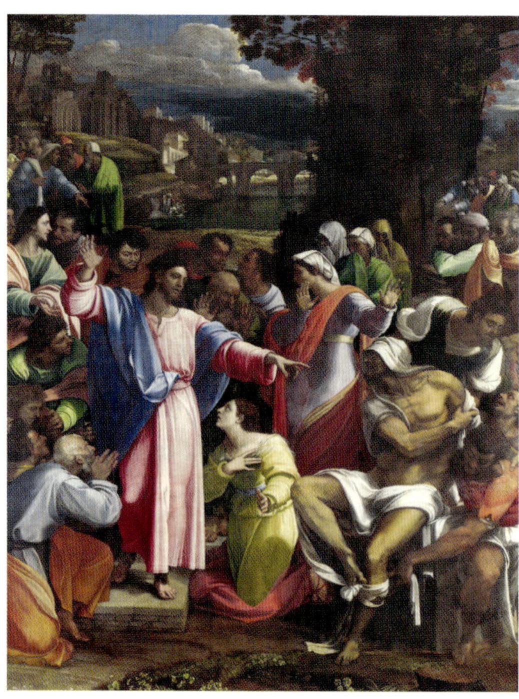

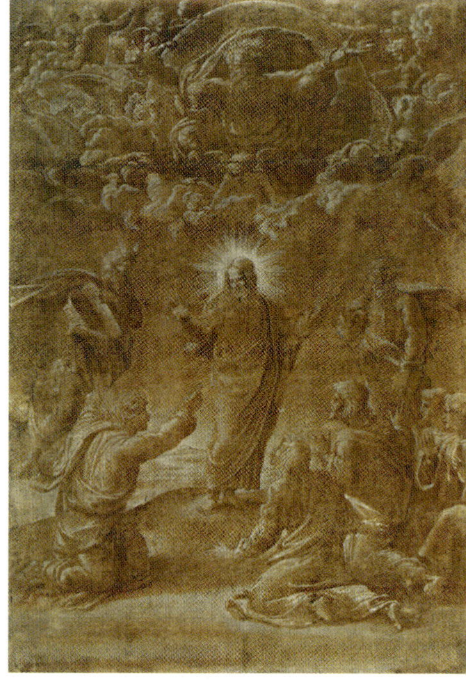

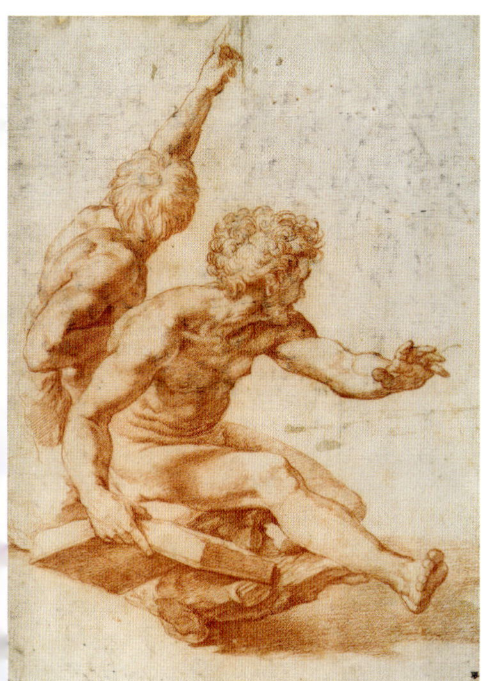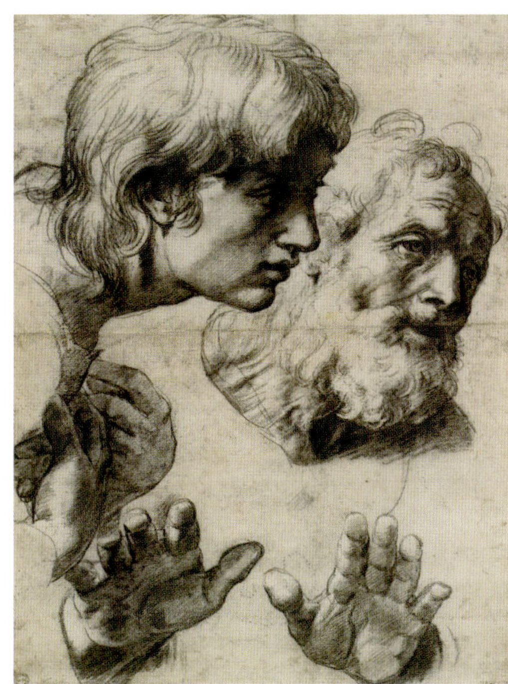

191 ABOVE LEFT Nude study for the two apostles at lower left
of *The Transfiguration*, 1518–19
192 ABOVE RIGHT The heads and hands of two apostles, c. 1519–20

Sebastiano's painting pivots on the commanding figure of
Christ, who dominates the central axis. He completed his panel
by the end of 1518 and wrote to Michelangelo that Raphael had
not yet begun. But Sebastiano's promptness worked against
him, and Raphael, now aware of his rival's scheme and no
doubt benefiting from theological advice, changed course
radically. In his first design, known from a copy of the lost
modello, Christ, like Sebastiano's, was large and accompanied
by three kneeling Apostles, with the two deacons venerated
in Narbonne appearing at the right, as they do in the upper left.
Unlike Sebastiano, Raphael had planned to animate the upper
part of the pictorial field with a half-length God the Father,
watching over his son. It may be that he was recalling the
structure of his only other altarpiece on a similar scale:
The Coronation of St Nicholas of Tolentino.

Raphael now decided to develop his painting on two levels
and inserted another episode, described in the Gospels of Mark
and Matthew, which immediately succeeds *The Transfiguration*:
a family brings a boy possessed by demons to the Disciples, but

they are impotent without Christ's aid. Raphael's response to Sebastiano thus repeated their exchange in the Sala di Galatea: he countered Sebastiano's gigantism (and Michelangelo's potent Lazarus group) with an unparalleled complexity. The result was the same: Raphael won the contest, and *The Transfiguration* was retained in Rome while the *Lazarus* was sent to Narbonne. But it may be that the strain of competition contributed to Raphael's premature death: the painting's display above his bier may have been a triumph, but it was posthumous.

The expansion of the subject massively increased Raphael's workload. He had to design, characterise, integrate and execute – the painting is very largely autograph – around fifteen additional figures in the lower half of the painting, some of them complexly posed. This necessitated an intense graphic campaign, and from the survivals – meagre compared with the number of drawings he and his assistants would have made – the design of the lower part must have gone through several stages. The small nude sketch for the Apostle, probably St Matthew, who is seated at lower left (Vienna, Albertina) was clarified and adjusted in a detailed study from the nude model, for Raphael, reverting to a practice from which he had largely abstained after his first months in Rome, prepared all the figures in nude studies, in red chalk, before another series of drawings in black chalk – of which only one survives (Paris, Louvre) – added their draperies. Raphael was assisted by Giulio, who drew at least two sets of nude studies from the model (Vienna, Albertina; Milan, Ambrosiana). Giulio or Penni would presumably have made the cartoon, and Raphael then completed the graphic preparation with auxiliary cartoons, for the heads of the Apostles. Six survive, all in black chalk and/ or charcoal to establish appropriate tones; their combination of light and shade, texture and abstraction make these drawings seem Rembrandtesque, and they are among Raphael's supreme achievements as a draughtsman. They show, furthermore, his efforts at precise spiritual characterisation, recalling Leonardo's efforts in *The Last Supper*.

VII

These paintings followed Leonardo's dramatic chiaroscuro mode, which focuses attention on the figures and imbues them with sculptural relief. But, as illustrated by the Louvre's *Virgin and Child with St Anne* and by the ex-Lansdowne *Madonna of the Yarnwinder* (private collection), Leonardo also represented daylight and integrated his figures with their immediate ambience – softening contours and adjusting textures to

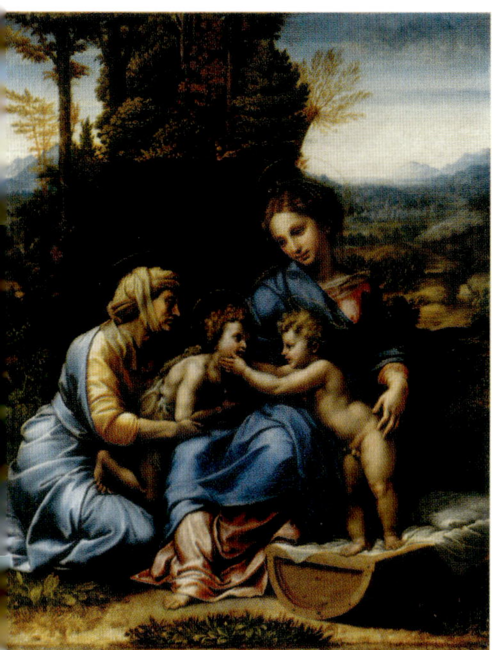 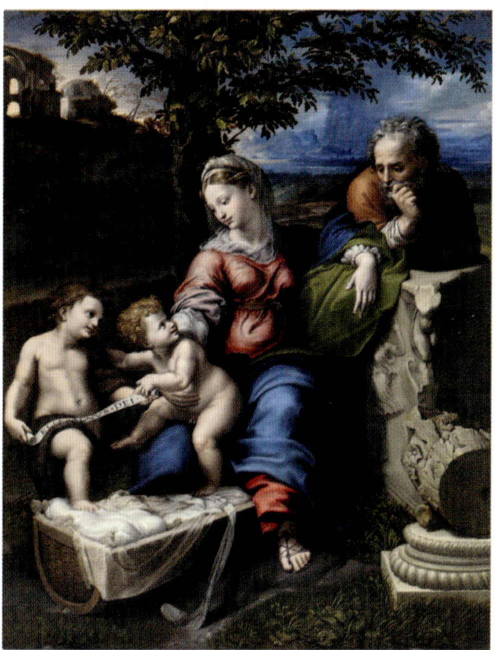

193 ABOVE LEFT Giulio Romano, *The Virgin and Child with Sts Elizabeth and John (La Petite Sainte-Famille)*, 1517–18
194 ABOVE RIGHT Giulio Romano, *The Holy Family with St John (The Madonna della Quercia)*, 1518–19

register out-of-doors illumination. He set them within astonishingly panoramic landscapes with great and varied detail and united all in tonally coherent colour schemes. Raphael himself may not have executed daylight paintings of this type in his last years, but his leading collaborator did. Giulio Romano must also have frequented Leonardo in the Belvedere and studied his work; he may, indeed, have formed his own friendship with Leonardo.

The Small Holy Family was painted, probably in 1517–18, for Cardinal Bibbiena, who at his death bequeathed it to Castiglione. It may depend on some sketch by Raphael, but the same-size preparatory drawing (Windsor, Royal Collection), later engraved by Jacopo Caraglio, is by Giulio. The painting is a daylight piece and, while Giulio made little effort to match the tones of the Virgin's and St Elizabeth's robes to the softened light, he includes a landscape in extreme depth that is unmistakably Leonardesque in conception and in detail.

He went further in *The Madonna della Quercia*, quintessentially Giuliesque both in planning and in its details, such as the

inclusion of recognisable antique ruins at the upper left
(the Temple of Minerva Medica and the circular mausoleum
beside St Peter's, as well as specific antique objects such as the
altar and the column base). The pudgy St John is characteristic,
as is the twisting pose of the Child. All the morphologies of
hands and heads are Giulio's and, while the design may have
had a starting point in a sketch by Raphael, the extended and
decentred figural arrangement is entirely his. Increasingly
desirous of loosening Raphael's compositions, in his slightly
later (1519–20?) *Madonna della Gatta* (Naples, Capodimonte)
Giulio manipulated Raphael's *Perla* by spreading it out and
posing the group obliquely.

The great oak (*quercia*) that shelters the Holy Family recalls
the tree in the centre of Leonardo's *Adoration*, which Giulio
might have known in a copy by Raphael or even from Leonardo
himself. The skyscape, in its representation of a passing storm,
irresistibly recalls Leonardo's drawings of alpine storms and
surely reveals knowledge of them. Certain aspects of this level
of attention to sky and landscape continued in Giulio's art
for a while after Raphael's death, for example in the *Deesis*
(Parma, Galleria Nazionale) or *The Stoning of St Stephen*, but
this interest represents a moment in his work rather than
a continuing preoccupation.

It may be that the iconography of *The Madonna della
Quercia* relates to the situation of the della Rovere in 1519.
Following its expulsion from Urbino in 1516 and subsequent
exile, negotiations were now beginning to restore the family
to its duchy. The Holy Family, having passed through a storm,
are sheltering under the tree that was associated with the
family, waiting hopefully for what is to come.

Chapter 13
Raphael's Architecture

I

On 11 April 1514 Donato Bramante died, aged about 70. He had dominated design under Julius and had marginalised Giuliano da Sangallo, the Florentine architect who had been a loyal servant to Julius when he was a cardinal. Bramante was responsible for the massive project of the Belvedere and had begun the multi-storey loggia at the west of the Vatican Palace. Elsewhere in Rome he had built – for the Spanish monarchs Ferdinand and Isabella – the circular neo-Roman monument known as the Tempietto, which marks the site of St Peter's martyrdom, in the courtyard of San Pietro in Montorio. He had also constructed a powerful Romanising cloister next to Santa Maria della Pace, and a grand choir for Santa Maria del Popolo. Both churches were Augustinian foundations and, in their modern form, constructions of Sixtus V and much favoured by Julius. Raphael was to work in both.

Bramante was also active in secular architecture. He had designed the innovative Palazzo Caprini in the Borgo, which, with its rusticated ground floor containing shops, *piano nobile* articulated by paired Doric half-columns standing on separate bases, and Doric entablature with metopes and triglyphs, looked more closely to the antique than any previous private building in Rome. The formula proved enormously influential. It projects strength in the lowest story and formality in the *piano nobile*; pediments, more commonly used above door-frames, give the windows a positive role.

Most importantly, Bramante was responsible, from late 1503 onwards, for designing the new church of St Peter's, of which the foundation stone was laid in April 1506. Raphael, who turned 31 only four days before Bramante died, was

195

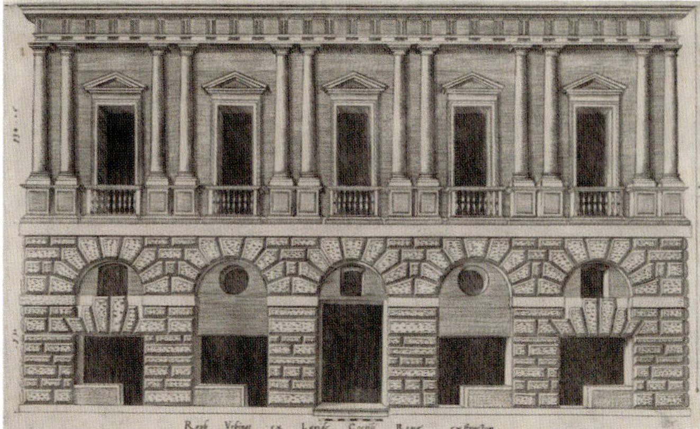

195 Donato
Bramante, the
Palazzo Caprini,
c. 1501 onwards;
demolished

immediately appointed his successor and the appointment
was confirmed in August.

To succeed Bramante as director of the most important
architectural project of the Christian world was a remarkable
accolade. According to Vasari, Raphael had been taken
under Bramante's wing and initiated into the 'secrets of
the profession' but, in the absence of some track record,
such an elevation is startling.

II

Given Giovanni Santi's intellectual bent, he was certainly
interested in the theories and practices of architecture. He
mentioned Vitruvius in his chronicle – although whether he
read him in any detail is another matter – and would naturally
have passed this interest to his son. This may have provided
the germ that later prompted Raphael to commission an
Italian translation of Vitruvius from the scholar Fabio Calvo
(1450–1527). The sketch of an arcade on the study for *The
Coronation of St Nicholas of Tolentino* suggests that Raphael
had some association with the polymathic Francesco di Giorgio
Martini (1439–1502), whom Giovanni had known and admired,
and perhaps had access to Francesco's studio, as he would
later to Leonardo's. It may have been at the commissioner's
request, but Raphael paid homage to Francesco's church of
San Bernardino – whose construction he and his father would
have witnessed – in the background of *The Small Cowper
Madonna*. Later Raphael was to recall a novelty of Francesco's
construction in that church.

Raphael's interest in architectural representation included
heavy forms as well as light ones, a range also found in the

painted architecture of Perugino. Thus the plastic and solid
formulation of the chamber in *The Nativity of the Virgin* in
Fano, its post-and-lintel construction articulated by applied
Doric columns bearing cross-beams, not arches, contrasts with
the arcuated setting of *The Annunciation* in the predella of the
degli Oddi *Coronation*. And in Raphael's painting the buildable
and the fantastic ran in parallel. The centrally planned sixteen-
sided temple in the *Sposalizio* could have been built only of
light materials and was a demonstration of virtuosity in
perspective construction rather than an archaeologising
attempt to recreate the Temple of Jerusalem. But in the pilaster
strips – or lesenes – that articulate the drum, Raphael shows an
early interest in merging separate forms, for they run into the
architrave. It also reveals the beginnings of Raphael's interest
in centrally planned buildings, a High Renaissance obsession.

It is *The Madonna del Baldacchino* that first presents solid
and buildable architecture: its broad niche, articulated by
unchannelled pilasters and flanked by smooth columns with
Corinthian capitals, derived from those in the Pantheon and,
with its coffered cove, creates an effect of great solidity – more
so than contemporary work by Fra Bartolommeo: it seems to
clasp the figures. It would have contrasted tellingly with the
Brunelleschian chapel that was to house it. It is notably Roman
in style, which may support the suggestion that Raphael visited
Rome before 1508.

Raphael's representation of buildings ran in tandem with
his increasing skill in the creation of invisible architecture: the
geometrical arrangement of human forms in a notional space
created by perspective. This is the mode of the upper part of
the San Severo *Trinity* and, spectacularly, *The Disputa*. Raphael's
employment of spatial geometry as an organising principle was
to be vital to his planning. But more immediately relevant for
Raphael's architectural career was *The School of Athens*, whose
backdrop, as always noted, must be influenced in its scale,
its giant order supported on high plinths, and its statue-filled
niches by Bramante's projects for St Peter's, although it does
not reproduce any of them. It is not buildable, for at the rear
there are no pendentives, only a wall that could not support a
drum and dome; but this was a by-product of formal concerns
and does not indicate ignorance of construction. The play of
wall levels, the excavation of niches and the energy of relief
are clearly invented by a mind thinking in monumental
architectural terms, and with organic unity in mind. It may
have been *The School of Athens* that created awareness in the
papal court of Raphael's potential as an architect.

Raphael's invention continues in the Stanza di Eliodoro.
In *The Release of St Peter*, the cell is a theatrically isolated block,
not a real gaol. Raphael is interested primarily in texture and
abstract shape: the heavy rustication of the pillars that enclose
it evoke the oppression, restriction and tyranny that the angelic
apparition dissolves. The fresco shows Raphael's deployment
of forms for association and emotional resonance, whereas
The Expulsion of Heliodorus fuses the potentially real and the
fantastic. In the choir we see a receding file of saucer domes,
covered in mosaic – like those of a Byzantine church – which
introduces colour and texture. And the domes are supported
directly on columns, an invention developed from Francesco
di Giorgio's San Bernardino, in which columns support
pendentives. The domes, too, recall Francesco, but more so
the ideas of the expert on Vitruvius and esteemed architect
Fra Giocondo (1433–1515), who was then making designs for
St Peter's.

In contrast to the rich surface effects of *Heliodorus*,
Raphael devised, at the same time, a painted architecture of
remarkable austerity and strength. The setting of the prophets
and sibyls in Agostino Chigi's Pace chapel, later overpainted,
is an open structure on two levels, consisting of square pillars
and heavy trabeation. The effect is severe and grand. The
contrast demonstrates Raphael's command of a wide range
of architectural forms and his freedom in their use: he was
never committed to a single manner.

III

While there is no evidence that Raphael had designed real
architecture before he arrived in Rome, the possibility cannot
be ruled out. But whatever experience he may or may not have
had, once in Rome he demonstrated his spatial awareness
in reorganising the vault of the Stanza della Segnatura.
He progressed rapidly, no doubt under Bramante's tutelage.
Whether Raphael attended Bramante as an unofficial assistant
in the Belvedere courtyard and at St Peter's is unknown, but
it seems more than likely. In any case, by the time he had
finished the Stanza della Segnatura he had begun his own
architectural projects.

It was probably in 1511–12, more or less contemporary with
The Expulsion of Heliodorus, that Raphael designed Agostino
Chigi's sepulchral chapel, opening off the north aisle of
Santa Maria del Popolo. Chigi, with his inexhaustible wealth,
his aesthetic perceptiveness – he was a Maecenas to Julius II's
Augustus – and freedom from institutional interference proved
an ideal patron for Raphael, affording him opportunities

otherwise unavailable. The Popolo chapel has a Greek cross plan, with three shallow arms and a short entrance passage, surmounted by a drum and dome. Two features may be emphasized. One is structural. The interior is treated as four tripartite or triumphal arches, in which a tall arched central field (that of the entranceway is open) is flanked by smaller arched niches. Taking up an idea of Bramante's, Raphael canted the niches at the diagonal, in part to expand the width of the drum and dome, in part so that each niche, in effect, flanks two arches: the corner does not divide one wall from

196 The Chigi Chapel, begun c. 1512

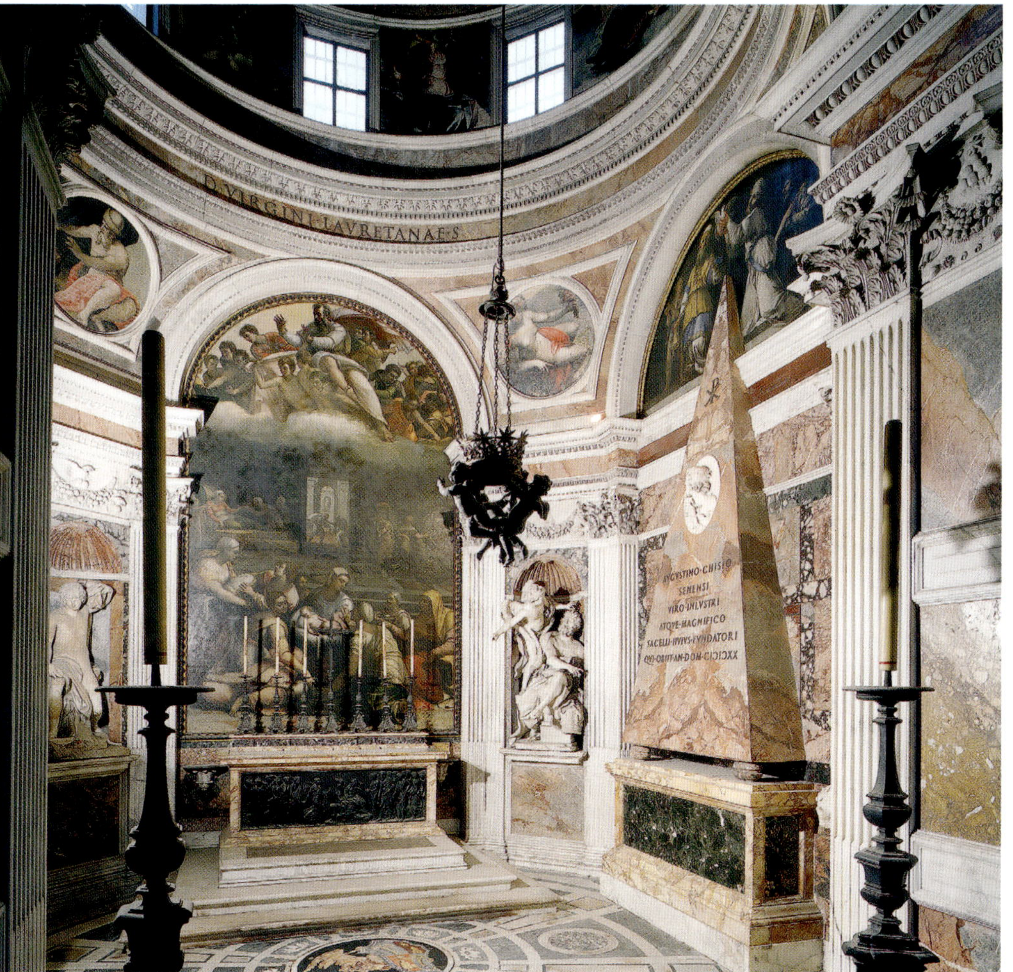

another but joins them. This illustrates that principle of elision that was to characterise much of Raphael's architectural thinking. In the chapel, it creates a cohesive space and, as in the Segnatura, the '+' axis of the entrance-altar and side walls is complemented by an '×' axis established by the niches. This latter is accentuated by the seated statues that were planned to protrude from their niches to energise the chapel's space.

The interior of Agostino's chapel was of a new richness. Although Raphael would, of course, have known the immensely costly multi-media Chapel of the Cardinal of Portugal at San Miniato al Monte, Florence, his project is at once more cohesive and sparer. Raphael exploits a wide range of material: a lavish use of costly coloured marbles on the walls, the floor and the monuments, white marble statuary, bronze reliefs, gilded bronze accoutrements, and mosaics, in addition to architectural carving of the highest quality. Structure and decoration are effectively fused. No doubt the disposition of the coloured marbles was prepared in now lost watercolours. A notable iconographic innovation is that the wall monuments – the sepulchres proper are in the crypt – are pyramidal; they are effectively abstract images of aspiration, embodying the hope of resurrection in their form and their penetration into the chapel's lunette zone. In his later letter to Leo X on the monuments of Rome, Raphael criticised Bramante for his use of plain materials, and it is evident that in this matter he was distancing himself from his architectural mentor even within Bramante's lifetime.

IV

To be appointed architect of St Peter's – 'il primo tempio del mondo', as Raphael called it – must have seemed the consecration of his reputation, but it proved a millstone. Raphael's melancholy is remarked upon in a letter of September 1519 and specifically in an architectural context. The project that Raphael took over had inherent flaws. Bramante had initially designed the church as centralised, and his project – which was admired by Michelangelo – was that shown on the foundation medal. But soon after construction commenced it was decided, both for liturgical and financial reasons, to add to it a nave to reinstate the length of the medieval church. It was also decided to retain the choir constructed by Bernardo Rossellino (1409–64) for Nicholas V, which Bramante's centralised project would have demolished. Tension between central and longitudinal plans became a constant throughout the church's building history; it was finally resolved only in the years around 1600 in favour of the latter.

Raphael's task was to regularise the fraught situation left by Bramante, who had made drawings for a nave extension but had not prepared a definitive model. As an advisor Raphael was allocated the elderly Fra Giocondo, who had recently published a corrected edition of Vitruvius. But Fra Giocondo, who died in July 1515, had little input into St Peter's. Giuliano da Sangallo too, who had revised Bramante's plan at an earlier moment and who was also salaried as co-advisor on the church, soon withdrew to Florence, where he died in 1516. He was replaced by his nephew, Antonio da Sangallo the Younger (1484–1546), another member of that extended family of architects and builders, who had been Bramante's assistant. We know little of the relation between Raphael and Antonio, but it seems, from the latter's occasional comments on drawings, that he was critical of certain features of Raphael's designs. He exercised some influence on him, especially since he had greater technical competence than Raphael.

The whole issue of St Peter's – the successive and overlapping projects, the number of architects involved, the endless discussions, the enormous body of visual and documentary evidence that survives but remains only partial, the traces of lements that were built and demolished – comprise one of architectural history's most complicated subjects, much of which is archaeological; it cannot even be summarised here. Little was constructed during Raphael's tenure of office, and what was built – an ambulatory designed to contain the outward thrust of the crossing piers and the dome that was to surmount them – was later destroyed. It is hard to avoid the conclusion that Raphael was, finally, overwhelmed by the project and failed to impose upon it a personal vision. Whether, had he lived, he might have done so is an unanswerable question.

We cannot trace the development of St Peter's from Raphael's drawings, for only a loose structural sketch of the interior dating from 1514 survives (Florence, Uffizi); there are otherwise no certainly connected autograph drawings. But from a synthesis of the available evidence, it seems that Raphael made three designs, each one of which would have required much thought and labour. The first, recorded by Sebastiano Serlio, would have eliminated the Nicholas V choir, and the exterior would have been articulated by giant pilasters, linking with those in the interior and giving the whole a degree of unity, but at the cost of a certain simplification. The chapels of the nave and ambulatory were to be lit by a series of serlian windows, or serlianas. The use of these openings, which became a favourite motif of Raphael, had been pioneered by Bramante. They consisted of a central arched window separated by thin columns or piers from flanking shorter rectangular windows, the three elements generally being gathered under a contiguous cornice. But Raphael soon turned – or was turned – against this plan and designed an exterior on two levels, with the lower articulated by Doric columns, based on those salvaged from the old basilica, carrying a heavy cornice. The second storey was again illuminated by serlianas, now pedimented, along the nave, but with only one lighting the ambulatory. What seems to be the latest project broadly followed the second, but at Antonio da Sangallo's prompting the lowest level was raised in height and the second, in which Diocletian windows are substituted for serlianas, correspondingly reduced. The exterior was now to be articulated by an endless row of applied columns, single on the ambulatories and paired on the nave walls. It would

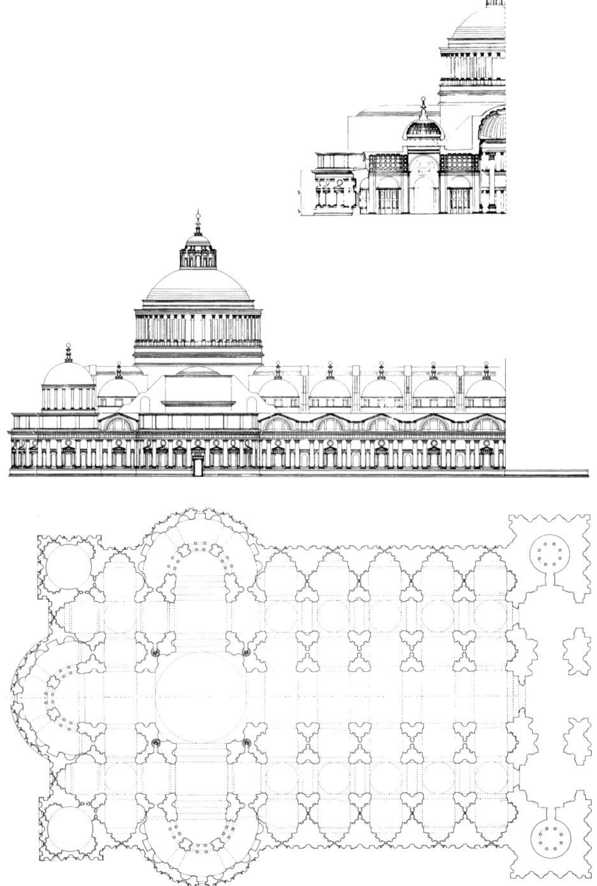

197 Raphael's third project for St Peter's, 1519–20. Reconstruction: plan, section and elevation; unexecuted

have lacked variety, and Raphael was clearly attempting to
impose unity on the body of St Peter's by accumulation and
repetition. In contrast, the façade entirely lacked unity. It was
to centre on a temple front, flanked by side bays with loggias,
each surmounted by a small dome. The sides were closed by
multi-storey belltowers that were accumulative rather than
unified in structure and that, surmounted by tall pyramids,
have an inadvertently 'Gothic' look. It is hard to see how the
façade could ever have been effective.

Raphael's final project was the starting point of Antonio da
Sangallo's much enlarged schemes, which carried multiplication
still further but more confidently, eliminating the weakness
of Raphael's exterior and raising the body of the building to
a uniform height. But his project was ungainly and, finally,
unbuildable. It required the imperious personality, impregnable
reputation and fearlessness of the 72-year-old Michelangelo,
appointed to St Peter's in 1547, to undertake the radical surgery
by which alone the project could be clarified.

V

It maybe that, before he was appointed to St Peter's, Raphael
designed the small church of Sant'Eligio degli Orefici for the
goldsmiths' guild (his friendship with the goldsmith Antonio
da San Marino might have opened his way to the commission).
The attribution is usually accepted but evidence is slight and,
if Raphael designed the church, he must have done so soon
after he arrived in Rome, even though construction began only
at the end of 1514 and was not finished until well after Raphael's
death. Sant'Eligio is coherent if impersonal, a Greek cross
plan with shallow arms and an apse at the east. Surmounted
by a drum and dome, it is of a type more familiar in Tuscany
than in Rome. But the nave is lit by a serliana, and the façade
has paired pilasters that carry small Ionic capitals linked by
a moulding running across their bases. Both motifs would
be appropriate for Raphael, but if the church is his it hardly
constitutes adequate preparation for St Peter's.

More interesting are the designs that Raphael submitted
for two other churches. The first, of 1515–16, which would have
brought about a direct confrontation with Michelangelo, was
for a monumental façade for the church of San Lorenzo in
Florence. Designed by Brunelleschi, San Lorenzo was the Medici
family church, thus dear to Leo X, who desired its completion.
Many architects competed for the commission, which called
for a strong, pedimented central element, corresponding to the
nave, and flanking wings closed at either side by a terminating
feature. A sketchy copy of Raphael's design shows that it would

198

have been a two-storey structure with a strong Doric lower storey supporting a high entablature, topped by a temple front enclosing a serliana for the reliquary display platform at the façade's centre. Raphael's was the most coherent of the known proposals for the church, and powerfully plastic. But the commission was allocated to Michelangelo, whose screen façade, carrying a multitude of statues and reliefs, proved impractical and massively costly. It was abandoned, and San Lorenzo remained – and remains – without a façade.

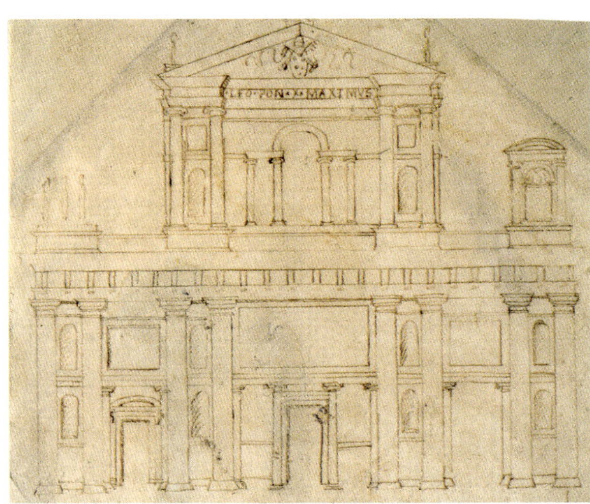

198 LEFT Unidentified draughtsman after Raphael, design for the façade of San Lorenzo, Florence, 1515–16; unexecuted
199 BELOW Unidentified draughtsman after Raphael, design for San Giovanni dei Fiorentini, Rome, 1518; unexecuted. This design is close to one prepared for the same project by Antonio da Sangallo

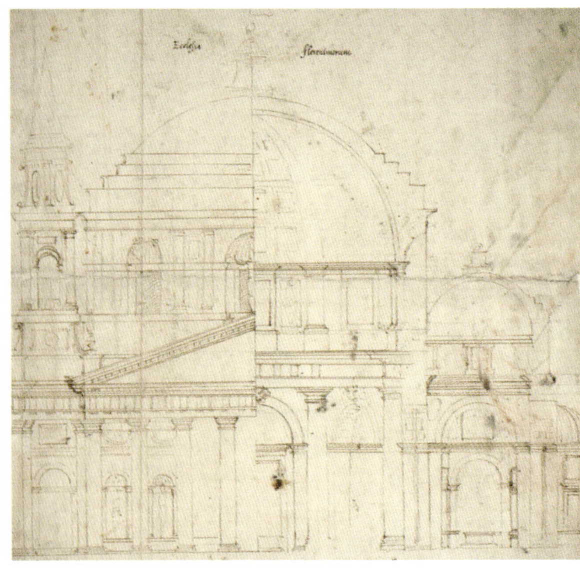

The other design, of 1518, was for San Giovanni dei Fiorentini, a new church planned for the Florentine community in Rome at the top of Via Giulia, opposite the palace Raphael intended for himself. Once more, several architects competed for the commission among them, reportedly, Giulio Romano. The most likely visual record of Raphael's design shows an octagonal building, with a dome inspired by the Pantheon, fronted by a Doric temple façade supported by eight columns. The façade seems low for the great volume of the dome, but this was surely deliberate, calculated to stress the church's geometry; perhaps coincidentally, Michelangelo considered a similar solution in his last idea for the façade of his (centrally planned) St Peter's. The façade of San Giovanni was to continue into the bases of two tall belltowers whose pinnacles reach the top of the dome. Like those planned for St Peter's, they are accumulative in structure but lighter and more elegant. In this project, Raphael sems to have released some of his frustrations with St Peter's.

VI

Raphael's inventiveness and the freedom of his architectural thought can be seen much more clearly in his surviving secular buildings or those that are known in visual records. It is probable that Raphael's first palazzo was for horses rather than humans: the stables that Agostino Chigi had built alongside the Farnesina, on the Via della Lungara. A page of sketches by Raphael of about 1511 – which includes the design of a fountain, maybe for the Farnesina's gardens – contains a ground plan probably for the stables. They would therefore date from the same period as the commissions for Chigi's chapels. The building was probably still unfinished by 1520 but, given its simplicity, could have been completed by any competent mason. It seems that in 1518 Agostino hosted a party in rooms draped with bunting and then surprised his guests by revealing that they were dining in a stable: horses cannot then have been in residence. Were it not for the blind lower storey, from the exterior the building could well be an apartment house.

The stables were lightly constructed and had so deteriorated by 1808 that they were demolished, leaving extant only part of the lower storey. Built of brick with stone dressing for the bases and the capitals of the pilasters, the stables were seven identical bays long and thus repetitive, but given some movement by the blind panels of the lower storey and, on the first floor, by rectangular windows with plain cornices that rise from the level of the pilaster bases. Perhaps the stables' most distinguished feature is their doubled pilasters, on separate bases, on both levels: Doric below, Corinthian above. Raphael

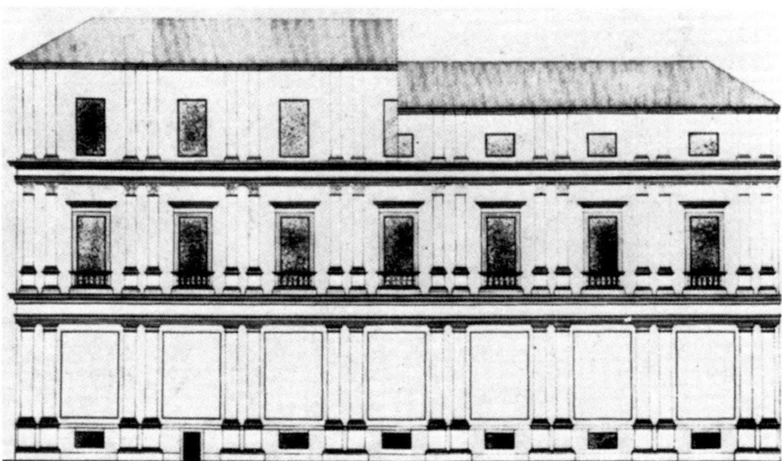

200 The Farnesina Stables, 1511 onwards; largely demolished

surely realised that the single pilasters with which Peruzzi had articulated the Farnesina seemed like appliqué decoration, parcelling up the building's surface but detracting from its volumes. In the stables the doubling creates a sense of weight and solidity.

201 In 1516 Raphael began the palazzo of Jacopo da Brescia, an important physician at the papal court. It occupied an awkward triangular plot, whence it was removed and reconstructed on a new site from 1937–40, but the original effect remains. In it, Raphael followed the formula of the Palazzo Caprini, which he himself acquired for 3,000 ducats in 1517. But he introduced variations to make Bramante's design sleeker. The ground floor is channelled horizontally, which encourages movement along the street and integrates the building with its setting. The *piano nobile* is cleverly articulated. Relatively narrow Doric pilasters set on pedestals are superimposed upon and partly merge with wider, flattened Doric piers that extend behind the pedestals. This conjunction gives the *piano nobile* great strength and enables Raphael to turn the corner fluently, for on the long façade the viewer sees a pilaster and half of a pier, and on the short side another pilaster and the other flank of the pier – effectively a further example of elision. The tabernacle windows alternate triangular and segmental pediments. Raphael surreptitiously diminished the bay widths on the *piano nobile* from right to left, presumably to accentuate the palace's authority when approached from the right, although it is hard now to see why. The problems its ground plan presented no

doubt stimulated Raphael's awareness of interior spaces, later to find virtuosic expression in the ground- and first-floor plans of 1519 for the new palace – never to be executed – that he projected for himself in Via Giulia (Florence, Uffizi). That complex project, which integrates two residences in a single block, includes both baths and indoor lavatories and shows how much attention Raphael paid to the services of his building – as well as testifying to his knowledge of hydraulics. In his planning of domestic interiors, Raphael turned to a wide variety of Roman models, eschewing the symmetrical and regularly disposed spaces characteristic of earlier Renaissance planning: he was, in fact, attempting to recreate a Roman seigneurial house with all its amenities.

The palazzo of Jacopo da Brescia was an exercise in Bramante's manner. Raphael's other surviving palace, the Palazzo Alberini-Cicciaporci, intended as an apartment house, is quite different. It was first mentioned in 1515 and worked on over the following years. The seven-bay façade employs very shallow rustication on the ground floor, which is divided horizontally by a simple rectangular moulding. It has six

201 The Palazzo of Jacopo da Brescia, 1515–19. Dismantled and reconstructed on a new site from 1937

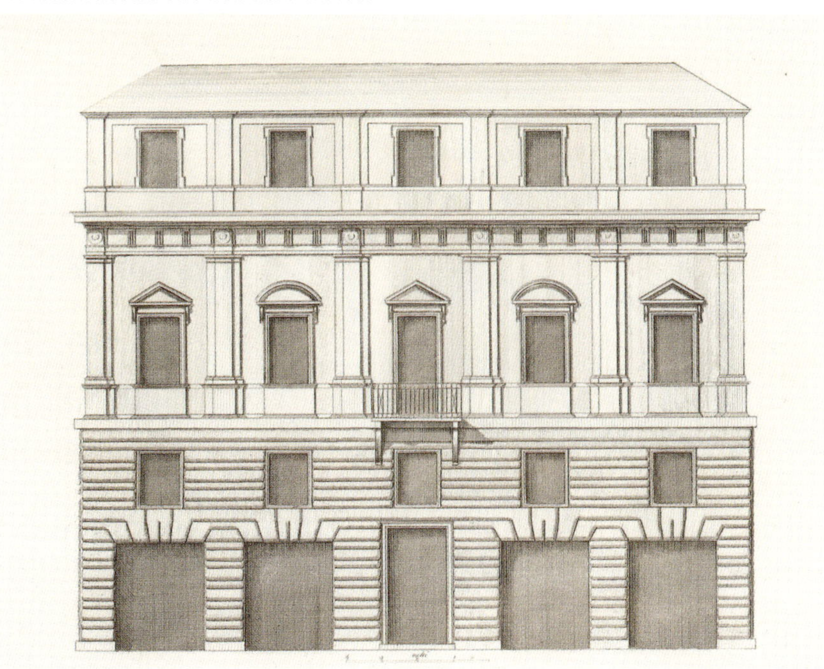

rectangular apertures for shops, and above the moulding
that delimits them are lunettes expressing the rooms above the
shops. But the lower storey can also be read as seven identical
arches, of which the central one is the palace's entrance.
The piers between the arches are set with vertical blocks that
serve as 'ghost' pilaster strips. These are taken up in the plain
and shallow Tuscan pilasters of the *piano nobile*. Raphael thus
established regular intervals across the two lower storeys of the
façade, with the lightest of touches. The *piano nobile*, eschewing
tabernacles, has rectangular windows with simple cornices
like those on the Chigi stables, and no balconies. The pilasters'
simple bases stand on the string course that runs across the
façade below the windows. They have residual capitals, yet
these do not support the compressed frieze but merge with it.
On the third level, the vertical emphases become panels with
neither bases nor capitals and indented rather than protuberant.
The already shallow lower levels are flattened still further, and
the whole façade becomes an exercise in low relief, suddenly
bursting into high relief in the imposing cornice. The façade
of Palazzo Alberini-Cicciaporci is extremely – one might
say infinitely – subtle, an exercise in rarefied minimalism.
Raphael treats it like a painter exploiting slight differences
among adjacent hues.

202   Raphael's third Roman palace, destroyed in the seventeenth
century, was again different – spectacularly so. Constructed
from mid-1518 for the papal protonotary Giovanni Battista
Branconio dell'Aquila (1473–1522), for whom Giulio and Penni
179 painted *The Visitation*, its five-bay façade displayed a plethora
of witty invention. The lower storey, again including shops, was
articulated by Doric half-columns on bases, evidently inspired
by the Colosseum. The relation of the ground floor to the *piano
nobile* was unprecedented and flouts a – perhaps the – axiom of
classical architecture, according to which solids and voids carry
solids and voids. One would expect the six half-columns to be
carried up as pilasters on the *piano nobile*: instead they become
six niches, housing statues in stucco. Thus the *piano nobile*
is closed at either side not by strong fields nor fields equal
in weight to those of the centre, but by weak ones. The five
windows are set in tabernacles based on those in the Pantheon,
with alternating pediments; the pediments are not carried on
the windows' frames, however, but on unfluted half-columns
with Ionic capitals, set on plinths, which effectively form a
canopy around and above them. The dance that Raphael
choreographed is too complex to analyse in detail, but two
other motifs may be mentioned. The triple-arch rhythm of five
windows flanked by six niches shows the same principle of

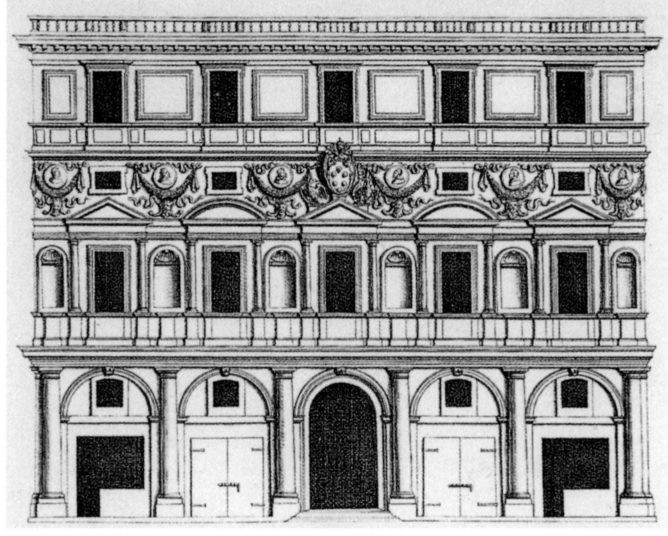

linking as the Chigi Chapel and Bibbiena's *loggetta*. And the
architraves of the window entablatures are extended across
the entire façade as a moulding tying it together. Above the
windows the wall, which fronts a low mezzanine, was peopled
with decorative forms – garlands, eagles, antique profiles, etc.
– in painted stucco, in a fusion of structure and decoration.
The upper storey too had figurative reliefs, again in painted
stucco, alternating with windows. Throughout, elements run
into one another. And at the top of the building there was a
balustrade, a grand element not seen in other Roman palaces
of this moment.

Many of the features were inspired by minor decorative
Roman architecture rather than major buildings. Painted
façades, such as Peruzzi's exterior frescoes on the Farnesina,
were becoming common in Roman building in the second
decade (according to Vasari, another contemporary palace, the
Palazzo Bracciaferro, was decorated by Pellegrino da Modena
with frescoes designed by Raphael), but extensive exterior
stucco work was new. No doubt executed by Giovanni da Udine,
this aspect of the façade looks forward to later sixteenth-
century Roman buildings such as the Palazzo Spada. The
theatrical and ultra-sophisticated membering of the Palazzo
Branconio dall'Aquila testifies to calm and confidence: it is
festive and invitingly playful, street scenery with no aura
of defensiveness. It instances a dimension of architectural
thought that one might not expect to find in Raphael:

202

features such as columns, architraves, etc. – which, even
if not structural, are generally used to represent notional
structure – are detached from their conventional roles and
used capriciously; representation is not anchored to the
convention of what is represented but expands into play.
The Palazzo Branconio dall'Aquila is Raphael's most
developed harbinger of glitzy postmodernism.

203   Raphael's unfinished Palazzo Pandolfini in Florence,
his only known building outside Rome, showed yet another
facet of his approach to design. It was planned as a nine-bay
structure closed by rusticated quoins at either side and
centred on a grand arched door. This is surrounded by
wide and inventive rustication, with tall blocks radiating
from the arch to reach cornice level. The walls are otherwise
unarticulated except at the base of the second storey, by a
moulding running the width of the façade, with the Greek
wave motif favoured by Raphael. The palazzo would have
contained a total of sixteen tabernacle windows, with
alternating triangular and segmental pediments on both
floors. Segmental and triangular pediments on the ground
floor are surmounted by triangular and segmental pediments
on the *piano nobile* to create a vertical zigzag. Above the door
would probably have been a large window, perhaps with a
balcony fronting a grand room, never constructed. The façade
has some similarities with that of the Palazzo Baldassini,

203 The Palazzo Pandolfini, Florence, c. 1516 onwards; unfinished

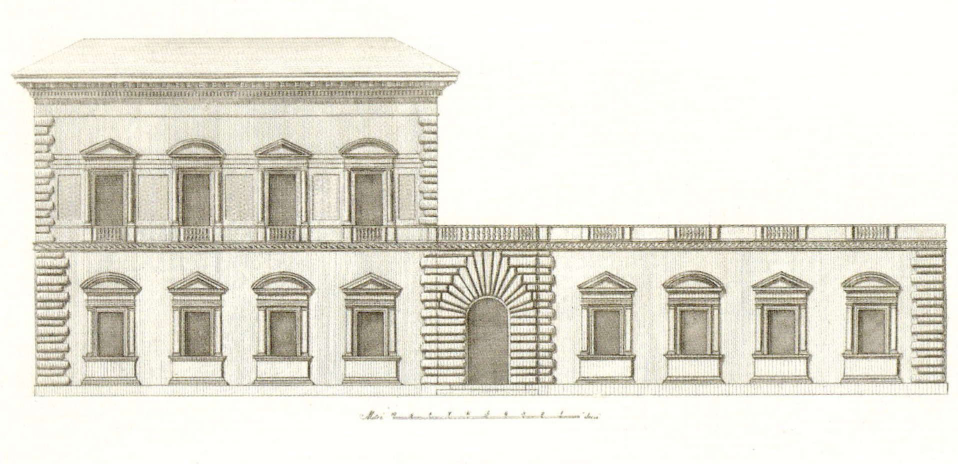

which Antonio da Sangallo began *c.* 1516, and there was presumably reciprocal influence.

VII

By far the most important of Raphael's secular projects was the enormous Villa Madama, commissioned by Leo X through Cardinal Giulio, on Monte Mario. Begun in 1517 on a difficult rising site, like the Villa Medici in Fiesole and the ducal palace in Urbino, its construction was an enormously costly engineering task. It was intended as a vast palace, its stables designed to house 400 horses, and one of its functions was to serve as a luxurious staging post for foreign dignitaries arriving at Rome. It was broadly inspired by Pliny's description of his villas and, uniquely, Raphael wrote an unfinished description of the Madama probably destined for the pope. It is, in effect, a guided tour, the only such document to survive by an architect of the period and evidence of his stature as a thinker and planner, although he was not a fluent writer. His account probably dates from late 1518 or early 1519. It was used by and amplified in a few details (the central loggia may have been intended to be frescoed with a biographical cycle of Leo X) in a long encomium of Cardinal Giulio and of the villa itself by the poet Francesco Sperulo (1463–1531), completed in March 1519.

Raphael's description itemises the villa's overall arrangement and its relation to its surroundings. He describes the rooms and spaces and elucidates their functions, their commodity and their beauty. He is alert to the needs of the horses who were to be housed in its stables. He is particularly concerned with the relation of rooms to the position of the sun and the uses of rooms at different times of the day and year. He demonstrates his close study of antique models in his discussion of the villa's frontal entrance, mentioning varieties of cryptoporticus, but the general emphasis is practical rather than formal: there is a detailed account of the planned baths, with hot and cold water and boiler rooms, revealing Raphael's careful thought about the bathers' comfort. All in all, the document shows a command of utility, organisation and display. It also demonstrates a strong awareness of the villa in relation to its prospects, whether of Rome, Monte Mario, the villa's gardens and their trees, or the fishpond below the terrace. At times Raphael seems to be thinking like a landscape painter of the following century or a landscape architect. He also refers frequently to the beauty of this or that space, notably the great loggia that opens onto the garden, always intended to be the villa's most spectacular space, and a modern equivalent of the richest kind of Roman architecture that Raphael so admired, notably the Golden

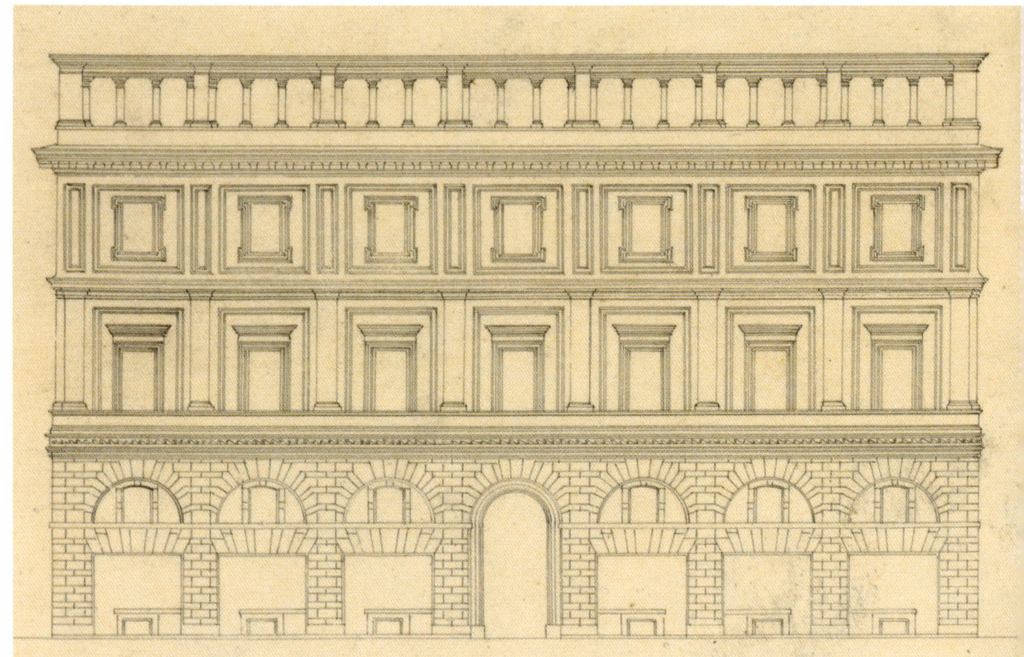

204 The Palazzo Alberini-Cicciaporci, c. 1515 onwards; completed by Giulio Romano

House of Nero. But with a few exceptions the account describes the building's interior and its amenities rather than the exterior. Raphael's description and analysis of the project make it clear that the villa was, in its fundamentals, an *all'antica* creation and the culmination of Raphael's use of ancient architecture in a modern context. Raphael's Roman buildings are rife with quotations from the antique, direct or indirect, large or small, and his knowledge was vast – supplemented, Vasari tells us, by drawings of ancient monuments sent to him by draughtsmen throughout the Mediterranean. But he used antique elements less as a programme than as a dictionary, from which to form his own, often witty, compositions. In the Villa Madama, the re-creation of an antique *locus amoenus*, a place of delight, was the generating idea (emblematic is the inclusion of an amphitheatre), and it represented the most complete assimilation of the antique of its period.

Construction of the Villa Madama seems to have proceeded rapidly, and huge resources were thrown at it. The energy of activity is mentioned in Sperulo's account of the villa, which is fused with an encomium of the glory of the House of Medici, making it clear that, whatever papal function it served, it was also a dynastic project, perhaps planned to remain as a Roman powerbase when the papacy passed to another family. This may account for Raphael's reference to the villa's defensive features, otherwise seemingly redundant but in the event sadly prophetic, for the villa was assaulted and badly damaged in a raid by the Colonna family in 1526.

The villa had reached something approaching its present state, about one-third finished, by the time of Raphael's death. Its intended appearance is most readily understood with the help of the great reconstruction model made for the *Raffaello architetto* exhibition of 1984. It was to be vast, with a large courtyard at the left and gardens of matching size on the right. The main body of the building is divided into three: a central block, which is fronted by three large arches, inspired by those of the Colosseum; and two side wings, each dominated by a large Diocletian window – open on the left, closed on the right – which stands above other windows arranged as a loose serliana (another example of Raphael's talent for fusion). Behind the main block is a circular courtyard, and behind that was to be an accurately Roman amphitheatre, set into the hill. Ostensibly it was to be a pleasure palace but also, one suspects, something of a Versailles, a centre of power distinct from, or an adjunct to, the Vatican. And as at Versailles, there is a disjunction between interior and exterior.

Despite the project's size and ambition, and the extreme intelligence of its organisation, there are curious lacks, and the impression is that, as at St Peter's, size obstructs cohesion. The three open arches in the centre of the *piano nobile* – perhaps intended as welcoming – create an uncomfortable void, and the columnar screens in the flanking arches seem too slight. The Diocletian windows – which Raphael included in his latest project for St Peter's – are overly modest in relief. Raphel did employ half-columns and pilasters spanning two storeys on the exterior, as he planned to do on his own projected palace, but this rather timid 'giant' order is surprisingly un-imposing and fails to unify the upper part of the building.

Put simply, the exterior of the Madama seems lacking in density and richness. Much of the articulation is thin, even spindly, and the building does not project a grandeur and authority commensurate with its size. There is little of that merging of parts that would help unify the building and that it would seem to invite. In general, there is a lack of physical substance and plastic relief in both the brickwork and the exterior articulation. To take one example, the frieze of the garden loggia is convex in section ('pulvinated'), and so are the bases of the pilasters: such forms register weight and imply

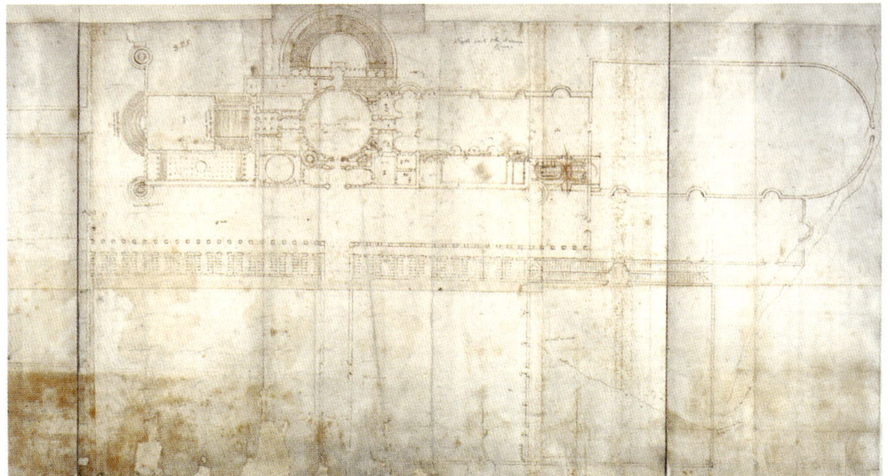

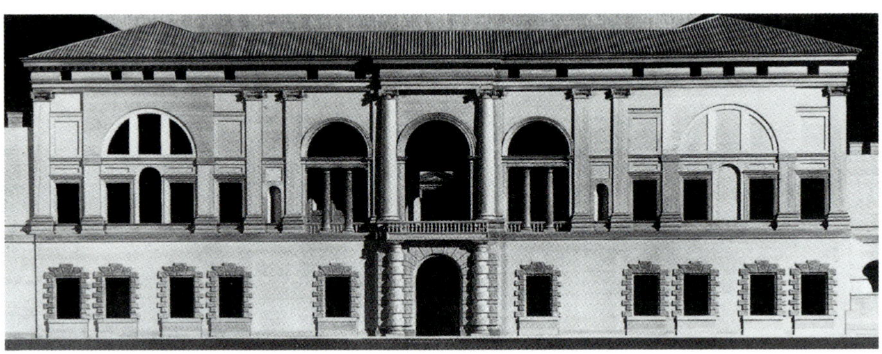

elasticity. But the pilasters that join them, which have perfunctory Ionic capitals, are shallow, overly thin for their height, and seem inappropriate to their positions. The masterly control of antiquising forms on the façades of Raphael's Roman palaces is not apparent at the Madama. Of course, Raphael clearly planned a contrast between a plain exterior and a rich interior, as exemplified in stucco by the magnificent decoration of the great loggia, and in articulation by the circular courtyard, with its heavy window lintels supported on half-columns. But, even allowing for intended contrasts, the prevalently shallow relief and unimpressive articulation of the exterior are hard to explain. It seems likely that Raphael's control of this project weakened and that much was left to

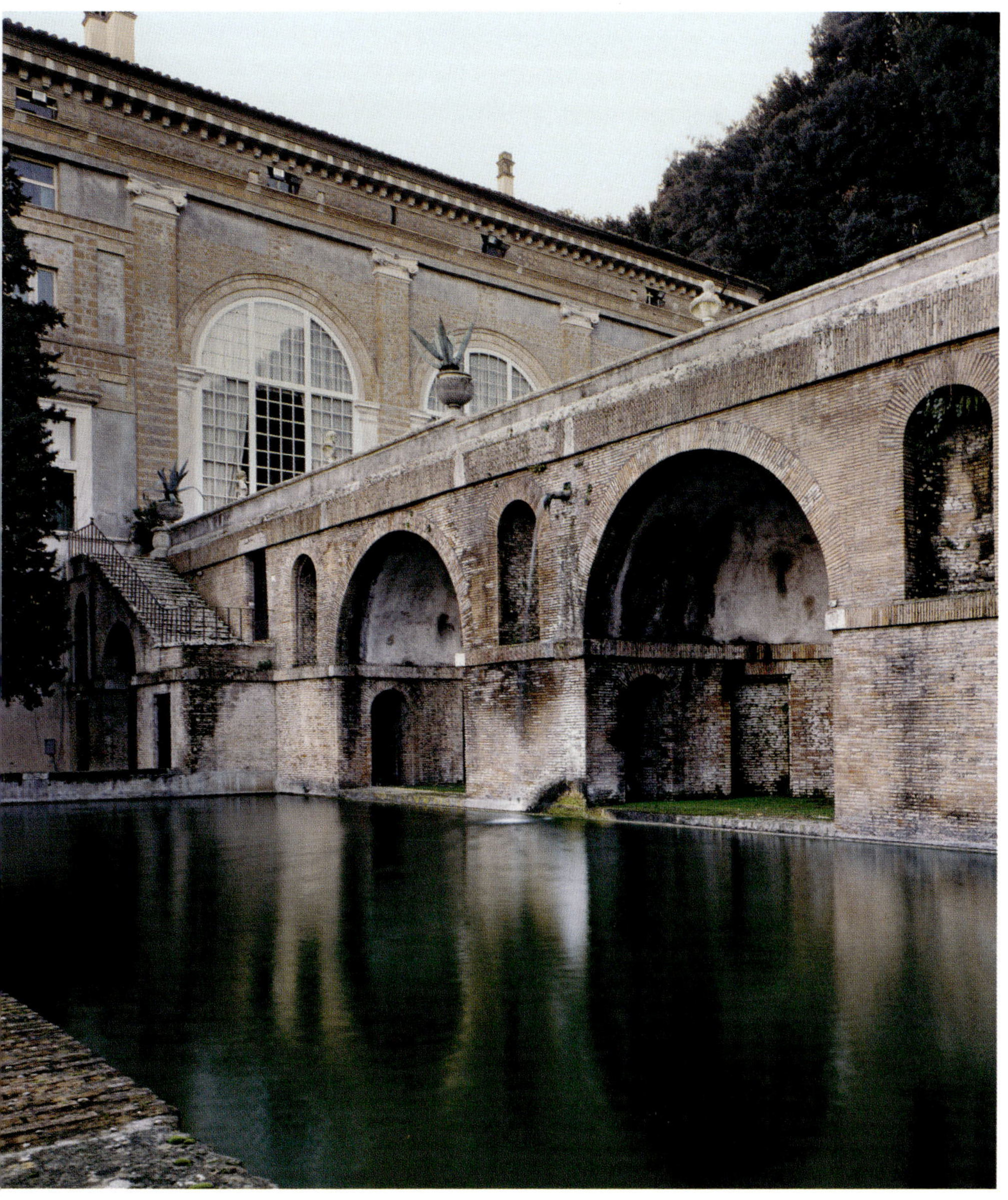

205 OPPOSITE ABOVE Antonio da Sangallo to Raphael's design, Villa Madama,
plan, c. 1516
206 OPPOSITE BELOW After Raphael, the Villa Madama, begun 1516
207 ABOVE The Villa Madama, begun 1516. Exterior view from the lower terrace

Raphael's Architecture

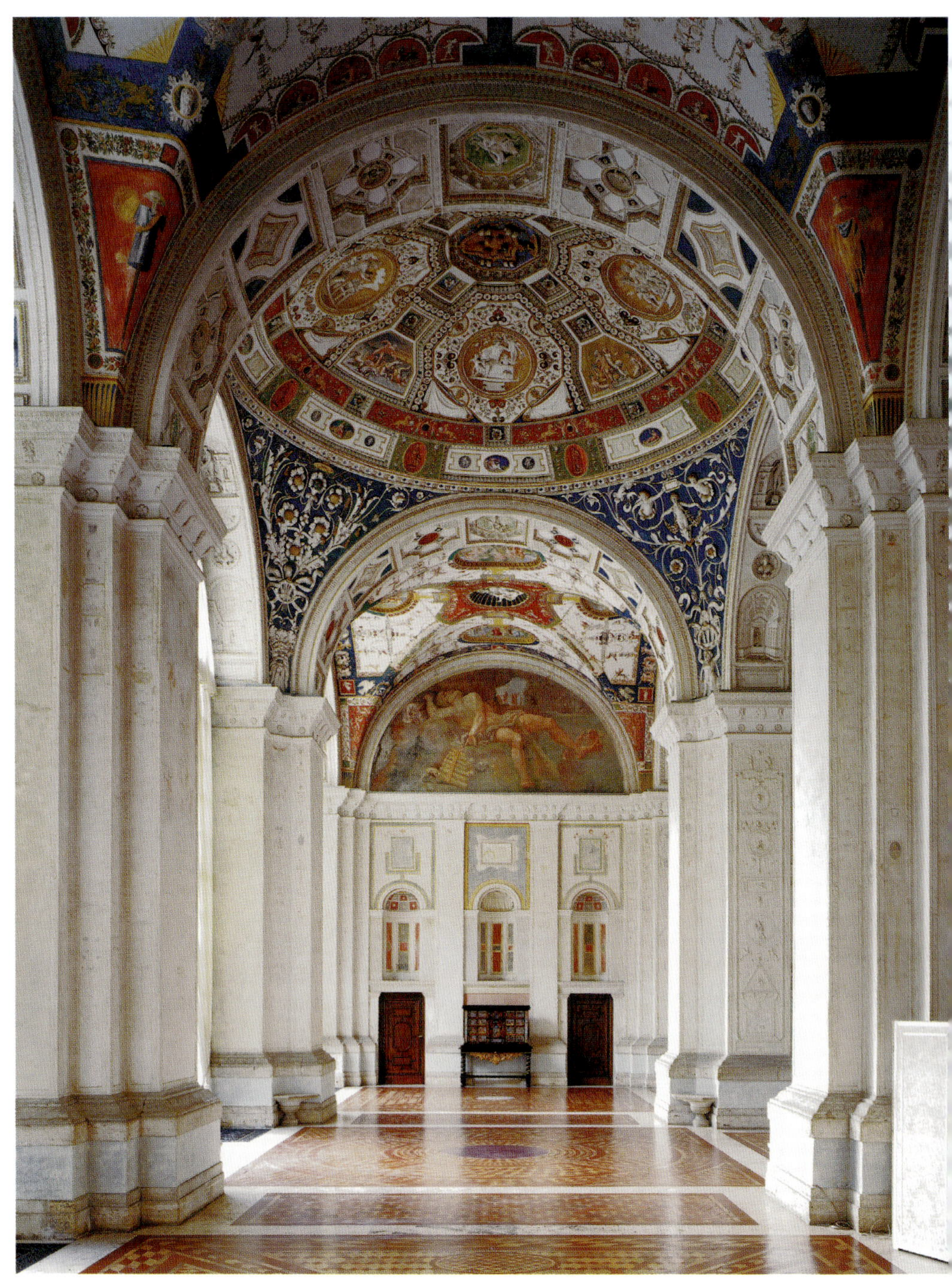

208 The Villa Madama, loggia. The decorative scheme, mainly executed in 1520–21 no doubt following Raphael's ideas, comprises stuccos by Giovanni da Udine and frescoes by Gianfrancesco Penni and Baldassare Peruzzi: *Polyphemus* on the end wall is by Giulio

Antonio da Sangallo and then to Giulio Romano. But such
features – or solecisms? – would be surprising from either.

VIII

Two thrusts of Raphael's account of the Villa Madama are the
building's antique credentials and its topography, especially
in relation to the roads that lead up to it from Rome. Such
concerns are found in his other extended piece of theoretical
writing, prepared in collaboration with Baldassare Castiglione
in 1519 but of which preliminary versions may date to 1516:
his famous report to Leo X. It is, centrally, a plea for the
preservation of Roman remains – which were steadily being
depleted for building materials – and for the reconstruction
of the ancient city in an early effort at visual archaeology.
In addition to careful study of the existing remains, Raphael
also stresses the need to study ancient texts and to relate
them to physical examination of the sites.

Much of the account is occupied with discussion of the
surveying instrument that Raphael was using – if not an
invention, then an improvement on existing types. He also
insists that it is necessary for all buildings to be drawn three
times, in ground plan, elevation and section, to ensure that
the information provided is undistorted. This seems to be the
first written formulation of such a programme, although
in practice it must have been adopted earlier. Raphael then
proceeds to a summary account of the historical development
of Rome's architecture and its periodisation, including a
condemnation of the 'German style' (in other words, Gothic).
However, Raphael's approach is not simplistic: citing the
Arch of Constantine, he points out that the style of later
Roman art underwent a decline. And he could separate art
and architecture: thus, while he deplores the quality of the
sculpture that decorated the Baths of Diocletian, he lauds
the majesty of the building. Raphael advocates the imitation
of Roman grandeur in modern buildings and pleads for the
restoration of Roman models; he also criticises Bramante
for neglecting rich materials.

The report is linked with an ambitious plan to provide
a map reconstructing the regions of ancient Rome, in which
Raphael enlisted the aid of various antiquarians. It seems
that only one section of it was brought to completion or near
completion at the time of his death, and the termination of
the project was lamented by his contemporaries. Had Raphael
lived, the measured drawings that he would have had made,
and the coordination of these with site maps, would have
advanced archaeology by many decades.

Paradoxically, in August 1515 Leo had appointed Raphael to take charge of securing ancient stones and marbles for use in St Peter's – in short, responsibility for cannibalising material from ancient buildings for new projects, precisely the practice Raphael deplores in the opening words of his report. But the power to cannibalise also implies the power not to cannibalise, and the selection process would have sharpened his awareness of what should be preserved.

The topography of Rome and its reorganisation were of vital importance to Raphael, and his reference to the lamentable state of the city is heartfelt. Julius had promoted the clarification of Rome's thoroughfares with projects such as the Via Giulia, a process that was continued by Leo. Raphael was also involved in this (it is inextricably connected with his reconstruction project), and he may have taken part in discussions surrounding the planning of streets that proceeded into the city from the Porta del Popolo, although little was done in his lifetime. But the dimensions of Raphael's activity as a town planner, in which he worked with Antonio da Sangallo the Younger and others, are complicated, left few traces and can hardly be investigated here. The central point, perhaps, is that by 1520 Raphael had acquired an authority over the visual–cultural life of Rome that was not to be equalled until Bernini was at the height of his career. At Raphael's death it was rumoured that Leo X had intended to make him a cardinal. Had he done so, Raphael would have wielded a political power achieved by no other artist. One can only wonder what he might have achieved had he been granted the longevity of Michelangelo.

Chapter 14
The Personal Touch

In parallel with his development of Leonardesque chiaroscuro and ultra-refined surfaces, Raphael was exploring an alternative manner. From 1516 until his death, he painted a series of portraits on canvas, a support previously used, as far as we know, only in the Città di Castello banner and the *Sistine Madonna*. It was employed only once more for a subject painting, the life-size *St John the Baptist in the Wilderness* (Florence, Uffizi) of *c.* 1517, which, although given by Vasari to Raphael, was designed and executed by Giulio Romano, who made no visual use of the fabric support.

It was in the 'painterly' *Sistine Madonna* that Raphael learnt to exploit the textures of canvas, and it is conjectural how he came to terms with its possibilities. Could he have seen paintings by Titian? Titian had not visited Rome, and there is no record that he had Roman commissions, but he and his work were known to the papal court for, in a letter of 31 May 1513, he stated that he had been invited to move to Rome. He does not say when or by whom, but the agent was surely his and Raphael's common friend Pietro Bembo – a key figure in both Rome and Venice and friendly with the major political and literary figures in both cities. Bembo seems to have been equally committed to Raphael and to Titian, to Roman and to Venetian art. Titian had painted a portrait of Bembo that the sitter may have taken to Rome, where Raphael would have seen it.

In Spring 1516 a significant conjunction occurred. On 3 April Bembo wrote to his friend and regular correspondent Bernardo Bibbiena that on the following day he was to revisit Tivoli, in the company of the poet Andrea Navagero (1483–1529), the

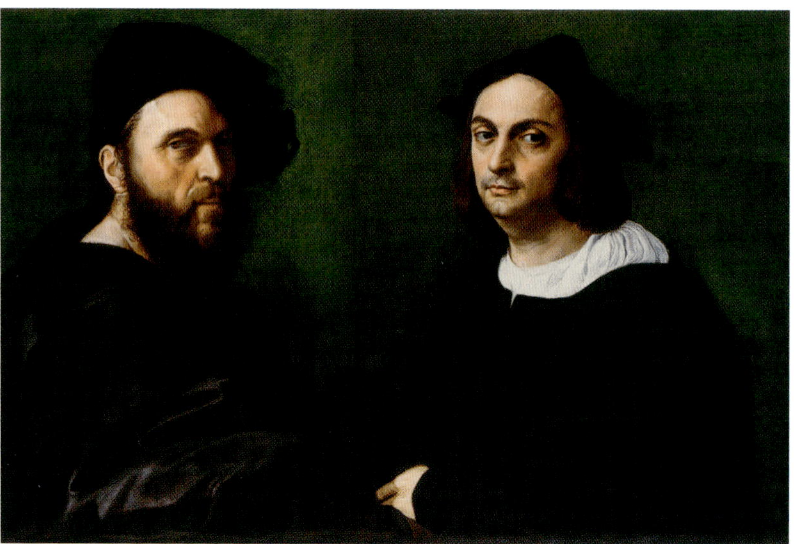

209 *Andrea Navagero and Agostino Beazzano*, 1516

ecclesiastic and papal diplomat Agostino Beazzano (*c.* 1490–
1549), Baldassare Castiglione and Raphael – all Bembo's close
friends. The aim was to examine Hadrian's Villa and, while the
length of the group's sojourn in Tivoli is unknown, it may have
lasted several days. One consequence of this meeting was that
Raphael portrayed Navagero and Beazzano on a single canvas,
destined for Bembo himself. Raphael treated his sitters as
juxtaposed busts rather than as a spatially coherent double
portrait – perhaps so that, if Bembo wished, the canvas could
be divided to show the sitters separately, as they are in an early
copy in the Prado. Navagero returned to Venice at the end of
April, and the double portrait was presumably begun – perhaps
even finished – before his departure.

Contemporaneously, Raphael portrayed another poet, the
Ferrarese Antonio Tebaldeo (1473–1537); his portrait, now known
only in a copy, is so Venetian in appearance that it was at one
time attributed to Giovanni Cariani. Bembo referred to it in a
further letter to Bibbiena, of 19 April, and admired it so much
that he said he was thinking of having his own portrait painted
by Raphael. He added that, in comparison with the *Tebaldeo*,
a likeness of Castiglione (evidently known to Bibbiena, which
dates it before mid-November 1515) seems to be the work of
one of Raphael's 'garzoni'. The great portrait in the Louvre
could not, under any circumstance, be described as looking
like assistant work, and Bembo must be referring to another

portrait of Castiglione, now lost or unidentified; this might have served Titian for his posthumous portrait of *Castiglione* of *c.* 1530 (Dublin, National Gallery of Ireland).

When Raphael became alert to a new and different kind of art and mastered its principles, he was able to develop them with unequalled speed and inventiveness. Nevertheless, the portrait of *Andrea Navagero and Agostino Beazzano* is not a wholly confident performance: the touch is overly solid and insufficiently aerated to exploit the blacks. It is, however, a passable interpretation of Titian's monochrome style of the middle teens; were it not certainly by Raphael it would probably be placed in Titian's orbit.

Raphael seems to have reserved canvas for portraits of intimates and otherwise used it only for special reasons: thus the 1517–18 portrait, painted with Giulio's help, of Lorenzo de' Medici, duke of Urbino, was probably executed on canvas – whose textures it does not exploit – because it had to be sent to France and then returned to Italy; the pictures intended to remain in France were all painted on wood.

Raphael's late portraits on canvas show extraordinary subtlety of characterisation and profound penetration of his

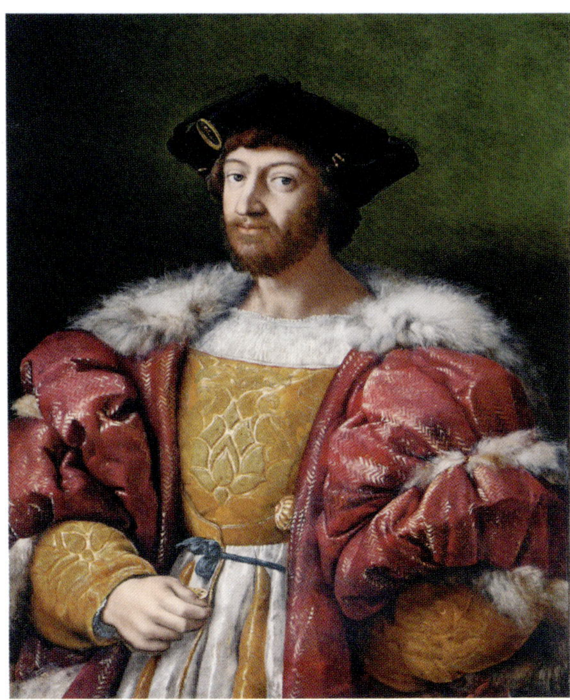

210 Raphael and Giulio Romano, *Lorenzo de' Medici, Duke of Urbino,* 1518

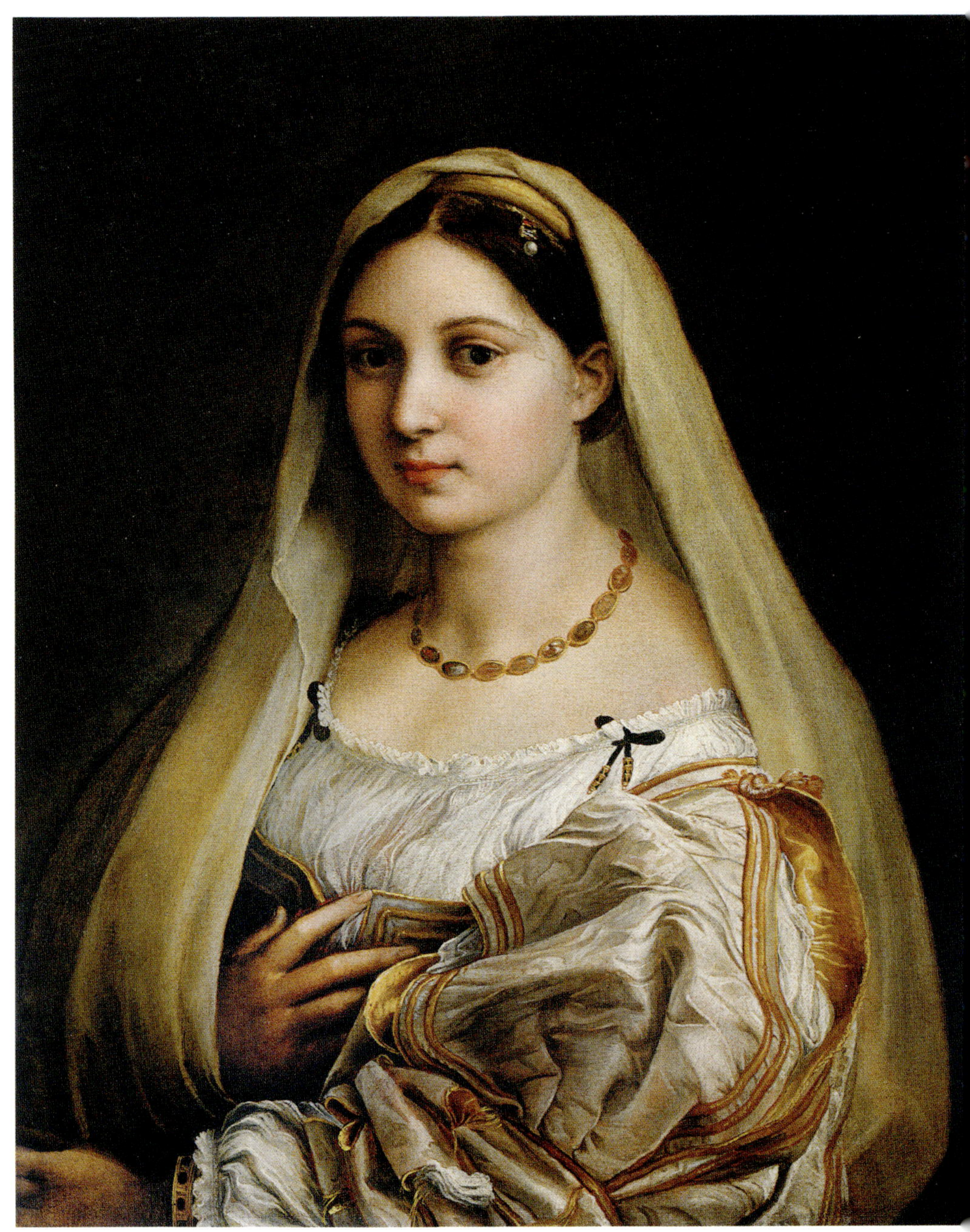

211 The 'Donna Velata', 1518

sitters' inner lives. Perhaps the most spectacular is the so-called *Donna Velata*, a painting that Vasari knew, admired greatly and believed to depict Raphael's mistress. It is likely to be of 1518: the exquisite play of the satin lining, sleek as mother-of-pearl, with the voluminous sleeve that swells like the sitter's body immediately recalls the play of a costume's interior and exterior seen in Giulio Romano's contemporary *Doña Isabel de Requesens*, but on a much higher level.

No other painting by Raphael makes so complex a use of texture or shows such variety of minimally differentiated hues. Raphael takes the *Donna Velata*'s costume as a surrogate for her body, its varied textures transmuted into softer and harder fabrics, and the strands of the sleeve perhaps evoking her bodily hair. Voluptuous and sumptuous, the portrait is simultaneously chaste, even reverent; it evokes love, not desire. Raphael has modelled the pose and attributes of his mistress, her face nested in its veil, on the prototype of virtue, the Virgin Annunciate: she places her right hand on her breast in acceptance of her lover, as the Virgin accepts divine will. The modulations of hue in her veil, varying minutely from part to part, comprise abstract painting of the highest order, the texture of the canvas attracting the slightest fluctuations of light to its surface. Few portraits convey so profoundly and intensely a painter's love for his sitter.

On 12 September 1519 Alfonso d'Este's ambassador in Rome told the duke that he had called on Raphael to enquire into progress on the duke's painting (by this time, presumably, the *Hunt of Meleager*) but had been refused entry because Raphael was painting a portrait of Baldassare Castiglione. There is no reason to doubt his statement: Castiglione had returned to Rome on 26 May 1519 after three years' absence and towards the end of that year was collaborating with Raphael on the letter to Leo X about the reconstruction of ancient Rome. Raphael and Castiglione would have spent many hours working together and, as we know from Castiglione's own testimony, the two men greatly enjoyed one another's company. This was the perfect moment for Raphael to have painted his friend, and their sympathy would have been enhanced by their common concern over the state of Rome and the affairs of the duchy of Urbino, seized for the house of Medici and for his nephew Lorenzo by the forces of Pope Leo X in 1516. That event certainly distressed Castiglione – and could hardly have left Raphael unaffected – but following Lorenzo's death on 4 May 1519 negotiations had begun with the aim of restoring the dukedom to Francesco Maria della Rovere.

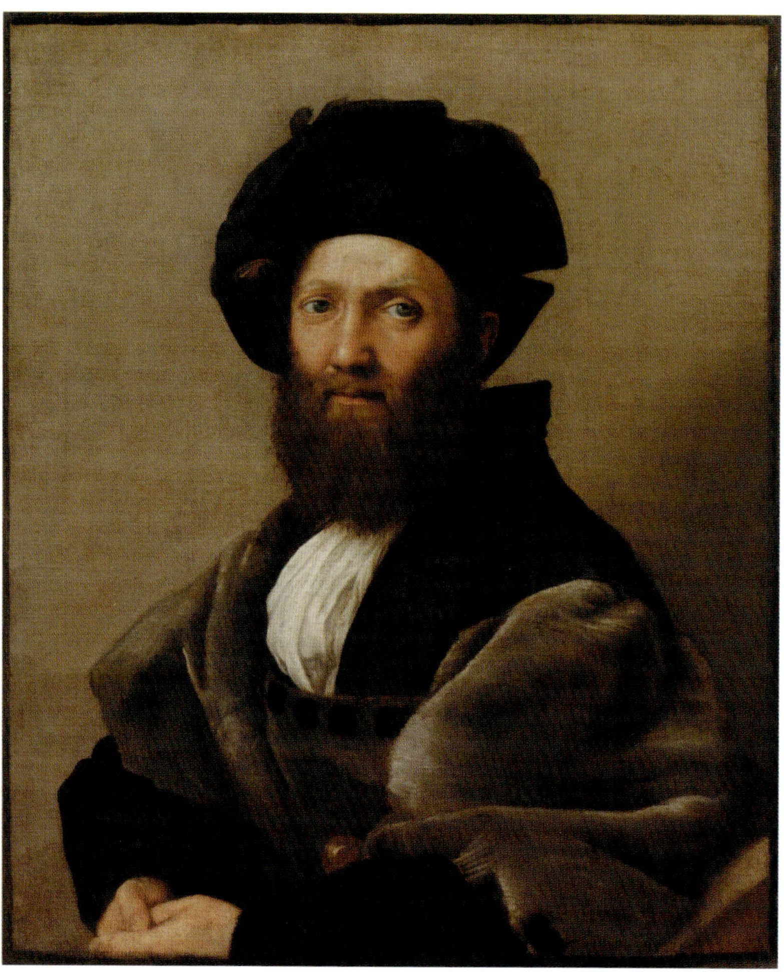

212   Raphael's portrait is an exercise in restraint. Pigment could
hardly be handled more sensitively, in colour, tone and touch.
Colours range from soft blacks to a sequence of browns:
the only strong hue is the mesmerising blue of Castiglione's
eyes, which sets off the warm tones of his flesh. Raphael maps
his sitter with apparent objectivity but also, simultaneously,
sympathetically, with appreciation but without flattery. The
head, in a device learnt by Raphael from Northern portraiture,
is a little enlarged so that it dominates the picture, set off
by the soft browns and greys that project the subtlety and
sensitivity of Castiglione's character. Raphael understood
as profoundly as Titian costume's metaphoric revelation

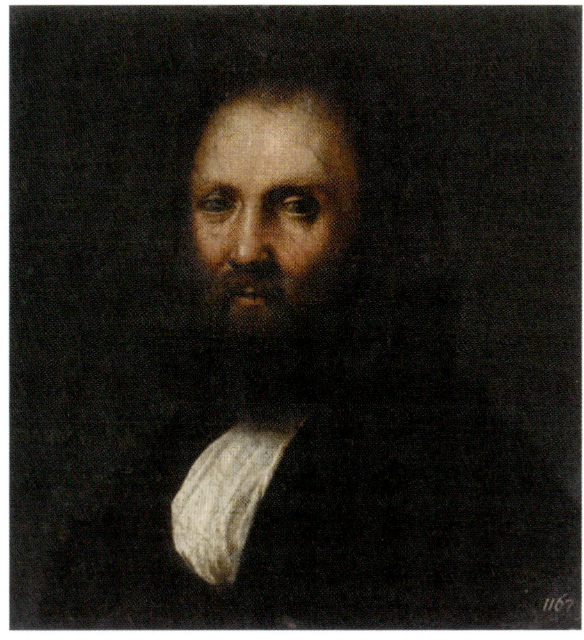

of interior life, and it has even been proposed that the
Castiglione influenced Titian's *Tommaso Mosti* (Florence, Pitti),
painted in 1526, after he had seen Raphael's portrait in Mantua.
But nothing in Titian's work quite resembles the *Castiglione*
in its softened, atmospheric contours and vaporous handling.
And while Raphael's *Castiglione* was copied in a drawing by
Rembrandt, who made use of its tonalities in his own work,
and in a painting by Rubens, neither attempted to emulate
its textures.

Castiglione had begun to go bald early, which depressed
him, and Raphael concealed his pate with a wide-brimmed
hat, which also acts as a frame for his face. But he prepared
the portrait in a lost study – probably on canvas, on the same
scale – that reveals Castiglione's sparse, receding hair. This
study is known from copies: one, on canvas and another
(Rome, Galleria Nazionale) painted on wood in Mantua after
Castiglione's death by a member of Giulio Romano's studio.

Whether Raphael made other portrait studies in oil
is unknown, but one by him in coloured chalks on paper
does survive: a head of a cardinal (Wilton House, Salisbury
Collection). It was probably made for a portrait – perhaps a
group portrait – that either was not painted or is lost. It has
been linked with the further of the two cardinals riding

behind Leo X in *The Repulse of Attila*, but the resemblance
is superficial, and the drawing is near 1520 in date. Raphael
may have been alerted to the possibilities of coloured chalks
by Leonardo or one of his entourage: its use was quite
common in Milan.

Raphael's intimate and friendship portraits contain a degree
of autobiography: his touch insinuates the painter into what
he paints, evokes his intimacy with his sitters, and pursues, by
reflection, a strain of self-analysis and self-presentation. Two of
Raphael's earliest surviving drawings are self-portraits, one of
c. 1500 a concentrated self-appraisal (London, British Museum),
the other, perhaps a little earlier, a presentational arrangement
inspired by Pinturicchio. The latter was adapted, probably
c. 1504, in his *Self-Portrait* as a sober student (Florence, Uffizi),
and in 1509 he reappears, again in sober garb, at the right of
The School of Athens. But close in date is a lost portrait (formerly
Kraków, Czartoryski Collection), known in many copies, in

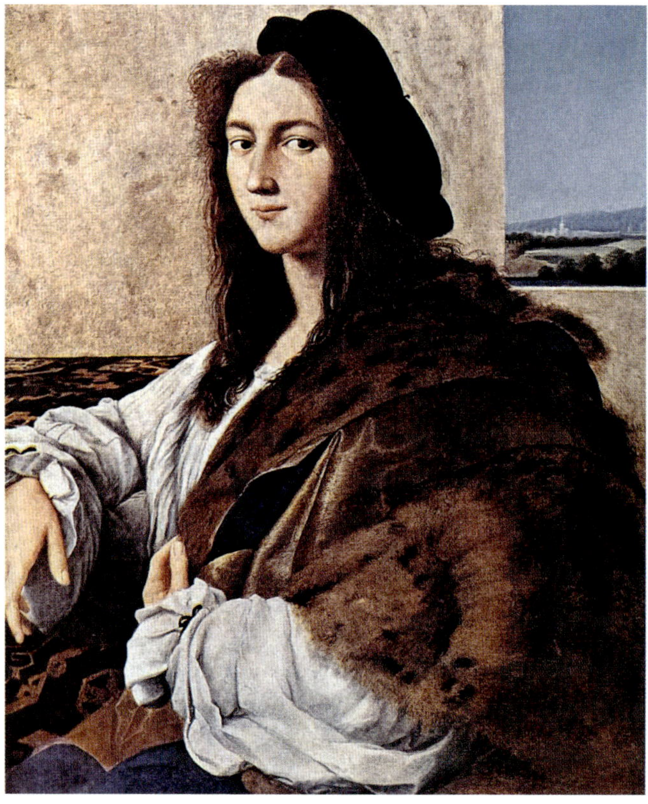

214 *Self-Portrait*, probably 1509

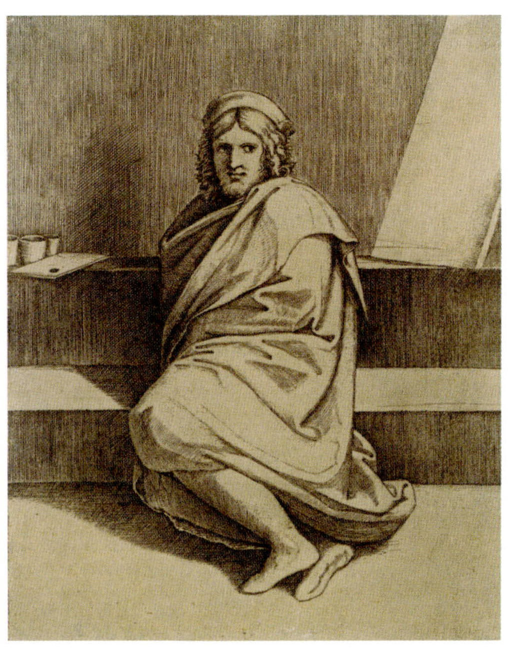

which Raphael shows himself as a luxuriously dressed young man about town, whose raiment uncannily recalls Dürer's comparably amorous self-regard of 1498 at a comparable age (Madrid, Prado). By 1513, the attentive scholar and the elegant playboy are both forgotten, and Raphael, now beginning to grow a beard, casts himself as a litter-bearer in *The Expulsion of Heliodorus*. We also have Marcantonio's engraved portrait of Raphael (probably *c.* 1518) huddled in a cloak, reclining in the studio: an innovative and informal image, shadowed with that melancholy remarked upon in a letter of September 1519 by Alfonso d'Este's ambassador. It was surely designed by Raphael and can hardly have been cut and published without his assent: the artist is contemplative and isolated.

From the very end of Raphael's life, we have the so-called *Raphael and his Fencing Master*, both a self-appraisal and a study in friendship. Unlike *The Navagero and Beazzano* it is a true double portrait in which Raphael – looking older than 36, standing back from the picture surface – places his left hand on the left shoulder of a younger man who turns to look up to him and gestures animatedly. While critics agree about the painting's date, they differ over the identity of the younger man; but he can only be Raphael's artistic heir, Giulio Romano, whose head type, large, fleshy nose and abundant curly hair are

still recognisable a decade and a half later in Titian's portrait
of him (Mantua, Ducal Palace).

In this double portrait, which may have taken a hint from
the double portrait in depth seen in Venice (but who was the
first to use the innovative arrangement is far from certain),
Giulio points forward, indicating something – an idea? a
model? a picture? – to Raphael. The younger man's energy,
enthusiasm and demonstrative eagerness (Vasari calls Giulio
'bold, resolute … and versatile') are evident; and these qualities,
matured, were conveyed also by Titian, who portrayed Giulio
displaying the ground plan of a centralised building.

Raphael's hand on Giulio's shoulder is paternal – following
Domenico Ghirlandaio's double portrait of *Francesco Sassetti
and his Son* (New York, Metropolitan Museum) – but the gesture
is simultaneously restraining, counselling moderation: an
intellectual exchange within an affective relation. Vasari says
that, had Giulio been his son, Raphael could not have loved
him more. The psychological and intellectual position of the
two men corresponds precisely to the relation between the two
late in Raphael's life, when it was obvious that Raphael was
relying ever more heavily on Giulio but was aware that Giulio
was champing at the bit. Spatially, the energetic organisation
of the picture is comparable to the lower left-hand corner of
The Transfiguration, then nearing completion. In the terms with
which debate and personal relations are depicted, this painting
develops – perhaps around an aesthetic issue – the kinds of
exchange seen in *The Disputa* and *The School of Athens* and, like
The Transfiguration, it is in part a reconsideration by Raphael
of elements of his first period in Rome. The painting evokes,
too, something of the two men's social status: Raphael, the
mature intellectual, classless; Giulio wearing a sword, which
implies membership of a relatively distinguished family (it may
not be coincidence that his father, Pietro Pippi, was referred to
as a 'nobilis vir' in 1518).

II

In Venice, painters sometimes equivocated in producing effects
'proper' to one kind of support on the other: canvas to wood,
or wood to canvas. Whether Raphael, who played compulsively
across boundaries and among different types and modes of
representation, decided on it consciously cannot be known,
but in his most majestic portrait – that of *Leo X with Cardinals
Giulio de' Medici and Luigi de' Rossi*, delivered to Florence in
September 1518, which is on wood – he emulated the kinds
of textural effect he achieved in portraits on canvas. Of course,
the picture is not monochrome, in the sense of being in black

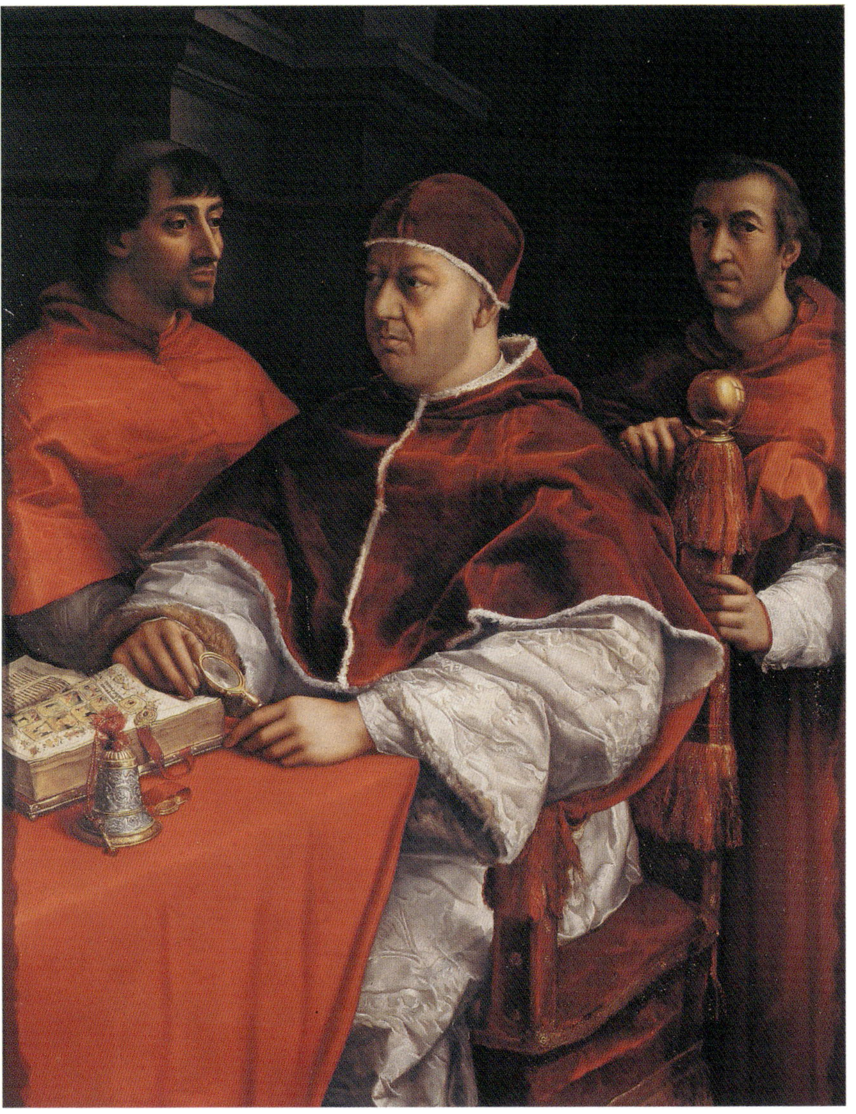

216 Raphael, with still-life elements by Giulio Romano, *Leo X with Cardinals Giulio de' Medici and Luigi de' Rossi*, 1518

and white, but its colours are largely restricted to varieties of red: the pope's thick and richly brocaded robe, the tablecloth and the robes of the two cardinals construct a suite of reds that Titian himself was not to achieve for a quarter of a century, in his own triple portrait of *Pope Paul III and his Grandsons* (Naples, Capodimonte).

Raphael probably began the portrait immediately after he had despatched the paintings to the French court, and it is likely to have been executed quickly. It was started as a portrait of Leo alone, and the two cardinals were added while it was under way. Leo is set obliquely within an imposing building that corresponds to nothing in the Vatican but seems to develop from the setting in *The Coronation of Charlemagne*. Perhaps it represents or recycles an otherwise unrecorded architectural project. This contrasts with the portrait of Julius, which even in the initial lay-in was to be contained by a hanging, whereas here Leo's ruminations expand and echo: as with *The School of Athens*, the spaces of architecture become chambers of the mind. Interestingly, neither of Raphael's papal portraits shows the sitter aggrandised, unlike Sebastiano's hubristic vision of *Clement VII* of *c.* 1525 (Naples, Capodimonte), mastering all he surveys. A power portrait of Leo was to be reserved for the Sala di Costantino.

Both Julius II and Leo X are shown in private, not in the public sphere, and both portraits contain an element of informality: the viewer approaches the sitters obliquely and is included in a circle of intimacy. Leo sits before a richly illuminated manuscript (the Hamilton Bible, now in Berlin), from which he looks up thoughtfully, his magnifying glass – he was severely myopic – momentarily put aside. Raphael pursues further a theme seen in the portrait of *Tommaso Inghirami*; the book is a prop designed to reveal some aspect of the sitter's character: creative in the *Inghirami*, contemplative in the *Leo*.

The addition of the cardinals – a further instance of Raphael's transforming a painting already under way – changed the picture's mood: the characterising function of the architectural setting diminishes, and the pope is now supported by the loyal ally who stands behind his chair and by his cousin Cardinal Giulio. De' Rossi (*c.* 1474–1519) was surely added first, for he is integrated easily into the space. Giulio, on the other hand, is included without plausibility: what might be an independent bust portrait is inserted into an inappropriate context. He interacts neither with his cousin nor with de' Rossi and, while his apartness stresses contemplation rather than confabulation, it weakens the painting's unity. Nevertheless, although the triple portrait is not wholly unified compositionally, it far surpasses in coherence Sebastiano's 1516 portrait of *Cardinal Bandinelli Sauli and his Attendants* that was no doubt in Raphael's mind (Washington, National Gallery of Art).

Raphael's triple portrait seems – with one qualification – to be entirely autograph; indeed, since so much of its effect

springs from the painter's visible touch, it might seem
impossible for Raphael to have imported work by an associate
without detriment. But he did so – very successfully – in one
area. In 1524 Federico Gonzaga requested the painting as
a gift, and Cardinal Giulio, now Clement VII, acceded. But
Vasari's mentor, Ottaviano de' Medici, considering the portrait
too important to Medicean status to relinquish, retained the
original in Florence, instead sending in 1525 a deceptive copy
by Vasari's master, Andrea del Sarto, to Federico. When, in 1538,
Vasari saw Andrea's copy in Mantua, where Giulio Romano
had lived since late 1524, he told Giulio the story but, until he
was able to supply proof, Giulio doubted him, for he believed
he could recognise his own work in the painting: his own
work, in this case, must be the bell, the magnifying glass,
and probably the open Bible.

Raphael obviously recognised Giulio's penchant for and
success in still-life painting, lavishly demonstrated in the
cover of *The Small Holy Family* (Paris, Louvre). This imitates a
sequence of coloured marble veneers and miniaturised cameos
surrounding a faux gilt statue of Ceres. It is miniaturist painting
of the highest level: precise, fully realised and revealing that
fascination with hard surfaces that runs through Giulio's
work and makes him one of the greatest of all designers of
metalwork. Even the most extreme pan-Raphaelisers have
proved reluctant to give the cover to Raphael, although it
bears his name. Raphael knew that in this area Giulio's
ability was the equal of his own in form, and more pungent
pictorially, and it is testimony to his judgment that he made
such acute use of Giulio's skills. The latter are seen also in
the 1518 portrait of *Lorenzo*, where Giulio executed most
of the drapery, rife with metallic threads.

In his textural approach Raphael was effectively characterising
Leo. As the drapery of the *Donna Velata* reveals the rich modesty
of her soul, so the drapery of Leo exposes his persona: luxurious
but complex, the apertures of his sleeve creating – as it were
– entrances to his mind. The purity of his linen is perhaps an
indication of the personal purity he wished to convey. The
abstracted gaze – a contrast to the porcine directness seen
in Giulio's drawn portrait of Leo (Chatsworth, Devonshire
Collection) made a year or two later for the Sala di Costantino
– shows up the differences in conception between Raphael and
his pupil.

Chapter 15
The Sala di Costantino

By October 1519, when there is a record of scaffolding being erected in the Sala di Costantino, Raphael had been working in the Vatican for a decade. Despite the magnitude of the task, he must have welcomed the opportunity to decorate the large, rectangular and relatively regular council chamber at the west end of the Stanze. It had been badly damaged in a storm in 1500 and had only recently been restored. It had a flat ceiling, installed earlier in 1519 by Antonio da Sangallo, perhaps to Raphael's design, and three uninterrupted walls. It would allow Raphael to execute an historical and dramatic cycle in which he could extend his previous achievements in a new and heroic direction. He would be able to vie in epic expansiveness, religious and human drama and representational range with the writers he had portrayed in the *Parnassus*, and in size and archaeological accuracy with Mantegna's *Triumphs*, which he would have known about, if not seen.

For two centuries the decoration of the Sala di Costantino has been undervalued and its achievement diminished. It was known that Raphael had not lived to paint the room, and it had even come to be doubted that he designed it. But it should be recognised as among one of Raphael's greatest and most influential schemes, one that realised a hugely significant historical sequence on an epic scale.

The room's compartmenting must have taken a while to determine but no lay-out drawings survive, and we do not know how Raphael arrived at the final arrangement. The order of the four narratives, all accurately sited in Rome, is chronological, running clockwise from the east wall. It starts with the *Allocution*, Constantine's address to his troops before the battle and his vision of the Cross, inscribed 'In this sign you shall conquer'; the scene is set before a reconstruction

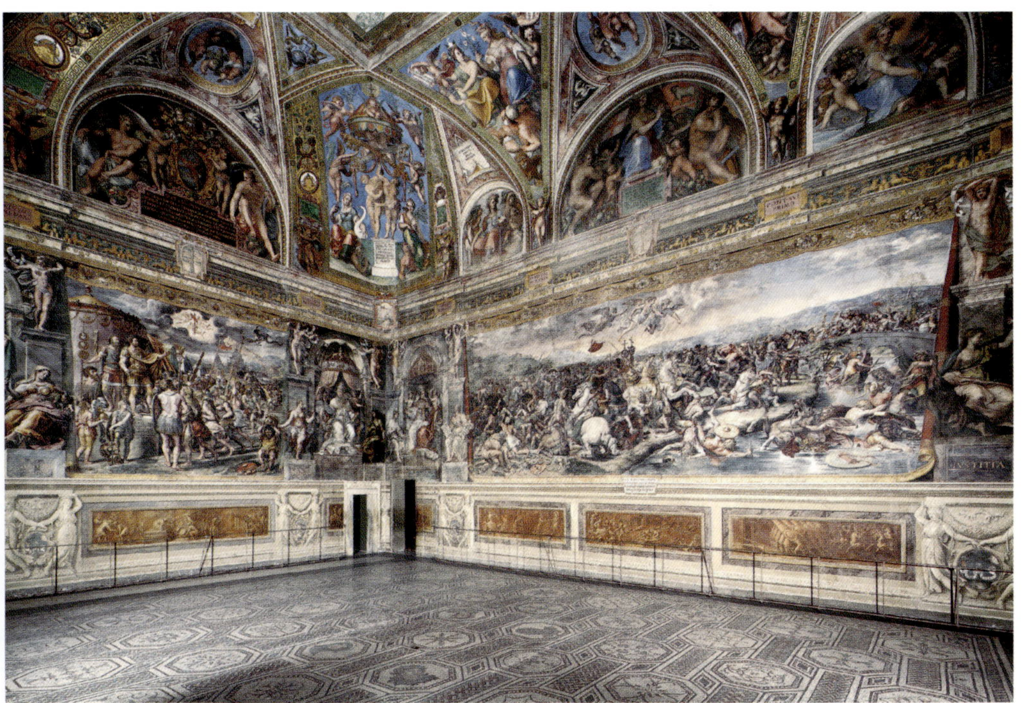

217 Giulio Romano and Gianfrancesco Penni, in part to Raphael's design,
The Sala di Costantino, 1520–24

of the Castel Sant'Angelo, the mausoleum of Hadrian. The
composition is based on reliefs on the Arch of Constantine,
a monument that Raphael had studied in depth.

On the south wall is *The Battle of the Milvian Bridge*. It is set
in its true location but includes a modern insert: a view of the
partially constructed Villa Madama at the upper left that shows
its circular courtyard under way. The third episode, designed
by Giulio with some intervention by Penni, is *The Baptism
of Constantine* by Pope Sylvester in the Lateran Baptistery.
The fourth, on the north window wall, was also designed
and painted by Giulio, with marginal interventions by Penni.
It shows Constantine's *Donation*, the emperor's gift of temporal
power to the papacy. The document that supposedly confirmed
this gift had been revealed to be a forgery as early as 1440, but
obviously this did not trouble Clement VII. This fresco and the
flanking papal groups were the last parts of the room to be
completed shortly before Giulio quit Rome for Mantua in
October 1524.

The components of the Sala di Costantino in part post-
date Raphael's death. Sebastiano, who attempted to secure

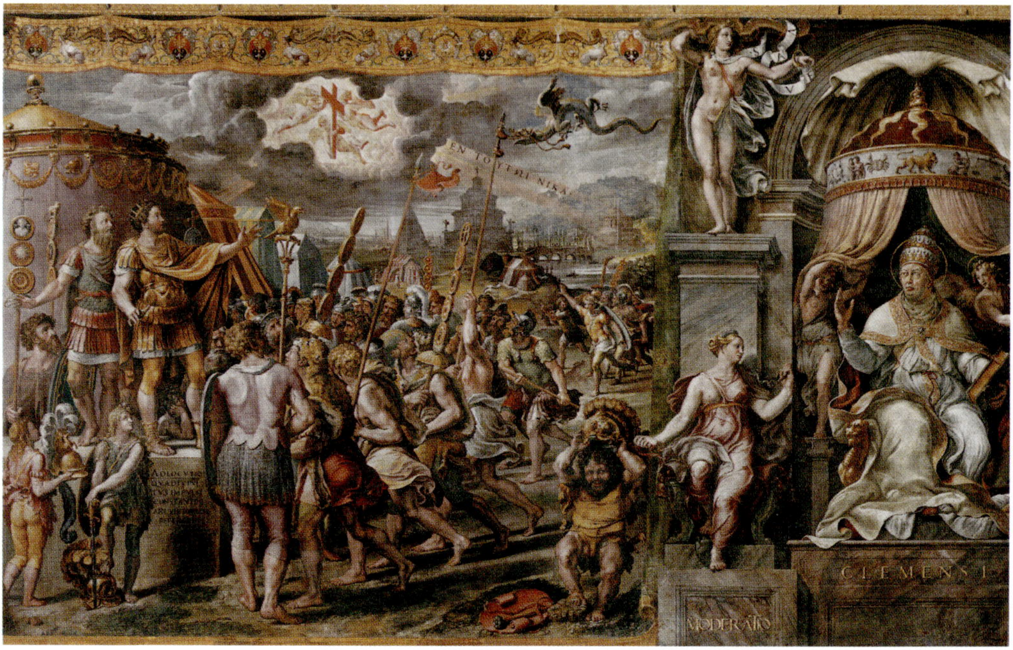

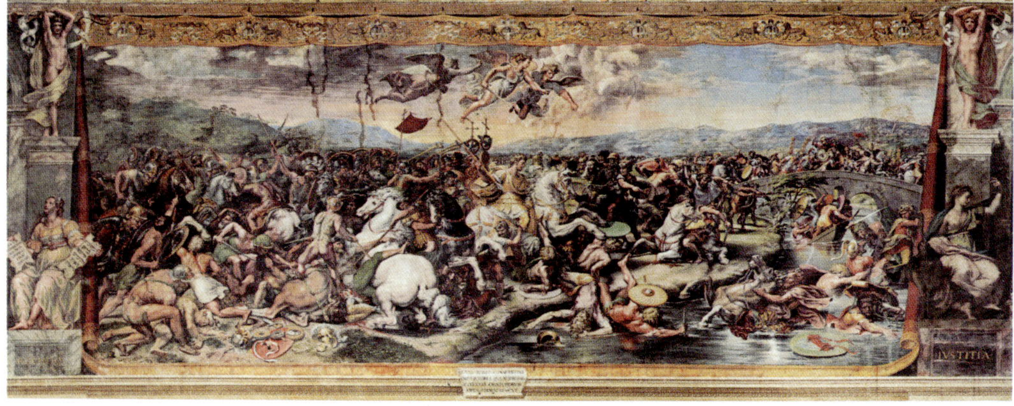

218 Giulio Romano, *The Allocution of Constantine*, 1520–21

219 Giulio Romano, *The Battle of the Milvian Bridge*, 1520–21

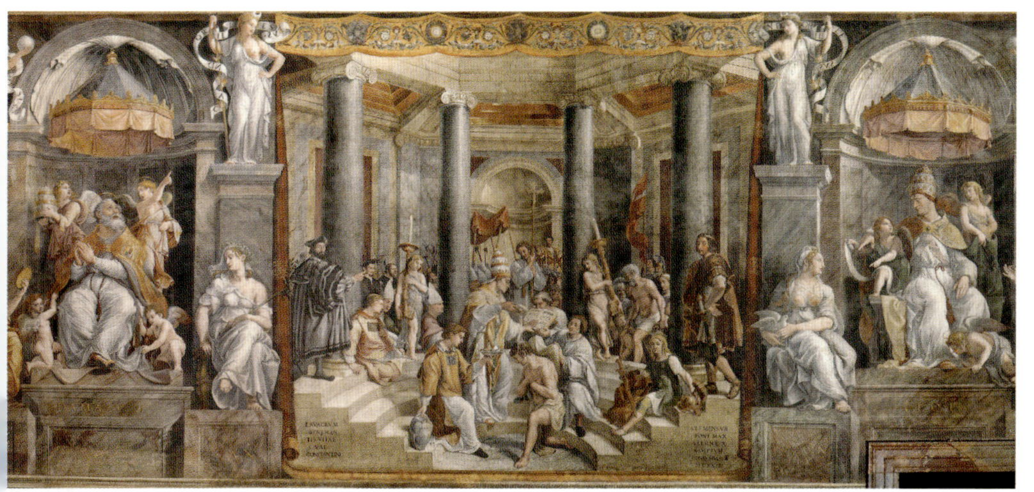

220 Giulio Romano and Gianfrancesco Penni, *The Baptism of Constantine*, 1521–24

221 Giulio Romano and Gianfrancesco Penni, *The Donation of Constantine*, 1524

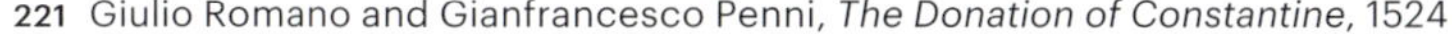

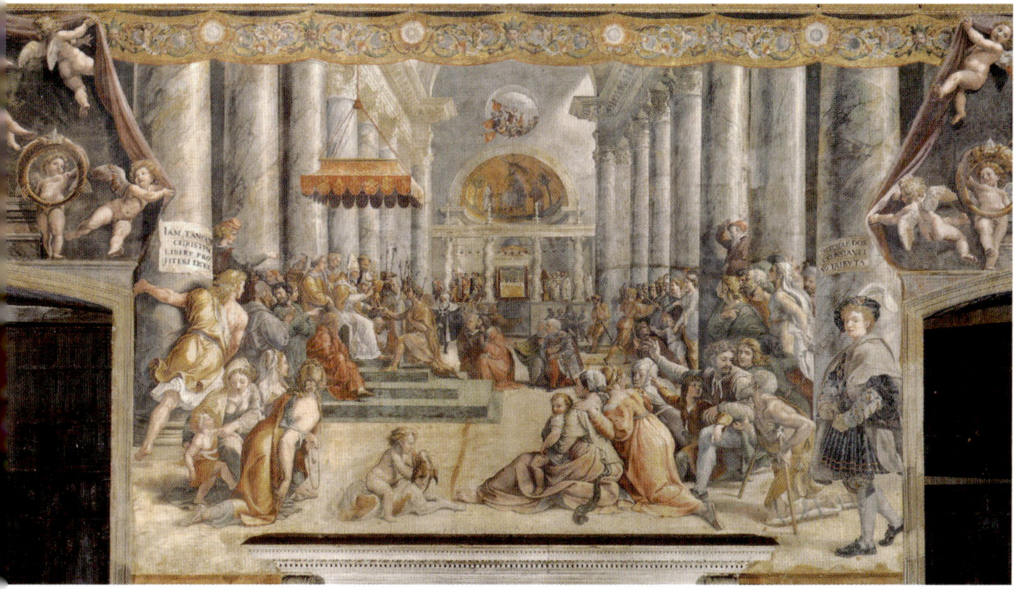

a portion of the scheme, describes the iconography in a letter of 6 September 1520 to Michelangelo. From it we learn two things. One is that his pupils claimed to possess Raphael's designs for the room – which was true, in part. The second is that one of the three subjects mentioned by Sebastiano – the others were *The Allocution* and *The Battle* – was to be a grisly scene of children about to be slaughtered to make a bath of blood to cure the emperor's leprosy. This might be dismissed as a misunderstanding, but a cartoon fragment survives by Giulio (unknown location) that would fit this subject. In the event, immersion in blood was replaced by aspersion by water.

The four episodes are framed by seated popes in niched pylons, flanked within the niches by angels and in the framing piers by Virtues seated on plinths. So eight popes in all, and fourteen Virtues (the groups on the north wall contain only one Virtue each), which led to the invention of some uncanonical ones. Above the Virtues stand caryatids and telamons who would notionally have supported the beams of Sangallo's ceiling. Whether Raphael planned figuration on the ceiling is unknown, but God the Father in the central compartment would be a possibility.

The Battle of the Milvian Bridge is by far the largest mural that Raphael devised. The space and subject gave Raphael the opportunity to challenge in energy and physical invention the aborted battle scenes planned by his mentor, Leonardo, and rival, Michelangelo, for the hall of the Great Council in the Palazzo Vecchio – projects whose fame had first attracted him to Florence and that continued to haunt him.

The battles planned by Leonardo and Michelangelo were ambitious and influential. But however much their designs transcended their subjects, those subjects were specific to the history of Tuscany: *Cascina*, a skirmish between Florence and Pisa of 1364; *Anghiari*, more consequential historically, Florentine curtailment of Milanese expansionism in 1440. They would not be remembered were it not for Leonardo and Michelangelo and, even by 1520, the historical events had become appendages to their representations.

Constantine's defeat of Maxentius at the Milvian Bridge was on a wholly different scale: a world-historical event embodying – to over-simplify – the overthrow of a pagan empire and its replacement by Christian rule, operating under divine guidance and based in the *caput mundi*. On stage were not mercenary commanders or regional heroes, but the first Christian emperor and his pagan adversary. There could hardly have been a more momentous subject, and the battle that Raphael designed, but did not live to see painted, would have been among his

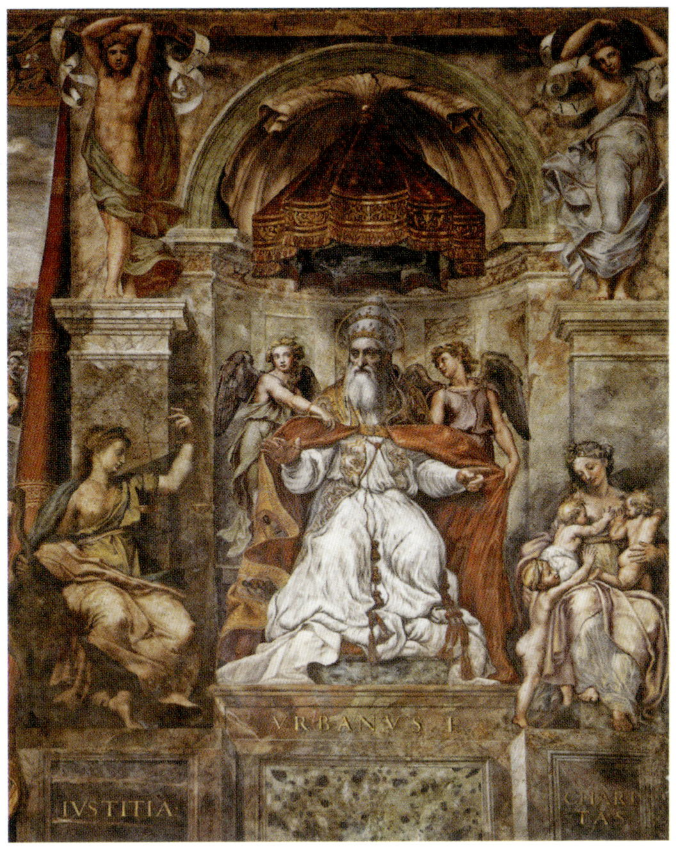

greatest achievements. Even as executed by Giulio Romano, who followed Raphael's plans with comparative loyalty, the *Battle* had an extended afterlife, as paintings by Peter Paul Rubens, Pietro da Cortona, Charles Le Brun, Théodore Géricault, Eugène Delacroix and many others can testify.

The pronouncedly horizontal picture field compelled Raphael to employ a relief format, and he took several ideas from the Arch of Constantine and from battle reliefs elsewhere. Among recent models, the projects of Leonardo and Michelangelo remained in his mind and affected elements of his composition, but his fundamental modern reference point was Piero della Francesca's fresco of the same subject at Arezzo – with qualifications. It was essential to Raphael's concept of historical drama that the protagonist, Constantine, and the antagonist, Maxentius, be readily identifiable, and that heaven's guidance of Constantine be clear; but whereas a victory

224

directed by grace must be irresistible, it should not, as in Piero's account, be an unopposed procession, exorcising paganism by the mere presentation of the cross. The pagan imperium will be vanquished but victory must be earned, its costs recorded. And for a victory to have meaning, the enemy should not be cowardly or contemptible but courageous and resilient. Within a scheme that describes the battle but that reifies that battle's outcome in its formal structure, Raphael aimed to evoke pity and terror, individual tragedy and *virtù*, as Piero had done in the companion composition of *Heraclius's Victory over Chosroes*.

The Battle of the Milvian Bridge, which also owes a profound debt to the famous bronze reconstruction of an ancient battle relief by Bertoldo di Giovanni (*c.* 1420–91; Florence, Bargello), extends to a depth of four planes and more at the left, diminishing plane by plane as the bank of the Tiber rises in the pictorial field and as the eye moves rightwards and inwards to the profiled emperor on his white stallion. Constantine's troops form a solid phalanx, inexorable in its advance, but elements of Maxentius's forces continue to resist. In the nearest plane, Raphael devised emblematic – and allusive – groups of soldiers or individuals, following Piero and Michelangelo. On the left, two brave infantrymen attempt to oppose Constantine's cavalry; they are arranged in a loose equilateral triangle at whose base a father, abandoned to grief, bends to lift the body of his son. Courageous and comradely – if doomed – endeavour combines with familial tragedy. A little to the right, a spearman straddling a fallen horse, steadfast but equally ill-fated, vainly attempts to withstand the Constantinian advance. Further right, two young cavalrymen tumble headlong into the Tiber, pagan angels, beautiful even in their fall. At the far right a soldier attempts to climb into an already overloaded boat, like a victim of the Flood, but he is about to be cut away by his erstwhile comrades: he and the exhausted friend who clings to him are both destined to perish.

A composition of such physical complexity and intellectual ambition would have required much research and study and many preparatory drawings. Although the *Battle* is not arranged in perspective, the different planes had to be focused with precision, and Raphael was faced with a plethora of problems: of detail, of spacing, and of the individuation of over fifty men and ten horses. The preparatory compositional sketches would probably have been made in pen and developed in red chalk, although pen may have been used for local accentuation. As in the Psyche Loggia, Raphael would not himself have made all the studies required. Few survive, but from them it is clear that he worked side by side with Giulio, but probably Penni too, at all stages of the *Battle*'s preparation. However, aware that his most recent fresco schemes had been derided by his most dangerous rival, Sebastiano – whose strictures were not unfounded and, no doubt, not isolated – Raphael was under pressure, both external and self-imposed, to produce an imposing ensemble.

Giulio's cartoon fragment (Ambrosiana, Milan) differs minimally from the section of *The Battle of the Milvian Bridge* that it prepares and was probably completed before Raphael's death. The most informative of the preparatory drawings for the *Battle* is Penni's large *modello* in which the whole scene is laid out. It was originally adhered at either side by companion *modelli* of papal groups, of which slivers remain at the right. In its complete state, adumbrating the decoration of the entire south wall, it was probably made to show to the pope, after which it was presumably divided so that its parts could be manipulated more readily. There are many minor differences between the *modello* and the *Battle* as painted – in placing and spacing and costume, for example – but it maps the *Battle* both as a whole and in its most important figures and groups.

We also have three studies – two by Raphael, one by Giulio – for individual figures in the *Battle*. All are drawn nude, although they were to be painted either draped or wearing armour, and all are in black chalk, not red, perhaps to simplify their forms. Rather than preceding the *modello*, as one might have expected, they seem to be successive, made to clarify the poses and physical expressiveness of key figures. An example is a tumbling warrior, by Giulio; in the fresco he is armoured, but differently from in the *modello*. This drawing should be compared with the sublime study by Raphael of the men attempting to enter the boat. The figures, set on the page in reverse order, were made from a single live model, who first wore and then doffed his cap. Raphael stumped the chalk to evoke the sheen of their wet backs. In the fresco the two men were clad, and the leading soldier given an unduly heavy helmet. These studies are the exiguous survival of a series that would certainly have run into double figures.

Raphael intended that the Sala di Costantino should be painted in oil. The technical possibility of painting in an oil mixture on a specifically prepared wall became an issue to painters in Rome late in the 1510s. Leonardo had attempted to paint the *Anghiari* in some kind of oil or encaustic medium and may have encouraged Raphael to experiment. And Sebastiano may already have been contemplating painting the Borgherini *Flagellation* in oil. Of course, Raphael had produced a simulacrum of oil execution in fresco in *The Miracle of Bolsena*, in which he had created effects that, in

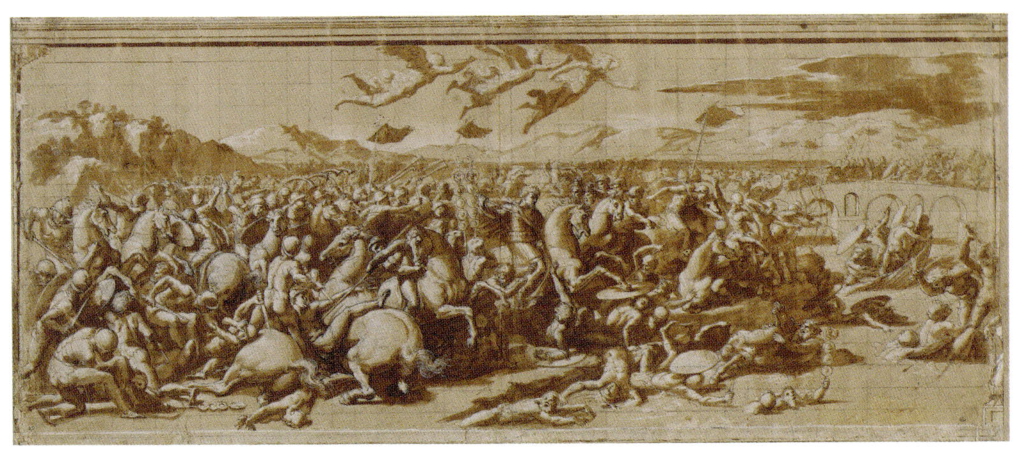

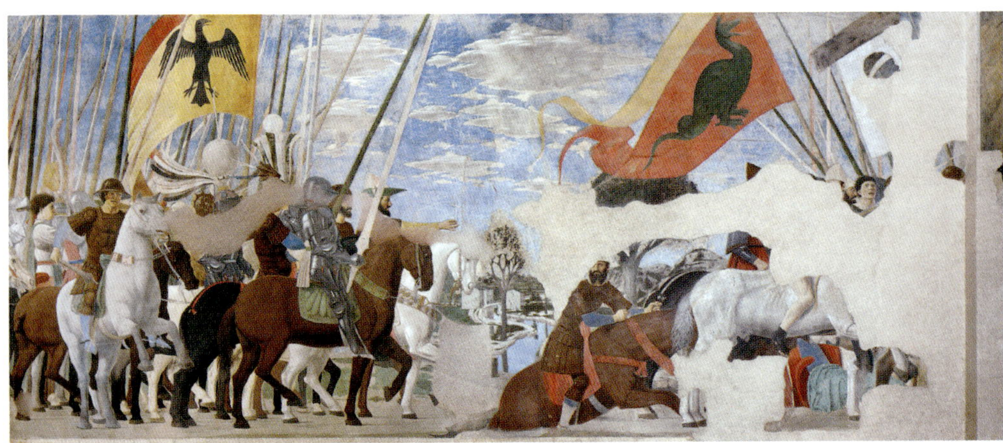

223 TOP Gianfrancesco Penni to Raphael's design, *modello* for *The Battle of the Milvian Bridge*, 1519–20
224 ABOVE Piero della Francesca, *Constantine's Victory over Maxentius*, mid-1450s

1512, were unprecedented. But *Bolsena* imitated an oil painting that was free, fluid and lush. The intended effect in the Sala di Costantino was different: Raphael aimed to imitate the densely modelled surfaces, purified and idealised, of the *St Cecilia* and the panels sent to France, seeking a smooth finish without visible brushstrokes, as in pigmented (or even glazed) sculpture. Two walls were prepared for oil, the south and east, which indicates that the project was not merely experimental, otherwise preparation would surely have been restricted to a single wall. While the two figures painted in oil, *Justice*

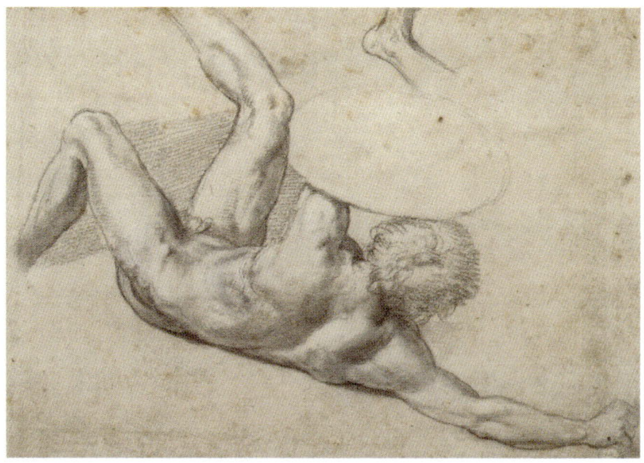

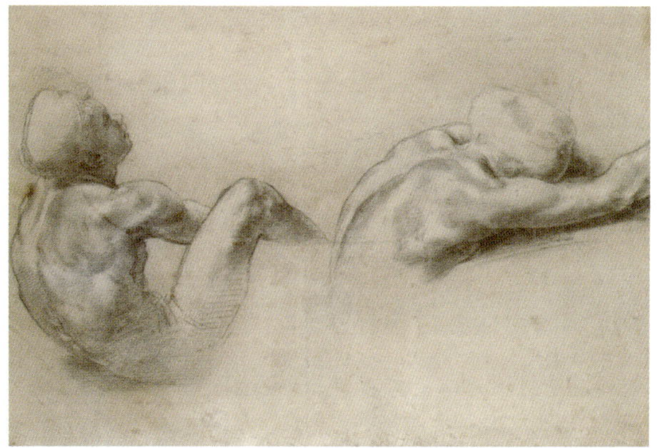

at the east end of the south wall and *Comity* at the south
end of the east wall, were retained, after Raphael's death the
results were judged insufficiently successful to justify the work
involved. The rest of the preparation was demolished, and the
scheme continued in fresco.

The test figures were both painted by Giulio (who tried
an oil-based technique again in the vault of the Sala di Psiche
in the Palazzo Te, Mantua), and this throws light on Raphael's
intentions for the room. Had he intended to take a major role,
he would surely have executed these figures himself: that he
did not implies that he planned to delegate the execution of
most, if not all, of the scheme to his assistants, in particular
Giulio, already a consummate painter in oils. But, more than
in the Psyche Loggia, Raphael seems to have controlled the

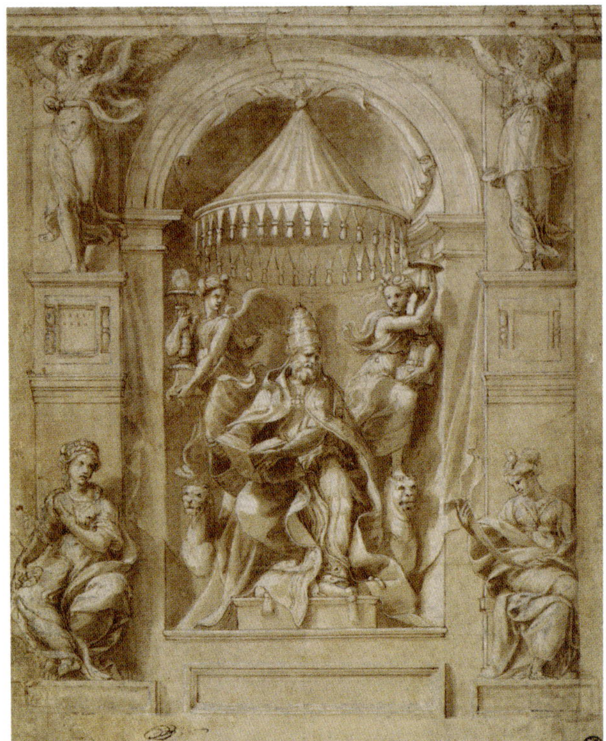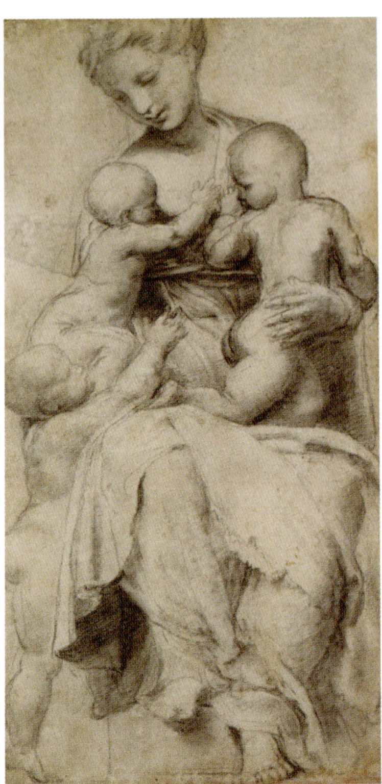

227 ABOVE LEFT Gianfrancesco Penni, *modello* for a *Papal Group*, 1519–20
228 ABOVE RIGHT Study for *Charity*, 1519–20

design stages with close attention. And that the scheme was to be executed in oil would allow him, to the extent that he wished to participate, to work slowly and, if necessary, to introduce revisions, free of the need for decisiveness imposed by fresco.

227   Penni's *modello* for a papal group is slighter than his *modello* for the *Battle* and it is not on the same scale. Although both were originally adhered to at either side they were not adhered to each other, and must be survivals from two different ensembles. The papal group is lit from the left, which indicates that it was planned to flank either *The Battle* or *The Allocution*. There are many differences between the *modello* and the groups as executed, but one that may be noted is that in the drawing the angels flanking the pope carry candelabra, as though illuminating statuary, while as painted they attend the popes directly. The papal groups were developed further, but we cannot trace their evolution. However, there survive two black chalk drawings, both by Raphael, made in preparation

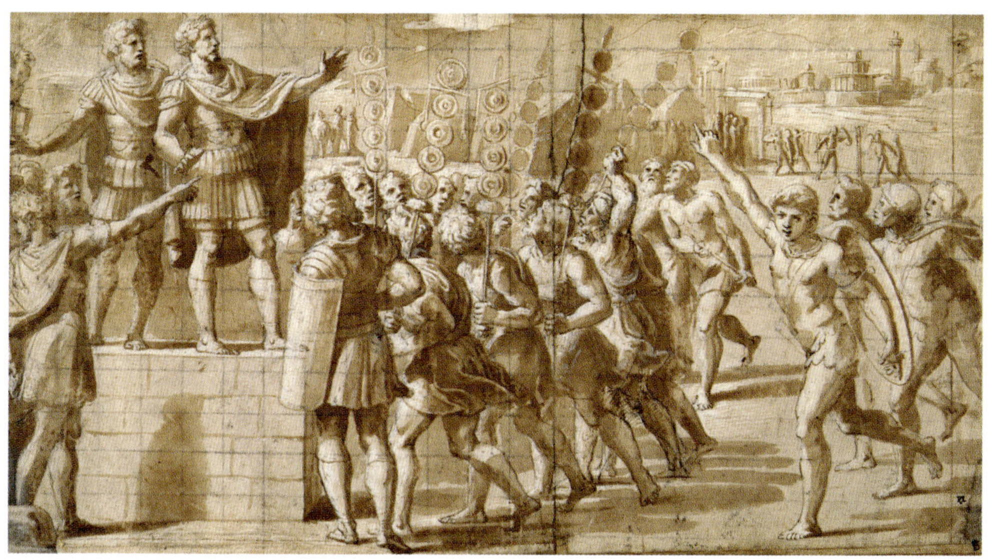

229 Gianfrancesco Penni, preliminary *modello* for *The Allocution*, 1519–20

228

for the final phase: one for the group of *Charity*, at the far right
of the south wall flanking Pope Urban and the counterpart of
Giulio's *Justice*, and the other for the caryatid immediately
above her who carries the papal arms (Frankfurt, Städelsches
Kunstinstitut). Both are in Raphael's softest, most evocative
style – an ideal preparation for oil painting because it allows
an infinite range of modulations across flesh and draperies
while simultaneously desensualising them. Giulio's approach
to a figure (in this case characterised as a hermaphrodite)
supporting Leo's arms on the east wall can be seen in a sheet
in the Rijksmuseum, of which the recto is executed in sharply
contrasting brush and wash, creating a marmoreal surface,
and the verso in hard pen line.

Another compositional study, a brush and wash drawing,
survives. It is by Penni and represents a penultimate stage in
the development of *The Allocution*; one of the soldiers follows
a figure study by Raphael (Paris, Louvre), and the composition
was presumably based on an ensemble sketch by him. The
design of *The Allocution* was probably not carried further
within Raphael's lifetime, which allowed Giulio to modify it
considerably. Giulio now seized the opportunity to express his
penchants and inserted anecdotal and picturesque details and
exaggerated movements that unbalance Raphael's composition
as recorded by Penni. He disrupted the original conception by

placing figures before the dais, situating a dwarf prominently in the foreground, pushing back the group on the right and disrupting the rhythms established by Raphael.

In the Sala di Costantino, Raphael employed a self-contradictory conceit, akin to the vault of the Psyche Loggia. Although the *Battle* and *Allocution* are treated as relief compositions with a strong base in classical sculpture, they are represented in the form of tapestries, which curl against the pylons. This fiction is maintained through all four frescoes. Whether it was intended that the stories of Constantine should also be woven as actual tapestries is unknown, but it is not to be excluded. One might have expected, had Raphael lived to supervise the decoration, that the manner of painting would have reflected the fiction of simulated tapestry, but the viewer is conscious of the conceit only by examining the edges of the scheme as executed: Giulio and Penni were less subtle than their master.

Work seems to have proceeded efficiently on the Sala di Costantino after the hiatus caused by Raphael's unexpected death: *The Battle* and *The Allocution* were completed by the time of Leo's death, also unexpected, in December 1521. Work then halted during the pontificate of Adrian VI but resumed after the election of Cardinal Giulio de' Medici as Clement VII in November 1523. *The Baptism* and *The Donation* must have been painted in less than a year. Castiglione wrote to Federico Gonzaga on 5 September 1524 to say that the room had been finished and had turned out very well; but one might wonder whether some of the subsidiary areas, such as the *basamento*, were entirely ready.

The *Baptism* had probably been designed before the interruption, for it is couched in broadly the same mode as *The Allocution*, with large figures performing a clearly readable action. But the addition of rather flaccid bystanders – merely observers and not involved in the drama – is probably due to Penni. Such bystanders occur too at the sides of *The Donation*, but the pseudo-historical event is conceived by Giulio in a different manner. The act of donation is set in the far background; performed by small figures, it is barely legible, and the significance of the event is conveyed by the interchanges within an eager crowd that includes men and women of different ages and conditions, and children. The arrangement takes further, in a 'realistic' direction, the principles of layout tried out in, for example, *The Incendio*. Giulio was no doubt thinking about the latter when he included an apparently accurate view of the interior of Old St Peter's, matching the exterior seen in *The Incendio*. In his foreground

121

screen of figures, Giulio equivocates between the observed and the emblematic, but the observed takes precedence: none of the figures has an historical identity, and none appears to be especially significant. Giulio's design set a pattern for many later treatments of historical ceremonies, including, perhaps most impressively, those by Federico Zuccaro (1540/1–1609).

The *basamento*, for which drawings by Penni are known, was executed in *brunaille*. It may be that Polidoro da Caravaggio played a role in its execution, but there are no obvious signs of his style. The simulated reliefs depict a series of events, mostly military, from Constantine's life and develop the ideas seen in the *basamento* of the Vatican Loggia.

A letter by Tommaso Vincidor to Pope Leo X of 20 July 1521 notes that the now-lost twenty-part tapestry series of the *Giochi di Putti*, for which some of Tommaso's *modelli* survive, was to hang in a room in which Giulio and Penni were working. This is commonly taken to be the Sala di Costantino. If the *Giochi* were intended for the Costantino, they would have been hung along the *basamento*, but this could only have been on festive occasions, for they are so discrepant in form and mood from the rest of the room's decoration that they could hardly have been integrated with it. A question mark must hang over their function.

Chapter 16
Epilogue: The Things of Raphael

I

Raphael died, following an illness lasting about a fortnight, to universal consternation, on his 37th birthday. Vasari, probably informed by Giulio, put his death down to a chill, caught after a night of exuberant lovemaking, which turned into a wasting fever when it was misdiagnosed by his doctors. The story is picturesque, but the underlying cause of Raphael's death was exhaustion, brought about by a workload that had expanded beyond human bounds and by the attendant psychological pressures. Raphael's death was received as the loss of a major public figure and occasioned an outpouring of grief and regret. Some contemporaries thought he had died at the same age as Christ, at 33 years old: it was widely felt that there was something divine about him. He was accorded the honour – unique for an artist – of burial in the Pantheon, something he must have requested: according to Vasari, Raphael left a detailed will – for which scholars are still searching – bequeathing a substantial sum for the care of his mistress and 3,000 ducats for the construction of his tomb, which features a tall standing Virgin and Child by Lorenzetto. Raphael also left his studio and its effects, plus his unfinished projects, jointly to Giulio Romano and Gianfrancesco Penni.

II

In October 1520, during his visit to the Netherlands, Albrecht Dürer met Tommaso Vincidor, who is first documented in Raphael's company in 1518 and who had worked with him on the Loggia and, no doubt, other projects. He had come north, probably in May 1520, to oversee production of the various tapestry series that Raphael had under way. But Tommaso was not merely a supervisor: active as a designer, he had become, after Giulio and Penni, Raphael's most significant collaborator, whose activities illuminate Raphael's entrepreneurship.

As well as the *modelli* and cartoons for the twenty-part *Giochi di Putti*, Tommaso was responsible for three figurative tapestries for Leo X's robing bed, placed in the Sala dei Palafrenieri. The first direct reference to this commission dates from 1521, but it was probably projected contemporaneously with the Sala dei Palafrenieri in 1516–17. At the head of the bed was an *Adoration of the Child*, of which we have only Vincidor's *modello* (Paris, Louvre), although the tapestry itself survived until the nineteenth century. *The Adoration*, in which Tommaso made use of a Raphael drawing of *c.* 1512 (Oxford, Ashmolean), included Leo X together with cardinals Giulio de' Medici and Innocenzo Cibo and was well advanced by 20 July 1521, when Tommaso wrote directly to Leo to request the pope's portrait and that of Cardinal Giulio, to be copied from Raphael's group portrait. The second tapestry, *The Meeting of the Two Holy Families* for the side of the bed, is also lost, but the cartoon, at Boughton House, shows that it in part followed *The Holy Family of Francis I*, to which Tommaso added several figures.

The most fascinating of the three, recently rediscovered and acquired by the Museo Nacional de Artes Decorativas, Madrid (Vincidor's cartoon is also at Boughton), is *The Trinity with Symbols of the Evangelists*, which formed the bed's canopy. It follows closely *The Vision of Ezekiel*, designed by Raphael and executed by Giulio *c.* 1516 as a small painting (Florence, Pitti). The subject and treatment of the *Ezekiel* are so novel that it is unlikely to have been intended for some other purpose and adventitiously borrowed by Vincidor. Giulio's panel (Vasari, followed by many modern scholars, believed it to be by Raphael) is probably a pioneering example of what came to be called a *petit patron* – a fully coloured painting from which cartoon and tapestry could be developed. In this case Tommaso was left to add the angels who occupy the tapestry's corners.

Vincidor was no doubt involved with the production of the enormously costly and ambitious twelve-piece set of tapestries (known as the Scuola Nuova series) depicting four events (in six panels) from the childhood of Christ and six of the events following his Passion. Much about this project remains unclear, and the weaving of the set seems to have begun only with the election of Clement VII in 1523, continuing into the early

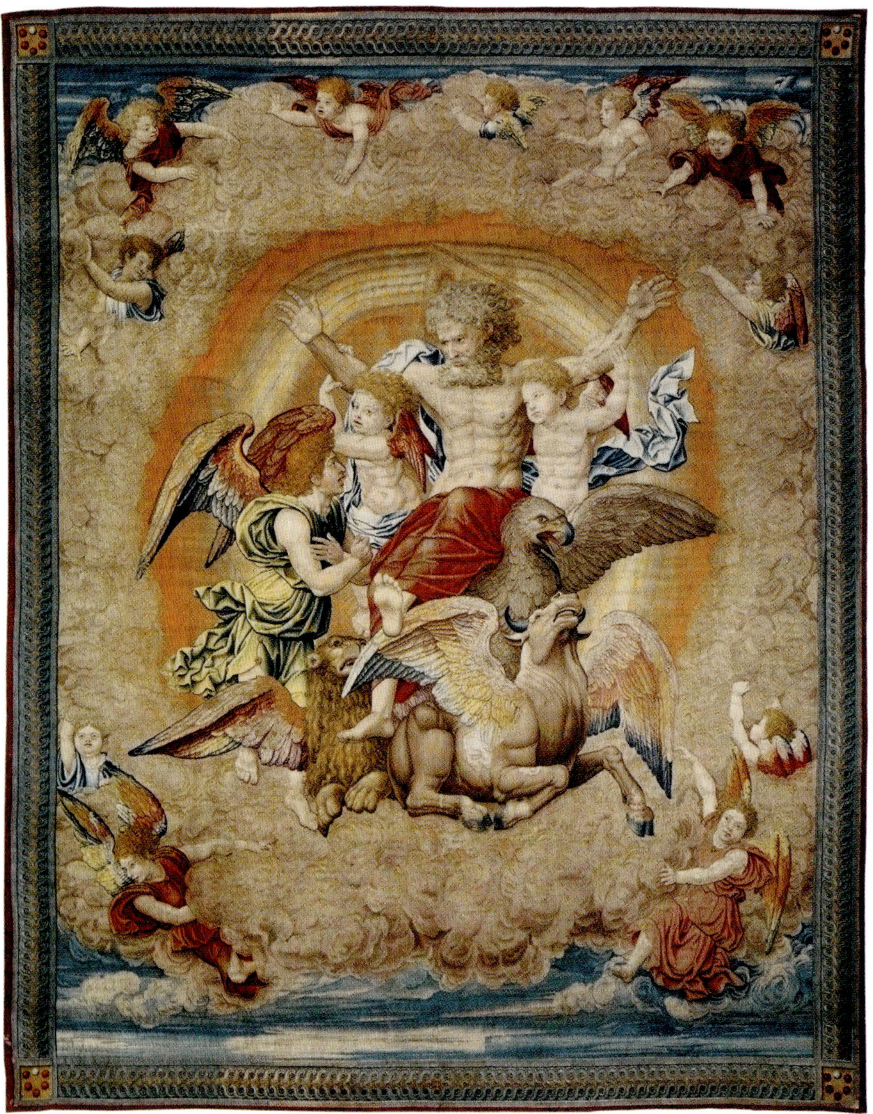

230 *The Trinity with Symbols of the Evangelists*, 1520

1530s. But Vasari says that the project was initiated in Leo's reign and, while we have no drawings for it by Raphael, he may have sketched out some ideas. While the final designs were no doubt the responsibility of Giulio and Penni working in Rome and Vincidor in Flanders (where he remained until his death), several of the tapestries make use of Raphaelesque inventions and they have traditionally been associated with him.

III

During their encounter Tommaso and Dürer spoke of Raphael, and Tommaso commented that 'Raphaels von Urbino Ding ist nach seiner Todt alls verzogen': 'The things of Raphael are all finished.' Six months after Raphael's death, Tommaso believed that the artistic conglomerate that Raphael had created was disintegrating. He may have been a little premature, but he was prescient.

Raphael's grandest Roman project, St Peter's, passed not to his heirs but to his former collaborator Antonio da Sangallo the Younger, probably Rome's most technically competent architect, who wrote a memorial shortly after Raphael's death criticising some aspects of his work. Antonio became the papal architect and was not eager to share responsibilities. In the Vatican, following a moment of uncertainty, Giulio and Penni continued work in the Sala di Costantino, while the vault of the Sala dei Pontefici was allocated to Perino del Vaga and Giovanni da Udine and was nearly finished by the time of Leo's death. In fact, there was no immediate decline in papal patronage, but internal problems were becoming evident. In the absence of Raphael's controlling intelligence, relations among members of his school began to fracture. The decoration of the Villa Madama occasioned a dispute between Giulio and Giovanni da Udine. A letter by Cardinal Giulio de' Medici written on 4 June 1520, less than two months after Raphael's death, describes Giulio and Giovanni da Udine as 'quei duo pazzi' – 'those two madmen' – quarrelling over the division of responsibility between design and execution. Reading between the lines, it seems evident that Giulio was pressing for design control. Although we do not know the outcome, it is unlikely that they worked together again.

Between December 1521 and November 1523 – the interregnum following Leo's death and the artistically barren pontificate of Adrian VI – Giulio and Penni switched their attention elsewhere. It was probably at this time that the chapel of the Magdalen in the church of Trinità dei Monti was completed, and the loggia of the Villa Mattei. But the Chigi commissions, which they might have expected to inherit, were thrown into disarray by Agostino's death, which followed Raphael's by a week. His heirs and executors hesitated, and there was some dissension – exacerbated by unexpected financial problems – between Agostino's widow, Francesca, and his brother and executor, Sigismondo. The lunettes and

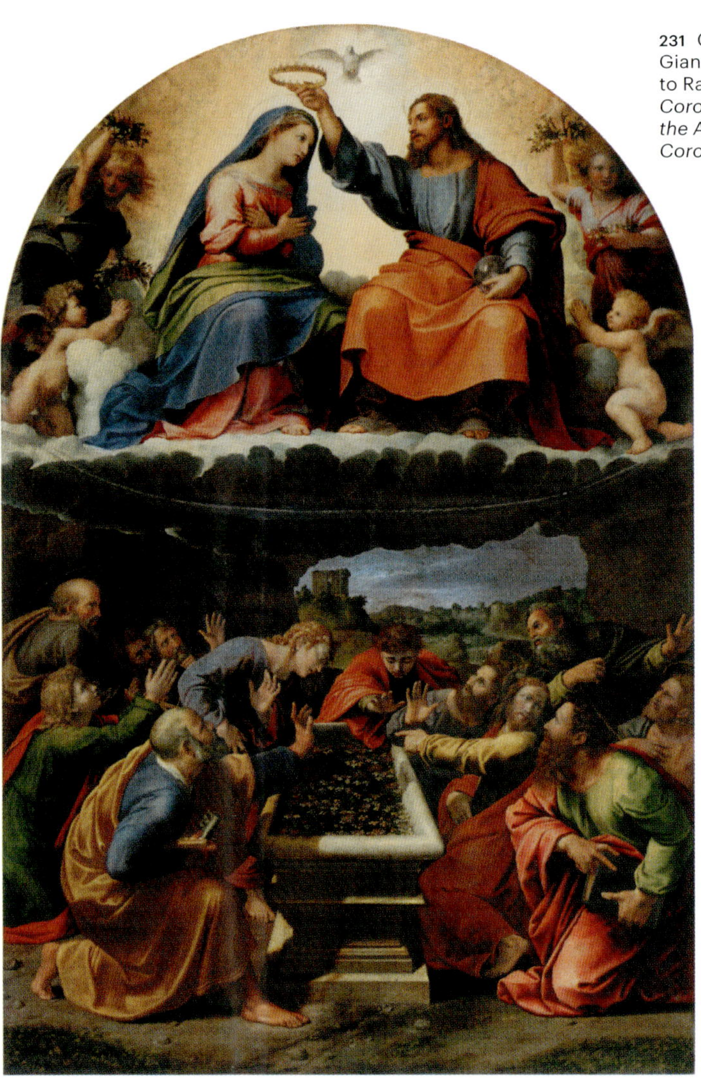

walls of the Psyche Loggia remained bare – it may have seemed inappropriate to finish so light-hearted a scheme – and there was no urgency to finish the Pace chapel; but Agostino's funerary chapel in Santa Maria del Popolo required completion. On 31 May 1520 Francesca Ordeaschi signed a contract with Luigi da Pace to execute the mosaic decoration of the drum and the roundels in the pendentives. But Raphael had left no drawings for these areas and, instead of consulting his heirs, Francesca turned to her fellow Venetian Sebastiano, by whom survive two drawings of episodes of *The Creation* perfectly fitting the fields in the drum (both Paris, Louvre). Sebastiano also made a design of *The Assumption of the Virgin* for the chapel's altarpiece. However, following Francesca's own (premature) death in November 1520, for unknown reasons the subject of the altarpiece underwent another change, and Penni and Giulio were reintroduced: both made large and elaborate drawings of *The Nativity of the Virgin*. But with Giulio's departure from Rome and Penni's evident limitations the project once more reverted to Sebastiano.

During the association between Giulio and Penni the former was the dominant partner. Penni's role in the Sala di Costantino is peripheral, and only one moveable painting, the *Noli Me Tangere* still in the chapel of the Magdalen, seems genuinely to be a joint production, with the artists sharing design and execution. More emblematic of the complexities outstanding at the time of Raphael's death and of emerging incompatibilities between Penni and Giulio is the Monteluce *Coronation*, that long-standing project contracted by Raphael in 1505, recontracted in 1516 and finally delivered to the nuns of Monteluce in Perugia only in 1525. The wood support is divided horizontally into two portions whose carpentry is discontinuous, showing that they did not originate as parts of the same panel. The lower section, with the Apostles clustered around the Virgin's sarcophagus, is by Penni, following a design by Raphael (an autograph drawing exists for three of its figures; Berlin, Kupferstichkabinett). But the upper part, with Christ crowning the Virgin between flower-scattering angels, is by Giulio, with some assistance. Penni's colouring is subdued, tonal and soft, while Giulio's is bright, aggressive and acidic, and his forms are hard. The upper section is bursting with barely contained movement. It is clarion painting, and extremely confident.

The final picture is iconographically problematic in the same way as Raphael's degli Oddi *Coronation*, which, we remember, was the result of a change made during execution. An earthly scene appropriate to an *Assumption* is surmounted by a *Coronation*. Many attempts have been made to explain such physical and iconographical anomalies, but perhaps the boldest hypothesis is that Giulio and Penni cannibalised two separate pictures. While this idea presents obvious difficulties – it implies that two altarpieces, one by Giulio, one by Penni, begun for different projects, were both sufficiently advanced for it to be more economical to divide and swap their parts than to overpaint one or the other – it does answer several of the questions raised by the final picture. The lower section,

231

however, cannot have formed the lower part of a putative
Assumption for the Popolo chapel as has been suggested:
it is too narrow by 1.3 m (4¼ ft) and is lit from the left.

IV

Penni remains shadowy as an artist. He likely remained active
as an administrator and organiser and for a while probably
acted as Giulio's *fattore*. In the few paintings that he executed
independently after Raphael's death, he was content to recycle
Raphael's forms, as in *The Rest on the Flight into Egypt* (Warsaw,
National Museum). Penni made some drawings, probably in the
mid-1520s, for groups of unidentifiable classical and, perhaps,
biblical scenes (he seems to have had a penchant for recondite
subject matter), but his conceptions are undramatic, and he
shows little ability either to integrate figures and space or to
play them against one another.

Penni's most important painting was a replica. When Cardinal
Giulio de' Medici decided to retain Raphael's *Transfiguration*
in Rome, Penni was assigned to make a full-sized copy for
Narbonne (Madrid, Prado). Never finished, it is a competent,
if pedestrian, performance, lacking Raphael's energy and
subtlety of modelling and colour.

By the end of work on the Sala di Costantino Giulio and
Penni had come to a definitive parting of the ways. Vasari
tells us that when, following the Sack of Rome in 1527, Penni
travelled to Mantua to seek employment from his supposed
friend, Giulio cold-shouldered him. Penni then found his
way to Naples, where he soon died, in 1528 or 1529, leaving
his *Transfiguration* copy (which must have accompanied him)
in the Ospedale degli Incurabili, whence it was eventually
transferred to Spain.

What else Penni might have painted after Raphael's death is
hard to assess, but Benvenuto Cellini, who allows us a glimpse
of Penni in Rome, banqueting with Giulio, describes him as
a good painter and executed a seal and some metalwork to his
designs, so Penni obviously had some activity as a designer of
decorative arts. However, it may be that future discoveries will
enlarge our view of him.

V

It was Giulio Romano who emerged as Raphael's most loyal
but simultaneously most disloyal follower. While Raphael lived
Giulio was held in check, eager to experiment but restrained by
his respect for the personality and mind of his master. But as
soon as he had a free rein, Giulio changed Raphael's modes.
Paralleling his redesign of *The Allocution of Constantine* is

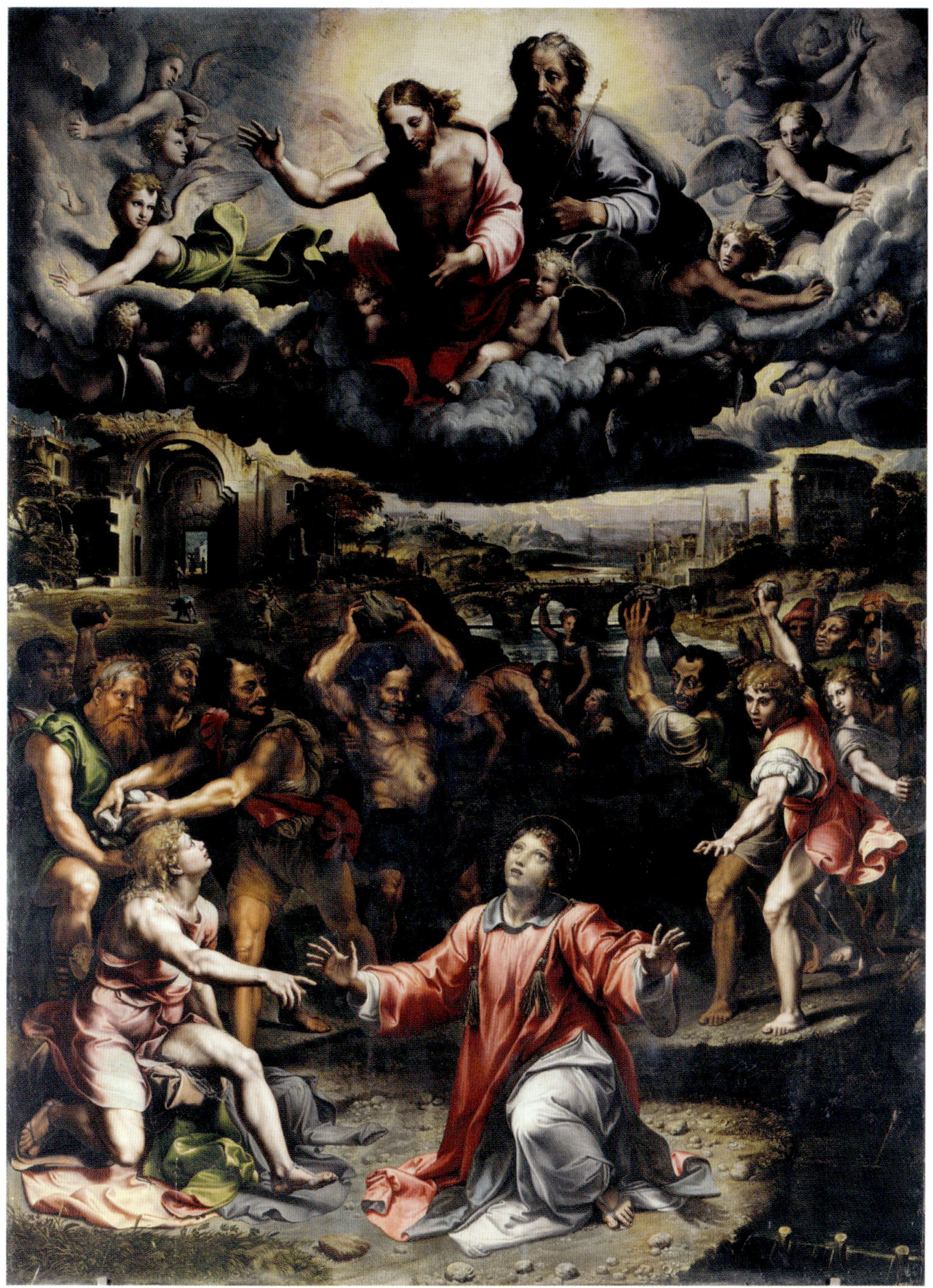

232 Giulio Romano, *The Stoning of St Stephen*, 1520–21

his redesign of a major moveable panel. In 1519–20 Raphael planned a grand narrative altarpiece, only marginally smaller than *The Transfiguration*, of *The Stoning of St Stephen*. It was commissioned by Leo X and Cardinal Giulio for the church of Santo Stefano in Genoa, where it remains, on behalf of Leo's secretary, the Genoese Matteo Giberti (1495–1543). A copy of Raphael's lost *modello* (Paris, École des Beaux-Arts) is known and, remarkably, the cartoon for the finished picture survives (Vatican, Pinacoteca). The cartoon's upper part, which is probably by Giulio, follows the *modello* closely and no doubt preceded Raphael's death. But the lower half, which seems to be a replacement rather than a completion, is drastically different. Patently by Giulio, it transforms Raphael's stately execution into a ferocious assault by an animalic mob: a conception quite alien to Raphael. The painting itself is entirely by Giulio, and it seems to have been finished before Leo's death. It is evidence of the speed and efficiency with which Giulio worked.

According to Vasari, Giulio soon formed his own team, employing several assistants – most notably Raffaellino dal Colle – and within a year or two of Raphael's death seems to have set up an independent practice to deal with such commissions as the famous Santa Prassede *Flagellation* and the famous and innovative altarpiece for the wealthy banker Jakob Fugger in Santa Maria dell'Anima.

Giulio was also advancing rapidly in his highly successful career as an architect. On Raphael's death he took over the partly built Palazzo Alberini-Cicciaporci and the Villa Madama, whose construction was about one-third finished. Giulio may already have designed the Villa Lante on the Janiculum for Raphael's friend Baldassare Turini, and was soon to design the Palazzo Stati Maccarani and the Palazzo Adimari.

Giulio's transfer in September or October 1524 to Mantua, where he enjoyed a stellar career at the Gonzaga court until his death in 1546, was engineered by Castiglione, whose friendship with Raphael Giulio had inherited. But his departure was probably accelerated by a scandal. He had made a set of drawings illustrating sixteen sexual positions (*I modi*); these were issued as engravings by Marcantonio and were accompanied and dramatized by equally explicit sonnets by Pietro Aretino. Marcantonio was briefly gaoled for the offence, and Giulio may have thought it advisable to remove himself from Rome.

In Mantua, like Mantegna before him, Giulio became the consummate court artist. But he extended Mantegna's reach to control every aspect of visual and cultural production, from architecture, frescoes and stuccos, to moveable paintings both secular and religious, sculpture in gesso and stone, decorative work and tableware. Although he sometimes regretted Rome and chafed at his employers' restrictions, he was free of competition and became a princely artist in the manner of his master. Although Giulio was personally confined to Mantua, his work, ideas and designs exercised a powerful influence throughout Northern Italy and the Veneto; and, outside the peninsula, as far as Bavaria (in the palace at Landshut) and, through his pupil Primaticcio, Fontainebleau. He occasionally made designs expressly for sites elsewhere, such as the choir of Verona Cathedral, but much of his influence was communicated via prints. Giulio encouraged an active school of engraving in Mantua that, naturally, reproduced many of his own compositions. In his later years, however, Giulio's style developed little and became repetitive; he rarely stooped to the execution of the paintings he designed, content with the production of an infinite number of scintillating drawings for every possible purpose. In the last analysis, Giulio lacked that restless and relentless commitment to exploration that fired Raphael's extraordinary intelligence and his devotion to the poetics of the brush.

Select Bibliography

General

Freedberg, Sydney, *Painting of the High Renaissance in Rome and Florence*, Cambridge, Mass. 1961

Frommel, Christoph, *The Architecture of the Italian Renaissance*, London and New York 2007

—— *Der Römische Palastbau der Hochrenaissance*, 3 vols, Rome 1973

Landau, David, and Parshall, Peter, *The Renaissance Print 1470–1550*, New Haven and London 1994

Il Rinascimento a Roma: Nel segno di Michelangelo e Raffaello, exh. cat., ed. Maria Grazia Bernardini and Marco Bussagli, Palazzo Sciarra, Rome 2011–12

Primary sources

Camesasca, Ettore (ed.), *Raffaello, gli scritti*, Milan 1994

Di Teodoro, Francesco P., *Raffaello, Baldassar Castiglione e la 'Lettera a Leone X'*, Bologna 1994

Falciani, Anna, 'Documenti urbinati sulla famiglia Santi', in *Raffaello e Urbino*, exh. cat., Lorenza Mochi Onori et al. (eds), Palazzo Ducale, Urbino 2009, pp. 268–84

—— and Marconi, Vincenzo, 'Apparato documentario', in ibid., pp. 285–333

Ferrari, Daniela, *Giulio Romano: Repertorio di fonti documentarie*, 2 vols, Rome 1992

Fontana, Vincenzo, and Morachiello, Paolo (eds), *Vitruvio e Raffaello: Il 'De Architectura' di Vitruvio nella traduzione inedita di Fabio Calvo Ravennate*, Rome 1975

Golzio, Vincenzo, *Raffaello nei documenti, nelle testimonianze dei contemporanei e nella letteratura del suo secolo*, Vatican City 1936

Shearman, John, *Raphael in Early Modern Sources, 1483–1602*, New Haven and London 2003

Vasari, Giorgio, *The Life of Raphael*, trans. and ed. Rick Scorza and Paul Joannides, London and New York 2020

Monographs

Bussagli, Marco, *Raffaello, nella pittura un dio mortale*, Florence, 2020

Ettlinger, Leopold D., and Ettlinger, Helen S., *Raphael*, Oxford 1987

Fischel, Oskar, *Raphael*, London 1948

Jones, Roger, and Penny, Nicholas, *Raphael*, New Haven and London 1983

Nesselrath, Arnold, *Raffaello!*, Milan 2019

Pope Hennessy, John, *Raphael: The Wrightsman Lectures*, London and New York 1970

Salmi, Mario (ed.), *Raffaello: l'opera, le fonti, la fortuna*, 2 vols, Novara 1968

Strinati, Claudio, *Raphaël*, Paris 2012

Talvacchia, Bette, *Raphael*, London and New York 2007

Vecchi, Pierluigi de, *Raffaello*, Milan 2003

Williams, Robert, *Raphael and the Redefinition of Art in Renaissance Italy*, Cambridge 2017

Exhibition catalogues

Hommage à Raphäel, vol. II: *Raphaël dans les collections françaises*, exh. cat., André Chastel, Sylvie Béguin and Françoise Viatte (eds), Grand Palais, Paris 1983–84

Late Raphael, exh. cat., Tom Henry, Paul Joannides et al. (eds), Museo del Prado, Madrid; Musée du Louvre, Paris, 2012

Raffaello 1520–1483, exh. cat., Marzia Faietti, Matteo Lafranconi et al. (eds), Scuderie del Quirinale, Rome 2020

Raphael: From Urbino to Rome, exh. cat., Hugo Chapman, Tom Henry and Carol Plazzotta (eds), National Gallery, London 2004–05

Roma e lo stile classico di Raffaello, 1515–1527, exh. cat., Konrad Oberhuber, Achim Gnann et al. (eds), Palazzo Te, Mantua; Graphische Sammlung Albertina, Vienna, 1999

Collections of essays and conference papers

Fagiolo, Marcello, and Madonna, Maria Louisa (eds), *Raffaello e l'Europa*, Rome 1990

Falomir, Miguel (ed.), *Late Raphael: Proceedings of the International Symposium*, Madrid 2013

Frommel, Christoph, and Winner, Matthias (eds), *Raffaello a Roma: Il convegno di 1983*, Rome 1986

Hall, Marcia B. (ed.), *The Cambridge Companion to Raphael*, Cambridge 2005

—— and Shearman, John (eds), *The Princeton Raphael Symposium: Science in the Service of Art History*, Princeton 1990

Jacoby, Joachim, and Sonnabend, Martin (eds), *Raffael als Zeichner/Raphael as Draughtsman*, Frankfurt am Main 2015

Paolucci, Antonio, Agosti, Barbara, and Ginzburg, Silvia (eds), *Raffaello a Roma: Restauri e ricerche*, Vatican City 2017

Sambucco Hamoud, Micaela, and Strocchi, Maria Letizia (eds), *Studi su Raffaello: Atti del Congresso internazionale di studi (Urbino–Firenze, 6–14 aprile 1984)*, 2 vols, Urbino 1987

Paintings

Camesasca, Ettore, *All the Paintings of Raphael: All the Frescoes of Raphael*, 4 vols, London 1964

Dussler, Luitpold, *Raphael: A Critical Catalogue of his Pictures, Wall-Paintings and Tapestries*, trans. Sebastian Croft, London and New York 1971

Ferino Pagden, Sylvia, and Zancan, Maria Antonietta, *Raffaello: Catalogo completo dei dipinti*, Florence 1989

Meyer zur Capellen, Jürg, *Raphael: A Critical Catalogue of his Paintings*, 3 vols, Landshut 2001–08

Oberhuber, Konrad, *Raphael: The Paintings*, Munich 1999

Vecchi, Pierluigi de, *The Complete Paintings of Raphael*, London 1969

Drawings

Ames-Lewis, Francis, *The Draftsman Raphael*, New Haven and London 1986

Clayton, Martin (ed.), *Raphael and his Circle: Drawings from Windsor Castle*, exh. cat., London and other venues 1999–2001

Cordellier, Dominique, and Py, Bernardette, *Raphaël, son atelier, ses copistes*, vol. V of *Inventaire général des dessins italiens, Musée du Louvre*, Paris 1992

Ferino Pagden, Sylvia, *Disegni umbri del Rinascimento da Perugino a Raffaello*, exh. cat., Uffizi, Florence 1982

—— *Gallerie dell'Accademia di Venezia: Disegni umbri*, Milan 1984

Fischel, Oskar, *Raffaels Zeichnungen*, 8 vols, Berlin 1913–41

Gere, J. A., and Turner, Nicholas, *Drawings by Raphael from the Royal Library, the Ashmolean, the British Museum, Chatsworth and other English Collections*, exh. cat., British Museum, London 1983

Gnann, Achim (ed.), *Raphael*, exh. cat., Albertina, Vienna 2017–18

Joannides, Paul, *The Drawings of Raphael with a Complete Catalogue*, Los Angeles and Oxford 1983

—— 'Raphael, his Studio and his Copyists', *Paragone*, vol. 44, nos 523–25, 1993, pp. 3–29

Knab, Eckhart, Mitsch, Erwin, Oberhuber, Konrad, Ferino Pagden, Sylvia, and Huber, E. W., *Raphael: Die Zeichnungen*, Munich 1983. Published in Italian as *Raffaello: I disegni*, Florence 1984

Oberhuber, Konrad, *Raphaels Zeichnungen*, vol. IX: *Entwürfe zu Werken Raphaels und seiner Schule im Vatikan 1511/1512 bis 1520*, Berlin 1972

Parker, Sir Karl, *Catalogue of the Collection of Drawings in the Ashmolean Museum, II: The Italian Schools*, Oxford, 1956

Pouncey, Philip, and Gere, John, *Italian Drawings in the Department of Prints and Drawings in the British Museum: Raphael and His Circle*, London 1962

Printmaking

Bernini Pezzini, Grazia, Massari, Stefania, and Prosperi Valenti Rodinò, Simonetta (eds), *Raphael Invenit*, exh. cat., Istituto Nazionale per la Grafica, Rome 1985

Getscher, Robert H., *An Annotated and Illustrated Version of Giorgio Vasari's History of Italian and Northern Prints from His 'Lives of the Artists' (1550 & 1568)*, 2 vols, Lewiston, Queenston, Lampeter 2003

The Illustrated Bartsch, vols 26–27: *The Works of Marcantonio Raimondi and his School*, ed. Konrad Oberhuber, New York 1978

The Illustrated Bartsch, vol. 28: *Italian Masters of the Sixteenth Century*, ed. Suzanne Boorsch and John Spike, New York 1985

The Illustrated Bartsch, vol. 28: Commentary by Madeline Cirillo Archer, *Italian Masters of the Sixteenth Century*, New York 1995

The Illustrated Bartsch, vol. 29: *Italian Masters of the Sixteenth Century*, ed. Suzanne Boorsch, New York 1982

The Illustrated Bartsch, vol. 45: *Italian Chiaroscuro Woodcuts*, ed. Caroline Karpinski, New York 1983

Joannides, Paul, 'Drawings by Raphael and his immediate followers made for or employed for engravings and chiaroscuro woodcuts', in Joachim Jacoby and Martin Sonnabend (eds), *Raffael als Zeichner/Raphael as Draughtsman*, Frankfurt am Main 2015, pp. 149–66

Pon, Lisa, *Raphael, Dürer, and Marcantonio Raimondi: Copying and the Italian Renaissance Print*, New Haven and London 2004

Shoemaker, Innis H. (ed.), *The Engravings of Marcantonio Raimondi*, exh. cat., Spencer Art Museum, University of Kansas, and various venues, 1981

Wouk, Edward, and Morris, David (eds), *Marcantonio Raimondi, Raphael and the Image Multiplied*, exh. cat., Whitworth Art Gallery, Manchester 2016

Urbino

Cleri, Bonita (ed.), *Timoteo Viti*, Urbino 2008

Giovanni Santi, exh. cat., Maria Rosaria Valazzi et al. (eds), Palazzo Ducale, Urbino 2018–19

Raffaello e gli amici di Urbino, exh. cat., Barbara Agosti, Silvia Ginzburg et al. (eds), Palazzo Ducale, Urbino 2019–20

Raffaello e Urbino, exh. cat., Lorenza Mochi Onori et al. (eds), Palazzo Ducale, Urbino 2009

Varese, Ranieri, *Giovanni Santi*, Fiesole 1994

Varese, Ranieri (ed.), *Giovanni Santi: Atti del convegno internazionale di studi, Urbino, Convento di Santa Chiara, 17/18/19 marzo 1995*, Milan 1999

Umbria

Fischel, Oskar, *Die Zeichnungen der Umbrer*, Berlin 1917

Henry, Tom, *The Life and Work of Luca Signorelli*, New Haven and London 2012

Perugino, il divin pittore, exh. cat., Vittoria Garibaldi and Francesco Federico Mancini (eds), Galleria Nazionale dell'Umbria, Perugia 2004

Raffaello giovane e Città di Castello, exh. cat., Mariangela Bocciolesi, Vittoria Garibaldi and Giuditta Rossi (eds), Pinacoteca Communale, Citta di Castello 1983–84

Scarpellini, Pietro, *Il Perugino*, Milan 1984

—— and Silvestrelli, Maria Rita, *Pintoricchio*, Milan 2003

Settis, Salvatore, and Toracca, Donatello (eds), *La Libreria Piccolomini nel Duomo di Siena*, Modena 1998

Florence

Joannides, Paul, 'Leonardo da Vinci, Peter-Paul Rubens, Pierre-Nolasque Bergeret and "The Fight for the Standard"', *Achademia Leonardi Vinci*, vol. 1, 1988, pp. 76–86

Meyer zur Capellen, Jürg, *Raphael in Florence*, London 1996

Raffaello a Firenze: Dipinti e disegni delle collezioni fiorentine, exh. cat., Palazzo Pitti, Florence 1984

Raffaello: da Firenze a Roma, exh. cat., Anna Coliva (ed.), Galleria Borghese, Rome 2006

Vatican

Pietrangeli, Carlo, et al., *Raffaello nell' appartamento di Giulio II e Leone X*, Milan 1993

Raffaello in Vaticano, exh. cat., Fabrizio Mancinelli et al. (eds), Vatican City 1984–85

Redig de Campos, Deoclecio, *I palazzi vaticani*, Bologna 1967

Shearman, John, 'Raphael's Unexecuted Projects for the Stanze', in Georg Kauffmann and Willibald Sauerländer, *Walter Friedländer zum 90. Geburtstag*, Berlin 1965, pp. 158–80

—— 'The Vatican Stanze: Functions and Decorations', *Proceedings of the British Academy*, vol. 57, 1971, pp. 369–424

Stanza della Segnatura

Emiliani, Andrea, and Scolaro, Michela, *Raffaello: La stanza della Segnatura*, Milan 2002

Hall, Marcia B. (ed.), *Raphael's School of Athens*, Cambridge 1997

Nesselrath, Arnold, 'Lorenzo Lotto in the Stanza della Segnatura', *Burlington Magazine*, vol. 142, January 2000, pp. 4–12

—— *Raphael's School of Athens*, Vatican City 1996

Stanza di Eliodoro

Ballarin, Alessandro, 'Raffaello 1511–1514: "Molto ancora resta da scoprire a proposito dell'attitudine di Raffaello verso la Natura"', in Antonio Paolucci, Barbara Agosti and Silvia Ginzburg (eds), *Raffaello a Roma: Restauri e ricerche*, Vatican City 2017, pp. 41–54

Shearman, John, 'The Stanza d'Eliodoro', in Christoph Frommel and Matthias Winner (eds), *Raffaello a Roma: Il convegno di 1983*, Rome 1986, pp. 75–88

Stanza dell'Incendio

Kaplan, Alice M., 'Raphael's Dürer Drawing Reconsidered', *Art Bulletin*, vol. 56, 1974, pp. 50–58

Nesselrath, Arnold, 'Art-Historical Findings during the Restoration of the Stanza dell'Incendio', *Master Drawings*, vol. 30, no. 1, Spring 1992, pp. 31–61

Loggetta and the Loggia

Caneva, Giulia, and Carpaneto, Giuseppe
M., *Raffaello e l'immagine della natura:
La raffigurazione del mondo naturale
nelle decorazioni delle Logge vaticane*,
Milan 2010

Dacos, Nicole, *The Loggia of Raphael: A Vatican
Art Treasure*, New York and London 2008

Davidson, Bernice F., *Raphael's Bible: A Study
of the Vatican Loggia*, New York 1985

Fernandez, Henry, 'Raphael's Bibbiena Chapel
in the Vatican Palace', in Tristan Weddigen,
Sible de Blaauw and Bram Kempers (eds),
*Functions and Decorations: Art and Ritual
at the Vatican Place in the Middle Ages and the
Renaissance*, Vatican City and Turnhout, 2003,
pp. 115–29

Sala dei Palafrenieri

Weddigen, Tristan, *Raffaels Papageienzimmer:
Ritual, Raumfunktion und Dekoration im
Vatikanpalast der Renaissance*, Berlin 2006

Sala di Costantino

Fehl, Philipp, 'Raphael as a Historian: Poetry and
Historical Accuracy in the Sala di Costantino',
Artibus et Historiae, vol. 14, 1993, pp. 9–76

Quednau, Rolf, *Die Sala di Costantino im
Vatikanischen Palast*, Hildesheim 1979

Sistine tapestries

Debenedetti, Ana (ed.), *The Raphael Cartoons*,
London 2020

Fermor, Sharon, *The Raphael Tapestry Cartoons*,
London 1995

*Raphael: Cartoons and Tapestries for the Sistine
Chapel*, exh. cat., Mark Evans, Arnold
Nesselrath, Clare Browne and Anna Maria
de Strobel (eds), Victoria and Albert Museum,
London 2010

Shearman, John, *Raphael's Cartoons in the
Collection of Her Majesty the Queen and the
Tapestries for the Sistine Chapel*, London 1972

Tapestry in the Renaissance: Art and Magnificence,
exh. cat., Thomas Campbell et al. (eds),
Metropolitan Museum of Art, New York 2002

Rome

Frommel, Christoph, 'Baldassare Peruzzi als
Maler und Zeichner', in *Römische Jahrbuch
für Kunstgeschichte* 11, supplement, Munich
and Vienna 1967–68

Sebastiano del Piombo, exh. cat., Claudio Strinati
et al. (eds), Rome and Berlin 2008

Church commissions for Agostino Chigi and others

Bonito, Virginia Anne, 'The Saint Anne
Altar in Sant'Agostino: Restoration and
Interpretation', *Burlington Magazine*, vol. 124,
no. 950, 1982, pp. 268–76

Gould, Cecil, 'Raphael at S. Maria della Pace',
Gazette des Beaux-Arts, vol. 120, 1992,
pp. 78–88

Hirst, Michael, 'The Chigi Chapel in S. Maria
della Pace', *Journal of the Warburg and
Courtauld Institutes*, vol. 24, no. 3/4, 1961,
pp. 161–85

Shearman, John, 'The Chigi Chapel in S. Maria
del Popolo', *Journal of the Warburg and
Courtauld Institutes*, vol. 24, no. 3/4, 1961,
pp. 129–60

The Farnesina

Caneva, Giulia, *Il mondo di Cerere nella Loggia
di Psiche*, Rome 1992

Frommel, Christoph, et al., *La villa Farnesina
a Roma*, Modena 2003

Oberhuber, Konrad, 'Raphael's Drawings for
the Loggia of Psyche in the Farnesina', in
Christoph Frommel and Matthias Winner
(eds), *Raffaello a Roma: Il convegno di 1983*,
Rome 1986, pp. 189–208

Shearman, John, 'Die Loggia der Psyche in der
Villa Farnesina und die Probleme der letzten
Phase von Raffaels graphischem Stil', *Jahrbuch
der Kunsthistorischen Sammlungen in Wien*,
vol. 60, 1964, pp. 59–100

Varoli-Piazza, Rosali, et al., *Raffaello: la loggia
di Amore e Psiche alla Farnesina*, Milan 2002

Roman paintings

Die Sixtinische Madonna, exh. cat., Andreas Hennin
et al. (eds), Gemäldegaleire, Dresden 2012

Fritz, Michael P., *Giulio Romano et Raphaël:
La vice-reine de Naples, ou la renaissance
d'une beauté mythique*, Paris 1997

Gould, Cecil, 'Raphael versus Giulio Romano:
The Swing Back', *Burlington Magazine*,
vol. 124, no. 953, 1982, pp. 479–87

—— 'Raphael's Double Portrait in the Louvre:
An Identification for the Second Figure',
Artibus et Historiae, vol. 10, 1984, pp. 57–60

Joannides, Paul, 'The Early Easel Paintings of
Giulio Romano', *Paragone*, vol. 36, no. 425,
1985, pp. 17–46

—— 'Giulio Romano in Raphael's Workshop',
Quaderni di Palazzo Te, vol. 8, 2000, pp. 35–46

—— 'Raphael and his Circle', *Paragone*, vol. 51,
no. 601, 2000, pp. 3–42

Weil-Garris Posner, Kathleen, *Leonardo and Central Italian Art, 1515–1550*, New York 1974

Architecture

Elet, Yvonne, *Architectural Invention in Renaissance Rome*, Cambridge 2017

Huppert, Ann C., *Becoming an Architect in Renaissance Italy: Art, Science, and the Career of Baldassare Peruzzi*, New Haven and London 2015

Lefevre, Robert, *Villa Madama*, Rome 1984

Raffaello architetto, exh. cat., Christoph Frommel et al. (eds), Palazzo dei Conservatori, Rome 1984

Ray, Stefano, *Raffaello architetto*, Bari 1974

Raphael's School

Castris, Pierluigi Leone de, *Polidoro da Caravaggio*, Naples 2001

Dacos, Nicole, Furlan, Caterina et al., *Giovanni da Udine, 1487–1561*, 3 vols, Udine 1987

Franklin, David, *Polidoro da Caravaggio*, New Haven and London 2018

Giovanni da Udine tra Raffaello e Michelangelo, exh. cat., Liliana Cargnelutti and Caterina Furlan (eds), Castello d'Udine 2021

Giulio Romano, exh. cat., Ernst Gombrich et al. (eds), Palazzo Te, Mantua 1989

Hartt, Frederick, *Giulio Romano*, 2 vols, New Haven 1958

Love, David, 'Gianfrancesco Penni: A Biographical and Iconographic Introduction to His Two Versions of 'The Holy Family with Saint John and Saint Catherine', *Journal of the National Museum in Warsaw*, vol. 3, no. 39, 2014, pp. 217–31

—— 'Gianfrancesco Penni: Designs for Overlooked Panel Paintings' in Miguel Falomir (ed.), *Late Raphael: Proceedings of the International Symposium*, Madrid 2013, pp. 136–49

Parma Armani, Elena, *Perin del Vaga, l'anello mancante: studi sul manierismo*, Genoa 1986

Perino del Vaga tra Raffaello e Michelangelo, exh. cat., Elena Parma Armani et al. (eds), Palazzo Te, Mantua 2001

Vannugli, Antonio, 'Un'altra "lettera rubata". La decorazione della Cappella di S. Maria Maddalena nella Ss. Trinità dei Monti e il vero "Noli Me Tangere" di Giulio Romano e Giovan Francesco Penni', *Storia dell'Arte*, vol. 111, 2005, pp. 59–96

Wolk-Simon, Linda, 'The Lost Decoration of the Chapel of the Magdalen by Giulio Romano and Giovanni Francesco Penni in SS. Trinità dei Monti in Roma: Some New Drawings', *Master Drawings*, vol. 49, no. 2, 2011, pp. 147–58

List of Illustrations

Measurements are given in centimetres and inches, height before width, where applicable
All works are by Raphael unless otherwise specified

1 *Self-Portrait with Giulio Romano*, probably 1520. Oil on canvas, 99 × 83 (39 × 32¾). Musée du Louvre, Paris (614)

2 *Self-Portrait*, 1499 or earlier. Black chalk with traces of white heightening, 38.2 × 26.1 (15⅛ × 10⅜). Ashmolean Museum, Oxford (WA1846.158)

3 Andrea Mantegna, *The Triumphs of Caesar*, third panel, *The Triumph with Elephants*, 1484–92. Tempera on canvas, 266 × 278 (104¾ × 109½). Royal Collection/Royal Collection Trust. Her Majesty Queen Elizabeth II, 2021/Bridgeman Images

4 Giovanni Santi, *The Virgin and Child Enthroned with Sts John the Baptist, Francis, Jerome and Sebastian (Pala Buffi)*, 1489. Tempera (and oil?) on wood, 330 × 221 (130 × 87⅛). Urbino, Galleria Nazionale delle Marche

5 Giovanni Santi, *Clio* (from the series *The Muses*), *c.* 1480. Tempera and oil on wood, 84 × 41 (33 × 16). Galleria Corsini, Florence

6 Giovanni Santi, *The Virgin and Child*, *c.* 1488. Tempera and oil on wood, 68 × 49.8 (26⅞ × 19⅝). National Gallery, London (NG751)

7 Giovanni Santi, *modello* for *The Muse Clio*, *c.* 1480. Wash and white heightening on a green preparation, 24.6 × 18 (9¾ × 7⅛). Royal Collection/Royal Collection Trust. Her Majesty Queen Elizabeth II, 2021

8 Piero del Pollaiuolo, *Tobias and the Archangel Raphael*, *c.* 1470. Tempera on wood, 232 × 165 (91⅜ × 65). Galleria Sabauda, Turin. Photo Musei Reali di Torino/Ernani Orcorte/Bridgeman Images

9 Giovanni Santi, *The Tiranni Chapel*, probably 1493. Fresco, 420 × 295 (165⅜ × 116¼). San Domenico, Cagli. Photo Gianni Dagli Orti/ Shutterstock

10 Pietro Perugino, *The Virgin and Child Enthroned with Sts Ercolano, Costanzo, Lawrence and Louis of Toulouse (Pala dei Decemviri)*, 1495–96. Oil on wood, 193 × 165 (76 × 65). Pinacoteca Vaticana, Vatican City

11 After Antonio Pollaiuolo, *Hercules and the Giants*, c. 1475. Engraving, 36.4 × 55.2 (14⅜ × 21¾). Metropolitan Museum of Art, New York. Harris Brisbane Dick Fund, 1925 (25.2.23)

12 *Virgin with the Sleeping Child*, 1495?. Fresco, 97 × 67 (38.1 × 26.3). Casa di Raffaello, Urbino. Photo Ivan Vdovin/Alamy Stock Photo

13 Perugino or Raphael, *The Nativity of the Virgin*, 1497 or later, predella panel from Pietro Perugino, the Altarpiece. Oil on wood, 25 × 50 (10 × 20). Photo Scala, Florence

14 Study for *The Birth of the Virgin*, 1497 or later. Pen, 16.3 × 12.1 (6½ × 4⅞). Gabinetto dei Disegni e delle Stampe, Uffizi, Florence (366)

15 Studies for *The Holy Family Groups*,1498–99. Pen over traces of black chalk, 25.4 × 21.6 (10 × 8⅝). Ashmolean Museum, University of Oxford (WA1846.145v)

16 *The Coronation of St Nicholas of Tolentino*, 1500–01. Fragments of *God The Father and The Virgin*. Oil on wood, 112 × 75 (44⅛ × 29⅝) (God the Father); 51 × 41 (20⅛ × 16¼) (The Virgin) Museo di Capodimonte, Naples (Q 50.)

17 *An Angel* (fragment), 1501. Oil on wood, 58 × 36 (22⅞ × 14¼). Musée du Louvre, Paris (RF1981–55)

18 *An Angel* (fragment), 1501. Oil on wood transferred on canvas, 31 × 27 (12¼ × 10¾). Pinacoteca Tosio Martinengo, Brescia.

19 Compositional study for *The Coronation of St Nicholas of Tolentino*, 1500. Black chalk over stylus, 40 × 26.3 (15¾ × 10⅜). Palais des Beaux-Arts, Lille (Pl.474). Photo RMN-Grand Palais/Hervé Lewandowski

20 Study for details in *The Coronation of St Nicholas of Tolentino*, 1500. Black chalk over stylus, 40 × 26.3 (15¾ × 10⅜). Palais des Beaux-Arts, Lille (Pl.475). Photo RMN-Grand Palais/Hervé Lewandowski

21 *Christ Crucified with God the Father, Sts Sebastian and Roch (Gonfalone della Santissima Trinità)*, 1499–1500. Oil on canvas, 167 × 94 (65¾ × 37⅛). Pinacoteca Comunale, Città di Castello. Photo Scala, Florence

22 *The Creation of Eve*, 1499–1500. Oil on canvas, 167 × 94 (65¾ × 37⅛). Pinacoteca Comunale, Città di Castello. Photo Scala, Florence

23 Study for *The Creation of Eve* (and a copy after an archer in Luca Signorelli's *Martyrdom of St Sebastian*, 1499–1500. Black chalk and pen, 25.4 × 21.6 (10 × 8⅝). Ashmolean Museum, Oxford (WA1846.145r)

24 *The Mond Crucifixion*, signed RAPHAEL VRBINAS P., 1502–03. Oil on wood, 283.3 × 167.3 (111⅝ × 65⅞). National Gallery, London. Mond Bequest, 1924 (NG3623)

25 *The Coronation of the Virgin with the Apostles (Pala degli Oddi)*, 1503–04. Oil on wood, transferred to canvas, 267 × 163 (105 × 64). Pinacoteca Vaticana, Vatican City

26 *Modello* for *The Coronation of the Virgin* (Upper part), 1503. Pen, 15.8 × 19.3 (6¼ × 7⅝). Szépművészeti Múzeum/Museum of Fine Arts, Budapest, 2021 (1779)

27 *Modello* for *The Coronation of the Virgin* (Lower part), 1503. Pen, 16.5 × 20 (6½ × 7⅞). Musée du Louvre, Paris (INV3970–recto). Photo RMN-Grand Palais (Musée du Louvre)/Michel Urtado

28 *The Adoration of the Magi and Shepherds*, 1503. Pen over stylus and traces of black chalk, 27.2 × 41.9 (10¾ × 16½). Nationalmuseum, Stockholm (296)

29 Predella panel, *The Annunciation*, from *The Coronation of the Virgin*, 1503. Oil on wood, 39 × 190 (15⅜ × 74⅞) by 27 × 50 (10⅔ × 19¾). Pinacoteca Vaticana, Vatican City (40335)

30 Predella panel, *The Adoration of the Magi and Shepherds*, from *The Coronation of the Virgin*, 1503. Oil on wood, 39 × 190 (15⅜ × 74⅞) by 27 × 50 (10⅔ × 19¾). Pinacoteca Vaticana, Vatican City (40335)

31 Predella panel, *The Presentation of Jesus in the Temple*, from *The Coronation of the Virgin*, 1503. Oil on wood, 39 × 190 (15⅜ × 74⅞) by 27 × 50 (10⅔ × 19¾). Pinacoteca Vaticana, Vatican City (40335).

32 *The Marriage of the Virgin (The Spozalizio)*, signed RAPHAEL VRBINAS and dated MDIIII (1504). Oil on wood, 170 × 118 (67 × 46½). Pinacoteca di Brera, Milan (336)

33 Perugino, *The Marriage of the Virgin*, 1499–1504. Oil on wood, 236 × 186 (93 × 73 ¼). Musée des Beaux-Arts, Caen

34 *The Virgin and Child with Sts John the Baptist and Nicholas of Bari (The Pala Ansidei)*, dated MDV (1505). Oil on wood, 216.8 × 147.6 (85⅜ × 58⅛). National Gallery, London (NG1171)

35 *The Virgin and Child with Sts John the Baptist and Peter, Paul, Cecilia and Catherine, with God the Father flanked by angels in the Lunette (The Pala Colonna)*, 1504–05. Oil on wood, 172.4 × 172.4 (67⅞ × 67⅞). Metropolitan Museum of Art, New York. Gift of J. Pierpont Morgan, 1916 (16.30ab)

36 Predella panel, *St Francis of Assisi*, 1504–05. Oil on wood, 25.8 × 16.8 (10¼ × 6⅝). Dulwich Picture Gallery, London

37 Predella panel to the Pala Colonna, *The Agony in the Garden*, 1504–05. Oil on wood, 24.1 × 28.9

(9½ × 11⅜). Metropolitan Museum of Art, New York. Funds from various donors, 1932 (32.130.1)

38 Predella panel to the Pala Colonna, *The Procession to Calvary*, 1504–05. Oil on wood, 24.4 × 85.5 (9⅝ × 33¾). National Gallery, London (NG2919)

39 Predella panel to the Pala Colonna, *The Lamentation over the Dead Christ*, 1504–05. Oil on wood, 23.5 × 28.8 (9⅜ × 11⅜). Isabella Stewart Gardner Museum, Boston

40 Predella panel to the Pala Colonna, *St Anthony of Padua*, 1504–05. Oil on wood, 25.6 × 16.4 (10⅛ × 6½). Dulwich Picture Gallery, London

41 *The Virgin and Child at Nones*, probably 1503. Oil on wood, 55.2 × 40 (21¾ × 15¾). Norton Simon Art Foundation, Pasadena (M.1972.2.P)

42 *The Virgin and Child with St John (Madonna Diotalevi)*, probably 1502. Oil on wood, 69 × 50 (27¼ × 19¾). Gemäldegalerie, Staatliche Museen zu Berlin (147). Photo Scala, Florence/bpk, Bildagentur für Kunst, Kultur und Geschichte, Berlin

43 *The Journey of Aeneas Silvius Piccolomini to Basel*, probably 1503. Pen with wash and white heightening over black chalk and stylus, 70.5 × 41.5 (27⅞ × 16⅜). Gabinetto dei Disegni e delle Stampe, Uffizi, Florence (520 E).

44 Pinturicchio, *The Journey of Aeneas Piccolomini to Basel*, c. 1505. Fresco. Piccolomini Library, Siena. Photo Gianni Dagli Orti/Shutterstock

45 *St George and the Dragon*, probably 1502–03. Oil on wood, 30.5 × 26.6 (12⅛ × 10½). Musée du Louvre, Paris (609)

46 *St Michael Vanquishing Satan*, probably 1502–03. Oil on wood, 29 × 25 (11½ × 9⅞). Musée du Louvre, Paris (608). Photo Scala, Florence

47 *An Allegory of the Choice between Virtue and Comfort (The Vision of a Knight)*, probably 1503–04. Oil on wood, 17.1 × 17.3 (6¾ × 6⅞). National Gallery, London (NG213)

48 *The Three Graces*, probably 1503–04. Oil on wood, 17 × 17 (6¾ × 6¾). Musée Condé, Chantilly (PE 38)

49 Peter Paul Rubens after Leonardo da Vinci's composition of 1504–05, *The Battle of Anghiari*, c. 1603, reworked later. Black chalk, pen and ink, wash and bodycolour, 45.3 × 63.6 (17⅞ × 25⅛). Musée du Louvre, Paris (DAG 20271r)

50 Aristotile da Sangallo after Michelangelo's composition of 1504–05, *The Battle of Cascina*, 1542. Oil on wood, grisaille, 76.5 × 129 (30⅛ × 50⅞). Holkham Hall, Norfolk

51 *The Holy Trinity with Saints*, 1505. Fresco, 389 × 175 (153¼ × 69). San Severo, Perugia

52 Study for *The Holy Trinity*, 1505. Metalpoint with white heightening, on a pale ground, 21 × 27.4 (8⅜ × 10⅞). Ashmolean Museum, Oxford (WA1846.176)

53 *The Virgin and Child (The Small Cowper Madonna)*, probably 1505. Oil on wood, 59.5 × 44 (23⁷⁄₁₆ × 17⁵⁄₁₆). National Gallery of Art, Washington, D.C. Widener Collection (1942.9.57)

54 *The Virgin and Child with Sts Bernard, Peter, James and Augustine (The Madonna del Baldacchino)*, 1506–08 (Unfinished). Oil on wood, 279 × 217 (109⅞ × 85½). Galleria Palatina, Palazzo Pitti, Florence.

55 *St George and the Dragon*, probably 1507. Oil on wood, 28.5 × 21.5 (11¼ × 8⁷⁄₁₆). National Gallery of Art, Washington, D.C. Andrew W. Mellon Collection (1937.1.26)

56 Leonardo, *The Virgin and Child with St Anne and a Lamb*, c. 1505–19. Oil on wood, 168 × 130 (66¼ × 51¼). Musée du Louvre, Paris (776)

57 Leonardo, *The Adoration of the Magi*, 1480–82 (Unfinished). Tempera and oil on wood, 246 × 243 (96⅞ × 95¾). Uffizi, Florence (1594)

58 *The Virgin and Child (The Madonna of the Pinks or La Madonna dei Garofani)*, probably 1507. Oil on wood, 27.9 × 22.4 (11 × 8⅞). National Gallery, London (NG6596). Photo Art Collection 2/Alamy Stock Photo

59 *The Virgin and Child (The Bridgewater Madonna)*, probably 1507. Oil on wood transferred to canvas, 81 × 55 (32 × 21¾). The National Gallery of Scotland, Bridgewater Collection Loan (NGL 065.46). Photo Eraza Collection/Alamy Stock Photo

60 *The Virgin and Child with Sts John and Thaddeus?* (The Terranuova *Madonna*), 1504–05. Oil on wood, diameter 88.5 (34⅞). Gemäldegalerie, Staatliche Museen zu Berlin (247A). Photo Scala, Florence/bpk, Bildagentur für Kunst, Kultur und Geschichte, Berlin

61 Studies for *The Madonna del Prato*, 1505. Pen and ink over stylus, 24.6 × 36.4 (9¾ × 14⅜). Albertina, Vienna (107r)

62 *The Virgin and Child with St John (The Madonna del Prato)*, dated MDV (1505). Oil on wood, 113 × 88.5 (44½ × 34⅞). Kunsthistorisches Museum, Vienna (175)

63 *The Virgin and Child with St John (The Madonna del Cardellino [goldinch])*, 1505–06. Oil on wood, 107 × 77 (42¼ × 30⅜). Galleria degli Uffizi, Florence

64 *The Virgin and Child with St John (The Belle Jardinière)*, signed RAPHAELLO VRB and dated MDVII (1507). Oil on wood, 122 × 70 (48⅛ × 27⅝). Musée du Louvre, Paris (602). Photo Prisma Archivo/Alamy Stock Photo

65 *The Holy Family with a Lamb*, signed RAPHAEL VRBINAS and dated MDVII (1507). Oil on wood, 28 × 21.5 (11⅛ × 8½). Museo Nacional del Prado (P000296)

66 *The Holy Family with Sts John the Baptist and Elizabeth (The Canigiani Holy Family)*, signed RAPHAEL VRBINAS but not dated; probably 1507.

Oil on wood, 131 × 107 (51⅝ × 42¼). Alte Pinakothek München, Bayerische Staatsgemäldesammlungen, Munich (476)

67 *St Catherine of Alexandria*, probably 1507. Oil on wood, 72.2 × 55.7 (28½ × 22). National Gallery, London (NG168)

68 Study for *The Entombment*, c. 1505–06. Pen and ink, 17.9 × 20.6 (7⅛ × 8⅛). Ashmolean Museum, Oxford (WA1846.170)

69 *The Entombment*, signed RAPHAEL VRBINAS and dated MDVII (1507). Oil on wood, 184 × 176 (72½ × 69⅜). Galleria Borghese, Rome (170). Photo Scala, Florence - su concessione Ministero Beni e Attività Culturali e del Turismo

70 The predella of *The Entombment* (detail) *Charity (Caritas)*, 1507. Oil on wood, each 18 × 44 (7⅛ × 1 7⅜). Pinacoteca Vaticana, Vatican City (40330)

71 Study for *Charity*, 1507. Pen and ink over lead-point, 37.8 × 27.5 (15 × 10⅞). Albertina, Vienna (IV 245)

72 *Hercules and the Hydra*, probably 1508. Pen and ink, 38.9 × 27.3 (15⅜ × 10¾). Royal Collection/Royal Collection Trust. Her Majesty Queen Elizabeth II, 2021/Bridgeman Images

73 The Stanza della Segnatura, 1508–11. Vatican Palace, Vatican City. Photo Scala, Florence

74 The Vault, Stanza della Segnatura, 1510. Fresco. Vatican Palace, Vatican City

75 *Parnassus*, Stanza della Segnatura, 1509–10. Fresco, 645 × 700 (254 × 276). Vatican Palace, Vatican City

76 *The Disputa*, Stanza della Segnatura, 1508–09. Fresco, 588 × 818 (232 × 322). Vatican Palace, Vatican City

77 *Justice*, Stanza della Segnatura, 1511. Fresco, 564 × 700 (222 × 276). Vatican Palace, Vatican City

78 *The School of Athens*, Stanza della Segnatura, 1509–10. Fresco, 588 × 818 (231½ × 322). Vatican Palace, Vatican City

79 Compositional study for the upper part of *The Disputa*, probably 1508. Wash with white heightening on buff preparation, 23.3 × 44 (9¼ × 17⅜). Ashmolean Museum, Oxford (WA1846.183)

80 Compositional study for the lower part of *The Disputa*, c. 1508. Wash with white heightening on buff preparation, 23.1 × 40.7 (9⅛ × 16⅛). Musée Condé, Chantilly (DE 53).

81 *A gesturing man*, probably 1509. Metalpoint on light-grey ground, 41.2 × 27.7 (16¼ × 11). Musée du Louvre, Paris (3869). Photo RMN-Grand Palais (Musée du Louvre)/Michèle Bellot

82 *Diogenes in the School of Athens*, probably 1509. Metalpoint on pink ground, 24.5 × 28.4 (9¾ × 11¼). Städelsches Kunstinstitut, Frankfurt am Main (380)

83 Marcantonio Raimondi after Raphael, *Parnassus*, c. 1513. Engraving, 35.6 × 47 (14⅛ × 18⅝). Metropolitan Museum of Art, New York. Bequest of James Clark McGuire, 1930 (31.54.166)

84 Unidentified draughtsman, *Parnassus*, copy after a lost drawing by Raphael, probably of 1509. Pen over black chalk, 29.2 × 45.8 (11½ × 18⅛). Ashmolean Museum, University of Oxford/ Bridgeman Images

85 Study for a Muse (probably Calliope) in *Parnassus*, 1509–10. Pen, 24.6 × 22 (9¾ × 8¾). Albertina, Vienna (219r)

86 *Justinian Receiving the Pandects*, 1511. Pen with wash over black chalk, 37.1 × 21.6 (14⅝ × 8⅝). Städelsches Kunstinstitut, Frankfurt am Main (381). Photo Scala, Florence/bpk, Bildagentur für Kunst, Kultur und Geschichte, Berlin

87 *The Prophet Isaiah*, 1512. Fresco, 250 × 155 (98 × 61). Sant'Agostino, Rome

88 Gianfrancesco Penni, compositional study for the Chapel of Agostino Chigi in Santa Maria della Pace, Rome, probably 1510. Metal point, pen and wash, with white heightening on brown preparation, 38.9 × 27.6 (15⅜ × 10⅞). Nationalmuseum, Stockholm (NMH 32⅝863). Photo Bodil Karlsson/Nationalmuseum 2011

89 Compositional sketch for the Chapel of Agostino Chigi in Santa Maria della Pace, probably 1510. Pen, 24.7 × 32.6 (9¾ × 12⅞). Ashmolean Museum, Oxford (WA1846.194v)/Bridgeman Images

90 The Chapel of Agostino Chigi, 1510–12 in Santa Maria della Pace; unfinished

91 Cesare (Cesarino) Rossetti to Raphael's design, *Christ's Descent into Limbo*, 1510–11. Bronze roundel, diameter 90 (35⅓). Abbey, Chiaravalle

92 *Pietà*, probably 1511. Wash and white heightening over black chalk, 30.4 × 21.5 (12 × 8½). Musée du Louvre, Paris (3858). Photo RMN-Grand Palais (Musée du Louvre)/Michèle Bellot

93 *The Resurrection*, probably 1511–12. Pen, 40.7 × 27.4 (16⅛ × 10⅞). Musée Bonnat-Helleu, Bayonne (NI1707). Photo RMN-Grand Palais/René-Gabriel Ojeda

94 The Sepulchral Chapel of Agostino Chigi, the dome was monogrammed by the mosaicist Luigi da Pace and dated 1516. Santa Maria del Popolo, Rome

95 Compositional study for an *Assumption*, probably 1510. Pen, 20.1 × 14.3 (8 × 5¾). Ashmolean Museum, Oxford (WA1846.195v)

96 Nude study for a soldier in a *Resurrection*, probably 1511–12. Black chalk, 32 × 25.5 (12⅝ × 10⅛). Royal Collection/Royal Collection Trust. Her Majesty Queen Elizabeth II, 2021

97 The Loggia di Galatea, general view showing Raphael's *Galatea* and Sebastiano's *Polyphemus*. Villa Farnesina, Rome. Photo Ghigo Roli/ Bridgeman Images

98 *Galatea*, 1512. Fresco, 295 × 225 (116¼ × 88⅝). Villa Farnesina, Rome

99 Marcantonio Raimondi after Raphael, *The Suicide of Lucretia*, probably 1510. Engraving, 21.2 × 13 (8⅜ × 5⅛). Rijksmuseum, Amsterdam (RP-P-1951-575)

100 Marcantonio Raimondi after Raphael, *The Massacre of the Innocents*, 1511. Engraving, 28 × 42.6 (11 × 16⅞). British Museum, London (1858,0417.1580)

101 The Stanza di Eliodoro, 1511–14. General view, Vatican Palace, Vatican City. Photo Scala, Florence

102 *The Expulsion of Heliodorus*, 1511–12. Stanza di Eliodoro. Fresco, 453 × 808 (178 × 318). Vatican Palace, Vatican City

103 *The Release of St Peter*, 1512–13. Stanza di Eliodoro. Fresco, 475 × 715 (187 × 281). Vatican Palace, Vatican City

104 Raphael and assistants, *The Repulse of Attila*, 1513–14. Stanza di Eliodoro. Fresco, 465 × 810 (183 × 319). Vatican Palace, Vatican City

105 *The Miracle of Bolsena*, 1512. Stanza di Eliodoro. Fresco, 471 × 712 (185 × 280). Vatican Palace, Vatican City

106 The vault, 1514. Stanza di Eliodoro. Fresco. Vatican Palace, Vatican City

107 Gianfrancesco Penni after Raphael, *The Vision of St John*, *modello* for a discarded scheme for the Bolsena wall of the Stanza di Eliodoro, 1511. Pen with wash and white heightening over black chalk, on buff preparation, 39.7 × 24.8 (15¾ × 9⅞). Musée du Louvre, Paris (3866r). Photo RMN-Grand Palais (musée du Louvre)/Michel Urtado

108 Sketch for *The Miracle of Bolsena*, 1511. Pen, 39.7 × 24.8 (15¾ × 9⅞). Musée du Louvre, Paris (3866v). Photo RMN-Grand Palais (musée du Louvre)/Michel Urtado

109 Unidentified draughtsman after Gianfrancesco Penni after Raphael, *modello* for *The Miracle of Bolsena*, original 1511. Pen and grey wash heightened with white. Ashmolean Museum, University of Oxford (WA1846.273)/Bridgeman Images

110 Circle of Nicolas Poussin after Raphael, compositional study for *The Expulsion of Heliodoros*, original 1511. Pen with brown wash, 25.2 × 41.5 (10 × 16⅜). Albertina, Vienna (24734)

111 Studies of a kneeling woman for *The Expulsion of Heliodoros*, 1511–12. Black chalk, 39.5 × 25.9 (15⅝ × 10¼). Ashmolean Museum, Oxford (WA1846.198r)

112 Unidentified draughtsman after Gianfrancesco Penni after Raphael, *modello* for *The Repulse of Attila*, original 1513. Pen with wash and white heightening on buff preparation. Ashmolean Museum, University of Oxford (WA1846.277)/Bridgeman Images

113 Gianfrancesco Penni after Raphael, *The Repulse of Attila*, probably 1513. Metalpoint, with wash and white heightening on parchment, 36.2 × 59.2 (14⅜ × 23⅜). Musée du Louvre, Paris (3873r). Photo RMN-Grand Palais (Musée du Louvre)/Michel Urtado

114 Sebastiano del Piombo, *St Louis of Toulouse*, 1511. Oil on canvas, 293 × 137 (115⅜ × 54). Accademia, Venice. Photo Cameraphoto/Scala, Florence

115 Julius II from *The Miracle of Bolsena*, 1512. Photo Scala, Florence

116 Sebastiano del Piombo, '*Dorothea*', 1511–12. Oil on wood, 78 × 61 (30¾ × 24⅛). Gemäldegalerie: Staatliche Museen zu Berlin (259). Photo Jörg P. Anders. Scala, Florence/bpk, Bildagentur für Kunst, Kultur und Geschicte

117 Stanza dell'Incendio, 1514–17, general view including the *basamento* by Giulio Romano. Vatican Palace, Vatican City. Photo Scala, Florence

118 Associate of Raphael, *The Battle of Ostia*, 1515. Stanza dell'Incendio. Fresco, 474 × 828 (187 × 326). Vatican Palace, Vatican City

119 Giulio Romano, Gianfrancesco Penni and others, *The Coronation of Charlemagne*, 1516. Stanza dell'Incendio. Fresco, 508 × 670 (200 × 264). Vatican Palace, Vatican City

120 Gianfrancesco Penni, *The Oath of Leo III*, 1516–17. Stanza dell'Incendio. Fresco, 500 × 715 (197 × 281). Vatican Palace, Vatican City

121 Raphael and Giulio Romano, *The Fire in the Borgo*, 1517. Stanza dell'Incendio. Fresco, 495 × 725 (195 × 285). Vatican Palace, Vatican City

122 Giulio Romano, nude study for *King Lothaire*, 1516–17. Red chalk, 40.5 × 26.3 (16 × 10⅜). Palais des Beaux-Arts, Lille (Pl.481)

123 Sketch for a figure group in *The Coronation of Charlemagne*, 1516. Red chalk, 31.8 × 26.1 (12⅝ × 10⅜). Museum Kunstpalast, Graphische Sammlung, Dusseldorf (FP 11)

124 Gianfrancesco Penni (?), a study for a man carrying a table in *The Coronation of Charlemagne*, 1516. Red chalk, 32 × 16 (12⅝ × 6⅜). Musée Condé, Chantilly (DE 57). Photo RMN-Grand Palais (domaine de Chantilly)/Thierry Ollivier

125 Study for the 'Aeneas' group in *The Fire in the Borgo*, 1517. Red chalk, 30 × 17.3 (11⅞ × 6⅞). Albertina, Vienna (4881)

126 Giulio Romano, study for the Appealing Woman in *The Fire in the Borgo*, 1517. Red chalk over stylus and traces of black chalk, 33.9 × 21.7 (13⅜ × 8⅝). Musée du Louvre, Paris (4008). Photo RMN-Grand Palais (Musée du Louvre)/Michèle Bellot

127 Study for the Protective Mother in *The Fire in the Borgo*, 1517. Red chalk over stylus, 33.8 × 25 (13⅜ × 9⅞). Albertina, Vienna (4878)

128 General view of the Sistine Chapel, with a selection of Raphael's tapestries as displayed in 1983. Vatican Palace, Vatican City

129 The Sistine Chapel: reconstruction of the original hanging order of the tapestries from John Shearman, *Raphael's Cartoons in the Collection of Her Majesty the Queen, and the Tapestries for the Sistine Chapel*, 1972 (fig. II, p. 25)

130 Marcantonio Raimondi after Raphael, *St Paul Preaching at Athens*, 1516. Engraving, 26.3 × 35.7 (10⅜ × 14¹⁄₁₆). Metropolitan Museum of Art, New York. Purchase, Joseph Pulitzer Bequest, 1917 (17.50.94)

131 *The Conversion of the Proconsul, c.* 1515–16. Watercolour and bodycolour over charcoal on paper, mounted on canvas, 344 × 446 (135½ × 175⅝). Victoria and Albert Museum, London. On loan from Her Majesty the Queen

132 *The Conversion of St Paul*, tapestry from the *Acts of the Apostles*, designed by Raphael 1515–16, woven in Brussels under the supervision of Pieter van Aelst, 1516–19. Wool, silk, and metal-warped thread, 466 × 634 (183½ × 249⅝). Vatican Palace, Vatican City

133 *Christ's Charge to Peter*, probably 1515. Watercolour and bodycolour over charcoal on paper, mounted on canvas, 344 × 534 (135½ × 210¼). Victoria and Albert Museum, London. On loan from Her Majesty the Queen

134 Two studies of a *Male Nude*, inscribed by Dürer and dated by him 1515. Red chalk, 40.3 × 28.1 (15⅞ × 11⅛). Albertina Museum, Vienna (17575)

135 Gianfrancesco Penni, *modello* for an alternative scheme for *The Miraculous Draught of Fishes*, 1514–15. Pen with wash and white heightening over black chalk, 22.8 × 32.7 (9 × 12⅞). Albertina Museum, Vienna (192r)

136 Sketch for *Miraculous Draught of Fishes*, 1514–15. Pen over black chalk, 22.8 × 32.7 (9 × 12⅞). Albertina Museum, Vienna (192r)

137 Compositional study for *St Paul Preaching at Athens*, 1515–16. Red chalk over stylus, 27.8 × 41.9 (11 × 16½). Gabinetto dei Disegni e delle Stampe, Uffizi, Florence (540E)

138 Gianfrancesco Penni, Giovanni da Udine and others, the Sala dei Palafrenieri, 1516. Vatican Palace, Vatican City

139 Giulio Romano, *St John the Evangelist*, from the suite of *Christ and the Twelve Apostles*, probably 1516. Red chalk over stylus, 20.1 × 13 (8 × 5⅛). The Devonshire Collections, Chatsworth. Reproduced by permission of Chatsworth Settlement Trustees/ Bridgeman Images

140 Giovanni da Udine, the *loggetta* of Cardinal Bibbiena, interior, 1516. Photo Scala, Florence

141 Giovanni da Udine and Giulio Romano, the *Stufetta* (bathroom) of Cardinal Bibbiena, general view, 1516. Photo Scala, Florence

142 Giulio Romano, *Venus and Cupid*, 1516. Red chalk over stylus, 21.1 × 17.2 (8⅜ × 6⅞). Royal Collection/Royal Collection Trust. Her Majesty Queen Elizabeth II, 2021/Bridgeman Images

143 Giovanni da Udine, Gianfrancesco Penni and others, to Raphael's design, the Loggia of Leo X, 1516–19. Vatican Palace, Vatican City

144 Assistant of Raphael (Perino del Vaga?) after a *modello* by Gianfrancesco Penni, *David and Bathsheba*, probably 1517. Fresco. Photo Scala, Florence

145 Marcantonio Raimondi after Raphael, *Joseph Fleeing from Potiphar's Wife, c.* 1520. Engraving, 20.7 × 24.1 (8¼ × 9½). Metropolitan Museum of Art, New York. Harris Brisbane Dick Fund, 1941 (41.8)

146 *David Beheading Goliath*, 1516–17. Black chalk, 24.2 × 32.1 (9⅝ × 12¾). Albertina, Vienna (178)

147 *Modello* for *Moses Receiving the Tables of the Law*, 1516–17. Wash and white heightening over black chalk, 25.5 × 27.9 (10⅛ × 11). Musée du Louvre, Paris (3849r)

148 Gianfrancesco Penni after Raphael, *modello* for *David and Bathsheba*, 1516–17. Wash and white heightening over black chalk, 21.4 × 26.5 (8½ × 10½). British Museum, London (1900,0611.2)

149 Marcantonio Raimondi after Raphael, *The Judgment of Paris, c.* 1514–15. Engraving, 29.1 × 43.7 (11⁷⁄₁₆ × 17³⁄₁₆). Metropolitan Museum of Art, New York. Rogers Fund, 1919 (19.74.1)

150 Conrad Martin Metz after Gianfrancesco Penni after Raphael, *The Indian Triumph of Bacchus*, 1798. Etching, 39.1 × 41.3 (15½ × 16⅜). British Museum, London (1855,0609.872)

151 Sodoma, *The Marriage of Alexander and Roxana*, 1517–18. Fresco, 370 × 660 (145¾ × 259⅞). Villa Farnesina, Rome

152 Raphael and Giulio Romano, study for the *Marriage of Alexander and Roxana*, probably 1517. Red chalk over stylus, 22.8 × 31.7 (9 × 12½). Albertina, Vienna (17634)

153 Raphael and assistants, the Psyche Loggia, 1518. Villa Farnesina, Rome

154 Raphael and assistants, the Psyche Loggia, Ceiling Narratives: *The Council of the Gods*. Villa Farnesina, Rome

155 Raphael and assistants, the Psyche Loggia, Ceiling Narratives: *Marriage of Cupid and Psyche*. Villa Farnesina, Rome

156 Compartment with a *putto* carrying the arms of Cupid, fresco. Villa Farnesina, Rome. Photo Scala, Florence

1516. Oil on wood, transferred to canvas, 238.5 × 155 (93⅞ × 61). Pinacoteca Nazionale, Bologna

181 Raphael and assistants, *The Virgin and Child with Sts John and Anne? (The Madonna of Divine Love)*, probably 1516. Oil on wood, 140 × 109 (55 × 43). Museo di Capodimonte, Naples

182 Marcantonio Raimondi after a lost design by Raphael, *The Holy Family with St John (The Madonna of the Long Thigh)* (date of design probably 1516), *c.* 1520. Engraving, 40 × 26.8 (15¾ × 10⁹⁄₁₆). Minneapolis Institute of Art. Bequest of Herschel V. Jones (P.68.247)

183 Giulio Romano, *Doña Isabel de Requesens*, 1518. Oil on wood transferred to canvas, 120 × 95 (47¼ × 37½). Musée du Louvre, Paris (612)

184 *St Michael Vanquishing the Devil*, signed RAPHAEL URBINAS PINGEBAT and dated MDXVIII (1518). Oil on wood transferred to canvas, 268 × 160 (105⅝ × 63). Musée du Louvre, Paris (610)

185 Raphael and Giulio Romano, *The Holy Family with Sts John, Elizabeth and two? Angels (The Holy Family of Francis I)*, signed RAPHAEL URBINAS PINGEBAT and dated MDXVIII (1518). Oil on wood, transferred to canvas, 207 × 140 (81½ × 55⅛). Musée du Louvre, Paris (604)

186 Giulio Romano to Raphael's design, *St Margaret*, 1518. Oil on wood, transferred to canvas, 184 × 116.5 (72½ × 45⅞). Musée du Louvre, Paris (607)

187 *The Virgin and Child with Sts John and Anne ('La Perla')*, probably 1519. Oil on wood, 147.4 × 116 (58⅛ × 45¾). Museo Nacional del Prado, Madrid

188 *The Transfiguration*, 1518–20. Oil on wood, 405 × 278 (159½ × 109½). Vatican Museums, Vatican City (333)

189 Sebastiano del Piombo, *The Raising of Lazarus*, 1517–19. Oil on wood, transferred to canvas, 381 × 290 (150 × 118). National Gallery, London (NG1)

190 Unidentified draughtsman after Raphael, *modello* for the first design of *The Transfiguration*, 1516–17. Brush and wash, with white heightening, on dark grey preparation, 40 × 27 (15¾ × 10¾). Albertina, Vienna (193)

191 Nude study for the two apostles at lower left of *The Transfiguration*, 1518–19. Red chalk over stylus, on paper, 32.8 × 23.2 (13 × 9¼). The Devonshire Collections, Chatsworth Settlement Trustees (904)

192 The heads and hands of two apostles, *c.* 1519–20. Black chalk with some white heightening over pouncing marks, 49.9 × 36.4 (19¾ × 14⅜). Ashmolean Museum, Oxford (WA1846.209)

193 Giulio Romano, *The Virgin and Child with Sts Elizabeth and John (La Petite Sainte-Famille)*, 1517–18. Oil on wood, 37.9 × 29.8 (15 × 11¾). Musée du Louvre, Paris (605)

194 Giulio Romano, *The Holy Family with St John (The Madonna della Quercia)*, 1518–19. Oil on wood, 144 × 110 (56¾ × 43⅜). Museo Nacional del Prado, Madrid (P-303)

195 Donato Bramante, the Palazzo Caprini, *c.* 1501 onwards; demolished. From Speculum Romanae Magnificentiae: House of Raphael, 1549. Engraving, 34 × 49 (13⅜ × 19⁵⁄₁₆). Metropolitan Museum of Art, New York. Harris Brisbane Dick Fund, 1941 (41.72-3.60)

196 The Chigi Chapel, begun *c.* 1512. Santa Maria del Popolo, Rome. Photo Scala, Florence/Fondo Edifici di Culto – Ministero dell'Interno

197 Raphael's third project for St Peter's, 1519–20. Reconstruction: plan, section and elevation; unexecuted. Drawings by E. von Branca, G. Kohlmaier, reproduced in C.L. Frommel, S. Ray, M. Tafuri, *Raffaello Architetto*, 1984, p. 305

198 Unidentified draughtsman after Raphael, design for the façade of San Lorenzo, Florence, 1516; unexecuted. Pen, 22 × 21 (8¾ × 8⅜). Gabinetto dei Disegni e delle Stampe, Uffizi, Florence (2048A). Photo akg-images/Rabatti & Domingie

199 Unidentified draughtsman after Raphael, design for San Giovanni dei Fiorentini, Rome, 1518; unexecuted. Pen on paper. Münchner Stadtmuseum, Graphische Sammlung (G-36/1928.b)

200 The Farnesina Stables, Rome, 1511 onwards; largely demolished. Reconstruction of the façade on the Lungara, from C.L. Frommel, S. Ray, M. Tafuri, *Raffaello Architetto*, 1984, p. 121

201 The Palazzo of Jacopo da Brescia, Rome, 1515–19. Dismantled and reconstructed on a new site from 1937. From *Opere architettoniche di Raffaello Sanzio, incise e dichiarate dall'Architetto Carlo Pontani*, published in two volumes in 1841 and 1845

202 The Palazzo Branconio dall'Aquila, Rome, *c.* 1518 onwards; demolished. Elevation from Pietro Ferrerio, *I Palazzi di Roma*, 2 vols (Rome, 1655–70), vol. 1, pl. 15

203 The Palazzo Pandolfini, Florence, *c.* 1516 onwards; unfinished. From *Opere architettoniche di Raffaello Sanzio, incise e dichiarate dall'Architetto Carlo Pontani*, published in two volumes in 1841 and 1845

204 The Palazzo Alberini-Cicciaporci, Rome, *c.* 1515 onwards; completed by Giulio Romano. From Paul Letarouilly, *Edifices de Rome moderne ou recueil des palais, maisons, églises, couvents et autres monuments publics et praticuliers les plus remarquables …dessinés, mesurés et publiés par Pl. Letarouilly* (vol. IV, 1840–1855), plate 106

205 Antonio da Sangallo to Raphael's design, Villa Madama, plan, *c.* 1516. Gabinetto dei Disegni e delle Stampe, Uffizi, Florennce. Photo Scala, Florence
206 After Raphael, the Villa Madama, begun 1516. Reconstruction by G. Dewez and C.L. Frommel, Foreign Ministry, Rome
207 The Villa Madama, Rome, begun 1516. Exterior view from the lower terrace. Photo © Massimo Listri
208 The Villa Madama, loggia. Photo Scala, Florence
209 *Andrea Navagero and Agostino Beazzano*, 1516. Oil on canvas, 77 × 111 (30⅜ × 43¾). Galleria Doria Pamphili, Rome (FC 130)
210 Raphael and Giulio Romano, *Lorenzo de' Medici, Duke of Urbino*, 1518. Oil on canvas, 97 × 79 (38 × 31). Private Collection, USA
211 The '*Donna Velata*', 1518. Oil on canvas, 82 × 60.5 (32⅜ × 23⅞). Galleria Palatina, Palazzo Pitti, Florence
212 *Baldassare Castiglione*, 1519. Oil on canvas, 82 × 67 (32⅜ × 26½). Musée du Louvre, Paris (611)
213 Unidentified painter after Raphael, copy of a lost study for *Baldassare Castiglione*, original, 1519. Oil on canvas, 53.5 × 48.3 (21⅛ × 19⅛). Musée du Louvre, Paris (204)
214 *Self-Portrait*, probably 1509. Oil on wood, 72 × 56 (28⅜ × 22⅛). Lost after 1939: Czartoryski Museum, Kraków, Poland. Photo incamerastock/ Alamy Stock Photo
215 Marcantonio Raimondi, *Raphael in his studio*, *c.* 1518?, Engraving, 13.8 × 10.7 (5½ × 4¼). British Museum, London (H,3.93)
216 Raphael, with still-life elements by Giulio Romano, *Leo X with Cardinals Giulio de' Medici and Luigi de' Rossi*, 1518. Oil on wood, 155.2 × 118.9 (61⅛ × 46⅞). Gallerie degli Uffizi, Florence
217 Giulio Romano and Gianfrancesco Penni, in part to Raphael's design, the Sala di Costantino, 1520–24. Vatican Palace, Vatican City
218 Giulio Romano, *The Allocution of Constantine*, 1520–21. Fresco, 710 × 1,213 (280 × 478). Vatican Palace, Vatican City
219 Giulio Romano, *The Battle of the Milvian Bridge*, 1520–21. Sala di Constantino, Vatican Palace. Fresco, 736 × 1,814 (290 × 714). Vatican Palace, Vatican City
220 Giulio Romano and Gianfrancesco Penni, *The Baptism of Constantine*, 1521–24. Fresco, 741 × 1,180 (292 × 465). Vatican Palace, Vatican City
221 Giulio Romano and Gianfrancesco Penni, *The Donation of Constantine*, 1524. Fresco, 720 × 1,720 (283 × 677). Vatican Palace, Vatican City

222 Giulio Romano, *Pope Urban I and allegorical figures*, 1520–21. Fresco. Vatican Palace, Vatican City
223 Gianfrancesco Penni to Raphael's design, *modello* for *The Battle of the Milvian Bridge*, 1519–20. Pen, wash and white heightening over black chalk, 37.6 × 85.1 (14⅞ × 33⅝). Musée du Louvre, Paris (3872r). Photo RMN-Grand Palais (Musée du Louvre)/Michèle Bellot
224 Piero della Francesca, *Constantine's Victory over Maxentius*, mid-1450s. Fresco, 322 × 764 (126⅞ × 300⅞). S. Francesco, Arezzo. Photo Scala, Florence
225 Giulio Romano, nude study for a fallen warrior in *The Battle of the Milvian Bridge*, 1519–20. Black chalk, 22.2 × 30.2 (8¾ × 12). The Devonshire Collections, Reproduced by permission of Chatsworth Settlement Trustees/Bridgeman Images (59)
226 Nude studies for two soldiers at the far right of *The Battle of the Milvian Bridge*, 1519–20. Black chalk with white heightening over stylus, 25.7 × 36.2 (10⅛ × 14⅜). Ashmolean Museum, University of Oxford (WA1846.210r)
227 Gianfrancesco Penni, *modello* for a *Papal Group*, 1519–20. Pen and wash, 37.6 × 29.5 (14⅞ × 11⅝). Musée du Louvre, Paris (4304)
228 Study for *Charity*, 1519–20. Black chalk with touches of white heightening, 31.3 × 15.2 (12⅜ × 6). Ashmolean Museum, Oxford (WA1846.294)
229 Gianfrancesco Penni, preliminary *modello* for *The Allocution*, 1519–20. Pen with wash and white heightening over black chalk, the left half of the composition squared, 23.2 × 41.5 (9¼ × 16⅜). The Devonshire Collections, Chatsworth. Reproduced by permission of Chatsworth Settlement Trustees/ Bridgeman Images
230 *The Trinity with Symbols of the Evangelists*, 1520. Tapestry, executed from a cartoon (Boughton House) by Tommaso Vincidor following Raphael's design for the main group. Woven in Brussels under the supervision of Pieter van Aelst. Wool, silk, and metal-warped thread, 425 × 347 (167⅜ × 136⅝). National Museum of Decorative Arts, Madrid
231 Giulio Romano and Gianfrancesco Penni in part to Raphael's design, *The Coronation of the Virgin with the Apostles (The Monteluce Coronation)*, 1516–25. Oil on conjoined wood panels, 354 × 230 (139⅜ × 90⅝). Vatican Museums, Vatican City (359)
232 Giulio Romano, *The Stoning of St Stephen*, 1520–21. Oil on wood, 420 × 288 (165⅓ × 113⅓). Santo Stefano, Genoa. Photo Scala, Florence

Index

'The single most influential series of art books ever published' *Apollo*

'Outstanding ... exceptionally authoritative and well-illustrated' *Sunday Times*

'World of Art delivers real knowledge with crisp, useful clarity' *Guardian*

Comprehensive in coverage and accessible to all, the World of Art series explores both the newest and the perennial in all the arts, covering themes, artists and movements that straddle the centuries and the gamut of visual culture around the globe.

You may also like:

Mary Cassatt
Griselda Pollock

Cézanne
Richard Verdi

Monet
James H. Rubin

Rembrandt
Christopher White

Sienese Painting
Timothy Hyman

The Thames & Hudson Dictionary of the Italian Renaissance
J. R. Hale

Turner
Graham Reynolds
Introduction by
David Blayney Brown

World of Art